AF644618

The Simplest Book for Learning Tally.ERP 9

Tally.ERP 9 Training Guide

Fourth Revised Edition Tally.ERP 9, Rel 6 with GST

by

Asok K Nadhani

BPB PUBLICATIONS
20 Ansari Road, Darya Ganj New Delhi-110002

REPRINT 2026

FOURTH REVISED AND UPDATED EDITION 2018

SECOND REVISED EDITION 2019

FIRST EDITION 2010

ISBN: 978-81-8333-339-9

Distributors:

BPB PUBLICATIONS
20, Ansari Road, Darya Ganj
New Delhi-110002
Ph: 23254990/23254991

BPB BOOK CENTRE
376 Old Lajpat Rai Market,
Delhi-110006
Ph: 23861747

DECCAN AGENCIES
4-3-329, Bank Street,
Hyderabad-500195
Ph: 24756967/24756400

COMPUTER BOOK CENTRE
12, Shrungar Shopping Centre,
M.G.Road, BENGALURU-560001
Ph: 25587923/25584641

MICRO MEDIA
Shop No. 5, Mahendra Chambers,
150 DN Rd. Next to Capital Cinema,
V.T. (C.S.T.) Station, MUMBAI-400 001
Ph: 22078296/22078297

Published by Manish Jain for BPB Publications, 20, Ansari Road, Darya Ganj, New Delhi- 110002 and Printed at Manipal Technologies Limited, Manipal

To

Kanta

Trademarks

Tally, Tally eis 5.4, Tally ees 6.3, Tally ies 7.2, Tally 8.1, Tally 9, TallyGold, TallySilver, TallyBronze, Accounting for Success, Power of Simplicity are registered Trade marks of Tally Solutions FZ-LLC / Tally Solutions P Ltd. All other trademarks are property of their respective owners and are hereby acknowledged.

Though care has been taken to publish correct information, neither the Authors, nor the Publishers are responsible for any mistake or omission in the book.

The information have been compiled from various sources. The authors or publishers do not guarantee for performance of any software, or any part thereof, described in the book.

Conventions Used in the book

Menu Path : Menu Path have been show with > indicator, like Display>Account Books>Ledger etc

Buttons : Buttons are indicated by the Function key or Letter and the Button Name, like F11:Features, P:Print, V:Voucher Types etc

Chapters : The book is divided in 3 Parts. Each Part contains several Chapters, identified by Part Number - Chapter Number : Chapter Name (e.g *Ch 01-03:Gateway of Tally*, indicating 3rd Chapter of Part 1 named *Gateway of Tally*). The Part Number (2 digits) & Chapter Number (2 digits) are separated by a hyphen, like 02-03.

Topic Reference : Each Topic is identified by a Ref Number, separated by a dot for each topic level (e.g 10.01). The complete topic reference consists the Chapter Number followed by Topic Reference Number, e.g 01-05.05.02 indicating Topic Ref Number 05.02 of Chapter 01-05. The Topic Reference Numbers are widely used to cross reference related topics, in *Table of Contents* and in *Subject Index*.

YouTube videos and FREE e-tutorial for Students & Tally Users

Play YouTube Videos & Subscribe to the YouTube Channel 'TallyGuru' to get regular updates for FREE e-tutorials & FREE job placement assistance services in Accounts Department of reputed business houses.

Make liberal use of the FREE Services

For details, e-mail to ***etallyguru@gmail.com***

Books of the Author

Computer Programming

Clipper Applications (1993)

Accounting Systems

BI Financial Management & Accounting (1997)*

Accounting with Tally 4.5 (1999)

REAL Accounting Software (2000)*

PURSE Payroll Software (2000)*

Implementing Tally 5.4 (2000)

Tally Tutorial 5.4 (2000)

Implementing Tally 6.3 (2001)

Tally Tutorial 6.3 (2001)

Implementing FACT (2002)

Implementing E.X.- NGN (2002)

Simple Tally 6.3 (2005)

Implementing Tally 7.2 (2005)

Implementing Tally 7.2 – Hindi (2006)

Simple Tally 7.2 (2006)

Tally Instant Reference (2006)

Simple Tally 7.2 Hindi - (2007)

Tally Payroll (2007)*

Implementing Tally 9 (2007)

Managing VAT with Tally 9 (2008)

Simple Tally 9 (2008)

Tally 9 Training Guide (2009)

Simple Tally.ERP 9 Hindi – (2011)

Tally.ERP 9 Training Guide (2010, 2013,2015)

Tally.ERP 9 Made Simple (2012)

Mastering Tally.ERP 9 (2012, 2013)

Implementing Tally.ERP 9 (2015)

CA (CPT/ IPCC)

Accounting Standards (2009)

Business Ethics & Communications (2009)

Business & Corporate Laws (2009)

Information Technology (2009)

Auditing & Assurance (2009)

Mercantile Laws (2009)

Tutorial CDs

Tally 6.3

Learn Tally 9 (Basic Financial Accounting – Level 1)

Learn Tally 9 (Traders Accounting – Level 2)

*With companion CD

Preface

It is heartening to find that the third edition of the book was highly acclaimed by students as well as Training Institutes, as ideal training manual for Basic Tally ERP 9 Training courses. The fourth edition brings the much waited rel 6 covering GST and incorporating many novel additions and enhancements.

The Tutorial has been divided into progressive training modules, viz, Accounting, Invoicing & Inventory, Taxation and Payroll. One can start with the first module, and may optionally proceed to next module. It is not essential to cover all the modules for everyone. So, the Training Institute may plan graded Training Courses according to Level & Course coverage. Self learning student can gradually proceed to the next module, as needed.

Basic Accounting

The first module entails the starting steps to learn basic essential features of *Accounting with Tally.ERP* 9. covering the complete cycle, viz, Creation of Company, Accounts Masters, Accounts Vouchers, Viewing & Printing of primary Books of Accounts, Trial Balance, Profit & Loss Statement, appropriation of Profit / Loss, Balance Sheet. Ratio Analysis. The steps of Back Up, Restore & Re-writing are also explained.

Basic Invoicing & Inventory

The second module explains creation of Inventory Masters (Unit of Measure, Stock Group & Stock Items), Inventory Vouchers & Invoicing, Stock Statements, Stock Ledger, Stock Analysis & Movement Reports, Order Processing etc, along with configuration options to set & customise the contents of Reports.

Tax Accounting

Majority of the Business organisations are to comply with statutory requirements to charge Tax in Invoices, deposit such Tax with Government under Tax Challans and submit Tax Returns. The Taxation aspects are covered in third module, elaborating the Company & Masters Set Up, Invoicing, Tax Deposit, Tax Challans and & related statutory reports printing in respect of GST, TDS & TCS, Uploading data and Statutory reports in GST Portal also explained in brief.

Payroll

All organisations have to prepare Paysheet, involving lot of computation for each employee, for each head. This module explains all the aspects of Payroll scheme set up, Employee & Statutory Masters, Attendance, Payroll Processing, Payslip, Paysheet and other Payroll Reports etc.

Practical Work Assignments

Accounting work cannot be learned without practical work. Selected sets of hand picked assignments, covering various typical and practical aspects, normally encountered in business process, are placed at the end of each chapter. Readers should work out these assignments to get thorough knowledge of maintaining Accounts with Tally.ERP 9

Installation of Tally.ERP 9 (latest release 6.0) software and keyboard shortcuts are covered in Appendices.

YouTube Videos

Students may also view complete videos tutorial at TallyGuru channel and post problems / comments on the videos. These videos will give a through knowledge of working with Tally.

I am sure, this book will help Students, Accountants & Businessmen to maintain Basic Accounts, Invoicing & Taxation compliance, and Payroll Maintenance, in Business.

The students, having done the Assignments appended at the end of each chapter, will gain enough understanding & confidence to tackle practical work in real life business environment.

Kindly give your opinion how much this small and elementary book has been able to help you, and your valuable suggestions to make it better.

Asok K Nadhani

Contents at Glance

Table of Contents

PART 1

Basic Financial Accounting

In this part, we explain the entire process of Accounting with Tally.ERP 9, from Creation of Company, Accounts Masters, Accounts Vouchers, Viewing & Printing of various Books of Accounts, to getting Final Accounts Statements (Profit & Loss Statement & Balance Sheet). The process of current years accounts closing are elaborately explained. Finally, the steps of Data Maintenance & various administrative tasks are also explained.

Company Creation explains the process of creation of a Company in Tally.ERP 9 to enter data and manage accounts of an accounting entity.

Gateway of Tally explains the entry (and exit) point of each component & ancillary tasks to work with Tally.ERP 9.

Accounts Masters discusses about the Reserved Accounts Masters auto created by Tally.ERP 9 & about Creation of Accounts Groups & Accounts Ledgers.

Accounts Vouchers explains the rules and steps of creation of various types of Accounts Vouchers, recording complete details of transactions. It also explains various novel short cut & quick methods of vouchers creation to save data entry time and ensure consistency & correctness of data.

Reports explains immediate display of reports on screen & seamlessly drill down & trace back through allied & subordinate areas, throughout the system, and printing of reports & vouchers.

Cash Bank Book explains Display & Printing of Cash / Bank Books, the primary Books of Accounts, showing details of daily transactions through Cash & Bank Accounts.

Journal Book explains the Display & Printing of Journal Books, including Sales & Purchase Journals.

Ledger Book shows the methods of Display & Printing of Ledger Account, printing of Multiple & selected range of Ledger Accounts in one shot.

Trial Balance shows Display & Printing of Trial Balance

Profit & Loss Statement shows Closing Stock Adjustment, printing of Profit & Loss Statement and appropriation of Profit / Loss.

Balance Sheet shows Display & Printing of Balance Sheet

Accounts Receivables & Payables explains tracking of Bill wise details of Open Accounts, Age Analysis etc

Banking explains various Banking Job like Cheque details entry in Voucher, Cheque Printing, Bank Reconciliation etc.

Cost Centre explains allocation of Revenue & Cost into Cost Centres & Cost Categories

Foreign Currency explains maintenance of Foreign Currency Accounts, transaction in Foreign Currency, Conversion & Reporting in Base & Foreign currency.

Tally Administration shows important chores of Back Up, Restore, Re-writing, Data Export/ Import, Reports e-mailing, Security & Passwords etc

Company Creation 01-01

01 Company in Tally

Having installed and loaded Tally.ERP (Appendix-B), the first task is to create a Company. The Term *Company* in Tally.ERP 9 means any Accounting Entity, for which a separate set of Accounting Records are maintained (referred as *Tally Company*). So, a *Tally Company* may be created for Personal Accounts, Business Organization of any form (Proprietorship, Partnership, Company), Association, Trust or any entity for which a separate set of accounts are maintained.

When separate set of Accounting Records of a Company (called *Business Entity*) are maintained for its various branches, warehouses, Sales / Purchase depots, collection centres etc, each of these separate *Accounting entities* will be called a *Company*, even if they are legally same Company or Organisation. Separate Tally Companies will be created for each of such accounting entity.

So, for one legal Company, say *ABC Company*, several *Companies* may be created, if separate accounts are maintained for its different Branches, Warehouses, Factories etc, such as:

- ABC Company (HO)
- ABC Company (Patna)

You may keep separate set of Data for each Financial Year, creating separate *Company* for each Year for the same Legal entity, such as :

- ABC Company 17-18
- ABC Company16-17

Or separate *Companies*, for each Branch, for each year, such as :

- ABC Company (HO) 17-18
- ABC Company (Patna) 17-18, and so on

02 Company Creation

On loading Tally for the first time, you get the *Company Info* menu (F-1A)

At *Company Info* menu (F-1A), click *Create Company* to get *Company Creation* Screen (F-2A)

F-1A Company Info Menu

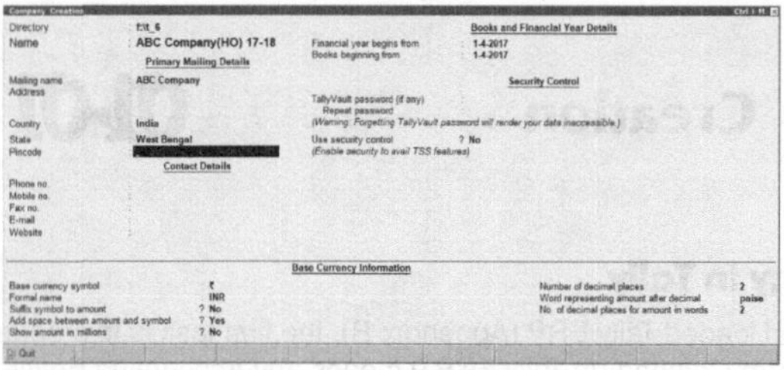

F-2A : Company Creation **F-2B: List of States**

For Quick Start, at *Company Creation* Screen (F-2A), you may just enter only the following basic Info about the Company

- **Name** : Enter Name of the Enterprise at the *Name* field. The Company is identified and selected by this Name (called *Tally Company Name*). To identify the Company for each Year, you may add the FY after the Company name (like ABC Company HO 17-18). So, in the next year, when you create separate Company for 18-19, you may name it like ABC Company HO 18-19., to identify Accounts of the respective year from the *Company Name*. The Company Name is carried in the next field Mailing Name. At Mailing name, keep only the Company Legal name (which would be printed in Invoice, Receipt etc), deleting the additional portion of name (like HO 17-18 etc).
- **State** : Select the State from the drop down list (F-2B). If you maintain GST, it is important.
- **Financial year from**: Normally you should enter beginning date of financial year (like 1-4-2017), to maintain accounts of the full financial year. Tally initially creates Accounting period of 1 year from Financial Year from date. For example, if you enter 14.10.2016 as books beginning date, the accounting period would be upto 13.10.2017 (which you may extend). Do not change this date after voucher entry.

Other Info: You may leave default values / blank in other fields (like *Address* etc) and all other options. You may set the options as desired through Company Modification.

Directory : At *Directory*, the default Data Path, as set by you at the time of Installation of Tally appears (the cursor skips this field). You should normally press <enter> to keep the Company Data at this folder. To change, (press Shift +Tab at *Name* to get back to *Directory* and enter the Directory Name where you like to keep Company data). This is useful only when you keep data of separate companies in separate folder.

Saving the Company

After entering the particulars, Click *Yes* at '*Accept Yes No*' button at the bottom right to save the Company profile . Alternatively, you may press *Ctrl+A* to save the Company profile directly (no confirmation required). Now a Tally Company gets created and you get Gateway of Tally (GoT) screen, after creation of first Tally Company. The created Company is shown at the left side of GoT, in the list of Selected Companies (F-3B).

This way, you may create multiple Tally Companies in your computer and maintain separate accounting records for each of them.

03 Modification of Company Profile

Later on, at any time (even after Voucher Entry/ Report Printing), you may modify the Company Details. You may also fill up the unfilled data fields in the Company Profile screen.

Click *F3: Company Info* button at Gateway of Tally to get Company Info Menu. Select *Alter*, select the Company Name from the list, to get Company Alteration screen, similar to Company creation screen (F-2A).

Place the cursor on the respective field and modify / enter any data of the Company Profile (Mailing Name, Address, Contact Details, Security Control, Base Currency Information) or fill up the blank data or options left out at the time of Company Creation, if any.)

At the lower part, at Base Currency, just leave the default values and do not change anything, as they have been properly set up for Indian Rupee Currency. These Advanced options are explained in the respective areas.

Having entered / modified the data, press *Ctrl+A* to save. Never change the '*Financial Year from*' Date after voucher entry.

04 Deletion of Company Data

Deletion of Company means removing the Company Profile data along with all voucher data of the company from the Disk. You may need to Delete a Company in certain cases, like, you have by mistake created one, or you have created a Company just for training or understanding it, or have moved the Company to another Computer (or Directory) and you do not need it any more.

Tally does not provide any direct option to Delete a Company. At Gateway, Click *F3: Company Info* to get Company Info Menu. Select *Alter*, Select the Company to be deleted to get Company Alteration screen. Now press *Alt+D* to Delete the Company

- You get a confirmation screen (Delete ? Yes / No). Click *Yes* (or type Y) to *Proceed to Delete* the Company data (click *No* if you do not want to Delete) .
- After you type Y at *Delete ? Yes / No* option, you get another prompt

'*Are You Sure ?*'. Click Yes (or type Y) to Delete the Company (to finally Delete the Company), else Type N, if you do not want to Delete.

On Deletion of the Company, not only the particulars stored at the Company Creation screen goes, all the data that you record for the Company, also get wiped out. Be careful!.

05 Selection of Company

To work with the desired Company, first you have to Select (Open) the desired Company. At Gateway of Tally (GoT), Click *F1 :Select Cmp* button and select the Company from the list (F-3A) (move the cursor on the Company Name and press <enter> or Double Click on the Company. Name).

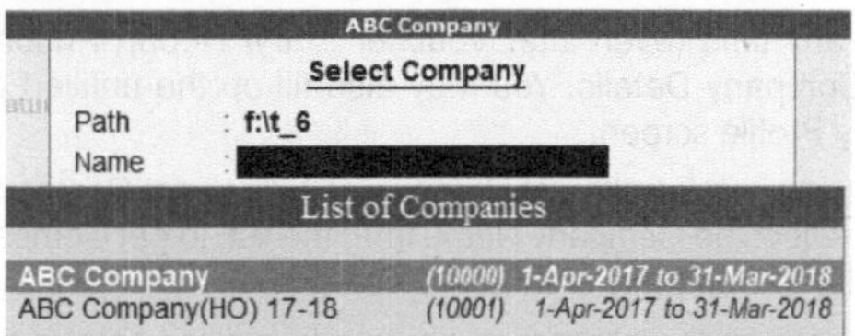

F-3A: Company Selection

This way, select any Company to work with. When you select another Company, the newly selected Company becomes the Active Company and is shown in Bold in the list of currently selected Companies (F-3B). At any point of time, you work with the currently Active Company *only* (shown in Bold). This way, you may switch selection between several Companies and work with the currently Active Company at any instance.

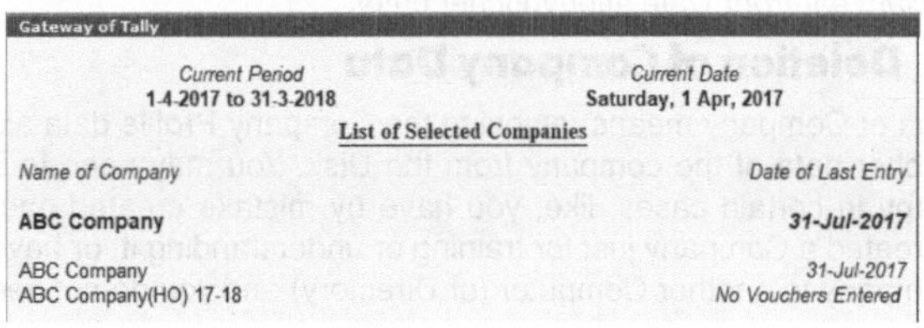

F-3B : Selected Company List

06 Re-selection of Companies

When you select a Company, it becomes the *Active* Company. The previously selected Companies remain as *Selected* Company but no more remain Active. To re-select any previous selected company (not yet shut) :

- **At Gateway of Tally**: At *Gateway of Tally*, click on the Company to be selected, from the list of Selected Companies at the left part (F-3B). The selected Company now becomes *Active* Company

- **At other Places** : From other places, Click *F3:Company* button (this button gets activated only when more than ONE Company is created) to get the list of selected Companies (F-3A). Select the desired Company from the list of selected Companies.

On re-selection, you get the same position in the next selected Company. For example, at *Display>Account Books Menu,* if you re-select another Company, you will get the same Menu (*Display>Account Books)* of the next selected (Active) Company

07 Shutting of Company

When you select a Company, the Company remains selected, even if another Company is selected next. So, if you have selected several companies one after another, each of them remains selected.

Shutting a company means de-selecting (or un-selecting) the company. You cannot work with a Shut Company, until you select it again.

To *Shut* a Company, at Gateway, select *F1: Shut Cmp* (or click *Alt+F1*) and select the company to Shut (if multiple Companies are selected). The company will be *Shut* and will no more appear in the list of selected companies. To work with that Company next time, *Select* the Company again.

Ideally, for no-frills fast work, *Select* a Company and work with that. To work with another company, it is often better to *Shut* the currently selected company and select the next company to work with. In this way, you normally keep only one Company selected at any point of time (unless specifically needed to keep multiple companies selected), so that you do not enter data in a wrong Company, by mistake!

Summary

- **Company Creation**
  - o **First Company creation** : When no company is created (you are going to create the first Company), you get Company Info Menu. Select Create Company. Create the Company. After creation of Company, you get *Gateway of Tally* (GoT).
  - o **New Company creation**:. Once a Company s created, to create a new Company, at GoT, click *F3:Comp Info* to get Company Info menu. Select Create Company. Create the Company.
- **Company Data Directory**
  - o **Default Directory :** At Directory, the first field in Company Creation screen, the default data directory specified at the time of Installation of Tally.ERP 9, is shown and the Directory field is skipped (the cursor comes to the next *Name* field). If you do not change the default Directory name shown at Directory field, the Company data will be stored at the specified default directory location.

- o **Changing Data Directory** : If you like to keep the data of the current company being created, in some other place (for any reason), then first go to *Directory* field (press Up Arrow or Shift+Tab key) and change the Directory Name (very correctly, and note down somewhere) typing the new directory name where you like to store the data of the current company being created. The Company data will then be stored in the specified directory.
- o **Company selection**: Next time, whenever you like to select the Company, you have to go to the Path field (at Select Company screen) and specify correctly the directory name, otherwise you will not find the company and cannot select it. It is important to decide the data directory location at the time of Company creation, as you will not be able to modify it later on, after the Company is created.

- **Essential Info**: To make the work of Company creation faster, just enter the essential info. 1. Company Name 2. State 3. Financial Year From.
- **Other Info** : Leave all other default values as it is, which you may enter / set up / change later on, through *Company Alteration*. Many of these options are too advanced, which you will not be able to understand or decide at the Company Creation stage, if you are new user of Tally. Once you understand the implications of these advanced features, set them as you need.
- **Base Currency Information** : Do not change any info in Base Currency section (bottom part of Base Currency Information). It is perfectly set for organisations with *Indian Rupee* as Base Currency.
- **Alteration of Company data** : To enter any data, or enter any left out field in Company Particulars at Company Creation screen, or set up any option, at GoT, click F3:Cmp Info, select *Alter* to get Company Alteration screen (like Company Creation screen) and enter / change/ set up data at any field
- **Switching between Companies**
  - o **Selection of Company located in default directory** :To work with any company, select *F1:Select Cmp* to get Select Company screen. The companies whose data are stored at the default directory at the *Path* filed are listed. Select the Company you want to work with, from the list.
  - o **Selection of Company from other directory** : If the Company you want select is stored in different directory, then move to the Path field (press Up Arrow key or Shift+Tab keys) to get to the Path field. Now type the directory name where the data of the Company you want to work with is stored. All the companies stored in the specified Path will be listed. Now you select the

desired Company from the list. This way, you may select any Company located in any Data Directory.

- o **Active Company** : The company you select last, remain as the currently *Active Company*. The name of Active Company is shown in bold at top of the list of Selected Companies, at the left part of GoT. You always work with currently Active Company only
- o **Switching to another Company** : To work with another Company, click the Company from the list of Selected Company. This becomes the currently active Company.
- o **Shutting Company** : Keeping too many companies selected at a time will clutter and inconvenience your work. You may, by mistake or oversight, enter data in a wrong company. So, Shut the Company for which you do not like to work with in the current session. The best policy is, during DATA ENTRY, you select only ONE Company.

- **Deletion of Company** : To Delete a Company, at GoT, select F3:Compay info, select Alter to get Company Alteration screen, press *Alt+D* to get Deletion Confirmation prompt, type Y at *Are you sure to Delete*. To Delete Type Y, All the data of the Company will be Deleted permanently. There is no option of recovery of deleted Tally data (however backed up data, if taken, will remain in the Back Up)

Gateway of Tally 01-02

01 Gateway of Tally (GoT)

On creation of the first Company, Gateway of Tally (GoT) Screen appears (F-1A). The Gateway of Tally is the main entry point from where any part of the Tally can be accessed to perform any task.

On entry to any operational screen from any Menu Item of Gateway, the Gateway screen goes out and the respective screen appears in place of Gateway screen.

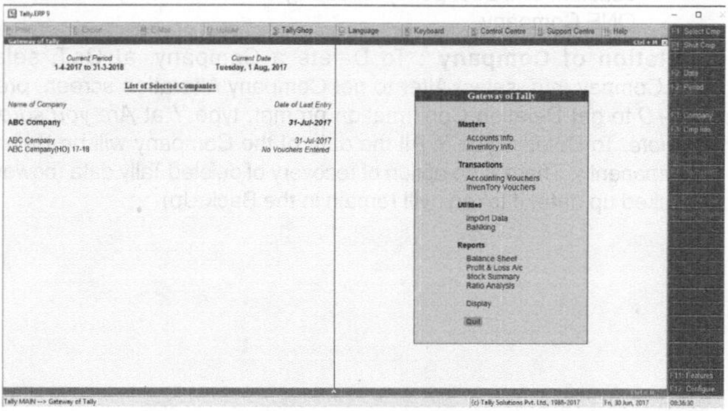

F-1A : Gateway of Tally

02 Components of Gateway of Tally

The Gateway of Tally (GoT) screen (F-1A) may be divided in following main sections:

- **Horizontal Button Bar:** Contains various Buttons to perform allied tasks:
    - **P:Printing** : Printing of Reports from Display screen
    - **E:Export :** Export of Reports and Data in various formats
    - **M:E-mail** : To e-mail a Tally Report
    - **O:Upload** : To Upload Reports into your website
    - **S:Shop** : To Shop various tally Add On Products
    - **G:Language** : To configure Interface Language

- o **K:Keyboard** : To set Tally's Phonetic Keyboard Operating System Keyboard for Language
- o **K:Conrol Center** : To access Control Centre through Remote Login
- o **H: Support Centre** : To access Tally's support Centre for supports
- o **H:Help** : To get Local & On-line Help

- **Main Area:** Tally Main area is divided into two parts.
  - o **Current Status** : Left Part is about the *Current status* (Current Period, Current Date, currently Active & Selected Companies
  - o **Tally Menu** : Right part shows the current *Tally Menu.*
- **Tally Product Info Part:** The bottom area contains details of Tally Software and Calculator area (F-1B). The Calculator may be invoked by Ctrl+N. The arithmetical formula may be typed to get instant result during work, without using external calculator. The Tally Info Part may be displayed / hidden using (X) and (^) handles.
- **Current Path (Task Bar):** At the bottom of the screen, the position and path of current screen from Main Menu is shown.

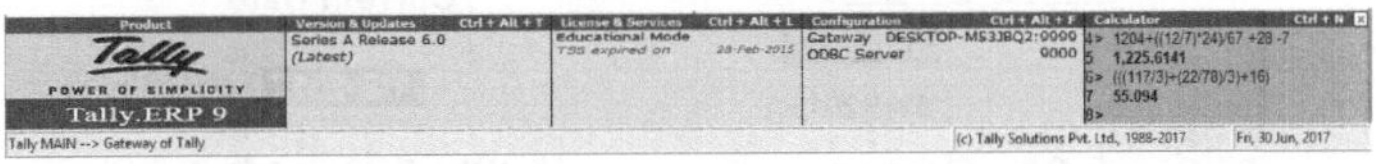

F-1B: Tally Product Info / Calculator part & Current Path

Vertical Button Bar: At the right part, a vertical Button Bar (F-1B) appears showing various buttons to quickly perform some associated / related tasks from within the current screen. The buttons keep on changing as per the context of the current screen.

At Gateway, the following buttons appear (F-1A)

- **F1: Select Cmp** : To select a Company from the list of Companies
- **F1: Shut Cmp** : To shut (de-select) a selected company
- **F2: Date** : To set the *Current Date.* Click *F2:Date* (or press F2 button) and enter the Current Date. This Date is carried as default current Date to the reports & vouchers being displayed / created The Current Date should lie within the Current Period.
- **F2: Period** : To set the *Current Period.* Click F2:Period (or press Alt+F2 button) and enter the *From* & *To Date* of Current Period. This Period is carried as default Current Period for the Report being displayed /Voucher being created
- **F3:Company** : To get the list of Companies on Disk, to select a Company

- **F3: Cmp Info** : To get the Company Info Menu to select the desired tasks related to Company Operation (like Create, Select, Shut, Alter, Back Up, Restore etc)
- **F11: Features** : To get Company Features Menu
- **F12: Configure** : To get Configuration Menu

03 Period & Date Setting

During working, set the Periods (Starting Date & Ending Date to cover a specified Period) and the Date (Voucher Date in Voucher Entry) as needed, through following buttons :

- **Voucher Date** : Click F2:Date (or press F2 button) during Voucher Entry. Enter the Date (F-2B)
- **Current Period** : Click F2:Period (or press Alt+F2 button) at any Menu screen to get the Change Period screen. Enter the Date From & Date To (F-2A)
- **Report Period** : Click F2:Period (or press F2 button) at any Display screen(F-2A).

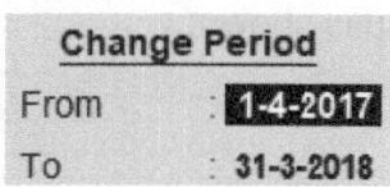

F-2A : Change

F-2B : Current Date

Rules of setting Period & Date

- **Current Period :** Current Period is the period for which you like to do any work in Tally (e.g enter voucher, display / print Report.). You cannot do anything beyond the Current Period.

  Click *F2:Period* button (or press Alt+F2 key) at Gateway (or at any Menu) to set the Current Period (F-2A).

  The current period is shown at the top line at the left part of Gateway of Tally (F-1A). The Current Period remains applicable to all the selected companies, until you reset it again. So, after doing some work in FY 16-17 (setting the Current Period as 1-4-2016 to 31-3-2017), when you select another Company, starting Financial Year from 1-4-17, still the previous current period (1-4-2016 to 31-3-2017) remains active. To work for the period 17-18 of the selected Company, you have to reset Current period accordingly (like 1-4-17 to 31-3-18). So, check the current period and re-set it accordingly whenever you do any work. Otherwise, you may sometimes get surprises / shocks to find blank report (if the current period is not aligned to the period of the active company).
- **Current Date** : It is the Date which you have set while making voucher entry. This helps to make continuous voucher entry for the same date.

Click *F2:Date* button (or press *F2 key*) and set the Current Date (by default, the next date is posed as Current Date, which you may accept or change (F-2B). Current Date applies to Voucher Date during new Voucher creation.

04 Accounting Features

At GoT (or at other menus), click *F11:Features* button to get Company Features Menu (F-3A). At Company Features Menu (F-3A), select *Accounting Features* to get Accounting Features Set up screen with default values set up for the currently selected Company(F-3B). You may change the options of any of the features as desired to change / activate / deactivate any feature.

F-3A: Company Features Menu

The options of Company Features Menu are applicable to the specific Company, for which you set up. So, you may set up different configuration for each Company, as per your requirements.

Other options of Company Features Menu (F-3A) are shown at the respective topic

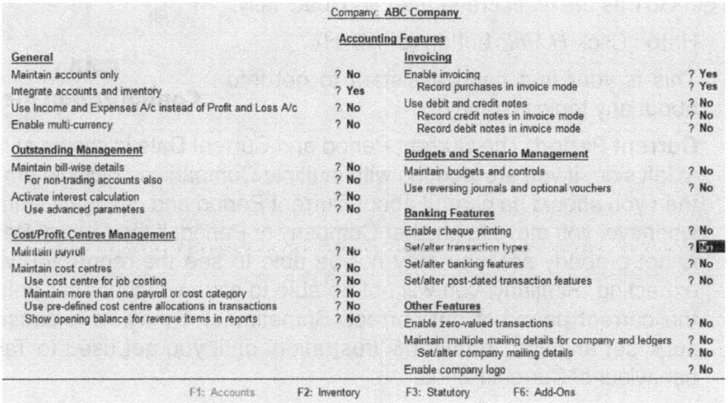

F-3B: Accounting Features Set up

05 Configuration Set Up

At GoT, click *F12:Configure* button to get Tally Configuration Menu (F-4A), which contains various configuration options with initial default values. You may change / set up the options to customise the behaviour / options of Tally as per user requirements. The options are applicable to all the Companies whose data reside in the same directory.

The Configuration options are explained at the respective topic in the book

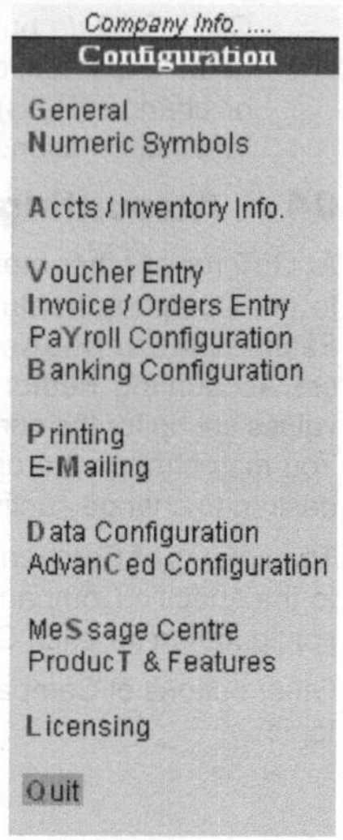

F-4A : Configuration Menu

06 Closing & Exiting Tally

To exit from current Menu (move to upper menu), *select Quit* (or press <Esc> key). This way, you reach to Main Menu. To finally exit and close Tally:

- Click on the rightmost Cross button,
- *Select Quit* in the Main Menu (or type Q at Gateway (or successively Press Esc key till you reach GoT)

A confirmation screen 'Quit Yes or No' appears. Click *Yes (*Press *Y)* to exit from Tally, else press *N* to continue to work with Tally.

Summary

Gateway of Tally (GoT) is the entry point to start working with tally. After the first Company is created, you get GoT as the first screen after you load Tally.

- **Help** : Click *H:Help* button (or Alt+H).

  This is your first hand assistant to get info about any topic instantly!
- **Current Period**: The Current Period and Current Date is shown at GoT at left side. If you are working with multiple Companies / Multiple period, then you should be careful about Current Period and change it suitably whenever you move to another Company or Period. If the Current Period is not properly set, you may not be able to see the report you were expecting. Similarly, you will not be able to save voucher after entry, if the current period is not correct. Sometimes, it may be a cause of surprise, anguish, irritation & frustration, until you get used to Tally's behaviour of Current Period.
- **Report Period** : Report Period & Current Period are separate aspects and are set by separate keys.
- **Company Features** : At the Gateway of Tally (or other screens), click *F11: Features* to get Company Feature Menu. Select the desired Menu and option to set the Feature of the current Company. The options set are specifically applicable to the Company. So you may set options in different ways for each Company as desired. For example, you will need only few basic options activated for your personal accounts whereas many more additional options for a Trading firm.
- **Configuration Set Up** : At GoT (at Main Menu or Sub Menu), click *F12:Configure* to get Configuration Menu. At other screens (e.g Entry, Report printing etc,),you get the Configuration options of the relevant

screen (not the main Configuration Menu). Now set the options in your own way, as required. The options set are applicable to all the companies residing in the directory.

- **Tally Info** : At the bottom part, the Tally Info panel displays few details of Tally Software installed.
- **Calculator** : At the rightmost part of Tally Info panel, you see the Calculator section.
  - **General Arithmetical Computation** : At any place of Tally Gateway Menu, you may press Ct+N to expand the Calculator pat in the Info panel (hiding other info part) and type any arithmetical expression (you may also use parenthesis pairs like (), but not braces like { } & [ ]), as per general arithmetical rules, to get results of arithmetical calculation. This is useful to make any computation, at any time during work, without any external calculator.
  - **In line computed input pasting** : At any numerical input field (e.g Amount), you may press *Alt+C* to invoke Calculator pane at the bottom of the screen and enter Arithmetical expression for calculation. The result will be carried at the numeric Input field from where the Calculator was invoked. It is is useful to enter some computed data in the field (e.g result of some arithmetic computation), without typing them again in the numeric input field.

Accounts Masters 01-03

01 Account Masters

Account Masters are the principal Accounting entities representing similar transactions (Account Ledgers) and similar Accounts (Account Groups) along which all transaction data are compiled, summarised and balanced, to be reflected in various Accounting Reports & Financial Statements (Profit & Loss Account & Balance Sheet).

After Creation of Company, the Account Masters are to be created first. Tally ERP 9 provides the means to organise and maintain Master data by user in their own way. To maintain the basic system, the following Accounts Masters are to be initially planned and respective master data to be created.

- **Account Ledgers** : Account Ledgers are entities representing similar transactions. For example Travelling Expenses Ledger contains all transactions (vouchers) related to Travelling Expenses. The transactions of a Ledger account are summed up (Debit & Credit) and balanced (net Debit / Credit).
- **Account Groups** : Account Groups are just convenient & systematic grouping of *Ledger Accounts* of similar nature. Account Group helps to present summarised Accounting Reports in systematic manner. The Account Group may be organised in multiple Levels to get accounting figures and report for each such sub level Groups.

02 Reserved Accounts Masters

During Company creation, Tally automatically creates 28 Reserved Account Groups and 2 Reserved Ledger Accounts

- **Reserved Groups** : Tally creates 15 Primary Groups and 13 Sub-Groups (known as Reserved Groups) for each Company (F-1A).

  For a small company (or individual accounts), the Tally created Reserved account groups (F-1A) may be adequate, and you may not need to create new Account Groups. However, for better organization of larger number of accounts, new Account Groups need to be created.

  The Reserved Groups carry their own characteristics. The Ledger Accounts placed under these Groups inherit the properties of the respective Reserve Group.
- **Reserved Ledger Accounts :** Tally also auto creates 2 Reserved Ledger accounts (Cash and Profit & Loss Account : F-1A). So, do not create

any new ledger for these Ledger Accounts. All other Ledger Accounts are to be created.

Branch / Divisions
Capital Account
  Reserves & Surplus (Retained Earnings)
Current Assets
  Bank Accounts
  Cash-in-hand
    Cash
  Deposits (Asset)
  Loans & Advances (Asset)
  Stock-in-hand
  Sundry Debtors
Current Liabilities
  Duties & Taxes
  Provisions
  Sundry Creditors
Direct Expenses (Expenses (Direct))
Direct Incomes (Income (Direct))
Fixed Assets
Indirect Expenses (Expenses (Indirect))
Indirect Incomes (Income (Indirect))
Investments
Loans (Liability)
  Bank OD A/c (Bank OCC A/c)
  Secured Loans
  Unsecured Loans
Misc. Expenses (ASSET)
Purchase Accounts
Sales Accounts
Suspense A/c
Profit & Loss A/c
28 Group(s) and 2 Ledger(s)

F-1A : Alphabetical list of Reserved Account Masters

Reserved Groups (Liabilities)

Capital Account
  Reserves & Surplus (Retained Earnings)
Current Liabilities
  Duties & Taxes
  Provisions
  Sundry Creditors
Investments
Loans (Liability)
  Bank OD A/c (Bank OCC A/c)
  Secured Loans
  Unsecured Loans

Reserved Groups (Assets)

Branch / Divisions
Current Assets
  Bank Accounts
  Cash-in-hand
    Cash
  Deposits (Asset)
  Loans & Advances (Asset)
  Stock-in-hand
  Sundry Debtors
Fixed Assets
Indirect Incomes (Income (Indirect))
Investments
  Unsecured Loans
Misc. Expenses (ASSET)

F-1B: Reserved Accounts Groups (Liabilities & Assets)

Reserved Groups (Income)

Direct Incomes (Income (Direct))
Indirect Incomes (Income (Indirect))
Sales Accounts

Reserved Groups (Expenses)

Direct Expenses (Expenses (Direct))
Indirect Expenses (Expenses (Indirect))
Purchase Accounts

F-1C: Reserved Accounts Groups (Income & Expenses)

The Reserved Account Masters cannot be deleted. The Parent Account Group of the Reserved Masters cannot be changed.

03 Account Master Creation

You can create new Account Group or Account Ledger in addition to the Reserved Groups or Ledgers (auto-created by Tally on creation of a Company).

Select *Gateway of Tally > Accounts Info* to get *Accounts Info* menu (F-2A).

Gateway of Tally ....
Accounts Info.
Groups
Ledgers
Voucher Types
STatutory Info.
Quit

F-2A : Accounts Info Menu

Account Group Creation

At *Accounts Info* Menu (F-2A) select *Groups* to get *Account Groups* Menu (F-3A). Now select *Create* under *Single Group* (F-3A) to get *Account Group Creation* screen (F-3B).

Groups
Single Group
Create
Display
Alter
Multiple Groups
CReate
Display
AlTer
Quit

F-3A: Accounts Groups Menu

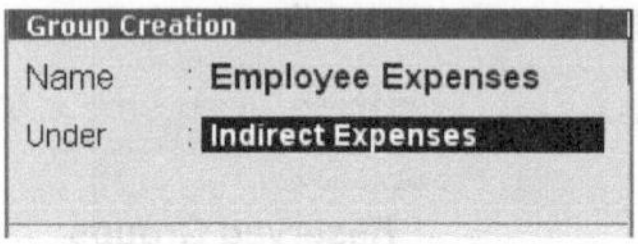

F-3B : Account Group Creation

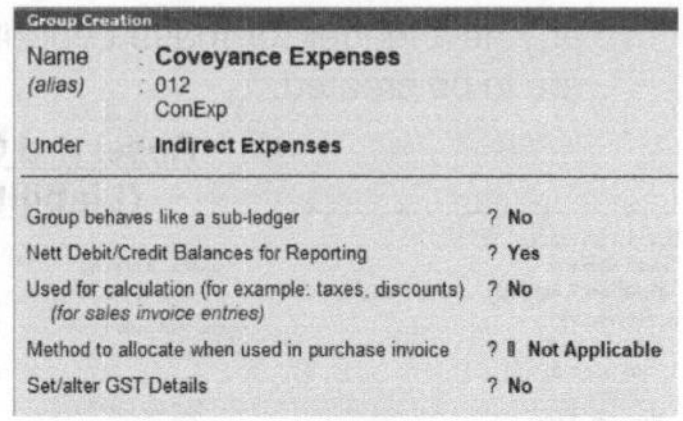

F-3C : Account Group Creation with Advanced options

At *Account Group Creation* Screen (F-3B), enter as follows :

- **Account Group Name :** At *Name*, enter unique Account Group Name.
- **Parent Group**: At *Under*, select the Parent Group from List of Groups already created. The new Group would be placed under the selected parent Group.

Multiple Account Group : For continuous entry of several Groups, it may be easier to make Groups Entry through Multiple Option. At *Account Groups* Menu (F-3A), select *Create* under *Multiple Group* to get *Multi Group Creation* screen. You get a columnar Table with columns for each field. Enter the data in the same way as explained.

Whether you enter through Single or Multiple mode, the Group records are saved in the same way.

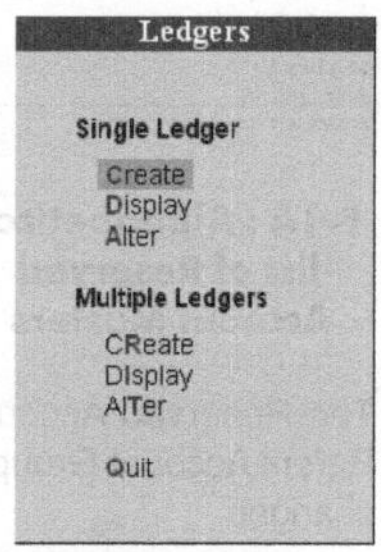

F-4A : Accounts Ledger Menu

Account Ledgers Creation

At *Accounts Info* Menu (F-2A), select *Ledgers* to get Accounts Ledger Menu (F-4A). Now select *Create* under *Single Ledger* (F-4A) to get *Account Ledger Creation* screen (F-4B).

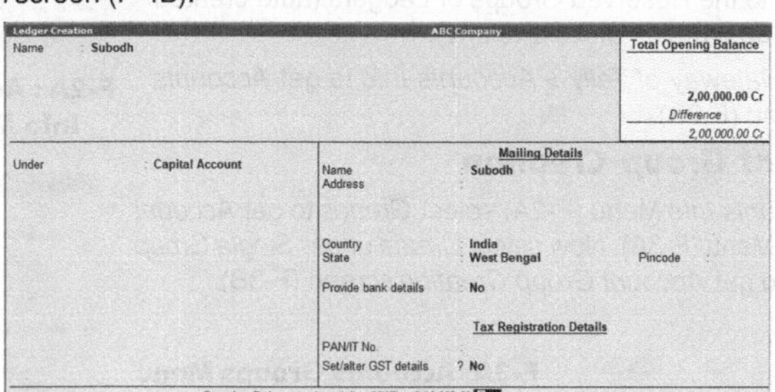

F-4B : Account Ledger Creation

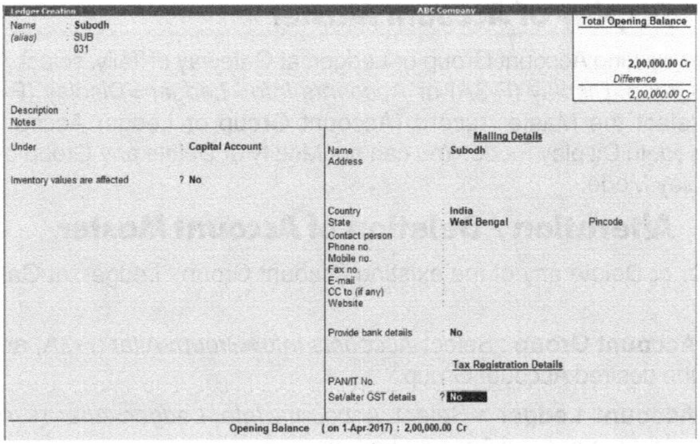

F-4C : Account Ledger Creation with Advanced options

At *Account Ledger Creation* Screen (F-3B), enter as follows :

- **Account Ledger Name :** At *Name*, enter the unique Name of the Ledger. This name will be printed in all internal records (like Ledger, Trial Balance etc) and will be available in drop down list for selection of Ledger.

  Ledger Opening Balance : You may enter Opening Balance, if any, specifying the nature of Opening Balance, Dr. (for Debit) or Cr. (for Credit). The appropriate Dr / Cr would be carried as default for convenience.

  When you start Accounts from the beginning of Financial Year, the Opening Balance of Nominal Ledger (Ledger Accounts appearing in Profit & Loss Account) would be zero.

- **Parent Group :** At *Under*, select the Parent Group of the Ledger from *List of Groups.*

Opening Balance Total : On entry of each Ledger Account, the cumulative Opening Balance (Debit & Credit) of all ledgers created are shown at the upper right corner. On entry of all ledgers with correct Opening Balance, the total Debit & Credit Balance should be equal.

Creation of new Parent Group during Ledger / Group entry

During Account Group or Ledger Account entry (F-3B/ F-4B), if you find that the parent group is not existing, press *Alt+C* at *'Under'* field to get *Account Group Creation (Secondary)* screen (like F-3B). Create the parent Account Group and select the parent group at *Under* field in Group Entry (F-3B), Ledger Entry (F-4B) as usual.

04 Display of Account Master

To view existing Account Group or Ledger, at Gateway of Tally, select *Accounts Info> Group>Display* (F-3A) or *Accounts Info> Ledger >Display* (F-4A) and then select the Master record (Account Group or Ledger Account) to be displayed. In Display mode. You can not Modify or Delete any Group or Ledger in Display Mode.

05 Alteration / Deletion of Account Master

To Alter or Delete any of the existing Account Group / Ledger, at Gateway of Tally :

- **Account Group** : Select *Accounts Info>Group>Alter* (F-3A) and select the desired Account Group
- **Account Ledger** : Select *Accounts Info>Ledger>Alter* (F-4A), and select the desired Account Ledger

  The selected Master record (Account Group / Account Ledger) appears in Alteration Mode (similar to creation screen).

  - o **Modification** : Now you may modify data of any field of the master record (Group or Ledger). Press *Alt+A* to save the changes made.
  - o **Deletion** : To Delete the Master Record, Press Alt+D and press Y at '*Delete? Yes or No.*' to confirm Deletion.

Restriction on Deletion of Master

An Account Master (Group or Ledger) cannot be deleted in following cases:

- **Deletion of Account Group**: An Account Group can not be Deleted, if there is any child ledger of the Group. The Tally created Reserved Group also cannot be deleted.
- **Deletion of Account Ledger** : An Account Ledger can not be Deleted if it is transacted in a Voucher. The Tally created Reserved Ledger Accounts (Cash and P& L A/c) also cannot be deleted.

Advanced Options : At Group / Ledger Creation screen, click F12:Configure to get respective Configuration screen. At respective Configuration screen, set *Yes* to activate the respective options in the Account Group / Ledger Accounts Groups (F-3C) & Accounts Ledger Creation screen (F-4C).

06 Chart of Accounts

Chart of Accounts is the organized list of All Account Groups & Account Ledgers (F-5A), represented in Hierarchical structure (arranged according to level in a multi level structure). Select *Display>List of Accounts* to view Chart of Accounts (F-5A).

The Reserved Groups appear in Alphabetical order and the subordinate groups appear below the respective Reserved Group in hierarchical order. Reserved Account Group appear in Bold, subordinate Account Group appear in Normal Font and Ledger Accounts appear in Italics.

To list Account Groups only, click *G:Groups* button at the vertical button Bar (click *Ledgers* to list Groups & Ledgers in hierarchical order). There is no option to list Accounts Ledger only

- **Branch / Divisions**
- **Capital Account**
  - **Reserves & Surplus** (Retained Earnings)
  - *Dr ABC*
- **Current Assets**
  - **Bank Accounts**
    - *Bank of India*
  - **Cash-in-hand**
    - *Cash*
  - **Deposits (Asset)**
    - *Calcutta Electric Supply*
  - **Loans & Advances (Asset)**
  - **Stock-in-hand**
    - *Stock of Medicine*
  - **Sundry Debtors**
    - *ABC Traders*
- **Current Liabilities**
  - **Duties & Taxes**
  - **Provisions**
  - **Sundry Creditors**
- **Direct Expenses** (Expenses (Direct))
- **Direct Incomes** (Income (Direct))
  - *Call Charges*
  - *Chamber Consultation*
- **Fixed Assets**
  - **Furniture**
    - *Chairs & Tables*
  - **Medical Equipment**
    - *Patient Bed*
- **Indirect Expenses** (Expenses (Indirect))
  - *Depreciation*
  - *Interest*
  - *Salary*
- **Indirect Incomes** (Income (Indirect))
  - *Interest on FD*
- **Investments**
  - *Fixed Deposit (SBI)*
- **Loans (Liability)**
  - **Bank OD A/c** (Bank OCC A/c)
  - **Secured Loans**
  - **Unsecured Loans**
  - *Mrs Gupta*
- **Misc. Expenses (ASSET)**
- **Purchase Accounts**
  - *Purchase*
- **Sales Accounts**
  - *Sales*
- **Suspense A/c**
- *Profit & Loss A/c*

30 Group(s) and **19 Ledger(s)**

F-5A:Chart of Accounts

Summary

- **Group Creation :** Tally creates 28 Reserved Groups, aligned with Standard Balance Sheet and Profit & Loss Statement. So, creation of new Chart of Accounts, for any organisation is a cool breeze. Tally created reserved Groups are normally good enough for small organisation. They may not need to create new Groups.
- **Primary Groups :** Normally all new groups created by user are placed under any of the Reserved Groups created by Tally. However, by setting Advanced Option in Account Master Configuration, you may create new Primary Group (at top level).
- **In line Parent entry at Account Group Master Creation:** Normally, at new Group creation, you select the parent Group (at Under field), from the list of existing Groups. However, if the parent group to be selected at Under field) is not currently existing (not yet created), you may create Parent Group in-line, from within the current Group Creation screen. At *Under* field, press *Alt+C* to get Secondary Group creation screen, similar to Group Creation screen. Now create the Group and save it. You will get back to the Group Creation screen. Select the newly created Group at *Under* field. This way, you may create a new Parent Group from within the current Group Creation screen.
- **Reserved Ledger Accounts** : Tally creates 2 reserved Ledger Accounts Profit & Loss Account & Cash. So, do not create these two Ledger Account. Enter the opening Balance of Cash, through *Ledger Alteration.*
- **In line Parent Group entry at Ledger Account Master Creation :** Normally, at new Ledger creation, you select the parent Group (at Under field), from the list of existing Groups. However, if the parent group to be selected at Under field) is not currently existing (not yet created), you may create Parent Group in-line, from within the current Ledger Creation screen. At Under field, press *Alt+C* to get Secondary Group creation screen, similar to Group Creation screen. Now create the Group and save it. You will get back to the Ledger Creation screen. Select the

newly created Group at *Under* field. This way, you may create a new Parent Group from within the current Ledger Creation screen.

- **List of Ledgers with Opening Balance** : Though you enter Opening Balance at the time of Ledger creation, the List of Accounts only gives a hierarchical list of Groups & underlying Ledger Names, without Opening Balance. After entry of Accounts Masters (Groups & Ledgers), to check the correctness of hierarchy and Opening Balance, print the Trial Balance (with Opening Balance alone), setting the Configuration options of Trial Balance, as described in Trial Balance chapter.

Accounts Vouchers 01-04

01 Accounts Vouchers

All business transactions are recorded and fully described in Voucher. Voucher is a complete & comprehensive record of all important details related to the transaction.

In fact, academically, all transactions (Cash or Non Cash) may be entered in Journal Voucher, which are recorded in Journal Book. However, for better control and division of accounting tasks to various persons, the Transactions are classified into several voucher types. Accordingly, different types of vouchers are used to record the transactions according to their nature.

02 Voucher Entry

Select *GoT>Accounts Voucher* and then click the respective Voucher button, to get the corresponding Voucher Entry screen.

Voucher Type Buttons : For convenience and error free entry, Tally provides following basic pre created account voucher types, according to nature of transactions. The specific type of Voucher is invoked through respective buttons (F-1A).

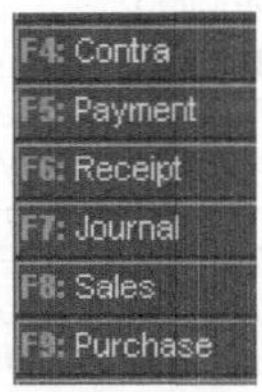

F-1A : Voucher Type Buttons

During voucher entry, Tally verifies that total of all Debits must be equal to the total of all Credits in each Voucher and does not allow to save the voucher if the total debits is not equal to total credits of the voucher

The basic rules for each Voucher Type are explained below :

Contra Voucher : Contra Voucher (click *F4:Contra*) is used to record transfer of fund from one Cash / Bank / Bank OCC to another Cash / Bank / Bank OCC a/c (like Cash Withdrawal from Bank, Cash Deposit to bank, Transfer from one Bank Account to another, Transfer between Main Cash and Petty Cash and Petty Cash). So, in contra voucher, you can transact only Cash / Bank / Bank OCC a/c ledgers.

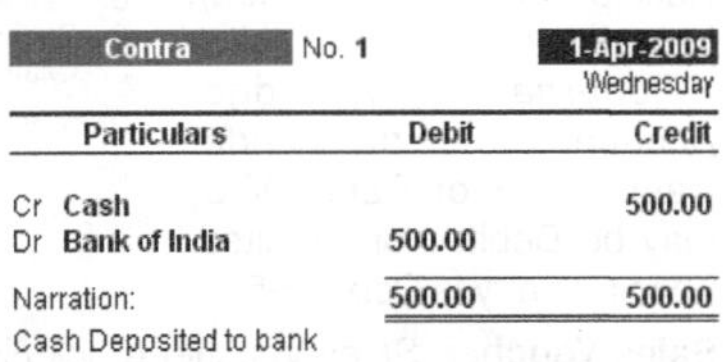

Contra No. 1 | 1-Apr-2009 Wednesday

Particulars	Debit	Credit
Cr **Cash**		500.00
Dr **Bank of India**	500.00	
Narration:	500.00	500.00

Cash Deposited to bank

F-2A : Contra Voucher

In Contra Voucher (F-2A), source of funds account (where the money is transferred from) is Credited and destination of funds accounts (where the money is transferred to) is Debited.

The first entry is always Credit (Source of Funds). From 2nd entry onwards you may Debit or Credit a ledger under Cash, Bank Accounts and Bank OCC group only.

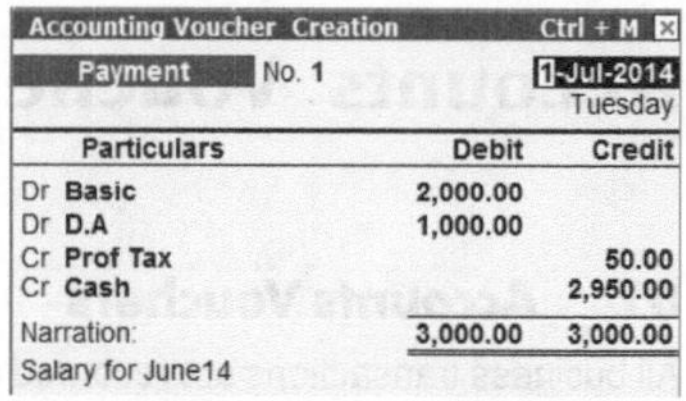

F-3A Payment Voucher

Payment Voucher : Payment Voucher is used for any sort of outgo of money (from Bank Account or Cash Account). In Payment voucher (click *F5: Payment)*, Ledger Account paid to is Debited and a Cash / Bank / Bank OCC A/c is Credited (F-3A).

The first entry is always Debit (other than Cash / Bank/ Bank OCC a/c) and second entry onwards you may specify Debit or Credit. The Cash / Bank / Bank OCC A/c must be Credited.

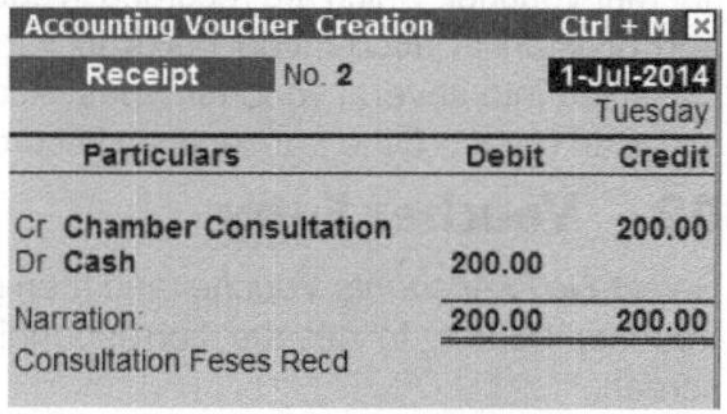

F-4A:Receipt Voucher

Receipt Voucher : Receipt Voucher is used for any sort of inflow of money (in Bank Account or Cash Account). In Receipt Voucher (click *F6: Receipt*), ledger account received from is Credited and Cash / Bank/ Bank OCC A/c is Debited (F-4A).

The first entry is always Credit (other than Cash / Bank Account), and second entry onwards you may specify Debit or Credit. The Cash / Bank / Bank OCC A/c must be Debited.

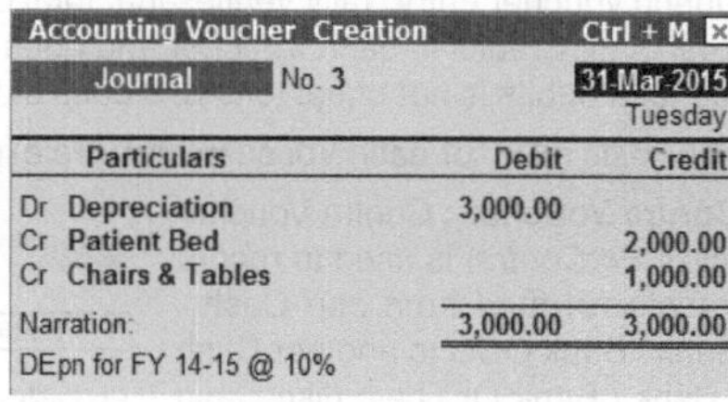

F-5A: Journal Voucher

Journal Voucher : Journal Voucher is used for all non cash transaction (other than Receipt, Payment & Contra). In a Journal Voucher (click *F7:Journal*), any Ledger Account (other than under Cash, Bank or Bank OCC) may be Debited or Credited. The first entry is Debit (F-5A).

Sales Voucher: Sales Voucher (Click *F8: Sales*): is created (F-6A) to record all sorts of Sales Transactions (Cash Sales or Credit Sales). At first ledger, you must select a Party Account (or Cash / Bank A/c) to be Debited. The next ledger account would be a Ledger under Sales Group and must be Credited. In subsequent entries, if any. In Sales Voucher, a ledger Account under Purchase Group cannot be entered.

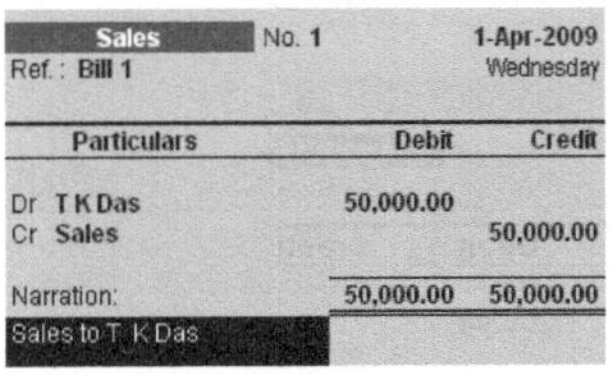

F-6A : Sales Voucher

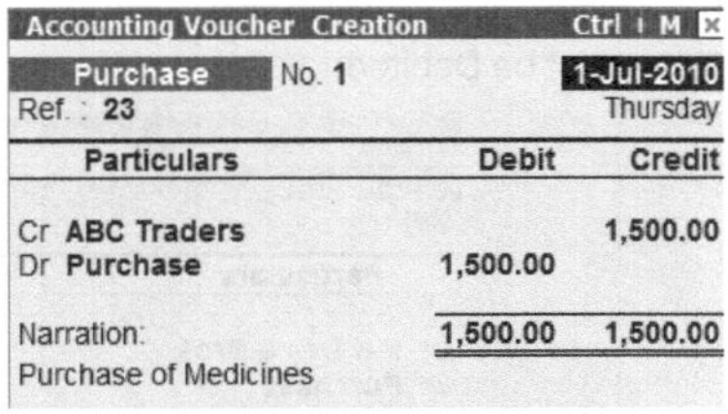

F-7A :Purchase Voucher

Purchase Voucher : Purchase Voucher (click *F9:Purchase*) is created (F-7A) to record all sorts of Purchase Transactions (Cash Purchase or Credit Purchase). At first ledger, you must select a Party Account (or Cash / Bank A/c) to be Credited. The next ledger account would be a Ledger under Purchase Group and must be Debited.

In a Purchase Voucher, a ledger account under Sales Group cannot be transacted.

03 Debit / Credit Note voucher

Debit & Credit note voucher are normally used for adjustment, supplementary bills, rebates, goods returns etc. These are supplementary Debits / Credits on Party, to Sales / Purchase Vouchers.

Activation of Debit / Credit Note Voucher : To enter Debit / Credit note voucher, click *F11:Features>Accounting Features* to get Accounting Features screen. At *Accounting Features screen*, set *Yes* at Use Debit / Credit Notes. Consequently, the buttons *F8:Debit Note* (F-8A) & *F9: Credit Note* (F-8B) buttons will get activated at the right side button bar at Accounts Voucher Entry screen.

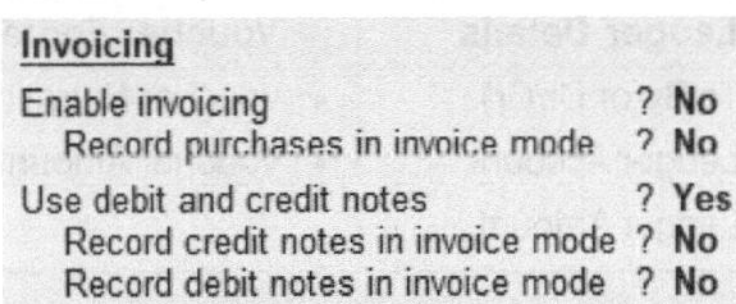

F-8A: Activation of Debit / Credit Note Voucher

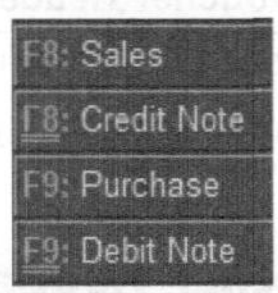

F-8B : Debit / Credit Note Buttons

Debit Note Voucher : Debit Note Voucher (click *F9:Debit Note*) is created (F-9A) to record supplementary Debits to the Party. Normally Debit notes are issued by customers on suppliers, for Goods returned to supplier, claims for damaged / defective goods, rebates allowed by supplier etc). However, sometimes, a Debit Note may also be issued as a supplementary Sales

Invoice on customer for further adjustments. The first ledger account in Debit Note must be Debited.

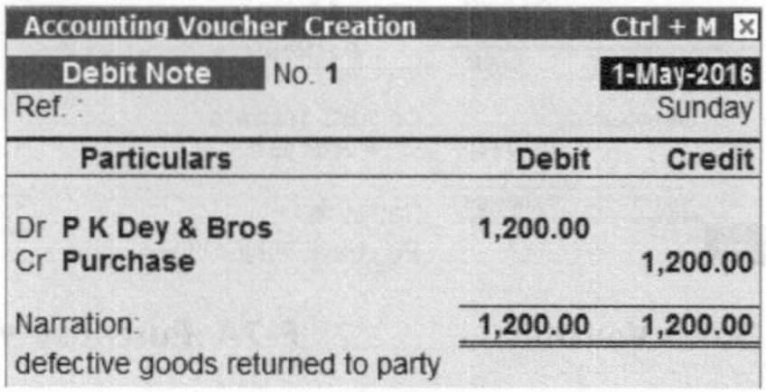

F-9A: Debit Note

Credit Note Voucher : Credit Note Voucher (click *F8:Cedit Note*) is created (F-9B) to record supplementary Credits to the Party. Normally Credit notes are issued by sellers in favour of customers, for Goods received back from customers, claims for damaged / defective goods, rebates allowed to customers etc). The first ledger account in Credit Note must be Credited.

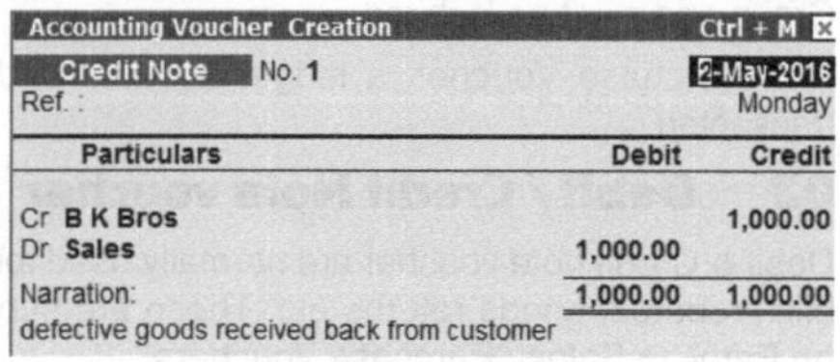

F-9B: Credit Note

04 Components of Voucher Entry Screen

Tally provides a standard Accounts Voucher entry Form for all types of Accounts Vouchers.

The Basic Accounts Voucher entry screen may be broadly divided into 3 areas:

Voucher Header	Ledger Details	Voucher Footer
• Voucher Type/Number • Voucher Date/Day	• To/By(or Dr/Cr) • Ledger Account • Ledger Amount	• Voucher Narration • Voucher Amount

Voucher Header

At Voucher Header, you enter the following :

- **Voucher Number**: Tally normally displays voucher number, serially generated in chronological order, for each Voucher type. For example, if the last voucher number was 5, the next voucher number will be 6. However, if you enter a back dated voucher, or delete a voucher, Tally will rearrange the voucher numbers in sequence of Date (However, you may change the Automatic voucher numbering option to Manual, No Numbering at Voucher Type creation / Alteration screen).

- **Voucher Date**: The Current Date is carried at this field as Date of Voucher
  - o To change the Voucher Date, press *F2: Date* button.The next Date is carried as default Voucher Date (F-2B/01-02). You may change it as needed.
  - o You may also press Shift+Tab to get back to the Date field and enter the Voucher Date, without changing the Current Date.

  Day of the Voucher Date (e.g., Tuesday) is displayed just below the Voucher Date

In *Sales* (F-6A) & *Purchase* (F-7A) Voucher, you may also optionally enter (or leave blank), some important document reference at *Ref* field at the header.

Voucher Ledger Account details

This is a tabular area where each Ledger Transaction data is entered .

- **Ledger Sign :** Press B (By for Debit) or T (To for Credit) at first column to indicate Debit or Credit the ledger that you select at *Particulars* Column. The Debit or Credit nature of the first Ledger Account in the Voucher is pre-determined by Tally according to Voucher Type . So, you have to enter To/By only from second entry onwards.

  To set the Ledger Sign, By/To to Dr / Cr , at Voucher Entry screen, click *F12:Configure* and set *Yes* at *Use Cr/Dr instead of To / By during Voucher Entry* to use Dr/Cr. Set No to get To/By. (we have used Dr/Cr throughout this book for better understanding). This is more convenient as it indicates the nature (Dr / Cr) of each entry instantly.
- **Ledger Account :** At Particulars field, select the Ledger Account from List of Ledgers pop-up.
- **Ledger Amount :** As per By / To or Dr/Cr entry in the first column, type the Ledger Amount in Debit or Credit column.

This way, you may enter many Debit and Credit entries in a voucher. The Ledger entries will be terminated as soon as the total of *Debit* and *Credit* is equal.

Quick Ledger Account selection in Voucher

Sometimes you write several vouchers continuously of similar transaction involving same ledger account. In such case, at Ledger Entry (particulars) field, press *Ctrl+R* to repeat the same first ledger entered in previous voucher. This way, if you are entering several vouchers for Salary payment for individual employees, Debiting Salary account, then after entering the first voucher for Salary, press Ctrl+R, the Salary account will be automatically carried, saving time for Ledger Account entry in Voucher.

New Ledger Accounts creation during voucher entry

During voucher entry, if you find that you need to create the ledger (the ledger account is not existing), press Alt+C at the ledger account field to get Ledger

Accounts entry screen, without exiting from the current voucher. Now create the new ledger account as usual. You will get back the voucher entry screen at the same point. Select the ledger account.

Voucher Narration

Enter Voucher Narration, describing the voucher transactions briefly but writing the essential details for future reference (long narration may get crumpled during entry).

To quickly rectify / insert words while entering Narration, use the following keys:

- **Home**: To reach beginning of the Narration.
- **End**: To reach end of the Narration.
- **Left & Right Arrow**: To move one character each time in the direction.
- **Cntl+ Left or Right Arrow**: To jump one word at a time Left or Right.
- **Insert**: To toggle between *Insert* (cursor is blinking line) and *Overwrite* (cursor is blinking block) mode.

Write complete details at Narration so that whole transaction and all important info are available in the Narration itself. You may enter the Cheque details also as part of Narration.

Narration carried from other voucher

To save time and write Narration Consistently & quickly, you may carry Voucher (Common) Narration entered in earlier voucher and just edit the required changes

- **Carry Narration of Previous Voucher** : At Voucher Narration field, press *Ctrl+R* to repeat the voucher Narration entered in the previous voucher. Now instead of writing the full narration again, just modify only the portion to be changed.
- **Carry the Narration of Similar Voucher** : At the voucher Narration field of the current voucher, press *Alt+R.* to carry Voucher Narration entered from earlier similar voucher (voucher with same first Ledger account). The Voucher Narration of a voucher having same first ledger account would be carried. This is quite helpful to quickly enter Voucher Narration of frequently occurred transactions, in a standard pattern (e.g, Narration of Conveyance Expenses will be of similar pattern). So, in Payment Voucher debiting Conveyance Expenses, press Alt+R at Narration field, the Narration of earlier Payment Voucher with Conveyance Expense as first ledger account, will be copied.

Ending Voucher Entry

After complete entry of the voucher, you get *Save Y/N* box to save the voucher

- **Saving the Voucher** : Press <Enter> or type Y at Accept*? Yes or No* to save the voucher. The current voucher will be saved.

To modify any data before saving, type N (or No) to go back to the top field, edit as desired and then save the voucher.

- **Quit without Saving** : To close the voucher entry screen without saving the current voucher being entered, press Q: *Quit* button at the bottom of the screen (or press Ctrl+Q).
- **Quick Saving** : To save the current voucher quickly (without confirmation), press A: *Accept* button at the bottom of the screen (or press Ctrl+A)

Terminating Voucher Entry

After saving the current voucher, a blank Voucher entry screen would appear to continue voucher entry. To terminate voucher entry, press <Esc>, and type *Yes* at *Quit? Yes or No.* to quit . To enter any other type of Voucher, click the respective voucher type button.

05 Voucher Alteration & Deletion

There is no Menu option for Alteration / Deletion of Voucher. You have to do it through Display mode.

After saving the voucher, to *Alter* any data in the voucher or to *Delete* Voucher, select *Display>Day Book*, click *F4:Chg Vch* button and then Click *F2:Date* (if you know the voucher date) or *F2:Period.* Enter the Voucher Date (at *F2:Date* prompt) or the Period (at *F2:Period* prompt) to get the list of the Vouchers (Day Book) for the selected Voucher Type for the selected Date / Period.

- **Voucher Deletion at Day Book** : At Day Book *Display*, select the Voucher (place the cursor on the desired Voucher) and click *Delete* button at the bottom button bar. Type *Y* to confirm *Voucher Deletion* (to quickly Delete the Voucher even without fully viewing it).
- **Voucher Alteration / Deletion :** At Day Book, drill down through the desired voucher (place the cursor on the voucher record and double click or press <enter>) to get the Voucher Alteration screen (similar to voucher entry screen). At Voucher Alteration screen:
    - o **Voucher Alteration** : Take the cursor on the desired field and make necessary alteration of data, as desired.
    - o **Voucher Deletion** : Press Alt+D and type Y to confirm deletion of the voucher. (you can view the entire voucher before confirming deletion)

06 Non Accounting Vouchers

We have so far discussed about vouchers which makes immediate effect in accounts. So, the entry is reflected immediately in ledger accounts, Trial Balance, Final Accounts etc.

However, tally provides following special purpose (Dormant) vouchers, which do not affect the accounts immediately.

- **Memo (F10) :** Such voucher is used to make entry for suspense account, to be converted to the respective voucher entry later on
- **Reversing Journal (F10) :** Used for inter period adjustments (like Depreciation) and to create scenarios
- **Optional (L:Optional):** These voucher are created to make provisional entry, to be regularized later on. Optional is state of a voucher, not any separate voucher type. Click L:Optional toggle button to convert to Optionl and vice versa
- **Post Dated (T:Post dated):** Entered in advance of the date of transaction. Often traders give post dated cheques, which are regularized when Banked. Post dated is state of a voucher, not any separate voucher type. Click T:Post Dated toggle button to convert to Post dated and vice versa

Activation of Non Accounting Voucher

To activate Non Accounting voucher, select *F11:Features>Accounting Features* to get Accounting Features screen. At *Accounting Features screen:*

- **Reversing Journal & Memo Voucher** : Set *Yes* at *Use Reversing Journal & Memo Voucher*. Consequently, the buttons *F10:Rev Jrnl* & *F10: Memos* buttons will get activated at Accounts Voucher Entry screen, to make entry for the respective voucher type
- **Optional Voucher** : Set *Yes* at *Maintain Budgets & Control*. Consequently the toggle button L:Optional & L:Regular will appear, through which you may convert the voucher to Optional & Regular State.

07 Voucher Type

Tally provides separate *Voucher Type* of for each type of transaction. Normally, you will not need to create any new *Voucher Type*. However, where needed, you may create a new Voucher Type, of any of the existing Voucher Type. The new Voucher Type inherits the properties of the parent Voucher type under which it is created

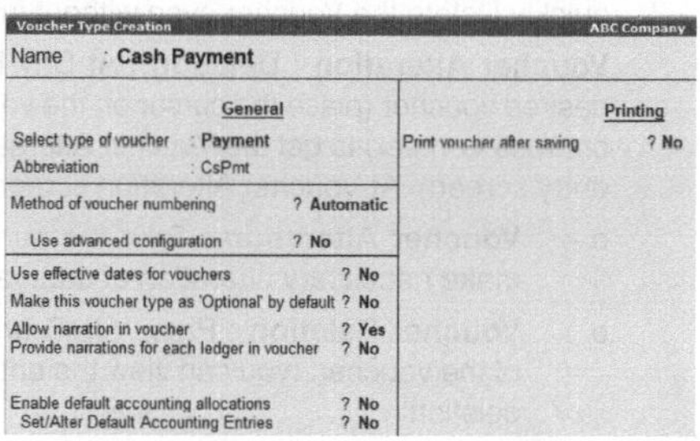

F-10A: Voucher Type cretaion

To create a new Voucher type, select *Accounts Info>Voucher Type>Create* to get Voucher Type creation screen (F-10A). At N*ame*, enter the Voucher Type Name, At Type of Voucher, select the Voucher Type from the list, At *Abbr*, enter the short name of the Voucher Type that would be printed in various reports for identification of voucher type, At *Method of Voucher Numbering*, select *Automatic* to get chronological auto serial number as per Date, select *Manual* to enter voucher number manually, select *None* to disable numbering (when you do not want voucher number to be maintained). Set other options as required.

08 Voucher Class

Voucher Class is a pre-defined Voucher Type Profile that helps to automate & expedite voucher entry and minimize errors. Voucher Class is just a way of voucher entry of a Voucher Type. The Voucher data is stored in the same way, and the Reports created are same whether you create a voucher through normal Voucher Type or through a Voucher Class. It does not make any difference in ultimate results or accounting process.

Voucher Class Creation

Select *Accounts Info > Voucher Type>Alter* and select the Voucher Type from the list for which you like to create a Voucher Class. Enter the details of Voucher Type (F-11A).

At *Name of Class* enter the unique Voucher Class Name (F-11A) to get Voucher Class set up screen (F-11B), for Ledger Account set up screen for set up of Voucher Class.

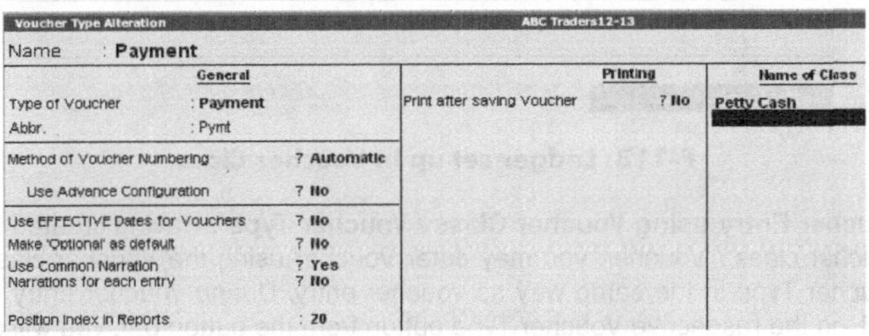

F-11A : Voucher Class Creation

Voucher Class set up

At Voucher Class set up screen (F-11B), you specify the Account Groups / Ledger Accounts, as follows:.

Account Groups : On the Upper 2 columns, specify the *Account Groups* to be Excluded / Included. You may select Multiple Groups in each section. Select *End of List* to terminate selection of Groups.

- **Excluded Groups** : At the Upper Left Part, specify the Cash / Bank Account Groups that you like to exclude in the Voucher Class. For example, if you want to create a Voucher Class for Cash Payments, you may specify the Bank Account Groups like Bank, Bank OOC etc.

- **Included Groups** : Having specified the Excluded Group, you may, if needed, include group some specific Group (among the sub groups of the Excluded Group).

Account Ledger : in the lower part, you may optionally specify the Ledger Account to be Included, or select Not Applicable

- **Selected Ledger Account** : The selected Ledger Accounts would be auto selected (carried) at the Header Account
- **No Ledger Account Selected** : When you set *Not Applicable* at Ledger Account, during voucher entry, at the header, you get the ledger accounts as per the Excluded / Included Groups (Ledger Accounts under Excluded Groups are not available for selection, but ledger accounts under the Included Groups are available.

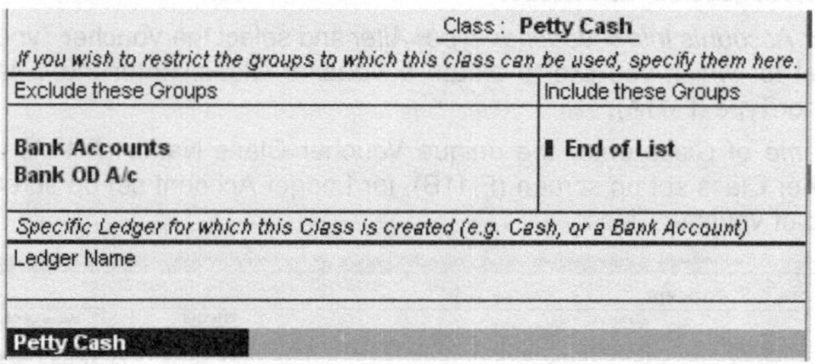

F-11B: Ledger set up in Voucher Class

Voucher Entry using Voucher Class / Voucher Type : Having created the voucher class / Voucher, you may enter Voucher using the Voucher class,/ Voucher Type in the same way as voucher entry. During voucher entry, on clicking the respective Voucher Type button from the button bar, you will get a list of Voucher Class / Type for the selected Voucher Type. Select the Voucher class / Type. The specified ledger Account, if set at Voucher Class, will be auto carried. Now enter the voucher as usual

09 Single Mode Voucher Entry

You may, alternatively enter Cash Vouchers (Receipt, Payment & Contra) in Single Mode. At Voucher configuration (click *F12:Config*), set *Yes* at *Use Single Entry Mode at Pymt/Rcpt/ Contra* to set Single Mode voucher entry option for Contra, Payment & Receipt Voucher Types.

In Single Mode, you have to enter Cash / Bank Account in Header and other Accounts in detail line. There is no Debit / Credit column in Single mode voucher entry, and you do not have to specify Dr / Cr sign. Tally internally sets the Dr / Cr sign for each entry according to the position (Header / Detail Line) and Voucher Types.

Tally stores the voucher in same manner, whether entered in Normal or Single Mode. You may edit / display a voucher in any mode, irrespective of the mode in which the voucher was created.

Summary

- **Voucher Entry** : Tally offers a standard interface to enter all types of voucher from a single interface. Just click the respective button to invoke the desired voucher type
- **Voucher Type** : Tally internally auto creates the Voucher Types. You may create new siblings of these voucher types (e.g a Cash Sales Voucher Type of Sales Voucher Type). The new Voucher Types inherits the properties of the parent voucher type. Tally created Voucher Types are good enough for normal accounting process. Normally, you may not need to create new Voucher Type or Voucher Class
- **Voucher Date** : Normally the Voucher Date field is skipped to make fast consecutive voucher entry for the current Date (click F2:Date button to enter next Date voucher). If you enter voucher of past dates randomly, then you my set the Voucher Configuration option to get the cursor at Date field, without skipping, and enter the Voucher Date for each Voucher.
- **Calculator** : Press Ctrl+N at numeric field (like Amount) to invoke calculator to make intermediate in line computation during voucher entry, and paste the computed value in any numeric filed (like Amount).
- **Narration Entry** : To make quick narration entry, you may carry Narration of previous voucher (press Ctrl+R) or similar voucher (press Alt+R) and edit the desired part of the narration without any need to write the whole Voucher Narration all over again
- **Duplicate Voucher** : For quick entry, instead of entering a new voucher, you may just copy a similar existing voucher (press Alt+2 at Voucher List / Day Book), make necessary changes and quickly save the voucher.
- **Voucher Numbering** : In automatic voucher numbering scheme, be careful about entry / date change of back dated voucher. All the successive vouchers may get renumbered.

Accounts Reports 01-05

01 Reports Display / Printing

As soon as you enter a voucher, its effect is immediately reflected in the respective places and you may view any report on screen or print on paper at any point of time to get the updated figures.

The top level reports like Balance Sheet, Profit & Loss Statement, Ratio Analysis, etc., are normally available at *Main Menu* of Gateway of Tally, while other reports are available through *Display* Menu (F-1A)

02 Display Menu

At Gateway of Tally, select *Display* to get *Display Menu* (F-1A). From *Display Menu* (F-1A), select the desired Report to get the respective Report Display screen (or the next level Report menu).

03 Accounts Books Display

At *Display* Menu (F-1A), select *Account Books* to get *Account Books Display* Menu (F-2A)

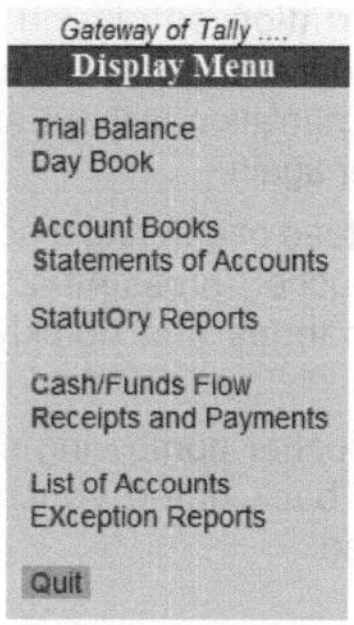

F-1A : Display Menu **F-2A : Accounts Books Menu**

At *Account Books Display Menu* (F-2A), select the option to get the respective report.

04 Drill Down & Trace Back

Tally provides a very convenient method to dill down through any Item in any Report Display to get next lower level details of the selected Item, and traverse back to get to the previous upper level Report

- **Drill Down**: From any on-screen report, press <enter>at any record to drill down, level-by-level to view the intermediary reports and reach to the vouchers constituting the Report.
    - o **Voucher in Alteration mode:** At lowest level, you may select a Voucher to get the voucher in *Alteration* mode where you may carry out *Alteration/ Deletion/ Cancellation* of voucher.
- **Trace Back**: Press <Esc> key to trace back (to the higher level report) in the same path through which you drilled down

05 Display Configuration

At any Report Display screen, click *F12:Configure* to get the respective Report Configuration screen (like F-3A), showing the options to customize the contents of the report as desired. The Configuration options vary according to the Report.

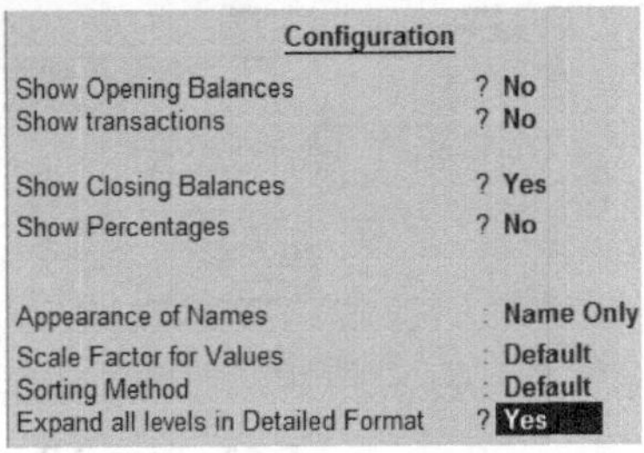

F-3A: Report Display Configuration (Trial Balance)

06 Reports Printing

The displayed report may also be printed on Paper. While the design of the Displayed Report is to conveniently allow drill down, the printed report is in the traditional familiar format of Books of Accounts and Accounts Statements.

Report Period : By default, the *Current Period* is initially set as *Report Period.* Click *F2:Period* button (or press F2 key) at the Report screen, to set the Report Period, in the same as you set Current Period. So, if you do not re-set the Report Period, the Report in Display would be shown as per Current Period.

The Report Period must be within the Current Period. So, Report Period may be same as Current Period (as default), or may be part of the Current Period (when Report Period is re-set). However, the Report Period set through *F2: Period* does not affect the Current Period (set through *F2:Period*).

To Print the Report shown in Display, at the current Report Display screen, click *P:Print* button to get the respective Report printing screen (like F-4A). The Report Printing screen contains the following major sections :

- **Printing Info** : At the top part, the current Printing Info displayed. You may re-set these values through Report Printing Buttons (F-5A).
- **Report Title** : At the middle part, the Report Title (and the respective Title Options activated / deactivated) are displayed for information. You may se the Reprt Title using *T:Titling* button.

- **Report Configuration** : At the lower Part, the default Report Printing Options are displayed (almost similar to the respective Display Configuration options). These options vary according to the Report. The report will be printed as per the options displayed. To re-set the Options, click *N* (No) at *Print Yes / No* option (F-4A), and change the options as desired.

Click *Yes* at *Print Yes / No* option to print the Report as per options set (F-4A)

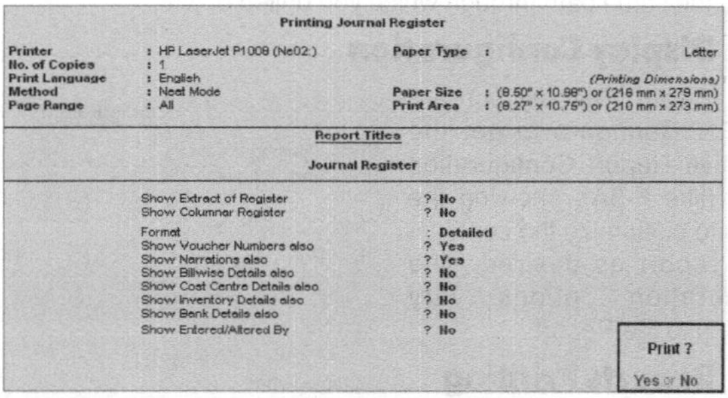

F-4A : Report Printing Screen

Report Printing Buttons

At the respective Report printing screen (like F-4A), click the button from the Report Printing Button bar (F-5A) at the right side, to change / set up respective Display/ Printing functions.

- L : Print Language - To set the Print language of the printed Report
- G: Page Number - To set the Page Number range of the report to be printed
- R : Pre Printed / Plain Paper- To set the Stationery type of the Report (Plain / Pre printed
- F: Print Format - To set the Report Format (Neat / Quick / Dot Matrix)
- C : Copies - To set Number of Copies of each report to be printed
- S : Select Printer – To select installed Printer for printing the current report
- T: Titling : To set the Report Title & other info to be printed at Report Header .
- I: With Preview / No Preview : To see / suppress the Preview of the Report on screen

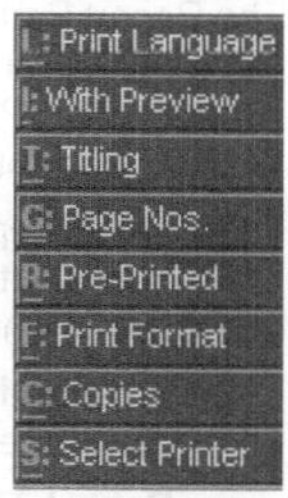

F-5A :Print Buttons

Report Title Setting

At Report Printing screen (like F-4A), click *T:Titling* button (or press *Alt+T*) at the button bar (F-5A), to get Report Title Set Up screen (F-5B) to set the Report Title options, as follows :

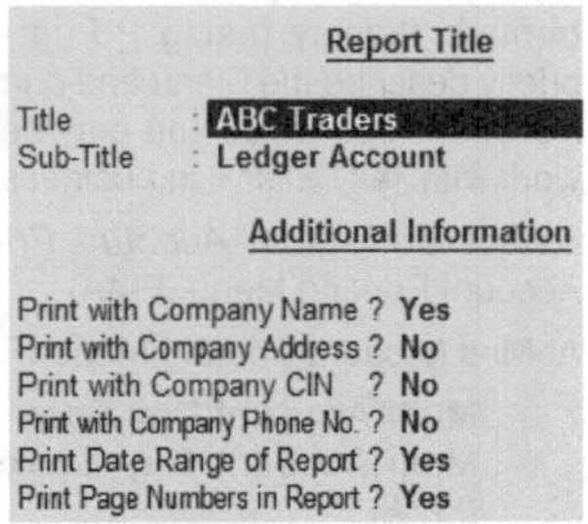

F-5B: Report Tile Set Up

- **Title** : The default Report Title is shown, which may be changed. This is printed in First Page of the Report
- **Sub Title** : Enter the Report Sub-Title to be printed in all the pages of the Report
- **Additional Information** : Set *Yes* at the respective option to print the info in the Report

Saving of Report in file

Instead of printing in paper, you may save the rport in file, in your desired format. At Report Display screen, click *E:Export* button instead of *P:Print* button. Select the desired format (PDF, Excel etc), specify the filename (with complete path) and save the report in selected format (F-5C). This allows you to print the report off line, send the digital file in e-mail or other means. This avoids printing to paper and is more suitable in current days digitally connected world, saving paper.

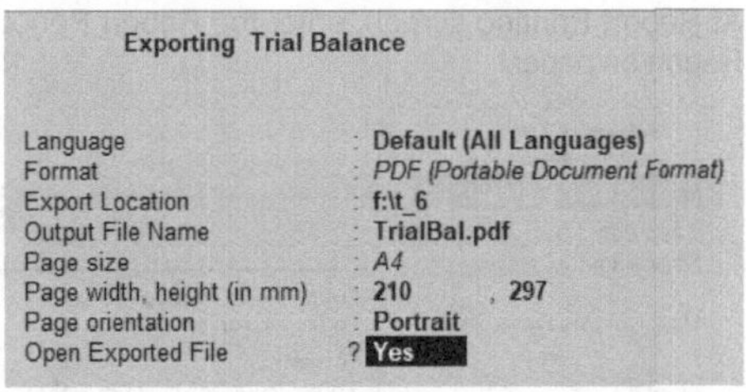

F-5C : Saving of Report in file

07 Multi Account Reports

So far, we have discussed Reports through Display, to view the Report on screen. Drill down & trace Back, Print the Report on paper/ or Preview the Report being currently viewed on screen. So, you get the Report for the selected Item only.

Multi Account Reports menu is useful to print the bulk reports like Accounts Books, on paper, offering Multi Account Reports more flexibility & selection facility for multiple items at a time, for printing in one shot. It is useful to print the Report on Paper for Record keeping / Distribution. The printing configuration options are similar to Display Configuration discussed earlier.

Multi Account Reports Menu is not available in Educational Version. During Training period, you may skip this option, as through Display option, you may

print all the Reports. The format & contents of the Multi Account Report are similar to Reports printed through Display (using P:Print) button. Here, we briefly describe the Menu and printing options of Multi Account Reports, as you may need them when you work with Tally ERP 9 in business environment.

Select *GoT>Multi Account Printing* to get Multi Account Printing Menu (F-4A)

At Muti Account Printing Menu (F-4A), select :

F-6A :Multi Account Printing Menu

- **Multi Account Day Book** : *Day Books* to get Multi Account Day Books Printing screen (F-7A)
- **Multi-Account Books** : *Account Books* to get Multi-Account *Account Books* Printing Menu (F-6B). Select the desired Account Book (F-6B) to get the Multi Account Printing screen for the respective Report (like F-7A)
- **Multi Vouchers** : *Multi Voucher Printing* to get Multi Voucher Printing screen (F-8A). Select the period, Voucher type to print al the Vouchers for selected voucher type, for selected period, in one shot.

At Report Printing screen, enter the Report Period and Click Yes to print the Report on paper.

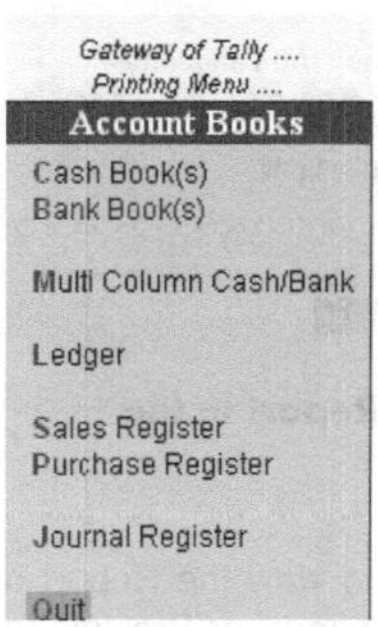

F-6B: Multi Account Books Printing Menu

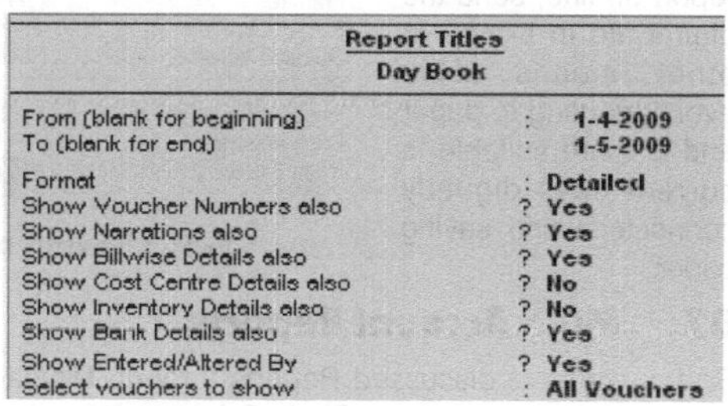

F-7A : Multi Account Report printing screen

08 Multiple Account Voucher / Invoice Printing

You may print several vouchers in a range, through Multi Account Voucher Printing. A Gateway, select *Multi Account printing > Multi Voucher printing* to get the Voucher printing screen (F-8A). Select the period and Voucher Type to print the Vouchers / Invoices in one shot.

09 Columnar Registers

You mat print some reports in columnar format setting the columns as desired. At Reports Display Screen, click the buttons *C:New column*, *A:Alter column*, *D:Del column*, *N:Auto Columns* (F-9A). You may set and configure the columns for Ledgers & Groups, in very compact and easy to use format.

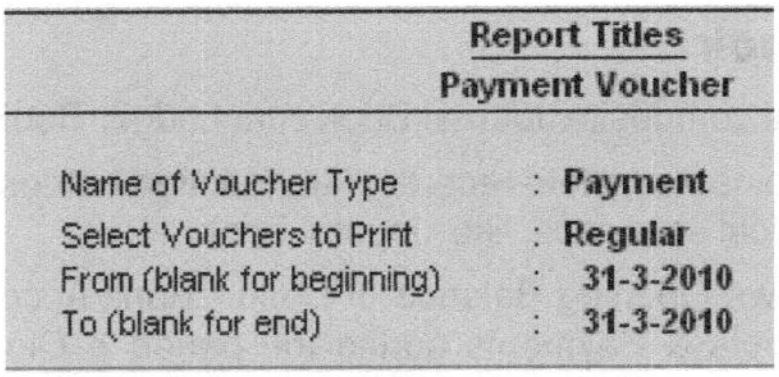

F-8A : Multi Account Voucher Printing

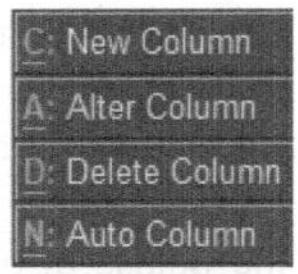

F-9A: Columnar Register button

Summary

- **Display :** You can Display all the reports from Display Menu (Balance Sheet & P L Statement from GoT). At Display screen, click respective report specific button as desired. Click *F12:Configure* to get the Configuration screen, to set the desired options. The options so set will be applicable to that instance of Report Printing and will be reset to default values after the current repot. So, you need to re-set the default Configuration, if required, at each time of report Display.
- **Printing** : At Display screen click *P:Print* button showing the current configuration. You may reset the Configuration options as desired and print the Report in printer.
- **Export** : Instead of printing in paper, you may export the report (click *E:Export* button instead of *P:Print* button at Report Display screen) and save the report in desired format, in a file.
- **Printing options Buttons** : At the right side of Report printing screen, select the desired button to set Number of Copies, Report Titles and other options.
- **Multi Account Printing** : Multi Account printing (not available in Educational Version), offers alternative method of printing in paper with additional options, to bulk printing of regular accounting reports (multiple account reports printing at a time in one shot).
- **Report Period** : In Display, the report is printed for current period set, as shown in right side of Reports Display screen (so you do not have to enter start and end date of report), while in Multi Account printing, you have to enter the report period (Start & End Dates).
- **Columnar Reports :** You may print some reports in columnar format. setting the columns as desired, through column buttons at button bar.

Cash Bank Book **01-06**

01 Cash / Bank Book

Cash / Bank Book is a special composite Journal Book cum Ledger Book :

- **Journal Book**: It contains complete record of transaction entries (i.e Vouchers) in chronological sequence, like Journal Book
- **Ledger Book**: It shows Opening Balance of Cash / Bank Account, the details of all Receipts & Payments during the period & Closing Balance of Cash / Bank Account (like a Ledger Book)

02 Cash / Bank Book Display

At Gateway of Tally, select *Display > Account Book > Cash & Bank Book.*

- The first screen shows the summary of each of the Cash Bank Accounts (Cash Bank Summary)
- At Cash Bank Summary screen, click on (Drill down) any Cash or Bank Account to get Ledger Monthly Summary (Ledger Monthly Summary) for the selected Cash / Bank Account
- At Ledger Monthly Summary, select a month and set the period to get the Cash Book of the selected Cash/Bank Account for the selected month (Ledger Vouchers)
- Click *F2:Period* and set the Period to get the Cash Book for the desired period(F-1A)

Ledger Vouchers — ABC Academy 9-10 — Ctrl + M

Ledger: Cash — 1-Feb-2010 to 28-Feb-2010

Date	Particulars		Vch Type	Vch No.	Debit	Credit
1-2-2010	A K Traders		Receipt	15	2,000.00	
1-2-2010	(as per details)		Receipt	16	2,850.00	
	Sales	3,000.00 Cr				
	Cash Discount	150.00 Dr				
20-2-2010	Bank of India		Contra	3		2,000.00
				Opening Balance :	19,189.50	
				Current Total :	4,850.00	2,000.00
				Closing Balance :	22,039.50	

F-1A : Cash Book Dislplay

The Cash Book (Ledger Voucher) shows the following main components and details (F-1).

- **Opening Balance** : Opening Balance of Cash & Bank Accounts for the specified period,

- **Voucher Details** : All transactions involving the selected Cash / Bank account, and complementary Ledger accounts in the voucher
- **Total Voucher Amount** : Total amount for cash / bank account in a separate column
- **Closing Balance** : Closing balance for the end of the period, for specified cash bank account.

Cash / Bank Book Display Configuration

At Cash Book Display screen (F-1A), click *F12:Configure* to get *Cash Book Configuration screen* (F-2A) showing the options to customize the contents of the Report, as desired.

03 Cash Bank Book Printing

At Cash / Bank Book Display (F-1A), Click *P:Print* button to get Cash / Bank Book Printing screen (F-3A).

Configuration

Select vouchers to show	: All Vouchers
Format	: Detailed
Show Billwise Details also	? No
Show Cost Centre Details also	? No
Show Inventory Details also	? No
Show Bank Details also	? No
Show Narrations also	? No
Include Opening Balances (*set as 'no' to remove from filtered reports*)	? Yes
Appearance of Names	: Name Only
Sorting Method	: Default
Show Running Balance	? No

F-2A: Cash Book Display Configuration

Report Titles

Bank of India Book

Style of Report	: Normal Ledger
Select vouchers to show	: All Vouchers
Format	: Detailed
Show Party's Address Details also	? Yes
Show Bank Account Details	? No
Show bill wise details	? No
Show Cost Centre Details also	? No
Show inventory details	? No
Show Bank Details also	? No
Show Additional Details	? No
Show Voucher Numbers also	? Yes
Show narrations	? Yes
Show Running Balance	? No
Include Opening Balances (*set as 'no' to remove from filtered reports*)	? Yes
Show Group Name	: No

F-3A: Cash / Bank Book Printing Screen

At Cash / Bank Book Printing screen (F-3A), set the options (mostly similar to Display Configuration : F-2A) and Type Y at Print Yes / No to print the Cash / Bank Book (F-3B)

Cash Book
1-Feb-2010 to 28-Feb-2010

Date		Particulars		Vch Type	Vch No.	Debit	Credit
1-2-2010	Cr	**Opening Balance**				**19,189.50**	
1-2-2010	Cr	**A K Traders**		**Receipt**	15	2,000.00	
	Cr	**(as per details)**		**Receipt**	16	2,850.00	
		Sales	**3,000.00 Cr**				
		Cash Discount	**150.00 Dr**				
20-2-2010	Dr	**Bank of India**		**Contra**	3		2,000.00
						24,039.50	2,000.00
	Dr	**Closing Balance**					22,039.50
						24,039.50	**24,039.50**

F-3B : Cash Book in Print

In Display form, the transactions are listed first, to enable easy drill down (F-1A). The Opening & Closing Balances are listed at the bottom . In Print Form (F-4A), the Opening Balance is shown first, transactions are listed next. The Closing Balance is shown at the end, like the traditional Cash Book.

04 Multi Account Cash / Bank Book

At GoT, select *Multi Account Printing > Account Books* to get Multi-Account Accounts Book Menu (F-6B/01-05). At Multi-Account Account Books Menu, select as follows, to get Multi Account Cash bank Book printing screen (F-4A).

- **Multi Account Cash Book(s)** : Select *Cash Books* and then the desired *Cash Account* (select *All Items* to print all Cash Books for all Cash Accounts one by one), to print Cash Book for the selected Cash Account only
- **Multi Account Bank Book(s)** : Select *Bank Books* and then the desired *Bank Account* (select *All Items* to print for Bank Books for all Bank Accounts one by one), to print Bank Book for the selected Bank Account only

Report Titles

Cash Book

From (blank for beginning)	: 1-4-2016
To (blank for end)	: 31-3-2017
Style of Report	: Normal Ledger
Select vouchers to show	: All Vouchers
Format	: Detailed
Show Billwise Details also	? No
Show Cost Centre Details also	? No
Show Inventory Details also	? No
Show Bank Details also	? No
Show Voucher Numbers also	? Yes
Show Narrations also	? No
Show Running Balance	? No
Include Opening Balances	? Yes
(set as 'no' to remove from filtered reports)	
Show Group Name	: No
Method of Balancing	: Yearly
Start fresh page for Balancing	? No

F-4A: Multi Account Cash / bank Book printing screen

The contents & format of Multi Account Cash / Bank Book is similar to Cash / Bank Book printed from Display (F-3B).

05 Multi Column Cash/ Bank Book

At *Multi Account Books* Menu, select *Multi Column Cash / Bank* to get *Multi Column Cash / Bank Printing* screen (F-5A), to print composite Cash / Bank Book with separate column for each selected Cash / Bank Account. of selected Cash Account (s).

Report Titles

Cash Book

From (blank for beginning)	: 1-4-2009
To (blank for end)	: 31-3-2010
Cash/Bank A/c for 1st Column	: Cash
for 2nd Column	: Bank of India
for 3rd Column	: State Bank of India
Format	: Detailed
Show Billwise Details also	? No
Show Cost Centre Details also	? No
Show Inventory Details also	? No
Show Bank Details also	? No
Show Narrations also	? Yes

F-5A : Multi Column Cash / bank Book printing screen

At *Multi Column Cash / Bank Printing* screen (F-5A), you may specify upto 3 Cash / Bank Accounts to include in the Multi Column Cash / Bank Book as follows:

- Cash / Bank A/c for 1st column
- Cash / Bank A/c for 2nd column
- Cash / Bank A/c for 3rd column

Click *Yes* to print the Multi Column Cash / Bank Book. The format of Multi Column Cash Book is similar to Cash Book. In Cash / Bank Book, only one column for Debit & Credit is provided and the transaction of the selected Cash Bank Ledger is printed. In Multi Column Cash Bank Book a separate column is created for each Cash Bank Account selected. Also, the Debit and Credit columns are shown in two sides. So, Multi Column Cash Bank Book becomes quite clumsy with too many columns

Summary

Cash Ledger : You may alternatively get Cash / Bank Book by Display of Cash / Bank Ledger for the selected Cash / Bank Account. The options and formats are similar.

Multi column Cash / Bank Book : In Multi Column Cash Bank Book (under Multi Account reports printing), the payment and receipts are shown in two sides. Avoid Multi column Cash Bank format as the Report becomes too cramped

Journal Books 01-07

01 Journal Books

Journal Books show list of non cash vouchers (other than Contra, Payment, Receipt vouchers). Here we discuss about following types of Journal Books :

- **Journal Register** : List of Journal Vouchers
- **Purchase Register** : List of Purchase Vouchers
- **Sales Register** : List of Sales Vouchers
- **Debit Note Register** : List of Debit Note Vouchers
- **Credit Note Register** : List of Credit Note Vouchers

02 Journal Register

Journal Register (also referred as *Journal Proper*) is a book listing Journal Vouchers.

At Gateway of Tally Menu, select *Display > Account Book > Journal Register* to get the Journal register Monthly summary screen (showing number of Journal Vouchers for each Month). Select a Month and set the Period (click *F2:Period* button) to get Journal Book (Voucher Register) for the specified Period (F-1A)

Voucher Register Ctrl + M

List of All Journal Vouchers — 1-Jan-2013 to 31-Mar-2013

Date	Particulars		Vch Type	Vch No.	Debit Amount	Credit Amount
1-1-2013	Pre Paid Expenses		Journal	1	1,500.00	
	Insurance Premia	1,500.00 Cr				
31-3-2013	Depreciation Account		Journal	2	32,000.00	
	Furniture Accounts	12,000.00 Cr				
	Building Account	20,000.00 Cr				
31-3-2013	P Kumar		Journal	3	2,300.00	
	Inerset Received	2,300.00 Cr				
31-3-2013	Interest Paid		Journal	4	1,250.00	
	D Sinha	1,250.00 Cr				
31-3-2013	Rent		Journal	5	2,500.00	
	Electricity Cahrges	1,250.00 Dr				
	Liabilties for Expenses	3,750.00 Cr				
31-3-2013	Salary		Journal	6	24,000.00	
	Prov Fund (Employee)	2,200.00 Cr				
	P Tax (Emloyee)	210.00 Cr				
	Loan (Employee)	2,500.00 Cr				
	Outstanding Net Salary	19,090.00 Cr				
31-3-2013	Bonus		Journal	7	3,000.00	
	Leave Salary	3,400.00 Dr				
	Outstanding Net Salary	6,400.00 Cr				

F-1A Journal Register Display

The amount of first Debit Entry only is shown in Debit Column. Amount of complimentary ledger accounts are shown in inner column only

Journal Register Configuration

At *Journal Register Display* (F-1A), click F12:Configure to get *Journal Book Configuration* screen (F-2A) to set the Configuration options.

Journal Register Printing

At *Journal Book Display* (F-1A), click *P:Print* to get Journal Book Printing screen (F-3A). Set the options (mostly similar to Journal Book Configuration screen (F-2A). Type Y to print Journal Book (F-4A).

Show Extract of Register	?	No
Show Columnar Register	?	No
Format	:	Condensed
Show Narrations also	?	No
Show Billwise Details also	?	No
Show Cost Centre Details also	?	No
Show Inventory Details also	?	No
Show Bank Details also	?	No
Show Entered/Altered By	?	No
Appearance of Names	:	Name Only
Sorting Method	:	Default

F-2A Journal Book Display Configuration

Report Titles

Journal Register

Show Extract of Register	?	No
Show Columnar Register	?	No
Format	:	Condensed
Show Voucher Numbers also	?	Yes
Show narrations	?	No
Show bill wise details	?	No
Show Cost Centre Details also	?	No
Show inventory details	?	No
Show additional description of Stock Item	?	No
Show Bank Details also	?	No
Show Additional Details	?	No

F-3A : Journal Register Printing

Journal Register
1-Jan-2013 to 31-Mar-2013

Page 1

Date	Particulars	Vch Type	Debit Amount	Credit Amount
1-1-2013	Pre Paid Expenses	Journal	1,500.00	
	Insurance Premia			1,500.00
	Proprtionate Insurance Premia for 1.4.12 to 30.6.12 adjusted			
31-3-2013	Depreciation Account	Journal	32,000.00	
	Furniture Accounts			12,000.00
	Building Account			20,000.00
	Depreciation on Furniture @ 10% on 1,20,000=12000, Building @ 5% on 4,00,000			
31-3-2013	P Kumar	Journal	2,300.00	
	Inerset Received			2,300.00
	Interest Receivable from Borrower for the Q/e Jan - Mar debited to his account			

F-4A : Journal Register Display in Print

- In *Journal Register Display* (F-1A), amount of only the first ledger account in the voucher is shown in Debit column. Amount of all other ledger accounts are shown in inner column with Dr / Cr indicator.
- In *Journal Register in Print* (F-4A), the amount for each ledger account in the voucher is shown in respective Debit column, the way we traditionally do in Journal Book.

03 Sales Register

Like Journal Book, Sales Register is chronological list of Sales Vouchers.

At Gateway, select *Display>Account Books* to get *Accounts Books* Menu. At Accounts Books Menu, select *Sales Register* to get Monthly Sales Summary. Select any month and Click *F2:Period* to set the period to Display the Sales Register (F-5A).

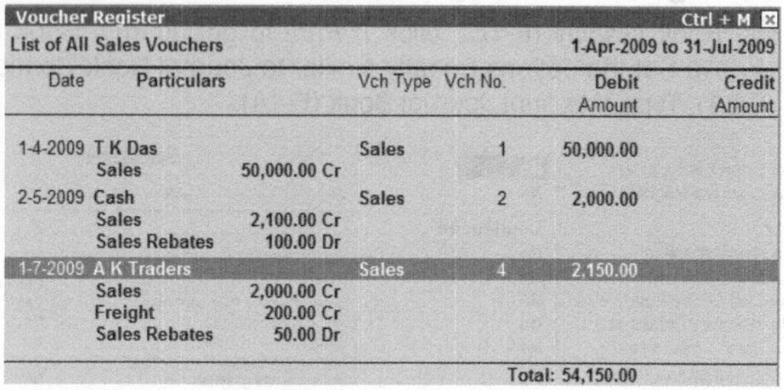

F-5A : Sales Register Display

Sales Register Configuration

At Sales Register Display (F-5A), click *F12:Configure*, to get Sales Register Display Configuration screen, to set the report display options

Sales Register Printing

At Sales Register Display (F-5A), click *P:Print* to get Sales Register printing screen (F-6A).

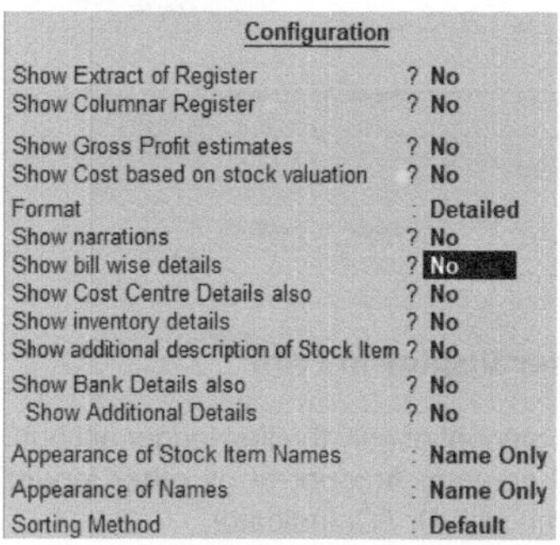

F-5B: Sales Register Display Configuration

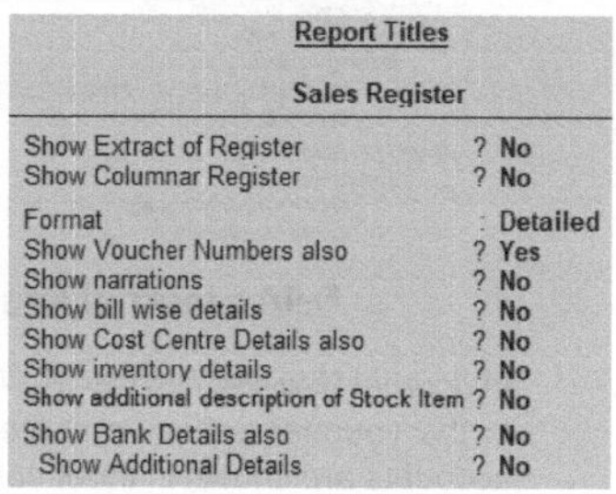

F-6A: Sales Register Printing

At Sales Register printing screen (F-6A), set the printing options (similar to Sales Register Display Configuration) to get Sales Register in Print (F-7A).

Sales Register
1-Apr-2009 to 30-Jun-2009

Date	Particulars	Vch Type	Vch No.	Debit Amount	Credit Amount
1-4-2009	T K Das	Sales	1	50,000.00	
	Sales				50,000.00
2-5-2009	Cash	Sales	2	2,000.00	
	Sales				2,100.00
	Sales Rebates			100.00	
2-6-2009	A K Traders	Sales	3	2,800.00	
	Sales				2,500.00
	Freight				300.00
			Total:	54,800.00	

F-7A:Sales Register in Print

- In *Sales Register Display* (F-5A), amount of only the first ledger account in the voucher is shown in Debit column. Amount of all other ledger accounts are shown in inner column with Dr / Cr indicator.
- In *Sales Register Display in Print* (F-7A), the amount for each ledger account in the voucher is shown in respective Debit / Credit column. The Grand total is shown only in Debit Column.

04 Purchase Register

Like Sales Register, Purchase Register is chronological list of Purchase Vouchers.

At Gateway, select *Display>Account Books* to get *Accounts Books* Menu. At Accounts Books Menu, select *Purchase Register* to get Monthly Purchase Summary. Select any month and Click *F2:Period* to set the period to Display the Purchase Register (F-8A).

Voucher Register — Ctrl + M

List of All Purchase Vouchers — 1-Oct-2009 to 31-Dec-2009

Date	Particulars		Vch Type	Vch No.	Debit Amount	Credit Amount
2-11-2009	B M Suppliers		Purchase	2		3,040.00
	Purchase	3,000.00 Dr				
	Freight	40.00 Dr				
2-11-2009	B M Suppliers		Purchase	3		3,040.00
	Purchase	3,000.00 Dr				
	Freight	40.00 Dr				
1-12-2009	B M Suppliers		Purchase	4		3,040.00
	Purchase	3,000.00 Dr				
	Freight	40.00 Dr				
						9,120.00

F-8A: Purchase Register Display

Purchase Register Configuration : At Purchase Register Display (F-8A), click *F12:Configure* to get Purchase Register Configuration screen, similar to Sales Register Configuration screen (F-5B)

Purchase Register Printing : At Purchase Register Display (F-8A), click *P:Print* to get Purchase Register printing screen (similar to Sales Register printing screen : F-6A). Set the printing options to get Purchase Register in print (F-9A).

Purchase Register
1-Apr-2009 to 31-Dec-2009

Page 1

Date	Particulars	Vch Type	Vch No./Excise Inv.No.	Debit Amount	Credit Amount
1-6-2009	B M Suppliers	Purchase	1		2,200.00
	Purchase			2,100.00	
	Freight			300.00	
	Discount on Purchase				200.00
2-11-2009	B M Suppliers	Purchase	2		3,040.00
	Purchase			3,000.00	
	Freight			40.00	
2-11-2009	B M Suppliers	Purchase	3		3,040.00
	Purchase			3,000.00	
	Freight			40.00	
1-12-2009	B M Suppliers	Purchase	4		3,040.00
	Purchase			3,000.00	
	Freight			40.00	
			Total:		11,320.00

F-9A: Purchase Register in print

- In *Purchase Register Display* (F-8A), amount of first ledger account in the voucher is shown in Credit column. Amount of all other ledger accounts are shown in inner column with Dr / Cr indicator.
- In *Purchase Register Display in Print* (F-9A), the amount for each ledger account in the voucher is shown in respective Debit / Credit column. The Grand total is shown only in Credit Column.

The contents, format, Printing screen & Configuration options (F-6A) of both the Sales & Purchase Register are similar.

05 Debit / Credit Note Register

Like Sales / Purchase Register, you may display / print Debit / Credit Note Register. At *GoT>Display>Accounts Books>Journal Register*, select:

- *Debit Note Register* to display Debit Note Register
- *Credit Note Register* to display Credit Note Register

The contents and options are similar to Sales / Purchase Register

06 Multi Account Registers Printing

At Gateway of Tally, select *Multi accounts Printing> Account Books* to get *Multi Account Books Printing* Menu.

Multi Account Sales / Purchase Register printing : At *Multi Account Books Printing* Menu, select :

- **Purchase Register** *:* Purchase *Register* to get Purchase Register printing screen (like F-10A)
- **Sales Register** *:* Sales *Register* to get Sales Register printing screen (like F-10A)

Multi Account Journal / Debit / Credit Note Register printing : At Gateway of Tally, select *Multi accounts Printing> Account Books>Journal Register* to get *Multi Account Journal Books Printing* Menu. At *Multi Account Journal Books Printing* Menu select :

- **Journal Register** *: Journal Register* to get Journal Register printing screen (like F-10A)
- **Debit Note Register** : To print display Debit Note Register
- **Credit Note Register** : To display Credit Note Register

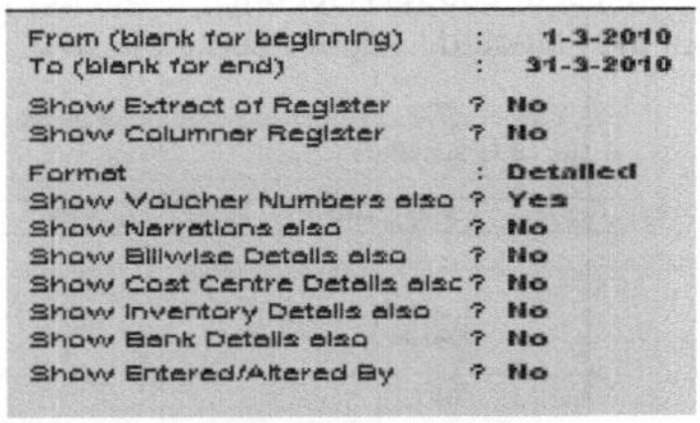

F-10A : Multi Account Journal / Sales / Purchase Register Printing screen

Set the Report Period and the printing options to get respective Register, with format and contents similar to the corresponding registers in print, shown earlier (like F-4A, F-7A, F-9A). However, columnar format is not available for Multi Account Registers.

Summary

- **Report Totals** : In Journal Register, you do not get Report Totals. However Sales / Purchase registers provide Report Totals for one of the columns (Debit / Credit).
- **Monthly Voucher Counts** : In Journal Register, first you get monthly voucher counts, from where you may drill down through any moth to get the Register for the selected month. To get the report for selected period, click *F2:Period* and set the current period.

Ledger Book 01-08

01 Ledger Book

Ledger is a report of assorted transactions related to a specified ledger account (F-2A). It shows Opening / Closing Balance & Transactions of the ledger account, in chronological order, for the specified period.

At *Account Books* Menu, select *Ledger* and then select the Ledger account from list of Ledger Accounts, to get Ledger account display (Ledger Vouchers) of the selected Ledger Account (F-1A).

Ledger Vouchers — Ctrl + M

Ledger: **B M Suppliers** — **1-Dec-2009 to 31-Mar-2010**

Date	Particulars	Vch Type	Vch No.	Debit	Credit
1-12-2009	**(as per details)**	Purchase	4		3,040.00
	Purchase 3,000.00 Dr				
	Freight 40.00 Dr				
			Opening Balance :		**4,130.00**
			Current Total :		**3,040.00**
			Closing Balance :		**7,170.00**

F-1A : Ledger Book Display

Ledger shows the following main components and details :

- **Opening Balance** : Opening Balance of Ledger Account for the specified period.
- **Ledger Account & Amount** : Ledger Account and the corresponding amount in respective Debit / Credit column /Sign
- **Closing Balance** : Closing Balance for the end of the period, for the specified ledger account

B M Suppliers
Ledger Account
1-Dec-2009 to 31-Mar-2010
Page 1

Date		Particulars	Vch Type	Vch No.	Debit	Credit
1-12-2009	Dr	**Opening Balance**				**4,130.00**
1-12-2009	Dr	**(as per details)**	**Purchase**	4		3,040.00
		Purchase	**3,000.00 Dr**			
		Freight	**40.00 Dr**			
		Materials purchased ag party's Inv No 12 dt 3110.11				
						7,170.00
	Cr	**Closing Balance**			7,170.00	
					7,170.00	**7,170.00**

F-1B : Ledger Book in print

Ledger Display Configuration : At Ledger Account Display (F-1A), click *F12;Configure* to get *Ledger Display Configuration* screen (F-2A), to set the options.

In Display, the opening & Closing Balances are shown at the bottom, after all the transactions (F-1A), while in Print format (F-1B), the Opening balance is shown at first, followed by transaction details and finally the Closing Balance, like in traditional ledger accounts.

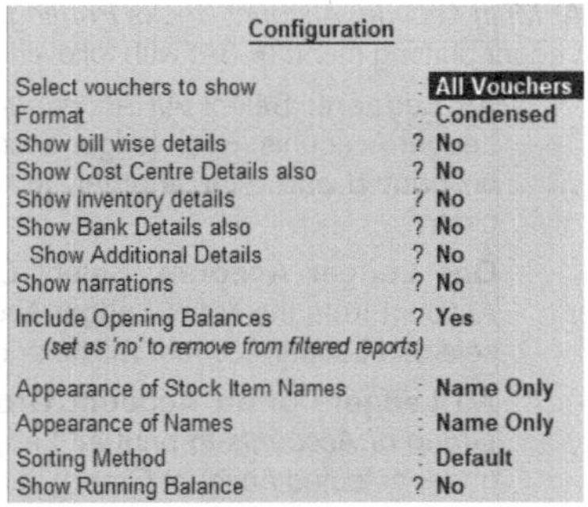

F-2A: Ledger Display Configuration

02 Confirmation of Accounts

In printing options (when you click P:Print at Ledger Display screen), you get additional option Style of Report (F-2B). Select *Normal Ledger* to print ledger Book, or *Confirmation of Accounts* to print statement of Confirmation of Accounts. This is normally for Parties (Sundry Debtors / Creditors), Loan Accounts, to match and reconcile the entries. Such statement is normally demanded by Auditors / Income Tax department to ensure that the Company's Books conform to that of the other Party.

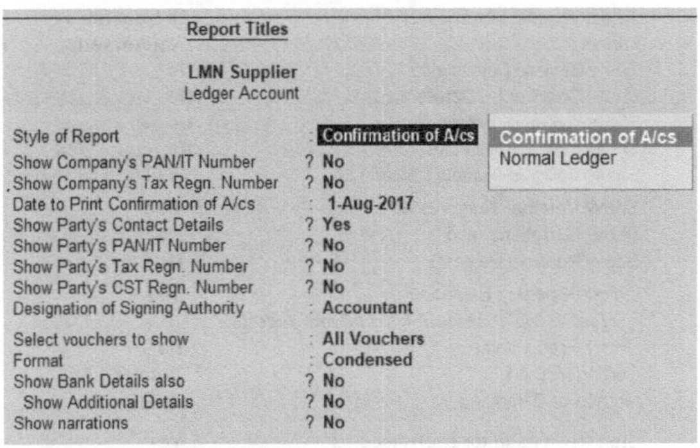

F:2B : Ledger printing options

03 Multi Account Ledger Book

Through Display, you can print only one Ledger Account at a time, whereas, through Multi Account Ledger option, you may print several Ledger Account of a Group (or all Ledger Account) at a time for the specified period

At *Multi Account Account Books Printing*, select *Ledger* to get Multi Account Ledger printing menu (F-3A) with following options :

- **All Ledgers**: Select *All Accounts* to print all Ledger Accounts. Each ledger accounts would be printed one after another, in alphabetical order
- **One Ledger Account**: Select *One* Ledger Account from the list of Ledger Accounts. The selected Ledger Account will be printed
- **All Ledgers of an Account Group**: Select *Group of Accounts* to print all Ledgers placed under selected Account Group, in alphabetical order, one after another.

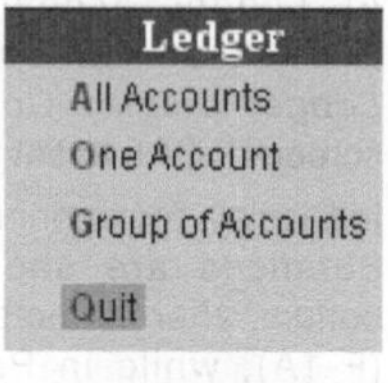

F-3A: Multi Account Ledger printing Menu

On selection of the desired menu Item as above, you get the Ledger Printing screen (F-4A). Set the period for which you like to print the Ledger Book.

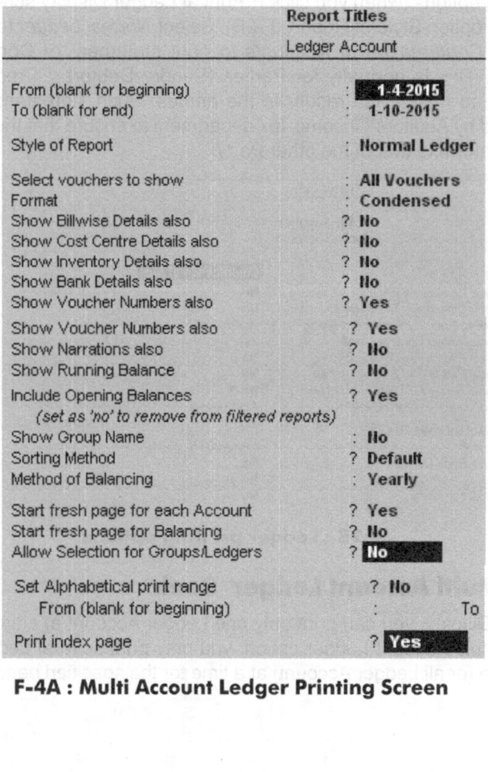

F-4A : Multi Account Ledger Printing Screen

When you select All Accounts or Account Groups (F-3A), you may select specific ledgers by filtering the Ledger Accounts through Range & selection of Ledger options (Include/ Exclude Groups / Ledgers).

Multi Account Ledger books printing (F-4A) provide a great deal of additional flexible option, than what you get in Printing from Ledger Display (F-2A), to selectively print specific ledger, ledger of specific groups, including / excluding, specified Ledger / Groups.

The format of Multi Account Ledger is similar to Ledger printed from Display. When Multiple Ledgers are printed (with All Ledgers/ Group of Ledgers option), several Ledger Accounts are printed in the same report, one after another, in alphabetical order, for the same period as specified at the Multi Account Ledger Printing screen.

Ledger Index : Ledger Index is alphabetical list of Ledger Accounts in the Ledger Book with page number for each Ledger Account, for quick finding of ledger pages manually, from printed ledger book.

To print alphabetical Index of Ledgers (helpful for printing the entire Ledger Book at Year ending on finalisation of Accounts), at Multi Account Ledger Printing screen (F-4A), set *Yes* at *Print Index Page.*

Summary

- **Ledger Display :** In Ledger Display, you may see the ledger of one selected Account only (useful to print a selective ledger on line).
- **Multi Account Printing :** Multi Account Ledger Printing allows to selectively print some specified ledger accounts in one shot (useful to print several ledgers at a time, at back end).
- **Cash / Bank Book** : You may print Cash / Bank of any selected Cash Bank through Ledger printing option also.
- **Ledger Index** : Through Multi Account Ledger Printing option, at the time of Ledger Printing, you may also print Index of Ledger showing the page number of each Ledger Account, like manual Ledger Book.

Trial Balance 01-09

01 Trial Balance

Trial Balance is a summary Statement showing the Net Balance of all Ledger Accounts. It is prepared to ensure that the Ledger Accounts are properly posted and balanced.

In Double Accounting System, every transaction causes equal Debit & Credit. Trial Balance is the Account wise summary of all the Transactions (Vouchers) & Balances. So, the total of Debits & Credits in the Trial Balance would also be equal (F-1A).

If the Trial Balance does not tally (i.e, the total of Debits & Credits of Trial Balance are not equal), there is mistake somewhere. As the equality of Debit / Credit in each voucher is ensured during voucher entry, carefully check the Opening Balance to make sure the total Debits & Credits of Opening Balance all ledger accounts are equal.

Trial Balance serves 2 major objectives:

- **Tallying the Trial Balance** : To check the arithmetic accuracy of Trial Balance ensuring Total Debits & Credits are equal (so the name Trial Balance).
- **Accounting Reports Preparation** : It shows the Account wise Balance of each Ledger Account. These figures are posted in various Financial Statements and Final Accounts (Profit & Loss & Balance Sheet) statements.

Trial Balance — Ctrl + M

Particulars	Dr ABC 14-15 1-Apr-2014 to 31-Mar-2015 Closing Balance	
	Debit	Credit
Capital Account		**1,00,000.00**
Dr ABC		*1,00,000.00*
Loans (Liability)		**37,900.00**
Mrs Gupta		*37,900.00*
Fixed Assets	**49,500.00**	
Furniture	22,500.00	
Medical Equipment	27,000.00	
Investments	**15,000.00**	
Fixed Deposit (SBI)	*15,000.00*	
Current Assets	**88,800.00**	
Opening Stock		
Deposits (Asset)	10,000.00	
Cash-in-hand	40,900.00	
Bank Accounts	37,900.00	
Sales Accounts		**1,100.00**
Sales		*1,100.00*
Purchase Accounts	**1,200.00**	
Purchase	*1,200.00*	
Direct Incomes		**32,000.00**
Call Charges		*17,000.00*
Chamber Consultation		*15,000.00*
Indirect Expenses	**16,500.00**	
Depreciation	*5,500.00*	
Interest	*3,000.00*	
Salary	*8,000.00*	
Grand Total	**1,71,000.00**	**1,71,000.00**

F-1A Trial Balance Display (Detailed)

02 Trial Balance Display

At Display Menu, select *Trial Balance* to get Trail Balance (F-1A), showing the Closing Balance of Major Accounts Groups.

The Top level Primary Groups are shown in Bold, the Account Groups are shown in Normal Font and the Ledger Accounts are shown in Italics.

Trial Balance Configuration

At Trial Balance Display (F-1A), click *F12:Configure* to get Trial Balance Configuration screen (F-2A) to set the contents of Trial Balance display.

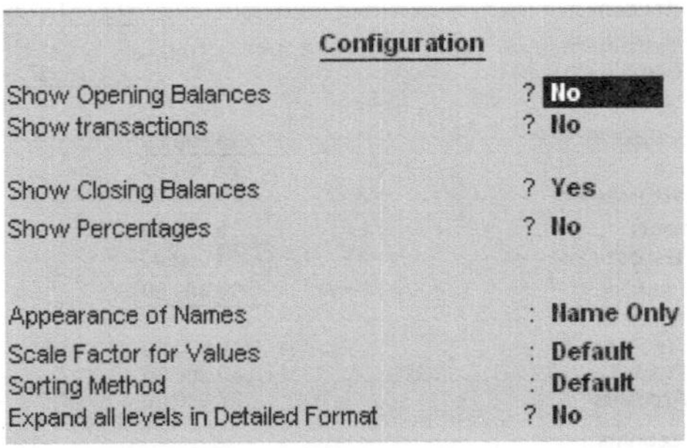

F-2A:Trial Balance Display Configuration

03 Trial Balance Printing

At Trial Balance Display (F-1A), Click *P:Print* (or press Alt+P) to get Trial Balance Printing screen (F-2A). Set the options to get Trial Balance in print (F-4A), similar to Trial Balance Display (F-1A).

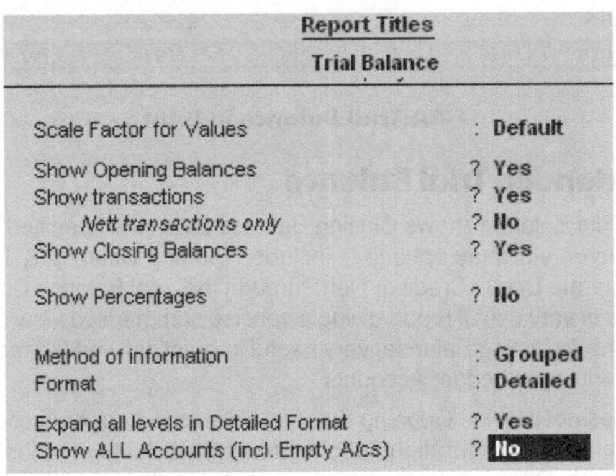

F-3A:Trial Balance Printing

Dr ABC
Trial Balance
1-Apr-2014 to 31-Mar-2015

Page 1

Particulars	Closing Balance	
	Debit	Credit
Capital Account		**1,00,000.00**
Dr ABC		*1,00,000.00*
Loans (Liability)		**37,900.00**
Mrs Gupta		*37,900.00*
Fixed Assets	**49,500.00**	
Furniture	22,500.00	
Medical Equipment	27,000.00	
Investments	**15,000.00**	
Fixed Deposit (SBI)	*15,000.00*	
Current Assets	**88,800.00**	
Opening Stock		
Deposits (Asset)	10,000.00	
Cash-in-hand	40,900.00	
Bank Accounts	37,900.00	
Sales Accounts		**1,100.00**
Sales		*1,100.00*
Purchase Accounts	**1,200.00**	
Purchase	*1,200.00*	
Direct Incomes		**32,000.00**
Call Charges		*17,000.00*
Chamber Consultatic		*15,000.00*
Indirect Expenses	**16,500.00**	
Depreciation	*5,500.00*	
Interest	*3,000.00*	
Salary	*8,000.00*	
Grand Total	**1,71,000.00**	**1,71,000.00**

F-4A:Trial Balance in Print

04 Extended Trial Balance

Normally Trial Balance shows Closing Balance as on the specified period end date. However, you may optionally include Opening Balance & Transaction details (separate Debit / Credit or Net), through the Trial Balance Configuration option. This is very useful report giving a concise summarised view of Opening, Transactions & Closing Balance, very useful in practical working, and to check Opening Balance of Ledger Accounts

As Tally does not provide Opening Balance entered in Ledger Account Master, the Trial Balance configuration options are very useful to print List of Ledger Accounts with Opening Balance, in your desired sequence (Groupwise Hierarchical, or flat alphabetical Ledger List).

Summary

- **Opening Balance Report :** After creation of Ledger Accounts, you can print the Trial Balance Ledger with Opening Balance (click F12:Configure and set the Configuration option), to manually check the correctness of Ledger Account entry (with Opening Balance). Click F5:Ledgwise button to get the Ledgerwise list.
- **Extended Trial Balance** : Extended Trial Balance (with figures of Opening Balance & Transaction totals) gives a summary of the Ledgerwise Transactions for a period. Just scrutinising the Extended Trial Balance, an expert Accountant may be able to locate wrong entries (Wrong Account, Wrong Debit / Credit etc).
- **Alphabetical Trial Balance** : Normally, in the Trial Balance, you get the Account Groups / Ledger Accounts orgnanised in hierarchical manner. To print Trial Balance in alphabetical order of ledger accounts, Click *F5:Ledgwise* button, at Configuration screen, set select *Alphabetical (A-Z)* at *Sorting Method.* However, in Alphabetical list, the Opening Stock ledger appears at the top. Difference in Opening Balance (if any), appears last, as usual.

Profit & Loss Statement 01-10

01 Profit & Loss Account

Profit & Loss Account shows the heads of all Nominal Accounts (Income & Expenses) and the net Profit / Loss, for the specified period (F-1A), the result of performance of the enterprise.

To get proper Profit & Loss Account, first you have to account for the value of Closing Stock at the end of accounting period, as explained next

02 Closing Stock Value

Unlike traditional method of Accounting, in Tally ERP9, you do not have to create a Journal Voucher for Closing Stock Value, at year end (so the *Closing Stock Value* does not appear in Trial Balance). Rather, at the end of the Year (e.g. 31.3.18), enter the value of Closing Stock at Stock Ledger Account.

Creation of Stock Ledger Account : Stock in Hand Ledger are created under the Reserved Group, in usual way, as explained in Ledger Creation. Opening Stock value are entered during creation (or later through Ledger Alteration) like other ledger accounts

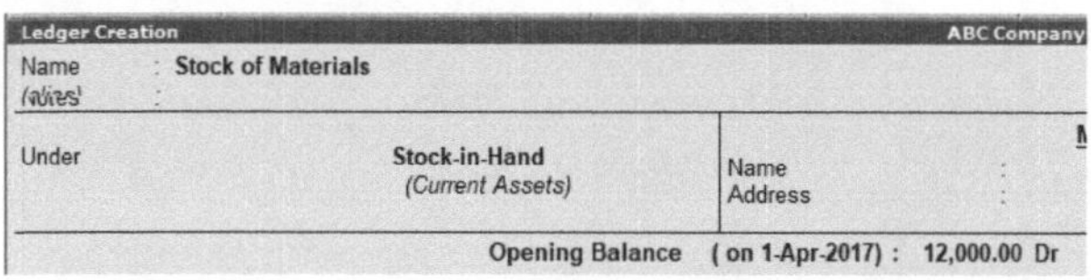

F-1A: Stock Accounts Ledger creation in Accounts

Entry of Closing Stock Value : At *Accounts Info>Ledgers>Alter*, select Stock Account to get Ledger Alteration screen (F-1B). At *Closing Balance*, enter the Date and the Closing Stock Value on the respective Date. You may enter multiple closing stock value for different dates (to prepare Periodical PL L statement and Balance Sheet)

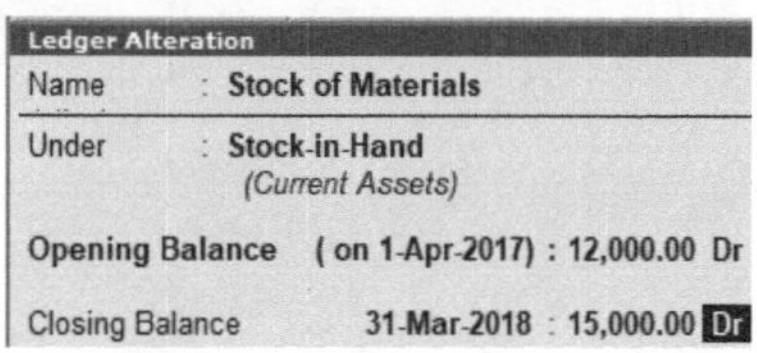

F-1B: Closing Stock value entry in Accounts

03 Profit & Loss Statement

The Profit & Loss Statement contains 2 parts, showing details of Expenses & Income Accounts, divided by a vertical line.

- **Expenses Side** (or Debit Side) :The Left Part shows the top level Expenses Groups (Direct & Indirect Expenses). The figures represent the total of Net Amount of all Ledger Accounts under the respective Group.
- **Incomes Side** (or Credit Side): The Right Part contains the top level Income Groups (Direct & Indirect Incomes). The figures represent the total of Net Amount of all Ledger Accounts under the respective Group.

  Net Profit / Loss : The Net Profit / Loss is computed as difference between Total of Income figures (Direct Income & Indirect Income) and the Total of Expenses figures (Direct Expense & Indirect Income).
- If the *Total of Income* figures is greater than *Total of Expense* figures, the difference is computed as *Net Profit* and is shown at left side of the Profit & Loss Statement
- If the *Total of Expense* figures is greater than *Total of Income* figures, the difference is computed as *Net Loss* and is shown at right side of the Profit & Loss Statement.

Profit & Loss Statement Display

Having entered the Closing Stock Value, you may display/ print Profit & Loss Statement.

Select *GoT>Profit & Loss Account* to get Profit & Loss Statement for the specified period (F-2A)

Profit & Loss A/c — Dr ABC 14-15 — Ctrl + M

Particulars		Dr ABC 14-15 1-Apr-2014 to 31-Mar-2015	Particulars		Dr ABC 14-15 1-Apr-2014 to 31-Mar-2015
Opening Stock			Sales Accounts		1,100.00
Stock of Medicie			*Sales*	1,100.00	
Purchase Accounts		1,200.00	Direct Incomes		32,000.00
Purchase	1,200.00		*Call Charges*	17,000.00	
Gross Profit c/o		32,400.00	*Chamber Consultation*	15,000.00	
			Closing Stock		500.00
			Stock of Medicie	500.00	
		33,600.00			33,600.00
Indirect Expenses		16,500.00	*Gross Profit b/f*		32,400.00
Depreciation	5,500.00				
Interest	3,000.00				
Salary	8,000.00				
Nett Profit		15,900.00			
Total		32,400.00	Total		32,400.00

F-2A: Profit & Loss Statement

Profit & Loss Statement Configuration

At Profit & Loss Statement Display (F-2A), click F12:Configure to get *P L Statement Configuration* screen (F-3A), to set the Configuration options

Configuration	
Show Vertical Profit & Loss	? No
Show Percentages	? No
Show with Gross Profit	? Yes
Exclude Particulars With Zero Closing Balance	? No
Appearance of Names	: Name Only
Scale Factor for Values	: Default

F-3A : P L Statement Configuration

Profit & Loss Statement Printing

At Profit & Loss Statement Display (F-2A), click *P:Print* to get the Profit & Loss Statement printing screen. (F-4A).

Set the printing options to get Profit & Loss Statement in print (F-5A)

Report Titles	
Profit & Loss A/c	
Scale Factor for Values	: Default
Format	: Detailed
Show Vertical Profit & Loss	? No
Show Percentages	? No
Show with Gross Profit	? Yes

F-4A: P L Statement Print

Dr ABC
27 Graham Rd
Topsia
Kolkata 700 999

Profit & Loss A/c
1-Apr-2014 to 31-Mar-2015

Particulars	1-Apr-2014 to 31-Mar-2015		Particulars	1-Apr-2014 to 31-Mar-2015	
Opening Stock			**Sales Accounts**		**1,100.00**
Stock of Medicie			*Sales*	*1,100.00*	
Purchase Accounts		**1,200.00**	**Direct Incomes**		**32,000.00**
Purchase	*1,200.00*		*Call Charges*	*17,000.00*	
			Chamber Consultation	*15,000.00*	
Gross Profit c/o		*32,400.00*	Closing Stock		**500.00**
			Stock of Medicie	*500.00*	
		33,600.00			33,600.00
Indirect Expenses		**16,500.00**	Gross Profit b/f		*32,400.00*
Depreciation	*5,500.00*				
Interest	*3,000.00*				
Salary	*8,000.00*				
Nett Profit		*15,900.00*			
Total		32,400.00	**Total**		32,400.00

P-5A: Profit & Loss Statement in Print

04 Profit / Loss Appropriation

You may transfer funds from Profit & Loss Account to Capital / Reserve Accounts (referred as Profit / Loss Appropriation), through Journal Voucher.

Create a Journal Voucher for Adjustment of Net Profit / Loss to Capital / Reserve Account (F-6A).

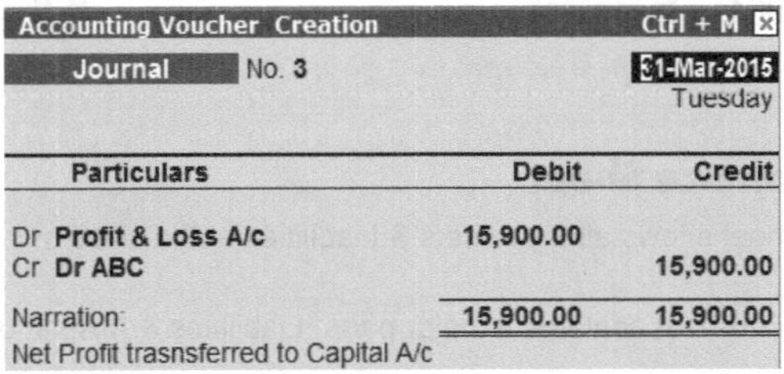

F-6A: Profit / Loss Appropriation Journal Voucher

Summary

- **Adjustment Journal Entries** : Before printing Profit & Loss Statement, you must make all adjustment entries for Income Receivables, Payables, Prepaid Expenses, Advance Income Receipts, Depreciation and all other adjustments affecting Income / Expenses & Provisions.
- **Closing Stock Value** : If you are maintaining Accounts only module, then you must make entry for Closing Stock value (if any), for the respective dates, otherwise you will get wrong Profit & Loss Statement

  If Inventory & Accounts are Integrated, then the Closing Stock Value will be carried from Inventory module, as explained in Inventory section.
- **P L Appropriation** : You may make P L Appropriation entry amount between Profit / Loss Account & Capital / Reserves Account
- **Configuration** :
  - o **Vertical P L Statement** : To get Vertical Profit & Loss Account (Income, Expenses & Net Profit listed one after another), at *Profit & Loss Configuration* (F-3A), set *Yes* at *Show Vertical Profit & Loss?*
  - o **Trading & Profit & Loss Statement** : To get Trading & Profit & Loss Statement showing Gross & Net Profit separately, at *Profit & Loss Configuration* (F-3A), set *Yes,* at *Show with Gross Profit?*

Balance Sheet 01-11

01 Balance Sheet

Balance Sheet shows all the Assets & Liabilities at the close of the specified Date

The Balance Sheet contains 2 major parts, Liabilities & Assets, divided by a vertical line.

- **Liabilities** (or Credit Side) : The Left Part shows the top level Groups of Capital (Funds *Owned*, by the organisation, like Capital & Reserves) & Liabilities (Funds *Owed*, by the organization, like Loans & other Liabilities).
- **Assets** (or Debit Side): The Right Part contains the top Assets Groups (all Assets possessed by the organization, like Fixed Assets, Investments & Current Assets).

The figures represent the total of Net Amount of all Ledger Accounts under the respective Group.

Current Year Profit Loss : The net Profit / Loss and appropriation therefrom are shown at Liabilities side (*Net Loss* is shown as negative figure).

02 Balance Sheet Display

Having done the P L Appropriation entry, you may get the Balance Sheet, as on the specified date.

Select *GoT>Balance Sheet* to get Balance Sheet (F-1A), as at the end of current period.

Balance Sheet		Dr ABC 14-15			Ctrl + M
Liabilities		Dr ABC 14-15 as at 31-Mar-2015	**Assets**		Dr ABC 14-15 as at 31-Mar-2015
Capital Account		1,15,900.00	**Fixed Assets**		**49,500.00**
Dr ABC	*1,15,900.00*		Furniture	*22,500.00*	
Loans (Liability)		**38,000.00**	Medical Equipment	*27,000.00*	
Mrs Gupta	*38,000.00*		**Investments**		**15,000.00**
Current Liabilities			*Fixed Deposit (SBI)*	*15,000.00*	
Profit & Loss A/c			**Current Assets**		**89,400.00**
Opening Balance			Closing Stock	*500.00*	
Current Period	*15,900.00*		Deposits (Asset)	*10,000.00*	
Less: Transferred	*15,900.00*		Cash-in-hand	*31,900.00*	
			Bank Accounts	*47,000.00*	
Total		**1,53,900.00**	**Total**		**1,53,900.00**

F-1A: Balance Sheet Display

Balance Sheet Configuration : At *Balance Sheet Display* (F-1A), click *F12:Configure* to get *Configuration screen* (F-1B), to set the Configuration options

Configuration	
Show Vertical Balance Sheet	? No
Profit or Loss, both as Liability	? No
Show Percentages	? No
Show Working Capital figures	? No
Method of showing Balance Sheet	? Liabilities / Assets
Exclude Particulars With Zero Closing Balance	? No
Appearance of Names	: Name Only
Scale Factor for Values	: Default

F-1B : Balance Sheet Configuration

03 Ratio Analysis

To display key performance ratios, at Gateway, select Ratio Analysis to get Ratio Analysis Report. You may further drill down to related reports through any of the figures in Ratio Analysis

Ratio Analysis — ABC Academy 9-10 — Ctrl + M

Principal Groups	ABC Academy 9-10 1-Apr-2009 to 31 -Mar-2010	Principal Ratios	ABC Academy 9-10 1-Apr-2009 to 31 -Mar-2010
Working Capital	1,09,136.78 Dr	Current Ratio	1.11 : 1
(Current Assets-Current Liabilities)		*(Current Assets : Current Liabilities)*	
Cash-in-Hand	9,88,939.50 Dr	Quick Ratio	1.11 : 1
Bank Accounts	71,826.78 Dr	*(Current Assets-Stock-in-Hand : Current Liabilities)*	
Bank OD A/c		Debt/Equity Ratio	0.79 : 1
		(Loans (Liability) : Capital Account + Nett Profit)	
Sundry Debtors	24,060.50 Dr		
(due till today)	37,260.50 Dr	Gross Profit %	1,672.89 %
Sundry Creditors	8,78,880.00 Cr	Nett Profit %	(-)206.00 %
(due till today)	8,83,030.00 Cr	Operating Cost %	306.00 %
		(as percentage of Sales Accounts)	
Sales Accounts	60,300.00 Cr		
Purchase Accounts	7,050.00 Dr	Recv. Turnover in days	127.90 days
Stock-in-Hand	2,000.00 Dr	*(payment performance of Debtors)*	
Nett Loss	1,24,220.00 Dr		
		Return on Investment %	156.80 %
Wkg. Capital Turnover	0.55	*(Nett Profit / Capital Account + Nett Profit)*	
(Sales Accounts / Working Capital)		Return on Wkg. Capital %	(-)113.82 %
Inventory Turnover	30.15	*(Nett Profit / Working Capital) %*	
(Sales Accounts / Closing Stock)			

F-2A : Ratio Analysis

Summary

- **Profit & Loss Appropriation** : To get proper Balance Sheet, you must make proper Appropriation entry for Profit & Loss (transfer Profit / Loss to Proprietor in case of Proprietorship Firm, transfer of share of Profit / Loss to Partners A/c in case of Partnership firm, Transfer to Reserves in case of Company etc
- **Balance Sheet Display** : At GoT select *Balance Sheet* to Display Balance Shet

- **Configuration** :
  - o **Source & Application of Funds**: To get Balance Sheet in modern style showing *Source & Application of Fund*, at *Balance Configuration* (F-1B), set *Yes* at *Show Vertical Balance Sheet?*
  - o **Working Capital** : To get Balance Sheet with Working Capital (Net of Current Assets & Liabilities), at *Balance Sheet Configuration* (F-1B), set *Yes,* at *Show Working Capital Figures*
- **Ratio Analysis :** At GoT select *Ratio Analysis* to get key performance figures. You may drill down from respective element do get further details of the underlying Ratio components.

Accounts Receivables & Payables

01-12

01 Accounts Receivables & Payables

Control of Receivables & Payables is the main concern for Debtors & Creditors Control & Financial Management. Accounts Receivables & Payables module deals with detailed records of Trade Transactions with Suppliers & Customers and Open Accounts (Outstanding Dues) for Party Analysis & Performance, tracking & control of Receivables & Payables

02 Activation of A/R A/P Features

Company Features Set Up : To maintain Billwise Details of Outstanding of Parties, *Click F11: Features > F1:Accounting Features,* set as follows (F-1A):

- **Bill Details Activation for Trader Accounts** : At *Maintain Billwise Details*, set Yes, to Activate Bill Ref Features, for Traders Accounts (Sundry Debtors & Creditors).
- **Bill Details Activation for Non-Trader Accounts** : Having set Yes at *Maintain Billwise Details*, you may further set Yes, at *For Non Trading Accounts also*, to activate Bill Features for Accounts other than Debtors & Creditors.

Outstandings Management

Maintain Bill-wise Details	?	Yes
(for Non-Trading A/cs also)	?	No
Activate Interest Calculation	?	Yes
(use advanced parameters)	?	No

F-1A: Accounting Features set up for AR/AP & Interest

Accounts Masters Features set up : Having activated the Billwise Features for the Company, set following options also at Ledger Account Master, for which you lake to maintain Billwise details of Receivables & Payables.

At Ledger Account Creation / Alteration of Accounts Ledger (*GoT>Accounts Info>Ledger*) and then select (Create to create a ledger account) , or Alter (to set Bill Features in an existing ledger Account) to get *Ledger Creation / Alteration* screen (F-2A). Now set as follows :

Ledger Alteration

Name	:	DEF Traders
Under	:	Sundry Debtors (Current Assets)
Maintain balances bill-by-bill	?	Yes
Default credit period	:	30 Days
Check for credit days during voucher entry	?	No

F-2A: Bill Features set up at Party Ledger Account

- **Bill reference** : Set *Yes* at *Maintain Bill By Bill* to activate Bill

Reference Feature for Ledger Accounts under Sundry Debtors, Sundry Creditors, Loans & Advance and Branch Accounts (F-1A), for which you like to maintain Bill details, to get Billwise Outstanding.

- **Interest** : You may also set *Yes* at *Activate Interest Calculation* to activate Interest Computation features.

03 Bill Details Entry

Consequently, you have to enter Bill details for Opening Balance entered in Ledger Account Master. You have also to enter Bill Details during Voucher Entry, for the amount entered in Voucher for the Party Ledger

Bill Details entry of Party Ledger Opening Balance

When you enter the Ledger Opening Balance of a Party Ledger, for which you have set Bill by Bill Option (F-1A) you get a screen to enter Bill Reference wise break-up of the Opening Balance amount as follows (F-3A)

Date	Enter Date of Bill (Prior to *Books Beginning From* date).
Name	Enter Bill Reference (normally Bill No.) or Advance (as the case be)
Due Date, or Credit Days	Enter the *Due Date* of the Bill or *Credit Days* – Bill Due Date would be arrived at by adding the Credit Days from Date of Bill.
Amount	Enter the Opening Outstanding Bill Amount (not original bill amount, if part paid).
Dr / Cr	Enter the sign, *D* (for Debit Balance) or *C* (for Credit Balance).

The Opening Balance may contain multiple references of several voucher types (like Bills, Debit Notes, Credit Note, etc). and may comprise of Bill References of Open Bills, Advance, On Account also. Each reference would be entered in separate row (F-3A).

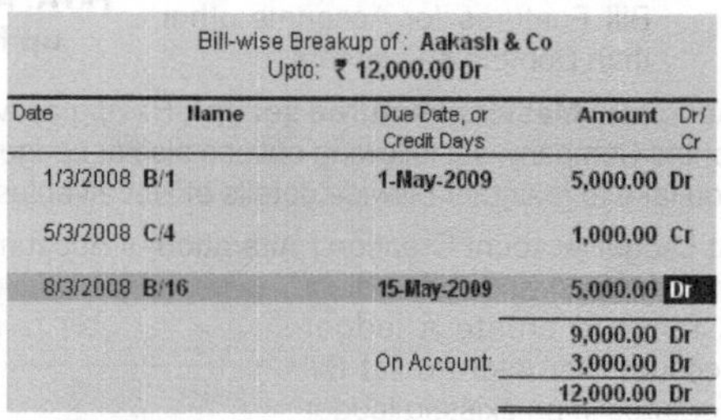

F-3A: Billwise details Opening Balance entry

Bill Details entry in Vouchers

During entry of Sales / Purchase Voucher (and Debit / Credit Note voucher, if activated) entry, you should enter following Bill Details for transaction :

- **Bill Ref Type** : Select the Bill Ref Type from the List, as described next
- **Bill Reference Number** : Enter / Select the Reference Number, as described next
- **Credit Period / Due Date** : Enter Credit Period or Due Date for New Reference (when Credit Period is entered, the Due date is computed from the Voucher Date & Credit Period and shown)
- **Bill Reference Amount** : Enter the Amount for the respective Bill Reference Number. In case of *Against Reference*, the Balance amount of Reference is auto carried (which may be changed)

The entry process of each of these elements are explained below in details

Voucher Entry Bill details in Voucher entry

Bill Reference Type : Select the relevant Type of Bill Reference at *Type of Adjustment field*, from the following list :

- **New Ref.**: Select it when a new Ref is created (normally a Sales or Purchase Voucher). Consequently, At *Name* field, the Ref Number from the voucher would be auto carried, which you may change.
- **Against Ref.**: Select it when the transaction is for adjustment of an existing reference (like payment is received or made against any existing Ref). All existing references are listed from which select the *Ref* to which the current entry relates.
- **Advance**: Select it when you make a Receipt or Payment as Advance (which would be adjusted against a reference later on).
- **On Account**: Select it (this option does not appear in Sales / Purchase Voucher) when payment is received or made but not against specific Bill or Advance (or Bill reference is not known). *On Account* amounts are not reflected in Interest Statement, Outstanding (Open Bills) Statements or Age Analysis Statement.

Bill Ref Amount : Enter the amount in respect of the reference Number.

In this way, you may make multiple entries of Bill Reference. However, the total net amount of all references must be equal to the net amount of debit / credit in the respective ledger account of the party, as entered in main voucher entry screen.

04 Outstanding Reports

Having entered the Bill Reference number in vouchers related to Parties, you may print Outstanding reports (List of Open Bills for which some amount is still due).

Outstanding Reports Menu : Select *Display > Statement of Accounts> Outstandings* to get Party *Outstandings Menu* (F-4A)

- *Receivables* menu gives you Reports for all Accounts receivables (from Customers)
- *Payables* menu gives you Reports for all Accounts Payables (to Suppliers).
- *Ledger menu* gives reports of outstanding reports of a selected Ledger Account of Customer/ Supplier.
- *Group* menu gives reports showing consolidated figures all ledger accounts of a selected Group Customer/Supplier

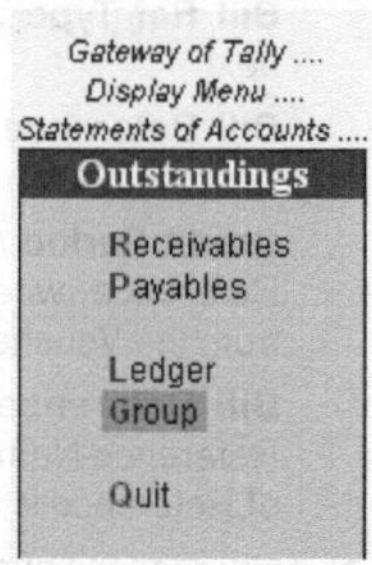

F-4A : Outstanding Reports Menu

Outstanding Bills Report

At *Outstanding* menu, select *Receivables* (to get the Outstanding Receivables), or *Payables* (to get the Outstanding Payables), showing the Billwise details of Outstanding (F-5A)

Bills Outstanding — Ctrl + M

Bills Receivable — 1-Apr-2009 to 31-Mar-2010

Date	Ref. No.	Party's Name		Opening Amount	Pending Amount	Due on	Age of Bill in Days
1-Feb-2009	S/5	M P Traders		12,000.00 Dr	5,000.00		423
1-Feb-2009	*Opening Balance*		*12,000.00 Dr*				
1-Jun-2009	*Receipt*	*1*	*7,000.00 Cr*				
31-Mar-2009	Advance	M P Traders		4,000.00 Dr	2,000.00	31-Mar-2009	365
31-Mar-2009	*Opening Balance*		*4,000.00 Dr*				
1-Jun-2009	*Receipt*	*1*	*2,000.00 Cr*				
2-Jun-2009	2	A K Traders		2,800.00 Dr	2,300.00	2-Jul-2009	302
2-Jun-2009	*Sales*	*2*	*2,800.00 Dr*				
1-Nov-2009	*Credit Note*	*2*	*500.00 Cr*				
1-Jul-2009	3	A K Traders		2,150.00 Dr	2,150.00		273
1-Jul-2009	*Sales*	*3*	*2,150.00 Dr*				
1-Nov-2009	4	M P Traders		42,000.00 Dr	42,000.00	31-Dec-2009	150
1-Nov-2009	*Sales*	*4*	*42,000.00 Dr*				
				62,950.00 Dr	53,450.00		

F-5A : Outstanding Bills (Receivables)

05 Age Analysis Report

At Outsatnding Report (Receivable or Payable), click *F6:Age wise* button to get Age Analysis Report (F-6A), showing the Age slabwise details of outstanding Bills

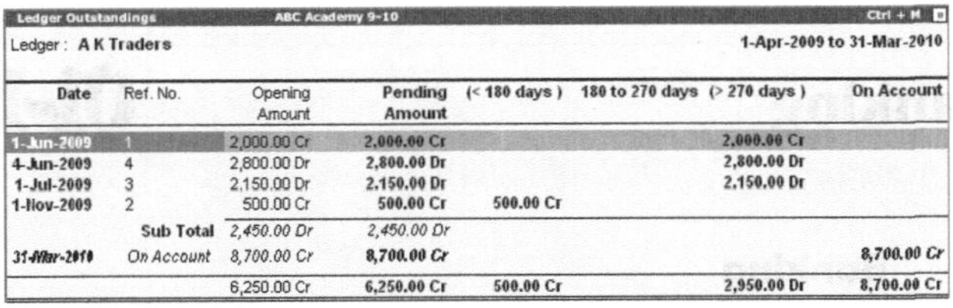

Ledger Outstandings — ABC Academy 9-10 — Ctrl + M

Ledger : A K Traders — 1-Apr-2009 to 31-Mar-2010

Date	Ref. No.	Opening Amount	Pending Amount	(< 180 days)	180 to 270 days	(> 270 days)	On Account
1-Jun-2009	1	2,000.00 Cr	2,000.00 Cr			2,000.00 Cr	
4-Jun-2009	4	2,800.00 Dr	2,800.00 Dr			2,800.00 Dr	
1-Jul-2009	3	2,150.00 Dr	2,150.00 Dr			2,150.00 Dr	
1-Nov-2009	2	500.00 Cr	500.00 Cr	500.00 Cr			
	Sub Total	2,450.00 Dr	2,450.00 Dr				
31-Mar-2010	On Account	8,700.00 Cr	8,700.00 Cr				8,700.00 Cr
		6,250.00 Cr	6,250.00 Cr	500.00 Cr		2,950.00 Dr	8,700.00 Cr

F-6A: Party Age Analysis Display

Summary

- **Initial Set Up for Accounts Receivable / Payables**
    - **Company Features Set Up :**Set Bill by Bill options at Company Features (GoT> F11:Fetaures> Accounting Features)
    - **Accounts Master Configuration Set Up** : At Accounts Master Configuration (at Accounts Master entry, click F12:Configure to get Accounts Master Configuration screen), set up Advance Features for Accounts Master
    - **Accounts Ledger Advanced options** : During Accounts Ledger Entry / Alteration, set up the respective options in Ledger Account of the Party for which want to enter Bill Details and other related options
    - **Accounts Voucher Configuration Set Up** : At Accounts Configuration (at Accounts Voucher entry, click F12:Configure to get Accounts Voucher Configuration screen), set up options to enter respective details during Voucher Entry)
- **Bill reference Details Entry**
    - **Ledger Opening Balance :** At ledger Account creation / Alteration, enter the Bill Reference details of Opening Balance (billwise break up of Opening Outstanding)
    - **Bill Reference :** Enter Bill Reference details in voucher entry. Enter New Reference in Sales / Purchase Voucher) and Against Reference (On Account) in Receipt / Payment Voucher by selecting the Reference Number from the list of open (outstanding) Bills
- **A/R & A/P Reports**
    - **Accounts Receivables & Payables :** Print Outstanding Reports, Party Ledger, Group Ledger, with Billwise Details of all Open(outstanding Bills).
    - **Age Analysis :** Print Age Analysis of Outstanding Bills, Party Age Analysis, Group Age Analysis

Banking

01-13

01 Banking

Every business organisation keeps at least one bank account for its business transactions. Tally.ERP 9 provides certain operation & features specially related to banking, like Cheque printing, Deposit Slip Printing, Bank Reconciliation etc.

02 Activating Banking Features

To activate Banking Features, *Click F11:Features >F1: Accounting Features* to get *Accounting Features screen (F-1A).* Under Banking Features section (F-1A), set Yes at the respective options to be activated to get the related set up screens (F-2A to F-2C).

Banking Features	
Enable cheque printing	? Yes
Set/alter transaction types	? Yes
Set/alter banking features	? Yes
Set/alter post-dated transaction features	? Yes

F-1A : Banking Feature Activation

Include/Exclude Transaction Types

Transaction Type	Payments	Receipts
ATM	No	No
Cash	NA	Yes
Cheque/DD	Yes	Yes
Card	No	No
ECS	No	No
Electronic Cheque	No	No
Electronic DD/PO	No	No
e-Fund Transfer	Yes	Yes
Others	Yes	Yes

F:2A: Banking transaction type set up

Banking Features	
Enable beneficiary code	? Yes

F-2B: Beneficiary Code set up

Post-dated Transaction Options

Link notional bank(s) : Bank of India

List of Banks
End of List
Bank of India

F-2C : Post dated Cheque set up

03 Bank Ledger Account set up

Accounts Ledger creation has been explained earlier. At Account Ledger Creation / Alteration screen (F-3A) of a Bank Ledger, set the respective options

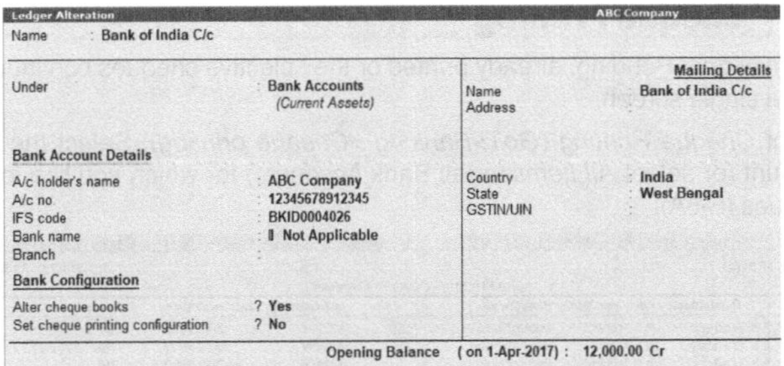

F-3A: Bank Ledger Account set up

You have to specify the additional information in respect of the Bank Account (F-3A)

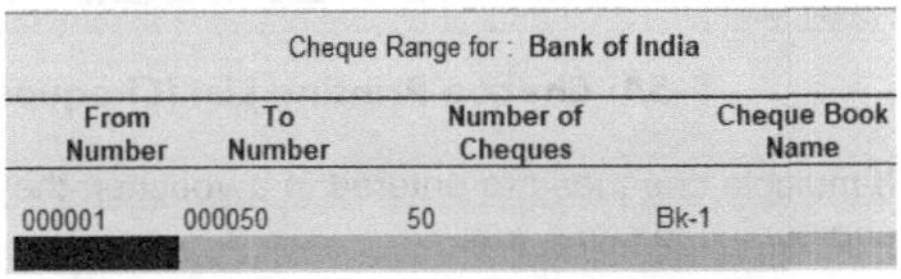

F-3B: Cheque Book etails set up

At Bank Ledger Account, set Yes at Alter Cheque Books and enter the Cheque Books issued by Bank to the Company. Enter the details (Cheque Book Range) of Cheque Books received by the company, issued by Bank (F-3B)

Banking menu

At Gateway, select *Banking* to get Banking menu (F-3C).

F-3C: Banking Menu

04 Cheque Details Entry in Voucher

Having set the Configuration as stated above at the respective voucher entry screen, on selection of a Bank Account, you get the Cheque details entry screen (F-4A)

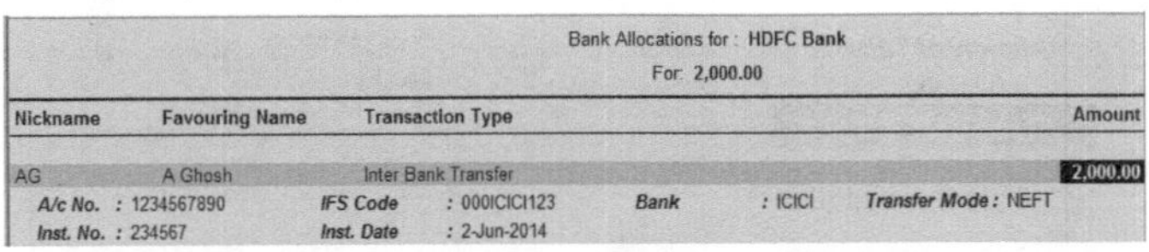

F-4A: Cheque details in Voucher Entry (Bank Details sub-screen)

If you have set Yes at Set Defaults at Bank Details screen of the Ledger Account, at Bank Allocation screen, enter the respective details

05 Cheque Printing

You may print Pending, already printed or the selective cheques continuously, from a single screen.

Select *Cheque Printing* (*GoT>Banking >Cheque printing).* Select the Bank Account (or select *All Items* for all Bank Accounts) for which you like to print cheques (F-5A).

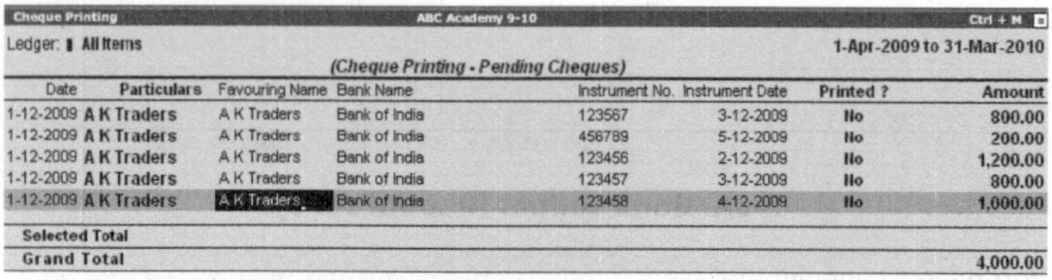

F-5A: Cheque Printing List (Cheques for all Banks)

If multiple cheques are entered in a voucher, they may be printed one after another in the same way.

Cheque Printing Configuration : At Cheque printing screen, click *F12:Configure* to get the Cheque Printing Configuration (F-6A) to set the desired option to facilitate cheques printing process as per users requirements

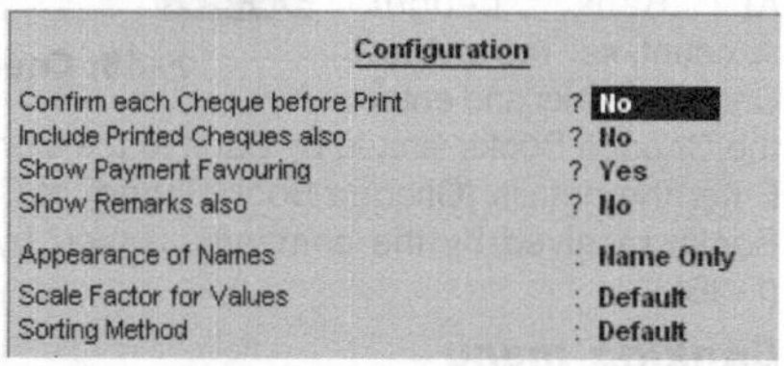

F-6A : Cheque Printing Configuration

6 Deposit Slip Printing

At Banking menu , select *GoT>Banking >Deposit Slip* to get *Deposit Slip* menu (F-7A). Select the option to print the respective deposit slip and then select the Bank for which you like to print the deposit slip.

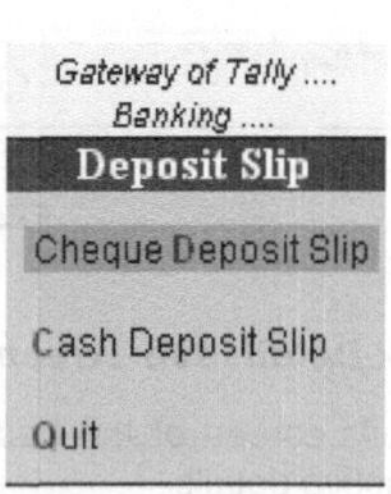

F-7A Deposit Slip Menu

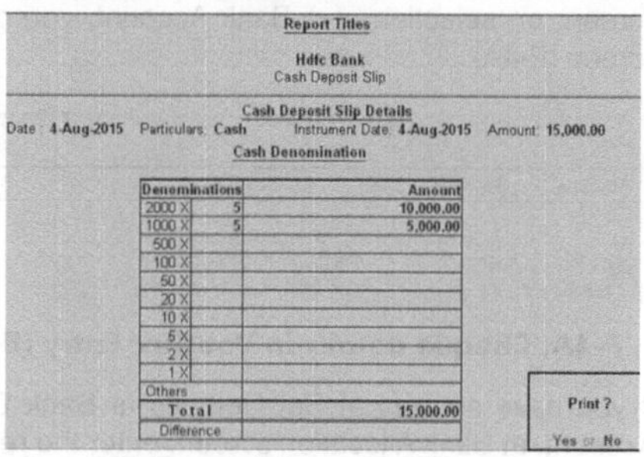

F-7B : cash Deposit Slip printing

07 Payment Advice

When a cheque is delivered to the receiver, a payment advice is also attached giving the details of Payment.

At Banking Menu, select *Payment Advice.* Then Select the Ledger Account (e.g Party Ledger Account) to get the Payment Advice List showing pending Advices List for the selected ledger (F-8A).

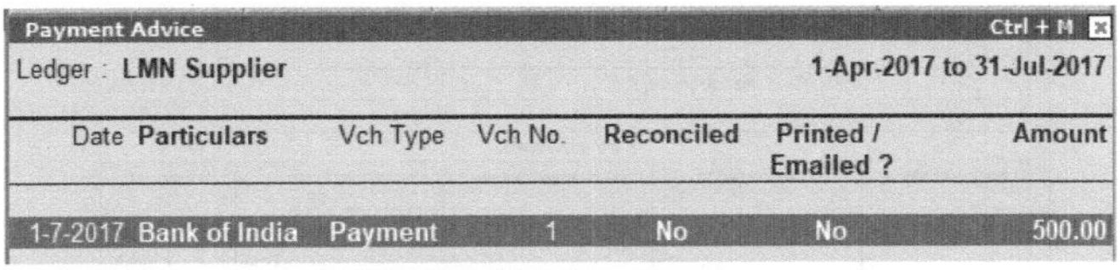

Payment Advice — Ctrl + M

Ledger : **LMN Supplier** — **1-Apr-2017 to 31-Jul-2017**

Date	Particulars	Vch Type	Vch No.	Reconciled	Printed / Emailed ?	Amount
1-7-2017	Bank of India	Payment	1	No	No	500.00

F-8A : Payment Advice List

Payment Advice Printing

At Payment Advice List (F-8A), select the Vouchers for which Payment Advice to be printed (select the required rows from the Payment Advice list and press spacebar on the row).

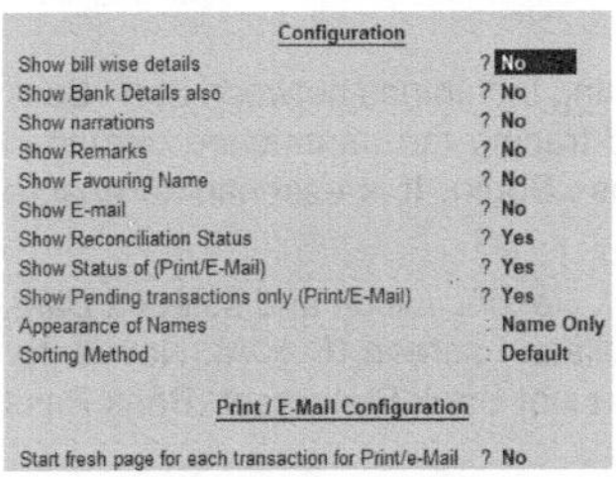

F-9A: Payment Voucher / Advice Printing Configuration

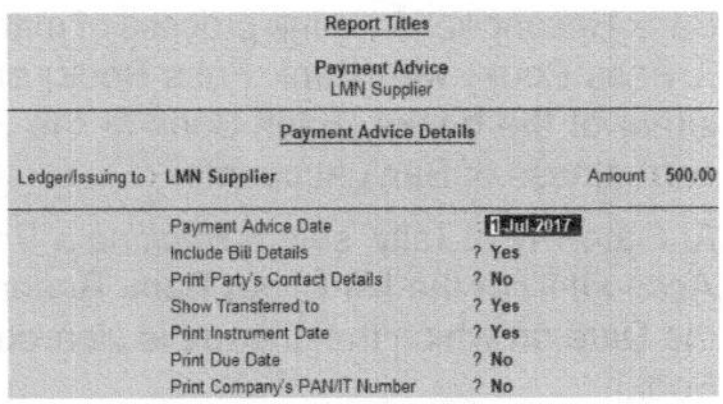

F-9B: Payment Advice Printing

At payment Advice list (F-8A), Click F12: Configure to set the Payment Advice printing Configuration (F-9A). Set the Configuration options.

Click P:Print button to get Payment Advice Printing screen (F-9B). Set the options and print the Payment Advice (F-9B).

ABC Company

Payment Advice

M/s. LMN Supplier Date : **1-Jul-2017**

West Bengal -

Dear Sir/Madam,

Please find below the payment details.

Bill Ref.	Bill Date	Amount
Agst Ref / 12	1-Jul-2017	500.00
	Nett Amount	₹ 500.00

Payment Details				
Payment Mode	Transferred to	Instrument Details	Issued From	Amount
Cheque		Dt: 1-Jul-2017	Bank of India	500.00
			Total	₹ 500.00

Kindly acknowledge the receipt.

Thanking You

Authorised Signatory Receiver's Signature

F-9B: Payment Advice

08 Bank Reconciliation

Bank Reconciliation is the process of matching the entries between Bank Book & Pass Book) with Bank Pass Book) and tracing the unmatched entries in either of the books (Bank Book or the Pass Book), It is essential to ensure correctness of Bank Accounts.

At Gateway of Tally, select *Banking > Bank Reconciliation* and select a *Bank Account* from the list to get Bank Reconciliation screen (F-10A). Now enter the Date on which the cheque is cleared as per Bank Statement (Bank Pass Book)

Bank Reconciliation — ABC Academy 9-10 — Ctrl + M

Ledger: **Bank of India** — (Reconciliation) — **1-Apr-2008 to 31-Mar-2010**

Date	Particulars	Favouring Name / Received From	Vch Type	Transaction Type	Instrument No.	Instrument Date	*Bank Date*	Debit	Credit
... 12 more									
1-6-2009	**A K Traders** *Paid for Bills after deducting TDS*		**Payment**	Cheque	239876	1-6-2009	*8-6-2009*		**1,980.00**
1-7-2009	**S Kurien** *Loan recived from S Kureint, @ 12% p. a. repaybale along with interest on 30. 6.10*		**Receipt**	Cheque/DD	875432	1-7-2009		**10,000.00**	
31-7-2009	**Rent Received** *Received from A K Traders, Rent for the m/o July 09*	A K Traders	**Receipt**	Cheque/DD	234567	31-7-2009	*3-8-2009*	**2,000.00**	
31-7-2009	**Rent Received** *Received from A K Traders, Rent for the m/o July 09*	A K Traders	**Receipt**	Cheque/DD	236761	3-8-2009		**1,000.00**	
1-8-2009	**ICICI Term Loan** *Ch# 123456 on ICICI Bank towards Term Loan @ 12% received from ICICI Bank . Interest to be charged on 31st March every year. Repayment Rs 10000 on 31st March every year.*		**Receipt**	Cheque/DD	345876	1-8-2009		**50,000.00**	
2-8-2009	**Cash** *Cash Deposited to Bank of India*	Disha Infotech	**Contra**	Cheque/DD	Cash	2-8-2009		**1,000.00**	
31-8-2009	**A K Traders**		**Payment**	Cheque	189743	31-8-2009			**1,000.00**
							Balance as per Company Books :	**28,520.00**	
							Amounts not reflected in Bank :	**71,700.00**	**44,300.00**
							Balance as per Bank :	**1,120.00**	

F-10A : Bank Reconciliation

At *Bank Reconcilitaion* screen, click *F12:Configure* to get *Bank Reconciltaion Configurtaion* screen (F-10B) to set the options, and click the desired button at the button bar (F-10C).

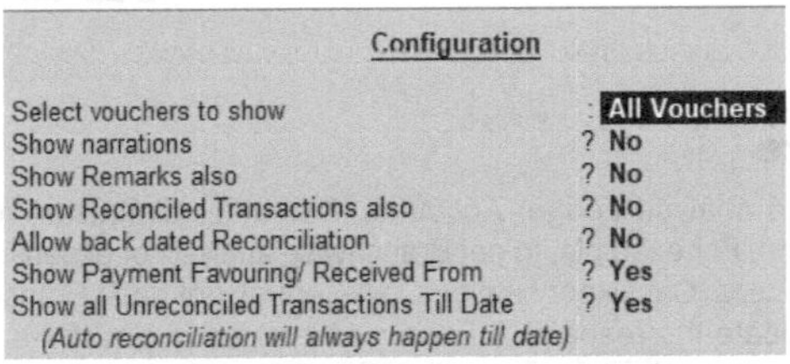

F-10B: Bank Reconciliation Configuration

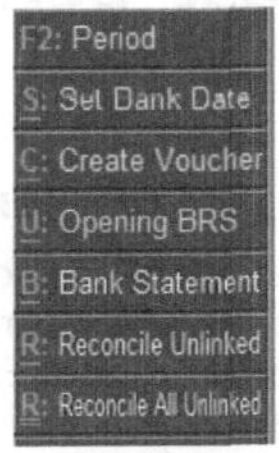

F-10C: Buttons

Opening Reconciliation entries : When you start accounting in Tally from a date when there are some unreconciled entries on *Books Beginning From* date, you have to create unreconciled entries relating to period prior to books beginning date.

At Bank Reconciliation screen, click *U: Opening BRS* button (F-10C) to get the Opening BRS screen.. Enter the details of pending entries as on the start date of Bank Reconciliation

Summary

- **Enabling Cheque Activities :** Set Up options to activate Banking Features
- **Bank Ledger set up for Cheque options and Bank details**
  - o Enabling Cheque Printing options
  - o Entering Cheque Book Range
  - o Designing Cheque Templates conforming to Bank's cheque stationery
- **Cheque details entry in Voucher :** Entry of cheque details (of cheques issued & received) in Vouchers
- **Cheque & Reports printing**
  - o **Cheque Printing** : Printing Cheques, Payment Advice and daily reports for cheques issued
  - o **Bank Deposit slips** : Printing Deposit slips for depositing Cash/ Cheques and daily reports of deposits into bank account
- **Bank Reconciliation :** Entry of Bank Clearing dates of cheques and reconciling the Pass Book & Bank Book Balances.

Cost Centres **01-14**

01 Cost Centre

Cost Centre is used to analyse Ledger Accounts in another dimension for management information. For example, to get Branchwise analysis of expenses (like Conveyance Expenses, Car Expense etc), Cost Centres (for each Branch) may be created to allocate the respective Expenses entered in Vouchers to the Cost Centres (i.e Branches). Thus, Travelling Expenses may be allocated to the respective Cost Centres (Branches), to get Cost Centrewise (Branchwise) analysis of Travelling Expenses at each level.

Cost Centre Activation

To activate Cost Centre feature, at Company Operations screen (*F11: Features >Accounting Feature*), set *Yes* at *Maintain Cost Centre* (F-1A).

Cost/Profit Centres Management	
Maintain Payroll	? No
Maintain Cost Centres	? Yes
Use Cost Centre for Job Costing	? No
More than ONE Payroll / Cost Category	? Yes
Use Pre-defined Cost Centre Allocations during Entry	? Yes
Show Opening Balance for Revenue Items in Reports	? No

F-1A: Cost Centre Activation

02 Cost Centre Masters Creation

At Gateway, select *Accounts Info> Cost Centre > Create* (under Single Cost Centre) to get *Cost Centre Creation* screen (F-2A).

Cost Centre Creation	
Name	: Computer
Under	: Primary

F-2A: Cost Centre Creation

Now enter as follows:

- **Cost Center Name**: At *Name*, enter Cost Centre Name.
- **Parent Cost Centre**: At *Under*, select the parent Cost Centre (or select Primary) under which you like to place the Cost Centre (for the first Cost Centre created, you must select *Primary* only*)*.

03 Cost Allocable Ledger Accounts

Ledger Creation	
Name	: Components Cost
Under	: Direct Expenses
Cost centres are applicable	? Yes

F-3A: Cost Centre activation in Ledger Accounts

Ledger Creation has been explained earlier. For Cost Allocable Ledger

Accounts (Ledger Accounts for which you like to enter Cost Centre allocation in Voucher), at Ledger Creation/Alter screen (F-3A), set *Yes* at *Cost Centres are Applicable*.

04 Cost Centre Allocation in Accounts Voucher

During voucher entry, on entry of a Cost Allocable Ledger (Ledger Accounts for which Cost entre has been activated (F-3A), and entering the Ledger amount (F-4A), Cost Allocation screen appears to enter the Cost Centre Allocation for the Ledger Amount (F-4B). At Cost Allocation screen (F-4B), enter as follows:

- **Cost Centre Name**: At *Name of Cost Centre*, select the Cost Center.
- **Cost Centre Amount**: At *Amount*, Tally proposes the balance amount allocable to Cost Centre. Press <enter> to allocate the balance amount or enter the amount allocated to Cost Centre.

This way, Ledger Amount is allocated may be allocated to Cost Centre. If the amount is to be allocated to multiple cost centres, continue to enter successive Cost Centres and allocate the amount, on by one, till the ledger amount is fully allocated to the Cost Centres.

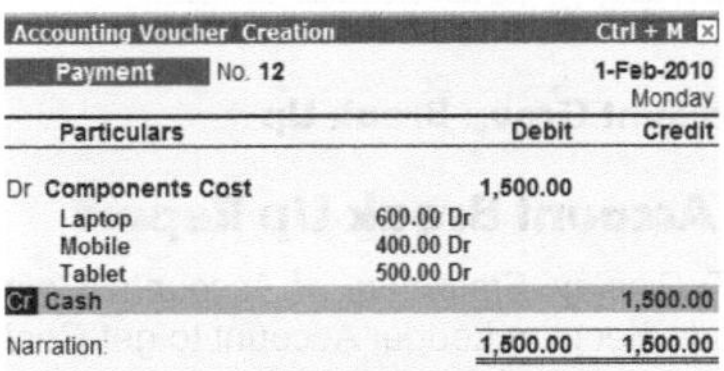

Accounting Voucher Creation — Ctrl + M

Payment No. 12 — 1-Feb-2010, Monday

Particulars		Debit	Credit
Dr Components Cost		1,500.00	
Laptop	600.00 Dr		
Mobile	400.00 Dr		
Tablet	500.00 Dr		
Cr Cash			1,500.00
Narration:		1,500.00	1,500.00

F-4A: Voucher Entry with Cost Allocations

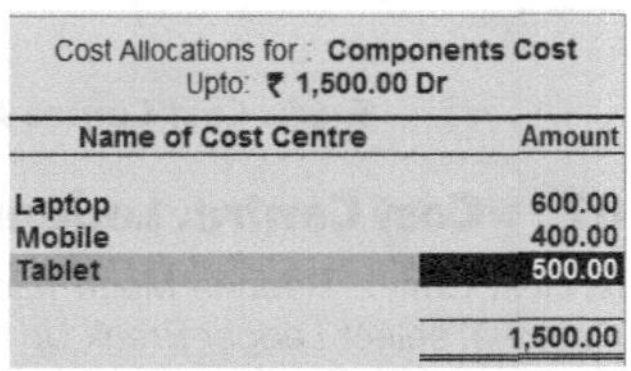

Cost Allocations for : **Components Cost**
Upto: **₹ 1,500.00 Dr**

Name of Cost Centre	Amount
Laptop	600.00
Mobile	400.00
Tablet	500.00
	1,500.00

F-4B: Cost Allocations in Voucher Entry

05 Cost Centre Break Up Report

Cost Centre Break Up Report shows Ledger Account wise break up of selected Cost Centre. At Cost Centre Reports Menu *(GoT>Display>Statement of Accounts>Cost Centres)*, select *Cost Centre Break Up* and select a Cost Centre to get Cost Centre Break Up Display (F-5A).

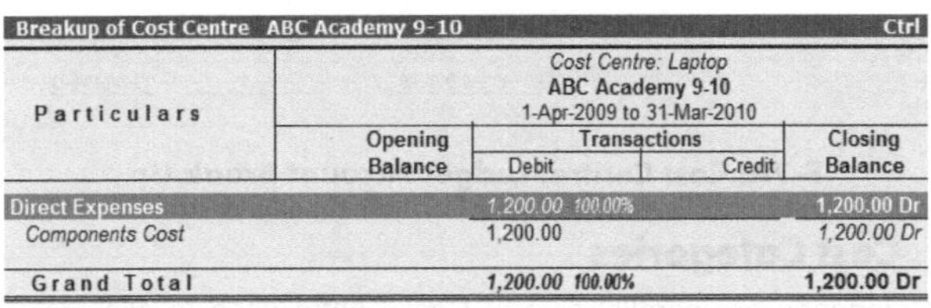

Breakup of Cost Centre ABC Academy 9-10 — Ctrl

Cost Centre: Laptop, ABC Academy 9-10, 1-Apr-2009 to 31-Mar-2010

Particulars	Opening Balance	Transactions Debit	Transactions Credit	Closing Balance
Direct Expenses		1,200.00 100.00%		1,200.00 Dr
Components Cost		1,200.00		*1,200.00 Dr*
Grand Total		1,200.00 100.00%		1,200.00 Dr

F-5A: Cost Centre Break Up

06 Cost Centre Account Group Break Up Report

Cost Centre Account Group Break Up shows Cost Centre wise break up of all vouchers in which the Ledger Accounts of the selected Account Group is transacted.

At Cost Centre Reports Menu *(GoT>Display>Statement of Accounts>Cost Centres)* , select *Group Break up* and then select the Account Group to get *Cost Centrewise Break up* of the selected Account Group (F-6A).

Cost Breakup of Group ABC Academy 9-10 Ctrl + M

Particulars	Opening Balance	Transactions: Debit	Transactions: Credit	Closing Balance
	Group: Direct Expenses ABC Academy 9-10 1-Apr-2009 to 31-Mar-2010			
Primary Cost Category		*3,000.00 100.00%*		,000.00 Dr *100.00%*
Computer		1,200.00		,200.00 Dr
Computer				
Laptop		*1,200.00*		,200.00 Dr
Mobile		800.00		800.00 Dr
Mobile		*800.00*		*800.00 Dr*
Tablet		1,000.00		,000.00 Dr
Tablet		*1,000.00*		*',000.00 Dr*

F-6A: Cost Centre Account Group Break Up

07 Cost Centre. Ledger Account Break Up Report

At Cost Centre Reports Menu *(GoT>Display>Statement of Accounts>Cost Centres*), select *Ledger Break Up* and select the Ledger Account to get *Cost Centre Ledger Break Up* of the selected Ledger Account (F-7A), showing the Cost Centrewise breakup of the selected Ledger Account.

Cost Breakup of Ledger ABC Academy 9-10 Ctrl + M

Particulars	Opening Balance	Transactions: Debit	Transactions: Credit	Closing Balance
	Ledger: Components Cost ABC Academy 9-10 1-Apr-2009 to 31-Mar-2010			
Primary Cost Category		*3,000.00 100.00%*		3,000.00 Dr *100.00%*
Computer		1,200.00		1,200.00 Dr
Computer				
Laptop		*1,200.00*		1,200.00 Dr
Mobile		800.00		800.00 Dr
Mobile		*800.00*		*800.00 Dr*
Tablet		1,000.00		1,000.00 Dr
Tablet		*1,000.00*		*1,000.00 Dr*

F-7A: Cost Centre. Ledger Account Break Up

08 Cost Categories

Cost Categories are parallel sets of Cost Centre used to allocate ledger accounts of same transactions to Cost Centres under each Cost Category simultaneously. For example, you may allocate ledger accounts of a voucher to Cost Centres under Cost Categories as follows:

- Products Type (Mobile, Tablet, Note Book, Laptop)
- Service Type (Board, Memory Card, AMC)

The allocation of Ledger Amount to Cost Centres under multiple Cost Categories simultaneously, are distinct and independent of each other.

Ledger Account Transactions in Voucher are allocated to Cost Centres only (NOT to Cost Categories). The Cost Category organizes the allocation to respective Cost Category

Activation of Cost Categories

Having activated Cost Centre, also set *Yes* at *More than one Payroll / Cost Category* (F-1A), to enable entry of Cost Categories.

Cost Category Creation

Select *GoT>Accounts Info>Cost Categories* >Create to get to get Cost Category creation screen (F-8A).

- **Cost Category Name**: At *Name*, enter Cost Category Name.
- **Cost Allocation Type**: You may specify the Ledger Account Types for Allocation to Cost Centres, as follows:
    - o **Allocation of Revenue Accounts Items** : At *Allocate Revenue Items*, set *Yes* to allocate amount of Nominal Ledger Accounts only (i. e. Ledger Accounts of Income / Expenses), else set *No* (Non Revenue Ledger Account cannot be allocated to the Cost Category).
    - o **Allocation of Non Revenue Accounts Items :** At *Allocate Non-Revenue Items* field, set *Yes* to allocate Non Revenue Ledger Account (i. e, Ledger Accounts of Assets / Liabilities) to the Cost Category, else set *No* (Non Revenue Ledger Accounts can not be allocated to the Cost Category

You may set *Yes* at either of the option (to allocate for selected type of Ledger Accounts, or both (to allocate all ledger accounts). Do not set *No* to both the option (No Ledger account would be allocated)

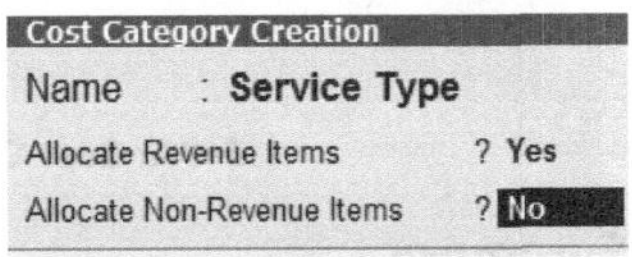

F-8A: Cost Category creation

Cost Centre creation under Cost Category : Cost Centre creation has been explained earlier . However, After you have created Cost Category (F-2A), you have to create a Cost Centre under a Cost Category only (F-9A)

During Cost Centre creation / alteration (F-9A) , enter as follows :

- **Parent Cost Category** : At *Category*, select the Parent Cost Category (if the cursor has skipped to next field, press Shift+Tab (or Up Arrow) to get to Category field and select the parent Category from the list.
- **Cost Centre Name** : At *Name*, enter the Cost Centre Name.
- **Parent Cost Centre** : At *Under*, select the Parent Cost Centre (or select *Primary*) from the list

Cost Centre Creation

Category : **Service Type**

Name : **Maintenance**

Under : Primary

F-9A Cost Centre creation

09 Cost Centre Class

Cost Centre Class is a defined set of Pre allocation of Cost Centre. Having activated Cost Centre, at *F11:Features > Accounting Features*, you may set Yes at *Use Pre Defined Cost Centre Allocation* (F-1A),to create Cost Centre classes and set the Cost Centrewise Pre allocation %. You may then use Cost Centre classes in Voucher Entry, to auto allocate the ledger amount to Cost Centre as per Cost Centre class.

Cost Category Summary

Select *GoT>Display > Statement of Accounts > Cost Centres > Category Summary* to get *Cost Category Summary*. It shows summary of all Cost Categories, displaying figures for underlying Cost Centres.

Cost Category Summary ABC Academy 9-10 — Ctrl + M

ABC Academy 9-10, 1-Apr-2009 to 31-Mar-2010

Particulars	Opening Balance	Transactions Debit	Transactions Credit	Closing Balance
Product Type		4,500.00 75.00%		4,500.00 Dr 75.00%
Computer		1,800.00		1,800.00 Dr
Computer				
Laptop		*1,800.00*		1,800.00 Dr
Mobile		1,200.00		1,200.00 Dr
Mobile		*1,200.00*		*1,200.00 Dr*
Tablet		1,500.00		1,500.00 Dr
Tablet		*1,500.00*		*1,500.00 Dr*
Service Type		*1,500.00 25.00%*		**1,500.00 Dr** *25.00%*
Maintenance		800.00		*800.00 Dr*
Repairs		700.00		*700.00 Dr*

F-9A: Cost Category Summary

Summary

- **Cost Centre Activation :** At *F11:Features > Accounting Features*, set the Cost Centre / Cost Category options.
- **Cost Category / Cost Centre creation** : Create Cost Category / Cost Centre Masters
- **Cost Allocation set up in Ledger Accounts** : Set the Cost Centre allocation options for the specified ledgers

- **Cost Centre allocation in Voucher** : In voucher, enter the Ledger account breakup (of Cost Allocable Ledger Accounts), as per Cost entre
- **Cost Centre Class** : Having activated Cost Centre, create Cost Centre classes and set the Cost Centrewise Pre allocation %. You may then use Cost Centre classes in Voucher Entry, to auto allocate the ledger amount to Cost Centre as per Cost Centre class.
- **Cost Category Reports :** Print Cost Category Summary & other Reports.

Foreign Currency 01-15

01 Foreign Currency

Normally organizations maintain accounts in currencies of that country (called *Base Currency*). However, Importers, Exporters, Money Exchangers, etc, who buy / sell or pay/ receive in foreign currency are required to enter transactions in Foreign currency also.

Activation of Foreign Currency : To activate foreign currency (to maintain amount in currencies other than base currency also), click *F11:Features> Accounting Features* to get Accounting Features screen. At Accounting Features screen, under section *General*, set *Yes* at *Enable Multi Currency*.

02 Foreign Currency Master Entry

Select *GoT>Accounts Info> Currencies>Create* to get Currency Creation screen (F-1A). Now enter as follows :

- **Currency Symbol**: At *Symbol*, enter the Foreign Currency Symbol of the Currency.
- **Currency Name**: At *Formal Name*, enter the Complete Name of the Foreign Currency (it must be different from Foreign Currency Symbol), as commonly used by International Trading Community & Bankers.
- **Currency Decimal Places**: At *Number of Decimal Places*, enter the number of decimal places required to express the amount in Foreign Currency (e.g 2 for Dollars, Pounds etc, 3 for Dinars etc).
- **Currency Amount Format**: At *Show Amount in Millions*, set :
    - *Yes* to show the Foreign Currency Amount formatted in Million Figures (like 9,999,999)
    - *No* to show the amount in Lacs format (like 99, 99,999).
- **Currency Symbol position**: At *Is Symbol Suffixed to Amounts*, set :
    - *Yes* to show the Foreign Currency Symbol after the Amount figure (like 152 $),
    - *No* to show the Foreign Currency Symbol prefixed to Amount ((like $152).
- **Currency Symbol Spacing**: At *Put a Space between Amount & Symbol,* set :
    - *Yes* to insert one letter space between the Foreign Currency Symbol and the Amount (like 152 $ or $ 152)

  o *No* to concatenate the Foreign Currency Symbol and the Amount ((like $152 or 152$).

- **Amount Delimiter**: At *Symbol for Decimal Portion of Amount* enter the delimiter for the decimal portion. Normally dot (.) is used. However, you may use any other symbol like (,).

Currency Creation

Symbol	: USD
Formal name	: U S Dollar
Number of decimal places	: 2
Show amount in millions	? Yes
Suffix symbol to amount	? No
Add space between amount and symbol	? No
Word representing amount after decimal	: Cents
No. of decimal places for amount in words	: 2

F-1A: Foreign Currency creation

03 Currency Exchange Rate Entry

Having created the new currency Master (F-1A), enter the Daily Exchange Rate of the currency with Base Currency. At Currencies Menu, select *Rate of Exchange*, to get *Exchange Rate* Entry screen (F-2A). At *Exchange Rate* Entry screen (F-2A), enter the Exchange Rate (with Base Currency) on the specified date, for the respective Currencies :

- **Date of Exchange Rate:** At *Date of Exchange Rate,* enter the *Date* for which you enter the Exchange Rate.

- **Exchange Rate Details** : Now enter the Exchange Rate details with base currency, in respect of each foreign currency, for the specified date, as follows :

  o **Foreign Currency Name:** At *Currency* column, select the Foreign currency from the list of Currencies

  o **Standard Exchange Rate:** At *Std Rate* column, enter the Exchange Rate (normally published by RBI), which is used to compute the Foreign Exchange Gain / Loss.

  o **Currency Selling Rate:** At *Last Voucher Rate* column, the Rate is carried from the last *Receipt* Voucher, if entered. At *Specified Rate* column, enter your Selling Rate, i.e, Rate in Base currency at which the Bank pays you in conversion of the Foreign Currency received by you.

Multi Currency Alteration Ctrl + M

Date for Rate of Exchange : 1-Jun-2013

S.No.	Currency	Std. Rate	Selling Rate		Buying Rate	
			Last Voucher Rate	Specified Rate	Last Voucher Rate	Specified Rate
1.	US$ (USD)	₹ 54.50/US$		₹ 55.20/US$	₹ 54.80/US$	₹ 54.49/US$

F-2A: Exchange Rate Entry

- o **Currency Buying Rate:** At *Last Voucher Rate* column, the Rate is carried from the last *Payment* Voucher, if entered. At *Specified Rate* column, enter your Buying Rate, i.e, Rate in Base currency at which you pay to Bank for remitting in Foreign Currency.

Enter the *Exchange Rate* for each Date whenever there is any change in any of the element of Rate entered. The Rate for the Date entered or immediately prior Date (if no Rate is entered for that Date) is applied to the voucher as default. For example for Date 5 Jun 2013, the Rate entered for 5 Jun 13 or immediately prior to that (e.g 1June 13) would be applied.

Currency Display : At *Currency* Menu, select *Display* and then select the Currency to be displayed from the list of Currencies. However, in Display screen, you just view the details, but you cannot make any alteration in the screen.

Currency Alteration : At Currency Menu, select *Alter* and then select the Currency to be Altered. You get similar screen as Display. Now, you can make any alteration in any field in the screen (take the cursor on the field by keyboard or click on the field by Mouse) and make alteration in the data as desired. After changing, Type Yes (at Yes No) or press Alt+A to save the changes made.

04 Currency Specification in Ledger Accounts

Accounts Ledger Creation has been explained earlier . Having activated Foreign Currency, at *Ledger Creation* screen, you get an additional Field *Currency of Ledger* (F-3A) . At *Currency of Ledger,* select the Currency in which you like to maintain for the ledger account, from the list of Currencies.

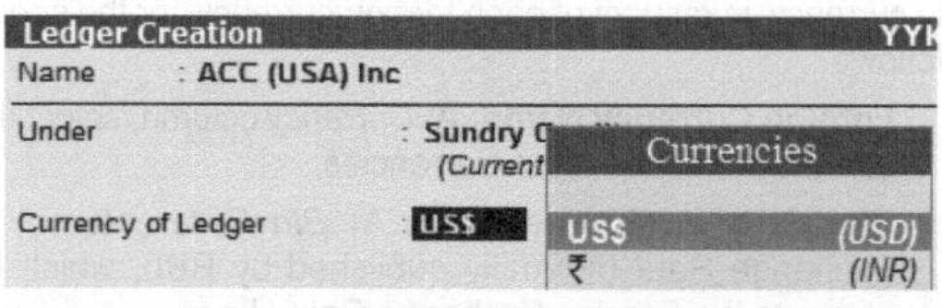

F-3A: Currency set up at Ledger Account Master Creation

05 Accounts Voucher entry in Foreign Currency

Accounts Voucher Entry has been explained earlier. Here we discuss about the entry of Amount in Foreign Currency.

Having selected the Ledger Account in Voucher entry (F-5A), enter the Ledger Amount details as follows (F-4A):

- **Amount in Foreign Currency** : To enter an amount in any Foreign Currency, at amount field enter currency symbol as specified in the respective currency master (e.g $, US$ etc.) before the amount (like $1200.00, US$2000 etc.).
- **Amount in Base Currency :** To enter amount in Base Currency, just enter the Amount as usual without any Currency prefix

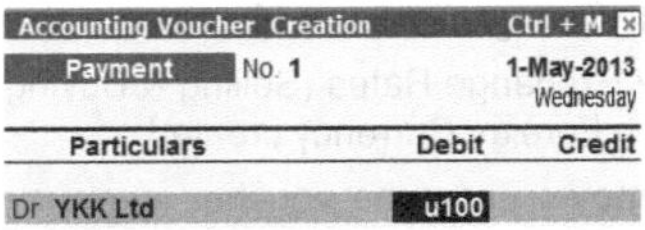

F-4A: Foreign Currency Symbol letter in Amount entry

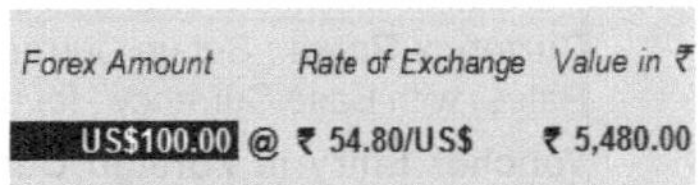

F-4B : Foreign Currency details entry

Foreign Currency Details : On entering Ledger Amount in Foreign currency, you will get *Forex Rate of Exchange* subscreen (F-4B), to enter the following details.

- **Forex Amount**: The Amount entered in Foreign currency is carried (you may change it in the window).
- **Rate of Exchange**: Tally proposes the Currency Rate (Selling Rate in Receipt Voucher, Buying Rate in Payment voucher or the Standard Rate), as the case may be, which you may change.
- **Value**: The computed value in Base Currency as per Exchange Rate entered is displayed, which you may change.

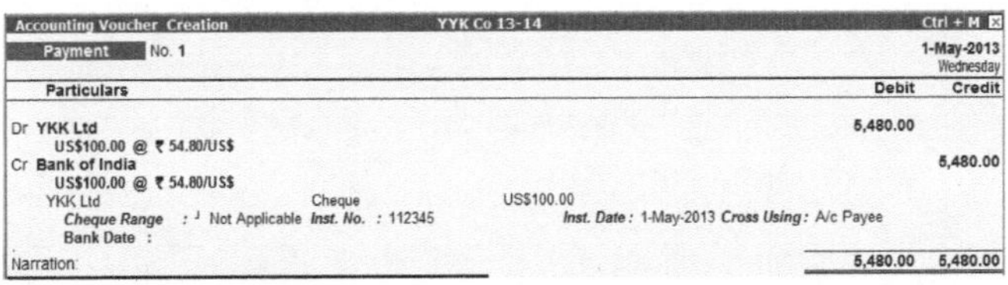

F-5A: Voucher entry in Foreign Currency

The Amount as entered in Value field in Base Currency at Forex Currency details screen (F-4B) is carried to the Amount column in Voucher Main screen (F-5A).

06 Forex Gain / Loss Adjustment

When the Bill is settled in Foreign Currency, any balance lying in Party Account, due to the difference in Exchange Rate, is to be adjusted to square off the Party Account and transferred to Forex Gain Loss , through a Journal Voucher . In case of Forex Loss, debit the Forex Gain/ Loss A/c and credit the Party Account. In case of Forex Gain, and Debit the Party Account & Credit the Forex Gain / Loss A/c.

Summary

- **Multi Currency Activation** : At *F11:Features>Accounting Features* , set the Multi Currency option to create Multiple Currencies (Foreign Currencies).

- **Foreign Currency Masters** : Create Foreign Currency Masters
- **Currency Rates** : Set up Currency Exchange Rates (Selling & Buying Rates) with Base Currency , for each Foreign Currency created.
- **Voucher Entry in Foreign Currency** : Enter the voucher, currency exchange rate and get the amount converted into Foreign / Base Currency as per Exchange Rates
- **Reports with Foreign Currency** : Having entered Forex details in voucher, you may get various Account Books with Forex details, by setting the Configuration option (Click *F12:Configure* at Report Display / Printing screen, and set Yes at the relevant Forex Options, like *Show Forex Transactions?)*
- **Forex Gain Loss** : You may enter Forex Gain /Loss voucher, to adjust the Forex Gain / Loss in Accounts.

Tally Administration 01-16

01 Tally Administration

Now we discuss briefly about maintenance of Tally Data and other salient features in Tally.ERP9, like:

- Data Back Up
- Data Restoration
- Data Rewriting
- Data Export & Import
- Reports e-mailing
- Message Centre
- Tally.Net
- Support Centre
- Password

02 Data Backup

Accounts Data are created with lot of efforts. So data are very valuable. Through Data Backup, a copy of data is kept at another place for safety. If the current working data is lost or damaged, the Backed Data may be restored and continue working.

At Gateway of Tally click <u>F3:</u> *Cmp Info* button (or press Alt+F3 keys) to Company Info Menu. Select *Backup* to get *Back Up* screen (F-1A)

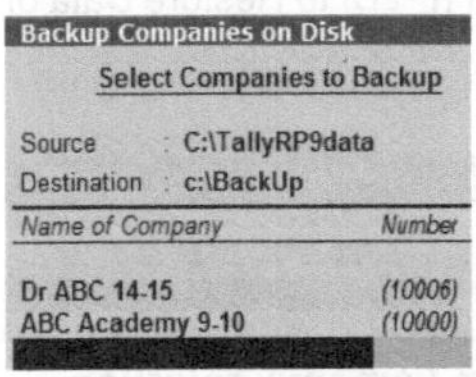

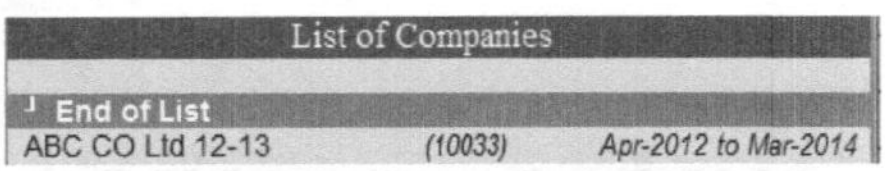

F-1A : Data Back Up **F-1B: Back Up Company selection**

Data Back Up Locations : At *Data Back Up* screen (F-1A), at the upper part, specify the locations of source & destination of data as follows:

- **Data Source Location :** At *Source*, the data directory of current company appears, from where data be Back up. Change it if Back Up is to be taken from other place (normally you need not change it).

- **Data Destination Location :** At *Destination*, enter the folder name (e.g c:\backup) where the Backed Up Data would be stored (you may define a folder, a network drive or another drive like Pen Drive / external disk). It is a good practice to keep data in external drive and then store in another computer system.

Data Back Up Process : At Data Back Up screen (F-1A), at the lower part, select the Company to be Backed Up, from the list of Companies in source directory (F-1B). Select *End of File* (F-1B) and Click *Yes* to start Back Up process to Back up data of all the selected Companies. This way, you may select any One or several Companies to back up in one shot.

All the selected Companies will be backed up one by one and placed together in ONE Back Up file (named TBK 900.001) in the destination drive (e.g c:\backup)

03 Data Restoration

If the current working data gets damaged, you should restore the backed up data to get the data back in the current working directory, in functional condition.

At Gateway of Tally click <u>F3:</u> *Cmp Info* button to *Company Info* screen. Select *Restore* to get Restore screen (F-2A).

Data Locations for Restoration : At Restore screen (F-2A):

- At *Destination* field, enter the current working data path where the Back Up data is to be *Copied To.*
- At *Source* field, enter the data path from where the Backed Data is to be *Copied From.*

Data Restoration Process : At Restore screen (F-2A), at *Name of Company* column, select the Companies whose data is to be restored (f-2B), one by one from the List of Backed Up Companies (you may select *All Items* to restore data of all available companies). Select *End of List* (F-2B) to Restore Data of selected Companies and click *Yes*.

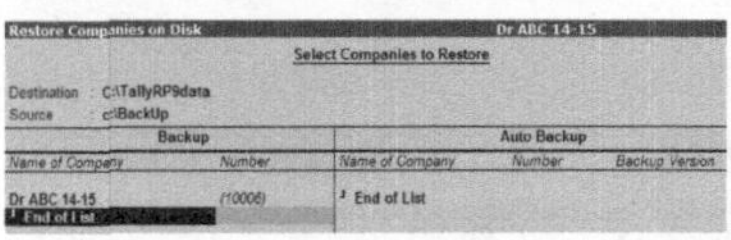

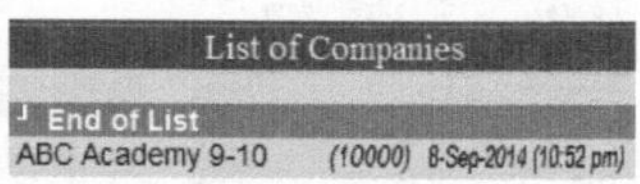

F-2A: Data Restoration **F-2B: Back up Compnay selection**

04 Data Rewriting

Rewriting means reconstructing inconsistent or older version Tally Data. When any part of data gets damaged and Tally fails to open a company, you should repair / reconstruct data through Rewrite Option.

At Gateway, press *Alt+Ctrl+R*, select the Company which you wish to rewrite, to get Rewrite Screen (F-3A). Press *Yes* to start Re-writing process.

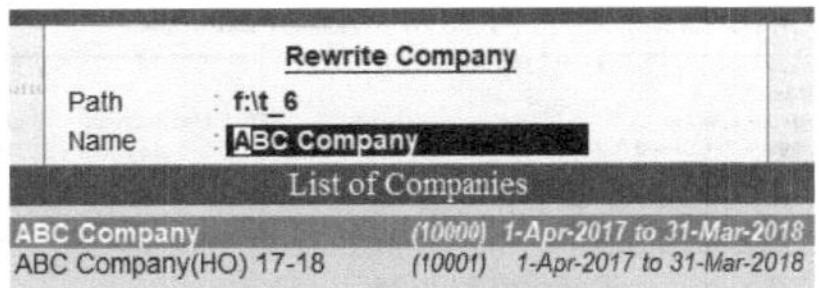

F-3A :Data Re-writing

05 Data Export

Data Export means extracting Tally data / Tally reports and storing in digital form for further processing / transmission.

At any Reports Display, click *E:Export* button to get Report Export screen (F-4A). At *Format*, select the Export Format from the list (F-4B).

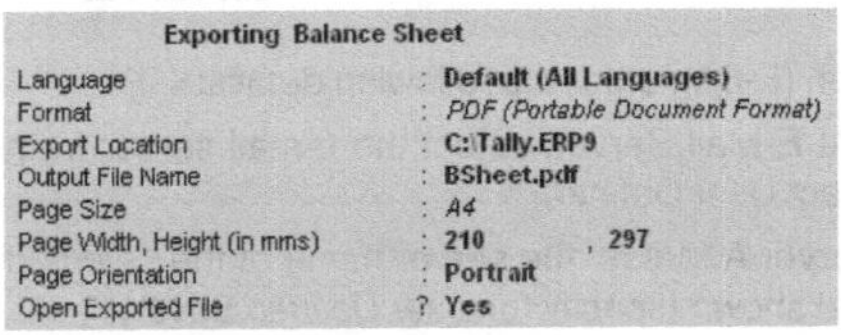

F-4A: Report Export

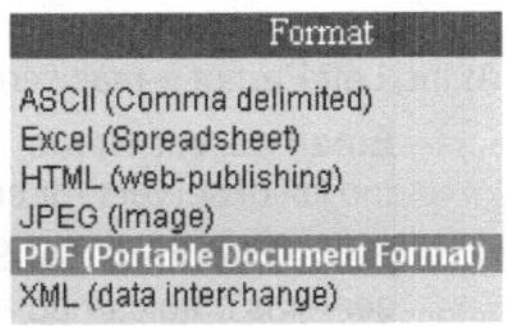

F-4B: Export Format

06 Data Import

Data Import means entering and storing Tally compatible Data in XML Format, from external Data file into Tally data base, without manually entering the Data through Tally.

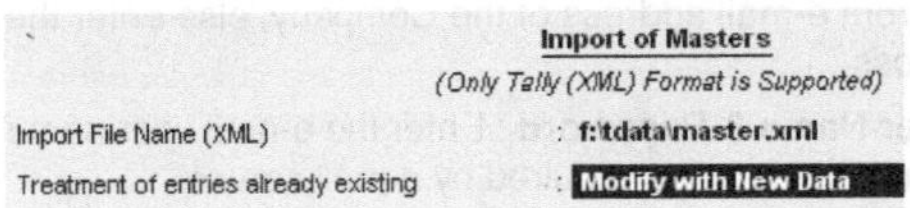

F-5A:Data Import screen

F-5B: Data Import Behavious list

Select *GoT>Import of Data* and then select *Masters* (to import Masters Data) or *Vouchers* (to Import Vouchers data) to get Data Import screen (F-5A). Enter the external file name (with Path). In case of import of Masters, you also have to select the treatment of imported data from the Behaviour List (F-5B).

07 Reports e-mailing

Instead of sending a printed report, you may e-mail a Report from Reports Display / printing screen, click *M:E-Mail* to get e-mail screen (F-6A).

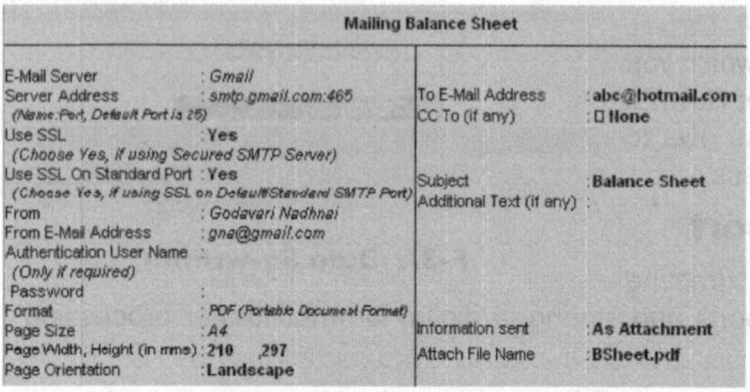

F-6A: e-mailing screen

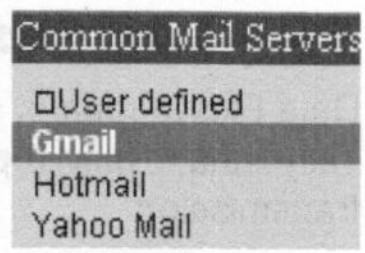

F-6B: e-mail server list

At the Left Part of e-mail screen (F-6A), enter the following details:

- **Email server Name** : At E-Mail Server, select the e-mail server from the list of servers (or select User Defined)
- **Server Address** : At Server Address, the server name of the selected server is auto carried and shown (specify for *User Defined* Sever)
- **Server Type** : At *Use SSL*, set *Yes* For SMTP Server Types
- **Standard Port** : At *Use SSL on Standard Port,* set Yes for SSL on Standard SMPTP Port
- **Sender Name** : At *From*, the Company Name is carried, as sender of the e-mail.
- **Sender e-mail address** : At *From e-mail address*, sender's e-mail address is Carried from e-mail address of the Company, else enter the sender's email address
- **Authentication User Name & Password** : Enter the e-mail user name & password, if the authentication is required by e-mail server
- **Attachment Page specification** : Enter / Select the Page size (at page Size), Page dimension (width & height in mm, carried for standard formats) and Page orientation, for the attachment.

At the Right Part of e-mail screen (F-6A), enter the following details

- **Receiver's e-mail address** : At *To E-mail address*, enter the receiver's e-mail address (or select e-mail address as entered from Ledger Accounts Master). In case of multiple receiver's, you may enter / select multiple e-mail address
- **Copy** : At *CC To*, you may further enter the e-mail address of the copy recipient
- **e-mail subject** : At Subject Enter the Caption (Subject) of the e-mail (the Report Heading is carried by default), which is carried at the subject field of the email

- **E-mail Text :** At Additional text, enter the text which is carried as the e-mail text in the e-mail (the report is sent as attachment)
- **Attachment File** : Enter the Attached Report Filename (default Report Name is carried)

Set up the Report optlons of the Report as usual, and Type Y to e-mail the report to the specified recipients

Another alternative (perhaps better) is to export the report (in PDF, JPEG, XLS etc) and send the report through your popular e-mail application.

08 Users & Password

For a Company, for which you have set up Security Features (at Company Creation / Alteration screen, you have set *Yes* at *Use Security Control*), you may further set up Users & Passwords, to provide better and consistent security features.

Passwords Policy Set Up : At GoT, Click F3:Cmp Info>Security Control to get Security Control Menu (F-7A). Select *Password Policy* to get Password Policy screen (F-8A) to set the Password Parameters.

F-7A: Security Contrl menu

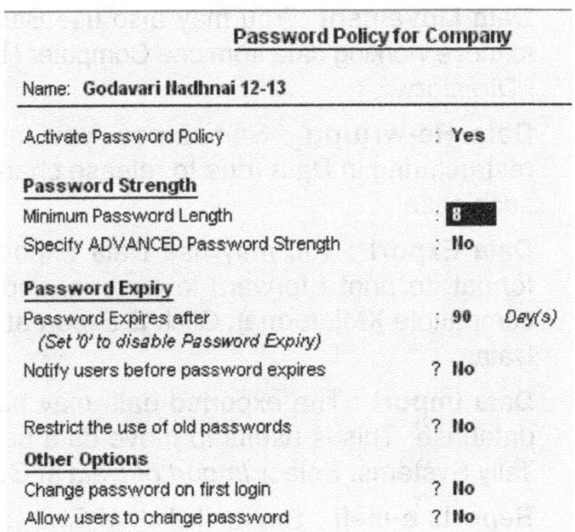

F-8A: Password Policy Set up screen

Users Creation & Password set Up: At Security Control Menu (F-7A), select *Users & Passwords* to get *Users List* (F-9A) to create Users and set Passwords.

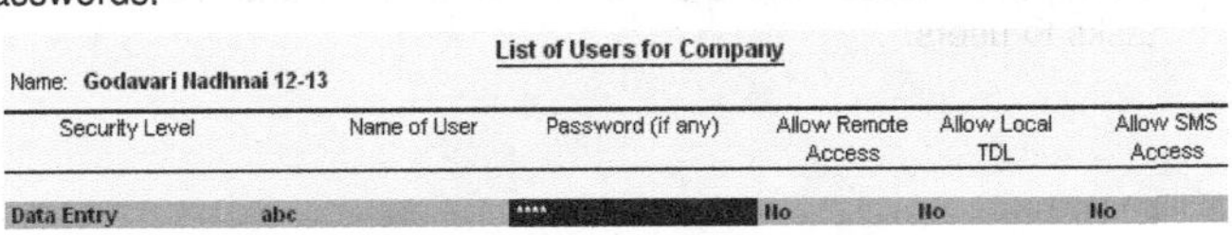

F-9A: Users & Password screen

Summary

- **Back Up :** To safeguard your valuable data, you should regularly take Data Back Up, from *F3:Comp Info* menu at GoT. If you take Back Up of all the companies at a time, select *All Items*, so that a complete Back Up of all the companies are created. Whenever you take Back Up, Tally would overwrite the earlier Back Up in the specified Destination Directory. So, if you omit any Company from Back Up, the Data Back Up of that Company would not be available.
- **Back Up Data Media :** To safeguard your data, it is advisable to Back Up data (or copy backed Up data file) in external media (like Pen Drive, External Hard Disk etc), so that your data is safe even if there is problem in Computer and you lose working data in the Computer. You should keep such Backed Up data in external media in very safe place, to protect from misuse.
- **Restore** : If the working Data is lost, you may restore the Backed up Data. You would lose the data updated after the last Back Up. Hover, you may get updated data on Restoring from Auto Back Up.
- **Data Movement** : You may also use Back Up / Restore combination to move working data from one Computer / Directory to another Computer / Directory.
- **Data Re-writing** : Sometimes, you may get errors due to some restructuring in Data (due to release change etc). Try rewriting data in such case.
- **Data Export** : You may use Data Export to store reports in desired format, to print / forward to anyone, and to extract raw data in Tally compatible XML format. Click *E:Export* at any Report screen to Export Data.
- **Data Import** : The exported data may be imported into another Tally database. This is useful to move data between various disconnected Tally Systems. Select *Import of Data* at GoT
- **Reports e-mail** : You mail click *M:Email* at any Report Display screen to send the Report by Email to nay email address. This saves and offers easy delivery of report to anyone. Alternatively, you may export report, as described, and then e-mail the exported report.
- **Users & Password**: At Company Creation / Alteration screen, set *Yes* at *Use Security Control* and set up Administrator. You may then set up Users, their access rights & Passwords to allow and restrict various tasks to users.

Assignments : Financial Accounting 01

01-01 Company Creation

Load Tally

[Click on Tally ion at desktop. In case of Educational Version, select *W:Work in Educational Mode>I:Silver Edition Moe (Single User)*

Create Company

- Create a Company of the name of your Roll Number (e.g 014 AK Sinha - Accnts), at folder d:/T/data, for Accounts Only. Change the Mailing Name, removing the Roll Number (e.g AK Sinha - Accts). Financial Year 01-4-2016 to 31-3-2017. Save the Company.

  [Select *GoT>F3:Cmp Info >Create Company* to get Company Creation screen. Press Shift+Tab (at name field) to go to *Directory* field and change the Directory Name to d:/T/data. At *Name*, enter your Roll Number, Name- Accts (e.g 014 AK Sinha – Accts). At *Mailing Name* , remove the Roll Number but keep the Name (e.g AK Sinha- Accts). At *Financial Year From*, enter 01-4-2016. Press Ctrl+A to save the Company]
- Shut the Company.

  [Hints : Click *GoT>F1:Shut Cmp*,(and select the Company from the list)]
- Exit from Tally.

  [Select Quit (or press <Esc> and finally select Y (Yes) to Quit.

Company Alteration (Company Address Entry)

- Select the Company

  [Select *GoT>F3:Cmp Info >Select Company* and then select the Company from List.
- Company info Alteration

  Select *GoT>F3:Cmp Info >Alter* and select the Company to get the Company Alteration screen. Now fill up the fields of Address etc with your own data]
- Save the changed data

  [Press Ctrl+A]

01-02 Gateway of Tally

- **Current Period Setting** : Set the Current Period as 01-4-2016 to 31-3-2017

  [Select *GoT>F2:Period.* At *From* enter 01-4-2016, at *To* enter 31-3-2017]

- **Accounting Features**

  [Select *GoT>F11:Features>Accounting Features* and set *No* at all the options]

- **Help :** Read the *Company Creation* topic at Local Help File

  [Select *GoT>Help>Local help* to view *Tally ERP 9 Reference Manual.* At *Contents* Tab, click on '*Creating Company*' link under the section *Maintaining Company data>Company Information*]

- **Tally Calculator**

  Compute the value of (12*(36+45)/ 20))+30

  [At Calculator field press <enter> (or press Ctrl+N) to expand Calculator field and enter the expression (12*(36+45)/ 20)+30 to get the result (=78.60). You may embed multiple level parenthesis , like ((12+30/7)+15), but cannot use braces like { } or [ ]. So, entering like [12*{(36+45)/ 20)}+30] will produce error].

01-03 Account Masters

- **Ledger Accounts Creation**
  - o Create following Ledger Accounts under existing Reserved Groups.
    - A K Sinha (under Capital), Opening Balance 1,00,000 Cr
    - HDFC Bank (under Bank Accounts) Opening Balance 10,000 Dr
    - SBI C/C A/c (under Bank OCC Accounts) Opening Balance 20,000 Cr
    - A K Enterprises (under Sundry Debtors), Opening Balance 30,000 Dr
    - B K Suppliers (under Sundry Creditors), Opening Balance 25,000 Cr
    - Furniture (under Fixed Assets), Opening Balance 60,000 Dr
    - Stock (under Stock-in-Hand), Opening Balance 35,000 Dr

- **Alter Account Ledger :** Select *GoT>Accounts Info>Ledgers>Alter* and the select:
  - o *Cash* account and enter Opening Balance 10000 Dr
  - o *A K Sinha, A K Enterprises & B K Suppliers* and enter the Address

and other particulars (like Address etc) as per your own assumed record.

- **Create Account Groups** : Select *GoT>Accounts Info>Groups>Create*

  Create Account Group - Freight Inwards (under *Direct Expenses*)

- **Ledger Creation with new Account Group (Secondary) Creation (at *Under* field).**
  - o Select *GoT>Accounts Info>Ledgers.* At Ledger Creation screen, at Under, press *Alt+C* to create Account Group creation (secondary) screen. Create the new Parent Account Group and select it at *Under*)
    - ▪ Salary (under *Employee Expenses*, under *Indirect Expenses*)
    - ▪ Handling Charges (under *Freight Outwards*, under *Indirect Expenses*)

- **List of Accounts / Chart of Accounts**
  - o **List of Accounts** : Select *GoT>Display>List of Accounts* to print List of Accounts
  - o **Chart of Accounts with Opening Balance** : Select *GoT>Display>Trial Balance*. Click F12*:Configure* to get Configuration screen. Set *Yes* at *Show Opening Balance*, set *No* at *Show Transactions, Show Closing Balance* and set *Yes* at *Expand All Levels in Detailed Format.*

01-04 Account Vouchers

Voucher Entry Configuration : Select *GoT>Accounting Vouchers* to get *Accounts Voucher Entry* screen. Click *F12:Configure* to get *Voucher Configuration* screen

- At *Skip date During Creation*, set *No*, so that the cursor goes at date filed to enter Voucher Date.
- At *Use Dr / Cr instead of To /By during entry*, set *Yes* to get Dr/ Cr sign instead of To / By sign, to indicate Debit / Credit Accounts more clearly in the voucher
- At *Use defaults at Bank Allocation*, set *Yes* so that bank details entry sub-screen does not appear (this makes voucher entry simpler)

Enter following Accounts Vouchers

- **On 1-5-16, A K Sinha (Proprietor) withdraws Rs 500 for personal expenses. From SBI C/C A/c, by cheque # 123321).**

  [This entry should be made through *Payment* Voucher as money is paid out. Since it is withdrawal for personal expenses, not an withdrawal of Capital, it is normally more appropriate to create a new *Drawings* Account under Capital Account, than debiting Capital A/c. Select *GoT>Accounting Voucher.* Click *F5:Payment* Voucher . Enter Voucher Date (1-5-16). At first ledger (Dr) entry, press Alt+C to get Ledger Creation screen. Create *Drawing* Account, select Capital Accounts at *Under* field and press *Ctrl A* to save the newly created *Drawing* Ledger Account and get back to the voucher entry screen. At Particulars column, select *Drawing* A/c from list of ledger accounts and enter 500 at Debit column].

Next select Cr. At *Particulars* column, select SBI C/C A/c and enter 500 at Credit column.

As the Debit & Credit columns are now equal, cursor will go to *Narration* field. Enter Ch No 123321 and enter the Narration in short (like Withdrawn by A K Sinha, proprietor). Press Ctrl+A and save the voucher]

- **On 2-5-16, Conveyance expenses of Rs 400 is paid in Cash to A K Sinha for attending a client**. Create a Payment Voucher (Select GoT>Accounting Voucher. Click *F5:Payment* button) Since Conveyance Expenses ledger account is not created, at first line, at *Particulars,* press *Alt+C* to get Ledger Creation (secondary)screen. Create the Conveyance Expenses ledger account (under *Indirect Expenses*) and select it. Enter 400 at *Debit* column. In next line, type C (for credit), select Cash A/c and enter 400 at *Credit* Column]. Write the Narration.
- **On 1-7-16 A K Sinha receives Rs 1000 in cash from a client as consultancy Fees.** Create a Receipt Voucher (Select GoT>Accounting Voucher. Click *F6:Receipt* button). Create a Ledger Account Consultancy Fees (under Direct Income) and Credit Rs 1000. Debit Cash Account Rs 1000, as explained above. Enter the Narration.
- **On 1-10-16 State Bank of India, charges Interest of Rs 650 on the C/C Account**. Create Interest Account under Indirect Expenses and debit Rs 650. Credit SBI C/C Account by Rs 650. Enter the Narration (e.g Interest Debited by SBI on CC A/c for 1-4-16 to 30-09-16)
- **On 1-12-16, A K Enterprises remitted 12000 against outstanding dues, into the HDFC Account by electronic transfer.** Create a Receipt Voucher. Credit A K Enterprises Rs 12000 and Debit HDFC Bank A/c Rs 12000.
- **On 1-1-17, cheque # 123322 was issued in favour of B K suppliers for Rs 10000, from HDFC bank, for outstanding dues payable to them.** Create a Payment Voucher. Debit B K suppliers Rs 10000 and Credit HDFC Bank A/c Rs 10000.
- **On 1-3-17, Stock Costing Rs. 12000 was sold in Cash for Rs. 15000.** Create a Sales Voucher . Credit Cash Sales Account (Create Cash Sales Ledger Account under Sales Group) Rs 15000. Debit Cash Account Rs 15000.
- **On 2-3-17, Rs 14000 Cash was deposited into SBI C/C Account.** Create Contra Voucher. Credit SBI C/C Account by Rs 14000 and Debit Cash A/c Rs 14000.

- **Interest on SBI C/C Account Rs 560 for 1-10-16 to 31-3-17 was debited by SBI on 4-4-17.** On 31-3-17, create a Journal Voucher for the Interest chargeable. Debit Interest A/c (under Direct Expenses) Rs 560 and Credit Interest Payable Account (under Current Liabilities) by Rs 560. Enter the Narration.

01-05 Reports

Preview Report on screen and print from Preview

At any Report Printing screen (when you click P:Print button), click *I:With preview* toggle button. Consequently, instead of printing on paper, a replica of the Report (called print preview) will be shown in screen for review, with few links at the bottom of the Report. Click *Zoom* to zoom the report to view. Click *Print* to print the report on printer. In case of wide / long reports, you may pan the report by Pg Dn, Pg Up, Pg Left, Pg Right links to view all the sections of the Report. A scale at the left and top indicates the print dimension of the Report.

01-06 Cash Bank Book

Print Cash / Bank Book in following Methods

- **Print Cash Bank Book for the period 1-4-2016 to 31-7-2016 after viewing Preview**

  Select *GoT>Display>Account Books>Cash / Bank Books.* Select *Cash* Account to get Monthly Break up of Cash Book Summary. Drill Down through any month. Click *F2:Period* and set the Period 1-4-2016 to 31-7-2016. Click *P:Print* Button. Click *I:With Preview* button. Set *Yes* at *Show Voucher Numbers also, Include Opening balance* and *Show Narrations also* (set *No* at other options). At *Method of Balancing,* select *Yearly.* Type Y (for Yes) to get the Preview screen.

  At preview screen, Click *Print* link to print the report on Printer

- **Print Cash Bank Book for the period 1-4-2016 to 31-7-2016 from Multi Account option.**

  Select *GoT>Multi Account Printing>Account Books>Cash Books.* Select *Cash* Account. At *From,* enter 1-4-2016, At *To,* enter to 31-7-2016. At *Format,* select *Detailed.* Set *Yes* at *Show Voucher Numbers also, Show Narrations also* and *Include Opening Balances.* Type Y (for Yes) to print the report on Printer.

  Whether you print through Display, Preview or Multi Account Methods, the output would be similar.

01-07 Journal Register

Print following Registers

- **Print Journal Registers for the period 1-3-17 to 31-3-17 from Display**

Select *GoT>Display>Account Books>Journal Register> Journal Register* to get the matrix of Monthly Number of Journal Vouchers. Select any month, click *F2:Period* and enter 1-3-17 & 31-3-17 for the Journal Register period. Click *P:Print* Button. At *Format*, select *Detailed.* Set *Yes* at *Show Voucher Numbers also, Show Narrations also.*

- **Print Sales Register for the period 1-3-17 to 31-3-17 from Display**

  Select *GoT>Display>Account Books>Sales Register* to get Monthly Summary of Sales Accounts . Select any month, click *F2:Period* and enter 1-3-17 & 31-3-17 for the Sales Register period. Click *P:Print* Button. At *Format*, select *Detailed.* Set *Yes* at *Show Voucher Numbers also, Show Narrations also.*

01-08 Ledger Book

Print the following Reports

- **Print Ledger Book for Sales Account & B K Suppliers for the period 1-4-16 to 31-3-17 from Multi Account printing.**
  - o As the Ledger Accounts to be printed are under different Group, it is quite difficult to print the both Ledgers from Multi Account Printing in one shot, even using the flexible combinations like Exclude / Include options.
  - o Select *GoT>Multi Account Printing>Account Books>Ledger>One Account* and the select the Ledger Account. Set the period as 1-4-16 to 31-3-17. At *Format*, select *Detailed.* Set *Yes* at *Show Voucher Narration Also.* This way, select Ledger Accounts (Sales Account & B K Suppliers) one by one and print the Ledger Account separately.
- **Print Confirmation of Accounts for A K Enterprises for 1-4-16 to 31-3-17 from Display option.**
  - o Confirmation of Accounts can be printed at Print option of Ledger Book Display or at Multi Account Printing of Ledger Book.
  - o Select *GoT>Display>Account Books>Ledger.* Click *F2:Period* and set the Period as 1-4-16 to 31-3-17. Click *P:Print* to get Ledger Printing screen. At *Style of Printing*, select *Confirmation of Accounts.* At *Format*, select *Detailed*, Set *Yes* at *Show Narrations Also.*

01-09 Trial Balance

- **Print Trial Balance showing Non zero Closing Balance of all Ledger Accounts, in Alphabetical Order**

  Select *Got>Display>Trial Balance.* Click *P:Print* button to get Trial Balance Printing screen. Set *Yes* at *Show Closing Balance* (Set *No* at *Show Opening Balance* and at *Show Transactions*). At *Method of*

Information, select *Itemwise*. Set *No* at Show All Accounts *(incl Non Empty Accounts)*.

- **Print Extended Trial Balance with Opening Balance, Transaction totals of Debits & Credits & Closing Balance of all Account Groups / Ledger Accounts (empty Ledger Accounts should be omitted) in hierarchical Format.**

  Select *Got>Display>Trial Balance*. Click *P:Print* button to get *Trial Balance Printing* screen. Set *Yes* at *Show Opening Balance, Show Transactions* (further set *No* at *Nett Transaction only)*, set *Yes* at *Show Closing Balance*. At *Method of Information*, select *Grouped*. Set *Yes* at *Expand All Levels in Detailed Format*. Set *No* at *Show All Accounts* (incl Non Empty Accounts).

- **Print Check List of Opening Balance of Account Groups / Ledgers in hierarchical order, to check the Ledger Accounts & Opening Balance.**

  Select *Got>Display>Trial Balance*. Click *F2:Period* and enter 1-4-16 to 31-3-17. Click *P:Print* button to get *Trial Balance Printing* screen. Set *Yes* at *Show Opening Balance*, Set *No* at *Show Transactions* & at *Show Closing Balance*. At *Method of Information*, select *Grouped*. Set *Yes* at *Expand All Levels in Detailed Format*. Set *No* at *Show All Accounts* (incl Non Empty Accounts).

01-10 P L Statement

- **Enter Closing Stock Value as on 31.3.17 Rs 23,000**

  Select *GoT>Accounts Info>Ledgers>Alter* and then select *Stock* Account (under Stock In Hand Group) from the list of Ledgers. At *Closing Balance*, at first column (without Label) enter Date 31-3-17 (DO NOT try to enter Amount in the first column). In next column, enter the Closing Stock Value (i.e.Rs 23,000) . The sign Dr appears alongside.

- **Print P L Statement for the period 1-4-16 to 31-3-17**

  Select *GoT>Profit & Loss A/c*. Click *F2:Period* and set the Dates 1-4-16 to 31-3-17. Click *P:Print* button to get Profit & Loss A/c printing screen. At *Format*, select *Detailed*, Set *No* at *Show Vertical Profit & Loss*. Type *Y* (for Yes) to print the Profit & Loss Statement on Printer.

- **Print P L Statement for the period 1-4-16 to 31-3-17 with Cost of Sales figures**

  Cost of Sales figure is shown in Vertical Format of Profit & Loss A/c. Select *GoT>Profit & Loss A/c*. Click *F2:Period* and set the Dates 1-4-16 to 31-3-17. Click *P:Print* button to get Profit & Loss A/c printing screen. At *Format*, select *Detailed*, Set *Yes* at *Show Vertical Profit & Loss*. Type *Y* (for Yes) to print the Profit & Loss Statement (in Vertical Format) on Printer.

01-11 Balance Sheet

- **Print Balance Sheet as on 31-3-17**

  Select *GoT>Profit & Loss A/c.* Click *F2:Period* and set the Dates 1-4-16 to 31-3-17. Click *P:Print* button to get Balance Sheet printing screen. At *Format*, select *Detailed*, Set *No* at *Show Vertical Balance Sheet*. Type *Y* (for Yes) to print the Balance Sheet on Printer.

- **Print Balance Sheet as on 31-3-17 in Vertical Format, with Working Capital figures**

  Select *GoT>Profit & Loss A/c.* Click *F2:Period* and set the Dates 1-4-16 to 31-3-17. Click *P:Print* button to get Profit & Loss A/c printing screen. At *Format*, select *Detailed*, Set *Yes* at *Show Vertical Balance Sheet*, set *Yes* at *Show Working Capital Figures* . Type *Y* (for Yes) to print the Balance Sheet on Printer.

01-12 Accounts Receivables / Payables

- **Activate AR/AP Features for the Company**

  Click F11: Features > F1:Accounting Features, and set *Yes* at *Maintain Billwise Details*

- **Create Customer Ledger Account - ABC Traders, Supplier Ledger Account - PQR Traders, and set Bill By Feature for these 2 accounts**

  Select *GoT>Accounts Info>Ledgers>Create* and then create following 2 Ledger Accounts:

  Enter ABC Traders at *Name.* Select *Sundry Debtors* at *Under.* Set *Yes* at *Maintain Balances Bill by Bill.*

  Enter PQR Traders at *Name.* Select *Sundry Creditors* at *Under.* Set *Yes* at *Maintain Balances Bill by Bill.*

- **On 1-6-2106, Goods purchased from PQR Traders for Rs 15000 by Bill No 125 dt 31-5-2016.**

  Select *GoT>Accounting Voucher.* Click *F9:Puchase* button to get Purchase Voucher entry screen.

  - o Click *F12:Configure* to get *Voucher Configuration screen* and set *No* at *Accept Supplementary Details.*
  - o Click *V:As Voucher* toggle button. Enter 1-6-2016 at Voucher Date. Enter 125 at Supplier Invoice No.
  - o At *Particulars* column, select *PQR Traders* and enter 15000 at Credit Column, to get *Bill Details* screen
  - o At Bill Details screen, At *Type of Ref* column, *New Ref.* select. from the list of *Method of Adj.* At *Name* column, the Party Bill Ref Number (i.e 125) as entered earlier is carried (press <enter> to accept it). At *Amount* column, the amount 15000 as entered earlier is carried (press <enter> to accept it).

- o In second line, Type Dr and select *Purchase* Account from List of Ledger Accounts (Press Alt+C and create Purchase Ledger A/c under Purchase Group, if necessary) and enter 15000 at Debit Column. Enter Voucher Narration (Goods Purchased from PQR Traders Bill No 125 dt 31-5-2016). Save the Voucher

- **On 1-7 -2016, Goods sold to ABC Traders Rs 12000 by Bill No 1**

  Select *GoT>Accounting Voucher*. Click *F8: Sales* to get Sales Voucher entry screen. Click V:*As Voucher* toggle button. The Voucher No 1 is shown. Click *F12:Configure* to get Voucher Configuration screen and set *No* at *Accept Supplementary Details*. Enter 1-7-2016 at Voucher Date.

  - o At *Particulars* column, select *ABC Traders* and enter 12000 at Debit Column, , to get Bill Details screen
  - o At Bill Details screen, At *Type of Ref* column, select *New Ref*. At *Name* column, the Voucher No 1 is carried (press <enter> to accept it). At *Amount* column, the amount 12000 as entered earlier is carried (press <enter> to accept it).
  - o In second line, Type Cr and select *Sales* Account from List of Ledger Accounts (Press Alt+C and create Sales Ledger A/c under Sales Group, if necessary) and enter 12000 at Credit Column. Enter Voucher Narration (Goods sold to ABC Traders Bill No 1 dt 1-7-2016). Save the Voucher

- **On 1-8-2016, Rs 4000 was received from *ABC Traders*, by cheque No 456789 on Canara Bank, Ballygunge Br., dt 31-7-16,against Bill Number 1. The cheque was deposited in SBI CC Account.**

  - o Select *GoT>Accounting Voucher*. Click *F6: Receipt* to get Receipt Voucher entry screen. Click *F12:Configure* to get Voucher Configuration screen and set *Yes* at *Use Defaults for Bank Allocations*, to suppress the Bank Details entry sub screen (to keep the things simpler). Enter 1-8-2016 at Voucher Date.
  - o At *Particulars*, select *ABC Traders* and enter 4000 at Credit column. You get *Bill Allocation* screen for allocation of Rs 4000. At *Type of Ref* select *Agst Ref*. At *Name*, select the Bill against which the payment is received (i.e Bill Number 1). At *Amount*, Rs 4000 (as entered in voucher) is carried. Press <enter>. You get back to main voucher entry screen.
  - o In next line, select the Bank Account in which the Cheque is deposited (i.e SBI CC Account). At *Amount* column, Rs 4000 is carried. Press <enter>. Since the Debit & Credit are equal, the Ledger entry is over. The cursor goes to voucher Narration. At Voucher Narration, enter Cheque details (i.e Ch No 456789, Canara Bk., Ballygunge Br., dt 31-7-16). Press Ctrl+A to save the voucher.

- **On 2-8-2016, Rs 6000 was paid to *PQR Traders*, by cheque No 123123 on HDFC Bank, against Bill Number 125.**
  - o Select *GoT>Accounting Voucher*. Click *F5: Payment* to get *Payment* Voucher entry screen. Click *F12:Configure* to get Voucher Configuration screen and set *Yes* at *Use Defaults for Bank Allocations*. Enter 2-8-2016 at Voucher Date.
  - o At *Particulars*, select PQR Traders and enter 4000 at Debit column. You get *Bill Allocation* screen for allocation of Rs 6000. At *Type of Ref* select *Agst Ref*. At *Name*, select the Bill against which the payment is received (i.e Bill Number 125). At Amount Rs 6000 (as entered in voucher) is carried. Press <enter>. You get back to main voucher entry screen.
  - o In next line, select the Bank Account from which the Cheque is issued (i.e HDFC Bank). At *Amount* column, Rs 6000 is carried. Press <enter>. Since the Debit & Credit are equal, the Ledger entry is over. The cursor goes to voucher Narration. At Voucher Narration, enter Cheque details (i.e 123123). Press *Ctrl+A* to save the voucher
- **Print Outstanding Bills Payables Statement, Age Analysis**

  Select *GoT>Display>Statement of Accounts>Outstandings>Payables*. Click *F1:Detailed* to display Billwise details of all Outstanding Bills Payables
  - o **List of all Pending Bills** : Click *F7:Billwise* toggle button to display Billwise details of all Outstanding Bills Payables
  - o **Partywise Pending Bills** : Click *F7:Bill-Partywise* toggle button to display Partywise details of all Outstanding Bills Payables
  - o **Age Analysis** : Click *F6:Agewise* button to get Age Analysis screen. Select *Ageing by Bill Date*, set the Ageing slab (30, 60, 90+ days) to view the *Age Analysis* Report with columns for each slab as set up.

  Click P:Print to preview the report on screen & / or print the report on printer (Click I:*With Preview / No Preview* toggle button).
- **Print Outstanding Bills Receivables Statement, Age Analysis**
  - o Select *GoT>Display>Statement of Accounts>Outstandings> Receivables*. Click *F1:Detailed* to display Billwise details of all Outstanding Bills Receivables
  - o **List of all Pending Bills** : Click *F7:Billwise* toggle button to display Billwise details of all Outstanding Bills Receivables
  - o **Partywise Pending Bills** : Click *F7:Partywise* toggle button to display Partywise details of all Outstanding Bills Receivables
  - o **Age Analysis** : Click *F6:Age wise* button to get *Age Analysis*

screen. Select *Ageing by Due Date,* set the Ageing slab (30, 60, 90+ days) to view the Age Analysis Report, with columns for each slab as set up.

- o Click *P:Print* to preview the report on screen & / or print the report on printer (Click *I:With Preview / No Preview* toggle button).

- **Print Reminder Letter to Customer for Payment of Due Bills Receivables**
  - o Select *GoT>Display>Statement of Accounts>Outstandings> Ledger* and select the Ledger Account of the party to whom the Reminder Letter for payment of outstanding dues is to be sent. Click *F1:Detailed.*
  - o Click *P:Print* button to get Party Outstanding Ledger printing screen. Set *Yes* at *Print Reminder Letter* and set Age Analysis slab (30, 60, 90+). Type Y (for Yes) to print the Reminder Letter (showing details of Outstanding Bill of Party in letter format) on printer. This letter can then be sent to the Party.

01-13 Banking

- **Set up Bank Account for Banking operations**
  - o Select *GoT>Accounts Info>Ledger>Alter* and select the Bank Account (e.g HDFC Bank) for which you like to perform Banking Operations (like Cheque Issue / Deposit, Bank Reconciliation etc). to get *Ledger Alteration* screen. Set *Yes* at *Set / Alter Bank Details* to get *Bank Details* entry screen.

- **Payment made to PQR Traders against Bill No 123 by Ch No 123125 on HDFC Bank, on 1-10-2016 for Rs 2000**
  - o Select *GoT>Accounting Voucher.* Click *F5: Payment* to get *Payment* Voucher entry screen. Click *F12:Configure* to get Voucher Configuration screen and set *No* at *Use Defaults for Bank Allocations* and other option under Bank Allocations Configuration to get Bank details screen during voucher entry).
  - o Enter 1-10-2016 at Voucher Date.
  - o At *Particulars,* select PQR Traders and enter 2000 at Debit column. You get *Bill Allocation* screen for allocation of Rs 2000. At *Type of Ref* select *Agst Ref.* At *Name,* select the Bill against which the payment is received (i.e Bill Number 125). At Amount Rs 2000 (as entered in voucher) is carried. Press <enter>. You get back to main voucher entry screen.
  - o In next line, select the Bank Account from which the Cheque is issued (i.e HDFC Bank). At *Amount* column, Rs 2000 is carried. Press <enter>. To get Bank Details entry screen. At Bank Details entry screen, At *Favouring Name* column, the Party Name (PQR

Traders) is carried. Press <Enter>. At Transaction Type, select *Cheque* from the list of *Transaction Type*. At *Instrument Number*, enter the Cheque Number (i.e 123125), At *Inst.Date*, the Voucher Date is carried (press <enter>). At *Cross Using*, Type *A/c Payee* (to Cross the cheque). You get back to the main voucher screen.

Since the Debit & Credit are equal, the Ledger entry is over. The cursor goes to voucher Narration. At Voucher Narration. Press *Ctrl+A* to save the voucher.

01-14 Cost Centres

- **Activate Cost Centre for the Company**

  Select *F11:Features>Accounting Features*. At *Maintain Cost Centre* (under the section *Cost / Profit Centres Management*) set *Yes*.

- **Create Cost Centre Patna Branch & Kolkata Branch**
  - o Select *GoT>Accounts Info> Cost Centre > Create* (under Single Cost Centre) to get *Cost Centre Creation* screen.
  - o At *Name*, enter Cost Centre Name (i.e Patna Branch), At *Under*, select *Primary*. Type *Y* to save. In the same way, next create *Kolkata Branch* under *Primary*

- **Create Cost Allocable Ledger Account (Legal Expenses)**

  Select *GoT>Accounts Info>Ledger>Create* to get *Ledger Creation* screen. At *Name*, enter Ledger Name (i.e Legal Expenses), At *Under*, select *Indirect Expenses*. At *Cost Centres are Applicable,* set *Yes*. Press *Ctrl+A* to save the Ledger Account

- **On 1-11-2016, Legal Expenses paid to S K Sinha advocate, for Rs 5000 by Cash (Rs 3000 for Patna Branch & 2000 for Kolkata Branch)**
  - o Select *GoT>Accounting Voucher*. Click *F5:Payment* to get Payment Voucher screen. Enter 1-11-2016 at Date. At particulars, select Legal Expenses. At Debit column, enter 5000 to get Cost Allocation screen. At *Name* column, *select Patna Branch, enter 3000 at Amount column and press <enter>*. In next line, at *Name* column, select *Kolkata* and enter 2000 at *Amount* column. You get back to man voucher entry screen.
  - o At *Particulars* column, select *Cash* Ledger Account and enter 5000. Enter Narration (Paid to S K Sinha Advocate for filing fees of documents of Patna Branch – 3000, Kolkata Branch – 2000)

- **Print Cost Centre Break Up report**

  Select *GoT>Display>Statement of Accounts>Cost Centres>Cost Centre Break* up to get the Cost Centre Break Up Report. Click *F1:Detailed* button

- **Print Ledger / Cost Centre Break Up report**

Select *GoT>Display>Statement of Accounts>Cost Centres>Ledger Break Up* and then select the Ledger Account (i.e Legal Expenses) to get the Ledger / Cost Centre Break Up Report. Click *F1:Detailed* button

01-15 Currencies

- **Activate Multiple Currency :** Click *F11:Features>Accounting Features* to get Accounting Features screen. Under *General* section, set *Yes* at *Allow Multi Currency.*
- **Create Currency Master for US$, with Symbol $**
  - o Select *GoT>Accounts Info> Currencies>Create* to get Currency Creation screen.
  - o At *Symbol*, enter $. At *Formal Name*, enter US$. At *Number of Decimal Places*, enter 2. At *Show Amount in Millions*, set *Yes.* At *Is Symbol Suffixed to Amounts*, set *No.* At *Put a Space between Amount & Symbol,* set *No.* At *Symbol for Decimal Portion of Amount* enter , enter (.). At *Decimal places for Printing Amount in Word*, enter 2.
  - o Press *Ctrl+A* to save the currency master
- **Enter Currency Exchange Rate**
  - o Select *GoT>Accounts Info> Currencies>Rates of Exchange* to get *Exchange Rate* Entry screen . At *Exchange Rate* Entry screen, enter the Exchange Rate
  - o At *Date of Exchange Rate,* enter 1-4-2016. Now enter the Rate particulars against the respective Currency. At *Std Rate* column, enter the Exchange Rate (normally published by RBI), which is used to compute the Foreign Exchange Gain / Loss. Under *Currency Selling Rate,* at *Specified Rate* column, enter Bank Selling Rate (Rate in Base currency at which the Bank charges you in conversion of the Foreign Currency received by you), i.e Rs. 62.00. Under *Currency Buying Rate,* at *Specified Rate* column, enter Bank Buying Rate (Rate in Base currency at which the Bank pays you in conversion of the Foreign Currency given by you to Bank), i.e Rs. 61.80
- **On 1-2-2017, Goods sold to UN Inc. for US $2000.**
  - o Select *GoT>Accounting Vouchers.* Click *F8:Sales.* Enter Date 1-2-2017. At *Particulars* column, press *Alt+C* to create *U N Corp* Ledger, under Group Sundry Debtor (At Currency of Ledger, select US$) and select the Ledger *UN Corp* at *Particulars* column. At Amount, type $2000 (you must first type $ and then 2000 immediately after it without space), to get the currency details entry screen. At *Forex Amount*, US$2000 is carried. At *Rate of Exchange*, enter Rs 61.80. The computed value (Rs 123600) is

displayed. Press <Enter>. The amount is carried at Debit column in the main voucher screen

- o Now, select (Type C at sign) *Sales* Account and enter 123600 in credit column. Enter *Narration* (sold to UN Corpn $ 2000) and save the Voucher.

- **On 1-3-2017, HDFC Bank credits Rs 125000 in respect of full payment of US$2000 against the sale bill**
  - o Select *GoT>Accounting Vouchers*. Click *F6:Receipt*. Enter 1-3-2017 at Voucher Date. At *Particulars* column, select U N Traders. At *Amount*, type $2000 At *Forex Amount*, enter US$2000. At *Value*, enter Rs 125000. The computed Rate (62.50) is displayed. Press <Enter>. The amount (125000) is carried at Credit column in the main voucher screen.
  - o Now, select (Type D at sign) *HDFC bank* Account and enter 125000 in Debit column. Enter Narration ($ 2000 from UN Corpn) and save the Voucher.
- **Create Journal entry on 2-3-2017 to adjust the Forex Gain**
  - o Select *GoT>Accounting Vouchers*. Click *F7. Journal*. Enter date 2-3-2017. At *Particulars* column, select *UN Corp* and enter 1400 at Debit column. At next line, type C (or Credit). At *Particulars* column, press *Alt+C* to create *Forex Gain* Ledger Account (under *Indirect Income* Group). Select *Forex Gain* Ledger Account and enter 1400 at Credit column.
  - o Enter Voucher Narration (Forex Gain of Rs.125000-Rs.123600=Rs.1400 on account of sale to U N Corp adjusted). Save the voucher

01-16 Tally Administration

- **Create Back Up at d:\Bkup :** Select *GoT>F3: Cmp Info> Backup* to get *Back Up* screen. At *Source*, the data directory of current company appears. Press <enter>. At *Destination*, enter d:\Bkup . At the lower part, select the Company, select *End of File* and Click *Yes* to start Back Up process. A Back Up file (named TBK 900.001) at (d:\backup) containing data of selected Companies is created.
- **Restore Back Up from d:\Bkup :** At GoT, *F3: Cmp Info* button. Select *Restore* to get *Restore* screen. At *Source*, enter d:\backup. At *Destination*, the current data directory is shown. At the lower part, select the Company, select *End of File* and Click *Yes* to start Restore process. The data from the source directory (i.e d:\backup) would be overwritten over the data (if existing) in the destination directory.

PART 2

Basic Invoicing & Inventory

So far we discussed about Financial Accounting (Accounting of Money). In this section, we discuss about Accounting of Materials, covering creation of Masters, Entry of Transactions, Printing of Invoices and various Inventory Reports.

Inventory Masters explains creation of Inventory Masters, like UoM, Stock Group, Stock Items, Stock Category and Godowns, to maintain Inventory System

Inventory Vouchers describes various types of transactions of materials. It describes how the Accounting & Inventory transactions (like in Sales, Purchase, Debit & Credit Notes) are entered and synched in one voucher. It also describes Pure Inventory Vouchers like Receipt Note & Delivery Note, Rejection In & Rejection Out Vouchers, Stock Journal Vouchers Physical Stock etc.

Invoicing is the most important task of Inventory system, taking most of the time and volume of Inventory work. The finer aspect of essential Invoice Data Entry & Configuration are explained.

Invoice Printing explains the process of configuring the contents of Invoice and printing the Invoice in various formats

Inventory Reports describes scores of Inventory reports Display & Printing,

Point of Sales describes quick entry printing of Retail Invoices.

Orders explains Orders entry, Orders processing, Pre Closure of Orders etc.

Inventory Masters 02-01

01 Inventory System

To maintain Inventory details also, Click *F11:Features > Accounting Features* to get Accounting Features screen (F-1A). At *Maintain Accounts only*, set *No.*

Consequently, in Company Features Menu (*F11:Features*), the option Inventory Features get activated to activate and set up various option related to Inventory.

Accounting Features

General		Invoicing	
Maintain accounts only	? No	Enable invoicing	? Yes
Integrate accounts and inventory	? Yes	Record purchases in invoice mode	? Yes
Use Income and Expenses A/c instead of Profit and Loss A/c	? No	Use debit and credit notes	? Yes
Enable multi-currency	? No	Record credit notes in invoice mode	? Yes
		Record debit notes in invoice mode	? Yes

F-1A: Company Features set up for Inventory & Invoicing activation

Inventory Features set up

At Company Features Menu (*F11:Features*) menu, select *Inventory Features* to get *Inventory Features* screen (F-1B), to activate and set up options relating to Inventory

Inventory Features

General		Invoicing	
Integrate accounts and inventory	? Yes	Enable invoicing	? Yes
Enable zero-valued transactions	? No	Record purchases in invoice mode	? Yes
Storage and Classification		Use debit and credit notes	? Yes
Maintain multiple Godowns	? Yes	Record credit notes in invoice mode	? Yes
Maintain stock categories	? Yes	Record debit notes in invoice mode	? Yes
Maintain batch-wise details	? No	Use separate discount column in invoices	? No
Set expiry dates for batches	? No	**Purchase Management**	
Use separate actual and billed quantity columns	? No	Track additional costs of purchases	? No
Order Processing		**Sales Management**	
Enable purchase order processing	? Yes	Use multiple price levels	? No
Enable sales order processing	? Yes	**Other Features**	
Enable job order processing (*Enables the options 'Maintain multiple godowns' and 'Use material in and out vouchers'*)	? No	Use tracking numbers (enables delivery and receipt notes)	? No
		Use rejection inward and outward notes	? No
		Use material in and out vouchers	? No
		Use cost tracking for stock item	? No

F-1B: Inventory Fetaures set up

02 Inventory Masters

To maintain Inventory System, first, you need to create Masters in respect of Unit of Measure (UoM), Stock Item. You may optionally also create Stock Group, Stock Category, Godowns, where needed.

Select *GoT>Inventory Info* to get Inventory Info Menu (F-2A), containing the options to create Inventory Masters.

F- 2A : Inventory Info Menu

03 Unit of Measure (UoM)

At Inventory Info Menu (F-2A), select *Unit of Measure > Create* to get Unit (UoM) Creation Screen (F-3A). Now enter the following Particulars.

- **Type**: Cursor normally skips showing at *Type* field, with *Simple* as selected, to create a Simple Unit. Otherwise press <shift+Tab> or <backspace> to get the cursor at Type field and select *Simple*.
- **Symbol**: At *Symbol* field, enter the Short Name of the Unit (e.g., Kg. Ltr.). In all reports, the Unit Symbol appears alongwith Quantity, to indicate the UoM of the Quantity.
- **Formal Name**: Enter full Name of the Unit (e.g., Kilogram, Litre etc) different from UoM Symbol, for internal Info about the UoM. The Formal name is displayed in UoM selection list (in parenthesis), beside the UoM symbol, to identify the correct Unit record.
- **Number of Decimal Places** : If the quantity is to be expressed in fractional values, enter the number of decimal places, to allow sufficient precision to avoid truncation of value.

Compound Unit of Measure : Compound Unit of Measure is combination of 2 unit of Measure (like Roll of 25 Mtrs).

To create Compound Unit of Measure, at Type field of Unit Master Creation, select Compound (press Shift+Tab to go up to Type field), to get Compound UoM creation screen (F-3B)

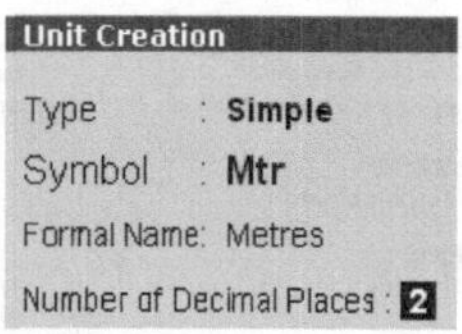

F-3A : UoM Creation

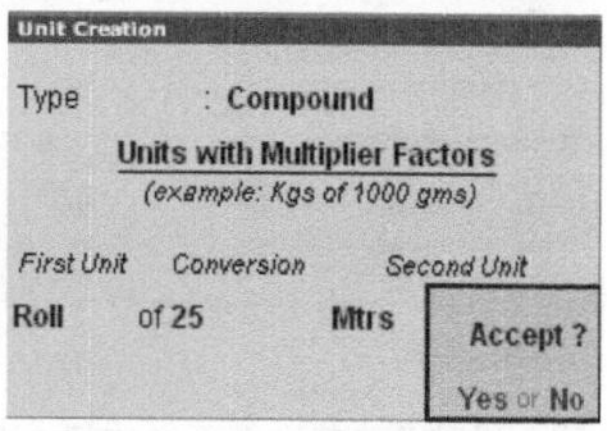

F-3B: Compound UoM creation

At Compound Unit creation screen (F-3B), at Main unit from the list of Units and enter the conversion factor (relationship) between Main & Tail unit. Next, select the Tail Unit. Now the Compound Unit (which is another Unit distinct from the 2 constituent Simple Units) is created.

04 Stock Group

Creation of *Stock Group* is optional. If you maintain a few Stock Items only (e.g Sugar), you may place the Stock Items under a Tally created Stock Group called *Primary* without any need to create new Stock Groups (*Primary* Stock Group is created by Tally when you create a Company). However, on most cases, creation of Stock Group is necessary to get organized reports with figures for each Stock Group

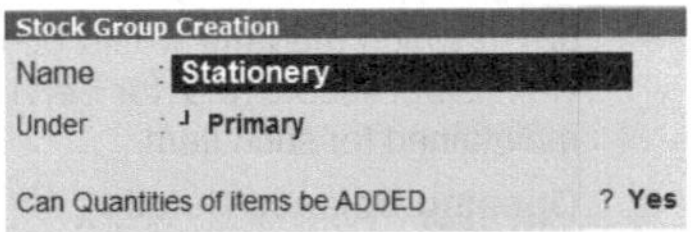

F-4A: Stock Group Entry

Select *Inventory Info > Stock Group > Create* under Single Stock Group to get Stock Group Creation screen (F-4A). Enter the following Particulars:

- **Stock Group Name**: Enter Name of Stock Group
- **Parent Stock Group**: At *Under* field, select the parent Stock Group for the Stock Group being created (select *Primary* to create top level Group). The first Group created must be placed under Primary.
- **Stock Group Quantity**: At the *Can Quantities of Items be Added*, set *Yes* to get Total Stock Quantity of the child Stock Items under the Stock Group (if all child Stock Items are measured in same UoM), else set *No* (Stock Group Quantity is not computed).

Multiple Stock Group creation : To quickly create multiple Stock Groups in a single screen, in tabular format, select *GoT> Stock Groups >Inventory Info > Create* at Multiple Stock Groups to get Multiple Stock Groups creation screen. Now enter data in same manner

05 Stock Item

Stock Item is the primary inventory entity and is the lowest level of information in Inventory system. Create a Stock Item for each Inventory Item that you want to keep separate transaction & stock account.

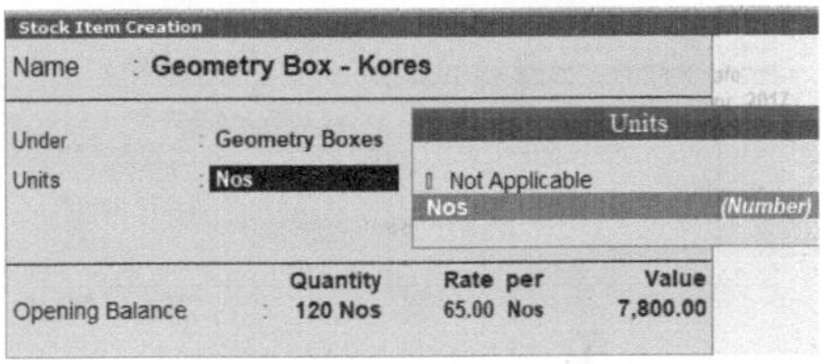

F-5A: Stock Item Entry

At *Inventory Info* Menu (F-2A), select *Stock Item > Create* under Single Stock Item to get Stock Item Creation screen (F-5A). Now enter the following particulars.

- **Stock Item Name**: At *Name*, enter a unique Name of the Stock Item.
- **Parent Stock Group**: At *Under*, select the Parent Stock Group. If the stock group is not existing. you may Create the Parent Stock Group instantly from Current Stock Item Creation screen itself. Press Ctrl + C to get Stock Group Creation screen. Enter the Stock Group date as explained and select the new Stock Group at under field of the Current Stock Item Master Creation screen.

- **Stock Item UoM**: At *Units*, select the Unit of Measurement (from pop-up) in which the Item would be measured. Select *Not Applicable* if no UoM is applicable (e.g, for Service Item) and quantity details will not be maintained for such Item.
- **Opening Balance Details** :
    - o **Opening Stock Quantity**: At *Quantity*, enter the Opening Stock Quantity as on *Books beginning from date.*
    - o **Opening Stock Rate**: At *Rate*, enter the Opening Stock Rate (if you do not know the Rate, leave it blank, enter the Opening Stock value, Tally will compute & fill up the Rate).
    - o **Opening Stock Value**: The Opening Stock value is computed from the Opening Stock Quantity & Opening Stock Rate as entered and displayed at Value field. However, you may change the Amount. The Rate will get changed accordingly.

Multiple Stock Item creation : To quickly create multiple Stock Items in a single screen, in tabular format, select *GoT> Stock* Items *>Inventory Info > Create* at Multiple Stock Items to get Multiple Stock Items creation screen. Now enter data in same manner

Stock Item creation with Advanced Options : At Stock Item creation / alteration screen, click *F12:Configure* and then set *Yes* at *Allow Advanced Entries in Masters* to get Advanced Stock Item entry screen (F-5B)

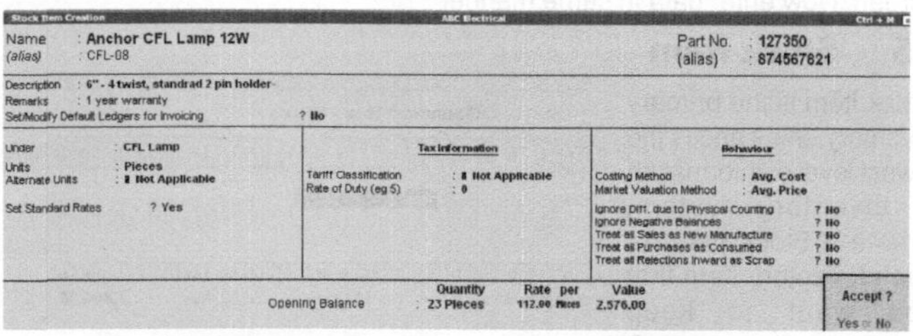

F-5B: Advance entry in Stock Item Master

06 Stock Category

Stock Categories are parallel classification to Stock Group for categorising Stock Items. For example, a book publisher may create Stock Group as per Subject and Stock Category as per Publisher, Author etc. So, he can find all the books of a specified topic, language, author or publisher. This way, stock categories can be created for manufacturer, model, brand etc to offer alternate Items and more choice to customers. So, if one book of a specific author is not available, he may find all other books on similar subject.

Stock Category Activation : Maintenance of Stock Category is optional. To maintain Stock Category, click *F11: Features > Inventory Features* and set *Yes at Maintain Stock Categories.*

Stock Category Creation : Select *GoT>Inventory Info > Stock* Category > *Create* at Single Stock Category to get Stock category creation screen (F-6A)

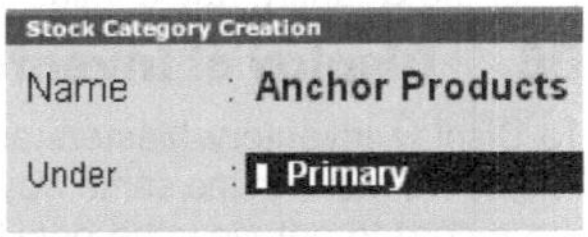

F-6A:Stock Category creation

- **Stock Category Name**: At *Name* field, enter Name of Stock Category
- **Parent Stock Category**: At *Under* field, select the Parent Stock Category from List of Categories (or select *Primary* to create top level Stock Category). The first Stock Category created must be Primary (F-6A)

Multiple Stock Category creation : To quickly create multiple Stock categories in a single screen, in tabular format, select *GoT>Inventory Info > Stock* Category > *Create* at Multiple Stock Category to get Multiple Stock category creation screen. Now enter data in same manner

07 Multiple Godowns

Godowns are location of materials storage. When Stock Items are stored in different locations (you do not need to create Godown, if all Stocks are maintained in one place, called *Main Location* which is internally created by Tally), you may maintain the transactions and stock of Items with location (Godownwise) details.

Activation of Multiple Godown : To activate Multiple Godowns, click *F11:Fetaures>Inventory Features*, set *Yes* at *Maintain Multiple Godowns.*

Creation of Godown Master : Select *Inventory Info > Godowns* to get Godown Master Menu. Select *Create at Single Godown* to get Godown Entry screen (F-7A). Enter the following particulars.

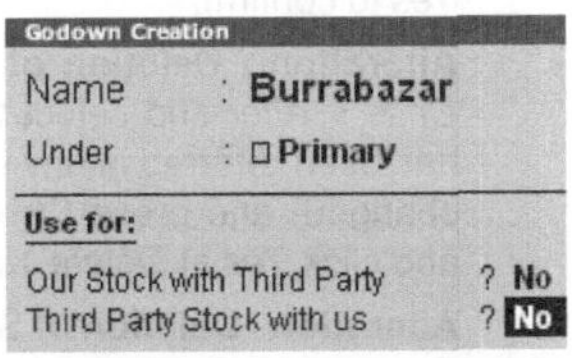

F-7A: Godown creation

- **Godown Name:** At *Name*, enter Name of the Godown.
- **Parent Godown:** At *Under*, select the Parent Godown (select *Primary* to create a top level Godown and the first Godown). Like Stock Groups, Godowns may be organized into various levels.

Multiple Godowns creation : To quickly create multiple Godowns in a single screen, in tabular format, select *GoT>Inventory Info >Godowns > Create* at Multiple Godowns to get Multiple Godowns creation screen. Now enter data in same manner.

Godown Details entry of Opening Stock : If you have created multiple Godowns, during creation / alteration of Stock item master, at entry of Opening Stock details, you get a screen to enter Godwnwise break up of Opening Stock. Enter the Quantity, rate & value of Opening Stock lying in each Godown.

08 Display of Inventory Masters

To Display Inventory Masters as discussed above, select Display from the respective Menu in the same way. All the records will be displayed. Now select the record to get view the details of selected record. In Display mode, you cannot modify the record.

- **Display of Stock Group**: Select *Inventory Info > Stock Group > Display* to view a Stock Group, choose the Group you wish to view from *List of Stock Group.*
- **Display of Stock Item**: Select *Inventory Info > Stock Item > Display* and select the Stock Item to Display.
- **Display of Stock Category**: Select *Inventory Info > Stock Category > Display* and select the Stock Category to Display.
- **Display of Stock Godown**: Select *Inventory Info > Stock Godown> Display* and select the Godown to Display.
- **Display of Unit of Measure**: Select *Inventory Info > Units > Display* and select the Unit to Display.

09 Alteration / Deletion of Inventory Masters

To Alter / Delete Inventory Masters as discussed above, select *Alter* from the respective Menu in the same way. All the records will be displayed. Now select the record to *Alter* or *Delete.* We now explain the Alteration / Deletion of each Inventory Master record discussed above.

- **Alteration / Deletion of Stock Group**: Select *Inventory Info > Stock Group > Alter. Select the* Stock Group. Make necessary modification and press Ctrl+A to save. To Delete the Group, press Alt+D and click *Yes* to confirm.
- **Alteration / Deletion of Units of Measure**: Select *Inventory Info > Units > Alter* and select the Unit. Carry out the Alteration (if the unit has been referred in any voucher, number of decimal places cannot be changed) and press Ctrl+A to save. To Delete any Unit, press Alt+D and click *Yes* at *Delete Yes or No?* to confirm Deletion.
- **Alteration / Deletion of Stock Category**: Select *Inventory Info > Stock Category > Alter* and select the *Stock Category.* Carry out the Alteration and press Ctrl+A to save. To Delete any Stock Category, press Alt+D and click *Yes* at *Delete Yes or No?* to confirm Deletion.
- **Alteration / Deletion of Godown**: Select *Inventory Info > Godwon > Alter* and select the *Godown.* Carry out the Alteration and press Ctrl+A

to save. To Delete any Godown, press Alt+D and click *Yes* at *Delete Yes or No?* to confirm Deletion.

- **Alteration / Deletion of Stock Item**: Select *Inventory Info > Stock Items > Alter* and select the Stock Item:
  - o **Alteration** : Carry out the Alteration (if the unit has been referred in any voucher, UoM cannot be changed). Alteration is also used to fill up the fields left blank at the time of Master Creation (like Opening Stock details). Press Ctrl+A to save.
  - o **Deletion** : To Delete any Stock Item, press *Alt+D* and click *Yes* at *Delete Yes or No?* to confirm Deletion.

Restriction in Deletion of Inventory Masters

In following cases, the Inventory Master Record cannot be Deleted.

- **Stock Group**: The *Stock Group* would not be deleted if it is parent of any Stock Group or Stock Item.
- **Stock Category**: The *Stock Category* would not be deleted if it is parent of any Stock Item.
- **Godown**: The *Godown* cannot be deleted if it has been referred in any Voucher
- **UoM**: The *UoM* cannot be deleted if it has been referred in any Stock Item.
- **Stock Item**: The *Stock Item* cannot be deleted if it has been referred in any Voucher.

10 Inventory Masters Lists

Master lists shows the list of respective Master records entered. It is useful to verify the correctness of Masters record entry (checklist) and also serves as a handy reference of structured lists of all Master records.

At GoT, select *Display > List of Accounts* to get Masters Lists display screen. Now select the respective button from the right side button bar to display / print the Master List

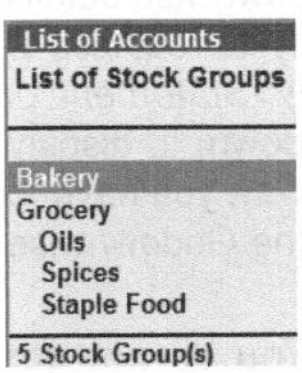

F-8A: Stock Groups

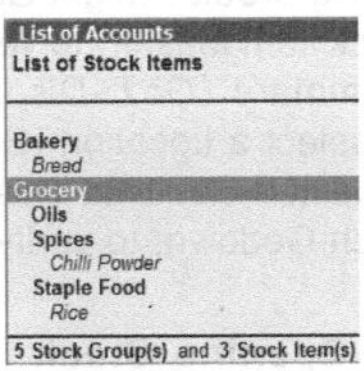

F-8B : List of Stock Items

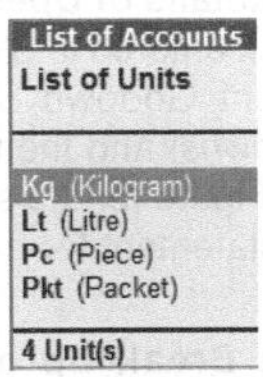

F-8C : List of UoMs

F-8D : List of Godowns (Locations)

- **Stock Groups List :** Click the button *T:Stock Groups* to get the List of Stock Groups in hierarchical order (F-8A). The list appears in alphabetical order of Primary Stock Groups, showing the total number of Stock Groups at report end.
- **Stock Items List :** Click the button *I: Stock Items* to get the List of Stock Groups & Stock Items (F-8B), in alphabetical order of Primary Stock Groups with sub groups and stock items in hierarchical order, showing the total number of Stock Groups and Stock Items at report end.
- **Units of Measure (UoM) List** : Click the button *N:Units* to get the List of UoM (F-8C) in alphabetical order of Unit Symbol (with Unit Name in parenthesis), showing the total number of UoMs at report end.
- **Godown (Locations) List** : Click the button *O:* Godowns to get the List of Godowns (F-8D) in hierarchical structure.

Summary

- **Activation of Inventory System**: At Company creation, select Accounts with Inventory at Maintain field
- **Creation of Inventory Masters**: Create UoM Master (Simple & Compound), Stock Group, Stock Item, Stock Category & Godown Masters in Single & Multiple Modes. Display & Deletion of Inventory masters. Print the lists of Inventory masters to check the records entered.
- **Godown wise details of Opening Stock** : At the time of Stock Item Master creation, you have to enter Opening Stock Details (Quantity, Rate, Value). If you have created Multiple Godowns also, then you have to enter Goownwise details of Opening Stock in Stock Item Master entry.
- **Stock item List with opening Stock figures** : To get the list of Stock Item with Opening Balance details (to verify the correctness of Stock Item Master entry details), you may Display / Print Sock Summary (*GoT>Stock Summary*) with Opening Balance only, setting the respective options at Stock Summary Configuration.
- **Godown wise details of Opening Stock** : To get Godownwise details of Opening Stock entered in Stock item Master (to verify correctness of data entry), print Godown Summary (*GoT>Display>Statement of Inventory>Godowns*) and then select a Location (Godown) to display Opening Stock Figure for the selected Godown. This way, you have to print separate statement for each Godown, to verify the Godownwise Opening Stock
- **Godown wise Break Up of Opening Stock** : You do not get Godownwise break up of a Stock Item (to check the Godownwise break up of Opening Stock) through Display option of Stock Item as in Display, as you cannot view the subordinate screen of Godownwise display (you may do it in Stock Item Alteration, check Godownwise Opening Stock on screen only, and make correction of mistakes detected).

Inventory Voucher 02-02

01 Accounts Voucher with Inventory Transactions

Having created Inventory Masters, you may start Inventory transaction (Vouchers) entry. Since, the trading transactions involving Inventory (like Sales, Purchase) affect Inventory & Financial Accounts, Inventory details are also entered in corresponding Accounts Voucher.

Now we discuss about Accounting Vouchers like Sales, Purchase, Debit Note, Credit Note with inventory details. Such transactions may be entered in Voucher Mode (as explained in this chapter) or invoice Mode (as explained in next chapter).

02 Invoice & Voucher Entry Mode

Inventory Transactions may be entered in Voucher mode and in Invoice Mode. In Voucher mode, the Ledger Amount is entered first and then the corresponding Item wise details are entered. In Invoice mode, the Item details are entered first, the computed Item value is posted into Ledger amount.

In Voucher Mode, you must have all the Amounts computed first. So, Voucher Mode is suitable when you have got all the amounts already computed (e.g you enter sales voucher from manual sales bills). Tally will not compute anything.

In Invoice mode entry, you enter the Stock Item Data first (Rate, Quantity etc). Tally computes the Item Value etc and other amounts (like Tax ec). Finally, Tally computes the Net Bill Amount and posts to the Party Ledger Account. So, Invoice mode is suitable for on-line billing (i.e you prepare the invoices from Tally only).

03 Inventory linked Accounts Ledger

When Inventory is activated for the Company, at Ledger creation screen, you get an option *Inventory Values are affected* to link certain Ledger Accounts with Inventory (like Sales, Purchase, Sales Return & Purchase Return etc.)

At Account Ledger entry /alteration of such Inventory related accounts (like Sales, Purchase, Sales Return & Purchase Return), set *Yes* at *Inventory Values are affected* at the respective ledger account (F-1A), to enter Inventory details for such ledger accounts in the Voucher.

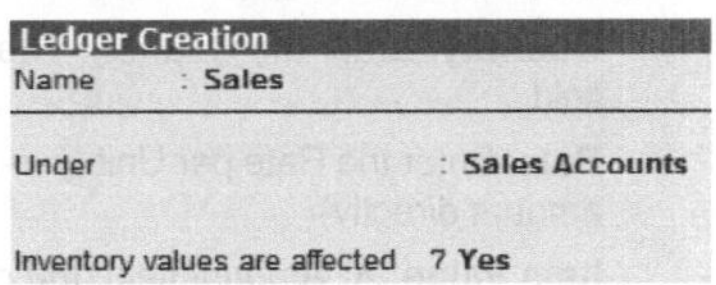

F-1A : Inventory Linked Ledger Account creation

Whenever you enter a voucher involving transaction with such ledger accounts, you will be prompted to enter the inventory allocations also (like Item Name, Quantity, Amount etc. : F-3A to F-3D) for the respective Ledger Account.

04 Party Ledger Accounts

You have to create Party Ledger Accounts (Customer / Supplier) to be entered in Sales / Purchase Voucher. At Party Account Ledger Entry / Alteration (like Buyer, Seller), set *No* at *Inventory Values are affected* at the respective Ledger Account (F-2A).

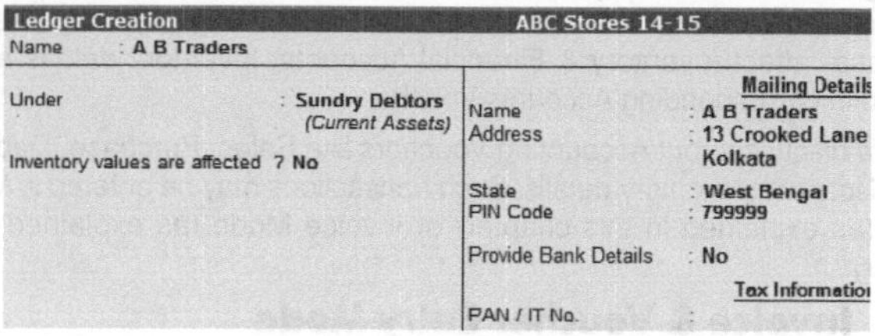

Ledger Creation ABC Stores 14-15
Name : A B Traders
Under : Sundry Debtors (Current Assets)
Inventory values are affected ? No
Mailing Details
Name : A B Traders
Address : 13 Crooked Lane Kolkata
State : West Bengal
PIN Code : 799999
Provide Bank Details : No
Tax Information
PAN / IT No.

F-2A: Party Ledger Account

05 Inventory Details Entry in Accounts Voucher

Entry of Accounts Voucher like Sales, Purchase, Debit Note, Credit Note has been explained earlier. At such voucher entry screen (F-3A), on entry of Inventory Linked Ledger Account (like Purchase, Sale Ledger Account etc), and amount in Voucher entry, you get the *Item Allocation* screen (F-3B) to enter the Item Details of the selected Ledger account, as follows:

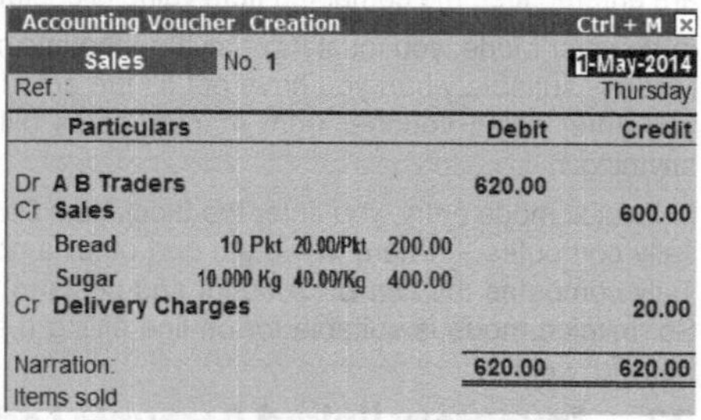

Accounting Voucher Creation Ctrl + M

Sales No. 1 1-May-2014 Thursday

Ref. :

Particulars				Debit	Credit
Dr A B Traders				620.00	
Cr Sales					600.00
Bread	10 Pkt	20.00/Pkt	200.00		
Sugar	10.000 Kg	40.00/Kg	400.00		
Cr Delivery Charges					20.00
Narration: Items sold				620.00	620.00

F- 3A: Sales Voucher entry

- **Item Name**: At *Name of Item* field, select the Stock Item
- **Quantity**: Enter the Quantity. The UoM of the Item is displayed at *Per* field
- **Rate**: Enter the Rate per Unit (you may leave the Rate column and enter amount directly)
- **Item Value**: At *Amount* field, the computed Amount (as per Quantity & Rate) is displayed, which you may change.

This way, enter the Items to complete the Ledger allocation. The total Item Value must match the entered Ledger Amount.

This way you may enter multiple ledger accounts and the Item allocations for each Inventory linked Ledger Accounts.

The ledger entries are terminated, when the total of Debits equals to total of Credits and the Item details are shown in the main voucher screen (F-3A).

Inventory Allocations for : **Sales**

Name of Item	Quantity	Rate	per	Amount
Bread	**10 Pkt**	**20.00**	**Pkt**	**200.00**
Sugar	**10.000 Kg**	**40.00**	**Kg**	**400.00**
				600.00

F-3B Item Allocation

06 Inventory Voucher Entry

Inventory Voucher affect only Inventory (Sock Item related details), but does not affect Accounts Reports.

Stock Journal Voucher

Stock Journal Voucher is used to make internal stock adjustments Stock Adjustment, e.g., due to shortage, wastage, excess or any other increase or decrease in stock,

Select *GoT> Inventory Voucher* and Click *F7:Stk Jrnl* (Alt+F7) to get Stock Journal Voucher entry screen (F-4A). Enter the Voucher Date.

Item Details in Stock Journal Voucher : At the left part, enter the Source (Consumption) Item details (i.e Items OUT, e.g for Shortages found, Transfer Out, etc), while at the right part, you enter the Destination (Production) Item details (Item name, Quantity, Rate & Amount), in the same way as explained above.

You may enter the Item details in both Source & Destination, or in any (or both) column. The quantity as entered for the Item in Source column is reduced from Stock and the quantity as entered for the Item in Destination column is increased. The Item, Quantity & Value may differ between Source (Consumption) & Destination (Production)

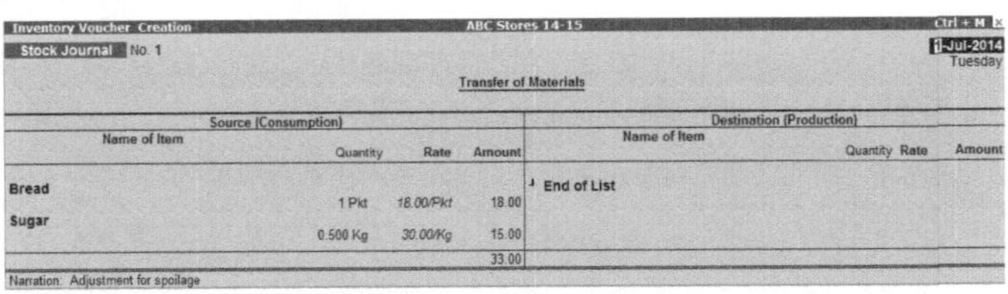

F- 4A: Stock Journal Voucher (for adjustment of Stock)

Other Inventory Vouchers

Apart from Stock Journal Voucher, you may also enter following Inventory Vouchers. At Inventory Voucher entry screen, click :

- **Rejection Vouchers** : *F6:Rejection In* (to enter Rejection In Voucher) & *F6:Rejection Out* (to enter Rejection Out Voucher). You must have set Yes at *Rejection Inward / Outward Voucher* at *F11:Features>Inventory Features*, to activate Rejection Vouchers.
- **Delivery Notes** : F8:Dely Note (to enter Delivery Note) & F9:Rcpt Note (to enter Receipt Note). You must have set *Yes* at *Use Tracking Number (Delivery / Receipt Notes)* at *F11:Features>Inventory Features*, to activate Delivery / Receipt Notes.
- **Physical Stock Voucher** : *F10:Phys Stk* to enter Physical Stock for any Item for any Date, as found on physical verification, to adjust the difference between Book Stock & Physical Stock. However, is is better to adjust Shortage / Excess on Physical Stock Verification, through *Stock Journal*.

Summary

- **Inventory Linked Ledger Accounts** : In Ledger Accounts creation / alteration of Sales, Purchase, set the Inventory Allocation option to allow Inventory allocation of the Ledger Accounts in Voucher.
- **Party Ledger** : In Party Ledger, enter the Party Details (Address etc),to be printed in Invoices
- **Accounts Voucher** : In Accounts Voucher of Sales, Purchase, Debit / Credit Note, enter the Inventory Allocation (Details of Stock Item, Quantity, rat, Value) of the Ledger, and other ledger accounts
- **Inventory Voucher** : Enter Inventory Vouchers , like Stock Journal, Rejection In & Rejection Out, Delivery Note & Receipt Note, Physical Stock Voucher etc

Invoicing 02-03

01 Invoicing

We have explained Inventory Voucher Entry in Voucher form, in which accounting details are entered first, and the Inventory allocation of the ledger account is entered. Now, we discuss Invoice Entry (Inventory Voucher in Invoice Mode), where, the basic data of computation (Item, Rate, Quantity etc) is entered. The computation of Invoice automatically gets done during entry (manual computation not needed).

Invoicing Mode Set Up

At *Inventory Features* screen (*F11:Features>Inventory Features*), set as follows (F-1A):

- **Sales & Purchase**: To set up Inventory details modes in Sales / Purchase transactions, under the section *Invoicing*, set as follows :
  - **Sales Invoice** : At *Allow Invoicing*, set Yes to enter in Invoice Mode also.

    Consequently, at Sales, Purchase, Debit Note & Credit Note Voucher entry screen, the following toggle buttons appear to set the entry modes:
    - *V:As Voucher / As Invoice* (Ctrl+V): To set the entry in Voucher Mode / Invoice
    - *I:Acounting Invoice / Item Invoice* (Alt+I): To set entry of Inventory Details
  - **Purchase Transactions** : Having set *Yes* at *Allow Invoicing* (activating Sales Invoice, as explained above), at *Enter Purchases in Invoice Format*, set *Yes* to enter Purchase Transactions in Invoice Mode also
- **Debit & Credit Notes**: Having activated Debit / Credit Note at *Inventory Features* screen, you may further set as follows:
  - **Credit Note** : At *Use Invoice Mode for Credit Notes*, set *Yes* to enter Credit Note in Invoice Mode also.
  - **Debit Note** : At *Use Invoice Mode for Debit Notes*, set *Yes* to enter Debit Note in Invoice Mode also

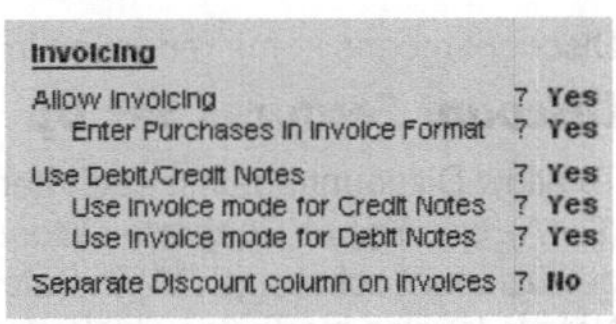

F-1A: Invoicing Features Set Up

02 Invoice Entry

At Gateway, select *Accounts Voucher* and click the respective Voucher Type button from the button bar, to get the Voucher entry screen. Click *V:As Invoice* & *I:Item Invoice* buttons (if you are in Voucher mode) to get Invoice Entry screen (F-2A, F-2B) in Item Invoice mode.

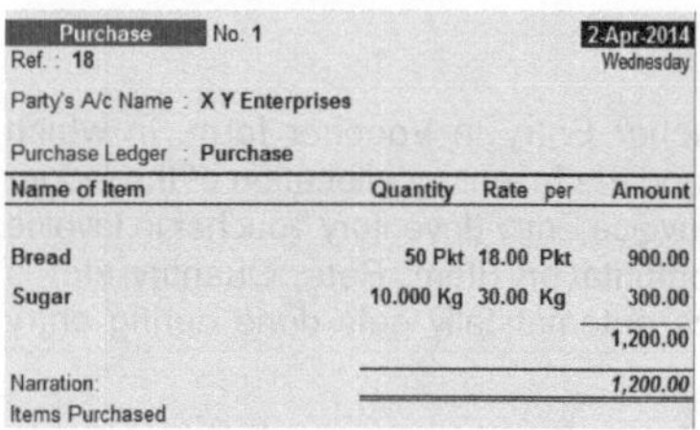

F-2A:Purchase Invoice

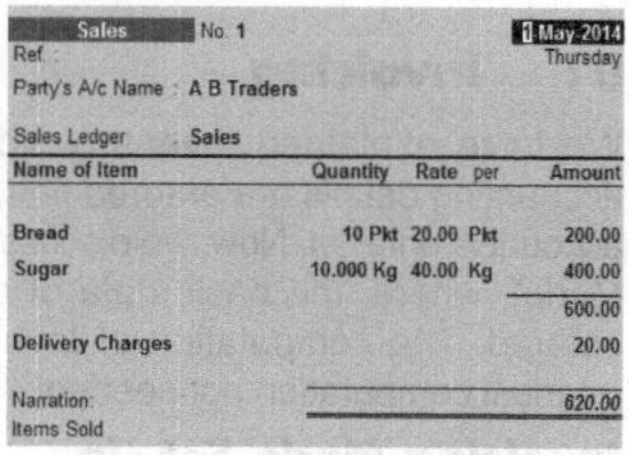

F-2B:Sales Invoice

Item Details Entry : Enter the Item details as explained in Voucher entry with Inventory details

- **Item Name**: At *Name of Item* column, select the Item Name
- **Item Quantity**: At *Quantity* column, enter the Item Quantity. The Item UoM is displayed along side.
- **Item Rate**: At *Rate* column, enter Item Rate
- **Item value**: The computed Item value is displayed, which you may change.

This way, enter Item details for all the Items. To terminate Items entry, press <enter> at *Name of Item* to enter Accounting Allocations (Ledger Account details), as explained below:

Ledger Account details :Now you may enter details of other ledger accounts (like Discount, Freight etc):

- **Ledger Account**: Select the Ledger Account from the list.
- **Ledger Amount**: Enter the Amount (to reduce the amount, e.g Discount, enter in negative figure).

03 Discount

Discount means some reduction in price offered by seller to customer.

Discount Features Set Up

To allow Discount against each Item in Invoice, at *Inventory Features screen* (F-1A), set *Yes* at *Separate Discount Column in Invoice*. Consequently, you get Discount column (F-3A) in Sales / Purchase Invoice entry & Debit / Credit Note in Invoice mode (for which you have set up Invoice Mode entry).

Discount Entry in Invoice

During Invoice entry, enter Discount Rate (in %) at *Discount* column against the respective Item, in Sales, Debit & Credit Note entry in Invoice entry. The Net Amount (Product value less Discount) would be posted in the respective Ledger Account (Sales, Purchase).

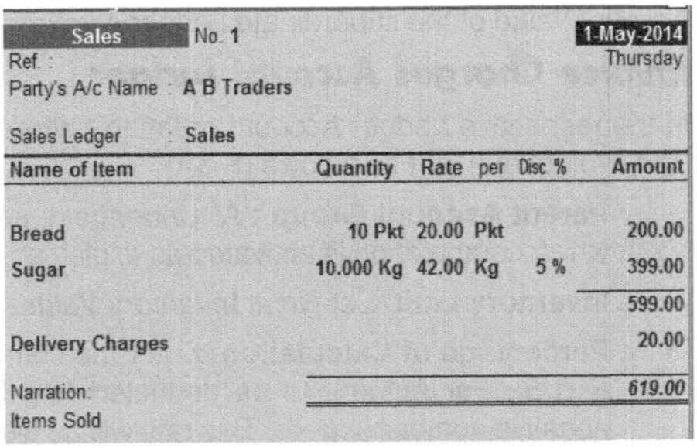

F-3A: Sales Invoice (with discount)

04 Invoice Additional Charges

We have shown above how to enter fixed value of any Additional Charges in Invoice. Here we shows how to compute other charges also (like Item Value), on the basis of Item Value. Additional Charges for Tax on Goods (like GST, TCS etc) have been explained in respective chapter. Here we discuss entry of about other Additional Charges like Freight etc.

Invoice Charges Account Group

To allow Computation of Invoice Charges on the basis of Item Value, you have to set the parameters and specify the rules of Computation at the parent Account Group of the respective additional charges Ledger Account.

So, you have to create a separate Account to place the computable Ledger Accounts under the Group.

Account Group Configuration Set Up : To allow advanced options of Account Group, at Account Group Creation / Alteration screen (F-4A), click *F12:Configure* to get *Account Group Configuration* screen (F-4B). At *Account Group Configuration* screen (F-4B), set *Yes* at *Allow Advanced Group Configuration*

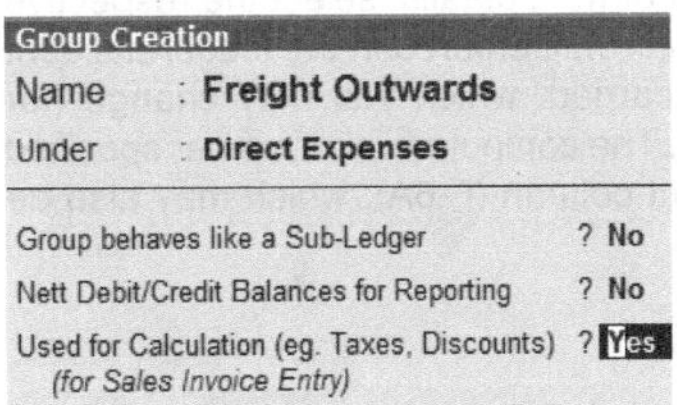

F-4A: Additional Charges Group creation (Advanced)

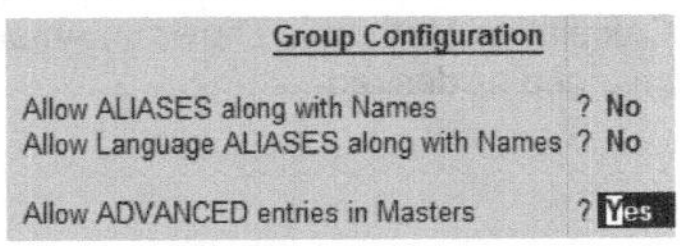

F-4B: Account Group Configuration

Account Group Creation : At *Account Group Creation / Alteration*(F-4A), set *Yes* at *Used for Calculation* (F-4A), to enable computation of value of the Ledger Account Value of the subordinate Ledger Accounts.

Invoice Charges Account Ledger

In the respective Ledger Account creation / alteration for additional charges (like Freight etc), set as follows (F-5A):

- **Parent Account Group** : At *Under* field, select the Parent Group (for which computation is activated as explained above).
- **Inventory Link**: Set *No* at *Inventory Values are affected*.
- **Percentage of Calculation**: Enter the standard Rate of Charges in % (e.g 5). For Amount to be deducted (e.g Discount), enter the % as negative number (e.g -5). This rate will be displayed as default in Invoice entry, which you may change in the Invoice
- **Method of Calculation**: After entering the *Percentage of Calculation*, select the method (e.g *On Total Sales* to compute Amount) at *Method of Calculation* from the list of Type of Duty (F-5B).

Ledger Creation

Name : **Freight**

Under	: **Freight Outwards** *(Direct Expenses)*
Inventory values are affected	? **No**
Percentage of Calculation (eg 5)	? **5 %**
Method of Calculation	: **On Total Sales**
Rounding Method	: ┘ **Not Applicable**

F-5A: Additional Charges Ledger creation

Type of Duty

- Additional Duty
- **On Total Sales**
- Surcharge on Tax
- Tax based on Item Rate

F-5B: Calculation Method List

Additional Charges Entry

Having created the Computable Charges Ledger Account, you may include such Ledger Account in Invoice entry, to get the amount computed .

During Invoice entry (F-6A), after entry of Item details, select the respective Additional Charges Ledger. The *Rate* (in %), if entered in the ledger account at *Percentage of Calculation* field is carried, which you may change (for Deduction, the Rate would be negative). The computed value, as per specified Calculation Method is shown in Amount column (F-6A), which may also be changed as desired.

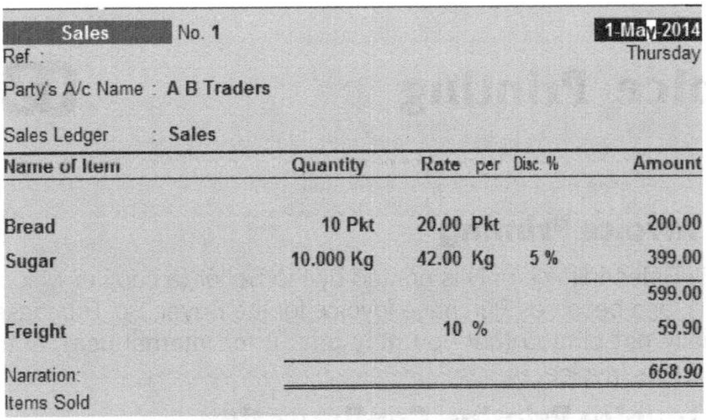

Sales No. 1 1-May-2014

Ref. : Thursday

Party's A/c Name : A B Traders

Sales Ledger : Sales

Name of Item	Quantity	Rate	per	Disc. %	Amount
Bread	10 Pkt	20.00	Pkt		200.00
Sugar	10.000 Kg	42.00	Kg	5 %	399.00
					599.00
Freight		10	%		59.90
					658.90

Narration:
Items Sold

F-6A: Additional Charges in Invoice

Summary

- **Invoice Mode Set Up** : At *Accounting Features* or *Inventory Features* screen (*F11:Features>Inventory Features*), set the Invoicing option for Sales, Purchase, Debit & Credit Note voucher, as required, to enter in Invoice Mode
- **Discount Column in Invoice** : Having set the Invoicing option, you may further set up Discount column to enter Discount % for each Item in the Invoice
- **Account Group creation for Invoicing** : To compute the amount for Ledger Accounts from the Item Vales, set up the options in respective parent Account Groups of the Invoice related Ledger Accounts.
- **Account Ledger creation for Invoicing** : To compute the amount for Ledger Accounts from the Item Vales, set up the computation methods and rates in respective Invoice related Ledger Accounts.
- **Item Details entry in Invoice** : Enter the Item details (Item, Quantity, Rate, Value)
- **Other Ledger Accounts** : Enter the details of additional ledger accounts (like Freight, Insurance, Bank Charges, Delivery Charges, Carriage, Handling, Entry Tax etc).

Invoice Printing

02-04

01 Invoice Printing

Normally Sales Invoice only is printed by the Seller (a copy of which is given to Buyer), and becomes Purchase Invoice for the Buyer. So, Purchase Invoice is normally not printed (but you may print it for internal use), in the same way, as Sales Invoice.

02 Invoice Printing Configuration

At Invoice *Entry / Alteration* screen, click *P:Print* button to get Invoice Printing screen (F-1A).

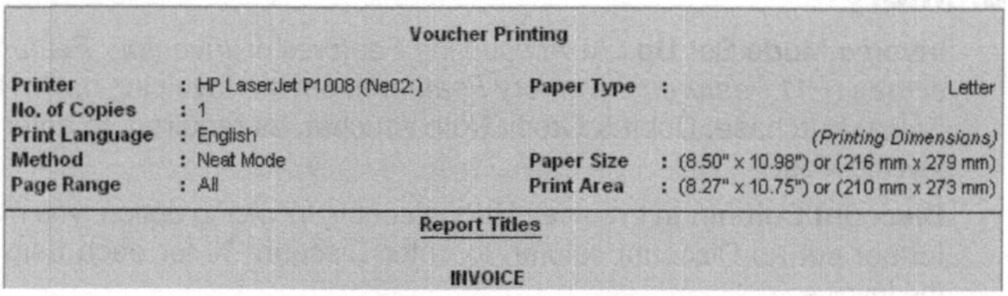

F-1A : Invoice Printing screen

Click *Yes* to print the current Invoice as per current Invoice Printing Configuration set.

Invoice Printing Configuration

At gateway, Click *F12:Configure*>Printing and then select the respective transaction printing option (like Sales Transaction, Purchase Transaction, Debit / Credit Notes etc) to get respective Invoice Configuration screen (F-2A). The option differ as per transaction selected (Sales, Purchase, Debit / Credit Note). Set the Invoice Printing options.

AT Invoice Configuration screen (F-2A), set *Yes* at Print in Simple Format to print in Simple Format (F-3A), set No, to print in Normal Format (F-3B).

Purchase Printing Configuration

Title of Document	: Purchase Voucher		
(for Optional Voucher)	: *INVOICE*		
Sub Title (if any)	:		
Height of Normal Invoice (inches)	: 10	Simple/Voucher :	10
Width of Normal Invoice (inches)	: 7.50	Simple/Voucher :	7.50
Space to leave on top (default 0.25)	: 0.25	Simple/Voucher :	0.25
Space to leave on left (default 0.5)	: 0.50	Simple/Voucher :	0.50

Print in Simple Format	? No	Print Serial No.	? No
Print in Voucher Format	? Yes	Print Part No.	? No
Print Cost Allocations in Voucher Format	? No	Print Quantity Column	? Yes
Print Voucher Reference	? Yes	Print Alternate Quantity	? No
Print Order Details	? No	Print as separate Column	? No
Print Company's PAN / Income Tax No.	? Yes	Print Actual Quantity Column	? No
Print Company's Tax Regn. Numbers	? Yes	Print Rate Column	? Yes
Print Supplier's Tax Regn. Numbers	? Yes	Print Batch Details	? No
Print Supplier's CST Regn. Numbers	? Yes	Print Godown Name	? No
		Print Godown Address	? No
		Print Rate of Duty with Items	? No
		Print Sub-Totals after each line	? No
		Print Narration	? No
		Print Narration for each entry	? No
		Print Base Currency Symbol for Total	? Yes

Method to use for Ledger Name : Name Only
Method to use for Stock Item Name : Name Only
Jurisdiction

F-2A: Invoice Printing Configuration

03 Sales Invoice Printing

At *Sales Invoice Printing* screen (like F-2A), type *Y* to print the Invoice (F-3A)

SUBJECT TO KOLKATA JURISDICTION

Invoice No. **1** Dated **1-May-2014**
Ref. No.

ABC Stores

INVOICE

Party : **A B Traders**

Description of Goods	Quantity	Rate	per	Disc. %	Amount
Bread	**10 Pkt**	20.00	Pkt		**200.00**
Sugar	**10.000 Kg**	42.00	Kg	5 %	**399.00**
					599.00
Delivery Charges					**20.00**
Total					**₹ 619.00**

Amount Chargeable (in words) *E & O.E*
INR Six Hundred Nineteen Only

for ABC Stores

F-3A: Sales Invoice in Print (in Simple Format)

INVOICE

ABC Company	Invoice No. **3**	Dated **2-Jul-2017**
	Delivery Note	Mode/Terms of Payment
	Supplier's Ref.	Other Reference(s)
Buyer **XYZ Traders**	Buyer's Order No.	Dated
	Despatch Document No.	Delivery Note Date
	Despatched through	Destination
	Terms of Delivery	

Sl No.	Description of Goods	Quantity	Rate	per	Disc. %	Amount
1	**Drawing Book -1**	**10 Nos**	72.00	Nos		**720.00**
2	**Gemetry Box -1**	**8 Nos**	48.00	Nos		**384.00**
	Total	**18 Nos**				**₹ 1,104.00**

Amount Chargeable (in words) E & O.E
INR One Thousand One Hundred Four Only

Declaration
We declare that this invoice shows the actual price of the goods described and that all particulars are true and correct.

for ABC Company

Authorised Signatory

This is a Computer Generated Invoice

F-3B: Sales Invoice in Print (in Normal Format)

In the same way, you may print Debit Note & Credit note (Purchase Invoice, if required) also.

Invoice Print Preview

At Invoice Printing screen button bar, you may use the toggle button 'With Preview / No Preview' to see the preview (exact copy of the Invoice on screen, with dimension scale at top & left side. The preview helps you to preview the Invoice (and each part, in case of multi part Invoice) on screen before printing. You may zoom, print and e-mail directly from Preview screen

04 Multiple Invoice Printing

We have described how you may print the current Invoice at the time of Entry. You may print multiple selected Invoices (which are already saved) in one shot, through *Multi-Account Printing.*

At Gateway, select *Multi Account printing > Multi Voucher printing* to get Multi Account Invoice printing screen (F-5A). Now select the period and Voucher Type to print the Invoices in one shot.

Report Titles

INVOICE

Name of Voucher Type	:	**Sales**
Select Vouchers to Print	:	**Regular**
From (blank for beginning)	:	**1-3-2010**
To (blank for end)	:	**1-3-2010**

F-5A: Multi Voucher Printing screen

Summary

- **Invoice Printing with current Printing Configuration**: On Invoice entry, click *P:Print* button to get Invoice Printing screen. Type Y to print the Invoice with current configuration
- **Invoice printing after Configuration setting** : On Invoice entry, click *P:Print* button to get Invoice Printing screen. Type N, set the Invoice Printing options and print the Invoice as per revised options set
- **Invoice printing Buttons** : Click the respective button to set print options like Number of Copies, Titling, etc.
- **Print Preview** : Preview the Invoice before printing. You may also print, e-mail the Invoice from Print Preview screen itself. Set the toggle button 'With Preview / No Preview'
- **Multi Account Printing** : Form Multi Account printing, may print all the Invoices of a specified Voucher Type, for a specified period.

Inventory Reports **02-05**

01 Accounts Reports with Inventory Details

Having entered the transaction vouchers (of Purchase & Sales) with Inventory Details, you may get various inventory reports instantly, like Registers, Day Books to Summary Statements. The reporting options are quite similar to Accounts Reports, discussed in previous section. These reports contain data of Vouchers of respective Voucher Type, with Inventory details.

Accounts Books with Inventory Details

Select *GoT>Display>Accounts Books* to get Accounts Books menu, as described earlier. At the respective report Display screen, click *F12:Configure* to set the following options (F-1A). Other configuration options may vary depending on the report.

- At *Show Inventory Details also*, set *Yes*, to get the report with Inventory.
- At *Format*, select *Detailed* (or Click *F1:Detailed* button) to get Accounts & Inventory details

By setting the above options at Configuration screen, you may get the respective Accounts Books with Inventory Details.

Configuration	
Format	: Detailed
Show narrations	? No
Show bill wise details	? No
Show Cost Centre Details also	? No
Show inventory details	? Yes
Show additional description of Stock Item	? No
Appearance of Stock Item Names	: Name Only
Appearance of Names	: Name Only
Sorting Method	: Default

F-1A: Inventory details set up in Reports

At Accounts Books menu

- **Sales Register :** Select *Sales Register* to get *Sales Register* showing Sales Vouchers with Inventory details (F-2A)
- **Purchase Register :** Purchase Register shows Purchase Vouchers with Inventory details, similar to Sales Register

Other Accounts Registers with Inventory Details : At *Accounts Books Menu*, select *Journal Register* to get Journal Register Menu (F-3A). At Journal Register Menu, select :

- **Journal Register** : To get *Journal Register*, showing Journal Vouchers with Inventory details
- **Debit Note Register** : To get *Debit Note Register*, showing Debit Note Vouchers with Inventory details

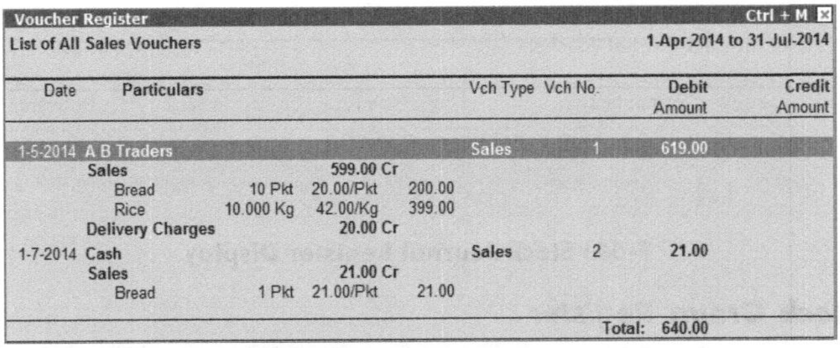
Voucher Register Ctrl + M
List of All Sales Vouchers 1-Apr-2014 to 31-Jul-2014

Date	Particulars					Vch Type	Vch No.	Debit Amount	Credit Amount
1-5-2014	A B Traders					Sales	1	619.00	
	Sales			599.00 Cr					
	Bread	10 Pkt	20.00/Pkt		200.00				
	Rice	10.000 Kg	42.00/Kg		399.00				
	Delivery Charges			20.00 Cr					
1-7-2014	Cash					Sales	2	21.00	
	Sales			21.00 Cr					
	Bread	1 Pkt	21.00/Pkt		21.00				
							Total:	640.00	

F-2A: Sales Register (with Inventory Details)

- **Credit Note Register** : To get *Credit Note Register*, showing Credit Note Vouchers with Inventory details

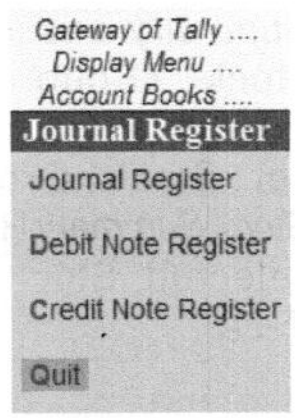

F-3A:Journal Register Menu

Other Accounting Reports

Tally has unique capability to include Inventory details also in Accounting Reports, as follows. For example, in Party Ledger, you can also get the details of Item details of Sales / Purchase, So, when talking with Parties regarding some disputes, you can immediately find out the complete details of the Items involved in the same statement. You do not have to look and flip through several reports together.

You may also print Inventory Details in following Accounting Reports also, by setting the respective configuration options, as explained.

- **Cash / Bank Book :** For Receipt (of Cash Sales) / Payment (of Cash Purchase) Voucher in Cash / Bank Book
- **Journal Book :** For Sales / Purchase Transactions recorded in Journal Voucher
- **Ledger Book :** For all Sales / Purchase transactions recorded

F-4A: Inventory Reports Menu

02 Inventory Books

The *Inventory Books* Menu provides reports of Item transactions and Stock. Select *Display>Inventory Books* to get *Inventory Books menu* (F-4A).

Stock Journal Register

At Inventory Reports menu (F-4A), select *Stock Transfers* to get monthly break up of number of *Stock Journal Register* Vouchers. Drill down through a Month and set the period (Click *F2:Period* and set the Dates) to get *Stock Journal Register* Display (F-5A).

Voucher Register						Ctrl + M
List of All Stock Journal Vouchers						1-Jul-2014 to 31-Jul-2014
Date	Particulars		Vch Type	Vch No.	Inwards Quantity	Outwards Quantity
1-7-2014	Bread		Stock Journal	1		1 Pkt
	Rice	(-)0.500 Kg				

F-5A: Stock Journal Register Display

Stock Group Register

At *Inventory Books* Menu (F-4A), select *Group Summary* and select a Stock Group (select *Primary* for all Groups) to get Stock Groupwise *Stock Summary* Report for selected Stock Group (F-6A).

Stock Summary			Ctrl + M
Particulars	ABC Stores 14-15 1-Apr-2014 to 31-Jul-2014		
	Closing Balance		
	Quantity	Rate	Value
Bakery	52 Pkt	18.44	958.75
Bread	*52 Pkt*	18.44	*958.75*
Grocery	37.500 Kg	33.47	1,255.10
Staple Food	37.500 Kg	33.47	1,255.10
Grand Total			2,213.85

F-6A: Stock Group Register

03 Movement Analysis

At *Inventory Books Menu* (F-4A), select *Movement Register* to get *Movement Analysis Menu* (F-7A). Movement Analysis shows the Stock Itemwise details of transaction for each Transaction Type with respective Parties.

Gateway of Tally ....
Display Menu ....
Inventory Books ....

Movement Analysis

- Stock Group Analysis
- Stock Item Analysis
- Group Analysis
- Ledger Analysis
- Transfer Analysis
- Quit

F-7A : Movement Analysis Menu

Stock Group Analysis : At *Movement Analysis Menu* (F-7A), select *Stock Group Analysis* and select a Stock Group from the list of Stock Groups (or select *Primary* for all Stock Groups) to get *Stock Group Analysis* Report (F-8A)

Movement Analysis						Ctrl + M
Particulars	ABC Stores 14-15 1-Apr-2014 to 2-Jul-2014					
	Inward			Outward		
	Quantity	Eff. Rate	Value	Quantity	Eff. Rate	Value
Bakery	50 Pkt	18.00	900.00	12 Pkt	20.08	241.00
Bread	*50 Pkt*	*18.00*	*900.00*	*12 Pkt*	*20.08*	*241.00*
Grocery	9.000 Kg	26.67	240.00	11.500 Kg	39.65	456.00
Staple Food	9.000 Kg	26.67	240.00	11.500 Kg	39.65	456.00
Rice	9.000 Kg	26.67	240.00	11.500 Kg	39.65	456.00
Grand Total			1,140.00			697.00

F-8A: Stock Group Analysis

Stock Item Analysis : At *Movement Analysis Menu* (F-7A), select *Stock Item Analysis* and select a *Stock Item* from the list of Stock Items to get *Stock Item Analysis* Report (F-9A).

Account Group Analysis : At *Movement Analysis Menu* (F-7A), select *Group Analysis* and select an *Account Group* from the list of Account Groups to get *Account Group Analysis* Report (F-10A).

Account Ledger Analysis : At *Movement Analysis Menu* (F-7A), select *Ledger Analysis* and select an *Account Ledger* from the list of Account Ledgers to get *Account Ledger Analysis* Report (F-11A).

Stock Journal Analysis : Stock Journal Analysis shows Item wise details of Stock Journal Vouchers, for the selected period. There is no concept of Parties in Stock Journal Analysis (Stock Journal is record of internal adjustment of Stock).

At *Movement Analysis Menu* (F-7A), select *Transfer Analysis* and select the *Stock Journal Voucher Type* from the list of *Stock Journal Voucher Types* to get *Stock Journal Analysis* (F-12A).

Item Movement Analysis Ctrl + M

Particulars	*Bread* ABC Stores 14-15 1-Apr-2014 to 2-Jul-2014 Movement Values			
	Quantity	*Basic Rate*	*Effective Rate*	Value
Movement Inward :				
Suppliers :				
X Y Enterprises	50 Pkt	*18.00*	*18.00*	900.00
	50 Pkt		**18.00**	900.00
Movement Outward :				
Buyers :				
A B Traders	8 Pkt		20.00	160.00
Cash	3 Pkt		21.00	63.00
	11 Pkt		**20.27**	223.00
Transfers Outward (Consumption) :				
Stock Journal	1 Pkt		18.00	18.00
	1 Pkt		**18.00**	18.00
	12 Pkt		**20.08**	241.00

F-9A: Stock Item Analysis Display

Group Analysis Ctrl + M

Particulars	*Sundry Creditors* ABC Stores 14-15 1-Apr-2014 to 31-Jul-2014					
	Purchases			Sales		
	Quantity	*Eff. Rate*	Value	Quantity	*Eff. Rate*	Value
Bread	50 Pkt	*18.00*	900.00			
Rice	9.000 Kg	*26.67*	240.00			
Grand Total			1,140.00			

F-10A: Account Group Analysis

Ledger Analysis Ctrl + M

Particulars	*X Y Enterprises* ABC Stores 14-15 1-Apr-2014 to 2-Jul-2014					
	Purchases			Sales		
	Quantity	*Eff. Rate*	Value	Quantity	*Eff. Rate*	Value
Bread	50 Pkt	*18.00*	900.00			
Rice	9.000 Kg	*26.67*	240.00			
Grand Total			1,140.00			

F-11A: Account Ledger Analysis

Transfer Analysis Ctrl + M

Particulars	*Stock Journal* ABC Stores 14-15 1-Apr-2014 to 2-Jul-2014					
	Goods In (Production)			Goods Out (Consumption)		
	Quantity	*Eff. Rate*	Value	Quantity	*Eff. Rate*	Value
Bread				1 Pkt	*18.00*	18.00
Rice				0.500 Kg	*30.00*	15.00
Grand Total						33.00

F-12A: Stock Journal Analysis

04 Stock Summary

At Gateway, select *Stock Summary* to get *Stock Summary* Report (F-13A)

Stock Summary			Ctrl + M
Particulars	ABC Stores 14-15 1-Apr-2014 to 31-May-2014		
	Closing Balance		
	Quantity	Rate	Value
Bakery	54 Pkt	18.44	995.63
Bread	*54 Pkt*	18.44	*995.63*
Grocery	**58.000 Kg**	*29.24*	**1,696.00**
Staple Food	40.000 Kg	33.40	1,336.00
Salt	*18.000 Kg*	20.00	*360.00*
Grand Total			**2,691.63**

F-13A: Stock Summary

Summary

- **Configuration Set Up** : In Report Configuration in various Accounts Reports, set Inventory details option to get Inventory details in the Report.
- **Stock Journal Register** : Print Stock Journal Register, showing list of Stock Journal Vouchers
- **Stock Group Register** : Print Stock Group Register, showing Stock Summary as per Stock Group, with subordinate Stock Item details
- **Stock Group Analysis** : Print Stock Group Analysis, showing the Transaction Summary for each Stock Item for a selected Stock Group
- **Stock Item Analysis** : Print Stock Group Analysis, showing the Vendor / Customer wise details of transactions for a selected Stock Item
- **Stock Journal Analysis** : Print Stock Journal Analysis showing Stock Item wise transaction details of Stock Journal Vouchers for a selected period
- **Account Group Analysis** : Print Account Group Analysis, showing Stock Item transaction Analysis for Item transacted with ledgers under the selected Account Group
- **Account Ledger Analysis** : Print Account Ledger Analysis, showing Stock Item transaction Analysis for Item transacted for selected Account Ledger.
- **Stock Summary** : Print Stock Summary showing the Opening, Transaction summary & Closing stock of each Stock Group / Stock Item for a specified period.

Point of Sales 02-06

01 Point of Sales (PoS)

PoS is an acronym for *Point-of-Sale*. Point of Sale can be a retail outlet, a checkout counter in a shop, or any other location where cash sale transactions take place. The seller prints the Sales Invoice, handing over the Invoice to the customer, and the customer makes full payment thereof, over the counter.

02 PoS Voucher Type creation

PoS Voucher Type is a special type of Sales Voucher type for preparation of quick cash sales memos. To create PoS Voucher type, at Gateway, select *Accounts Info>Voucher Types>Create* to get Voucher Type creation screen (F-1A). Now enter the particulars to create PoS (a Sales voucher type)

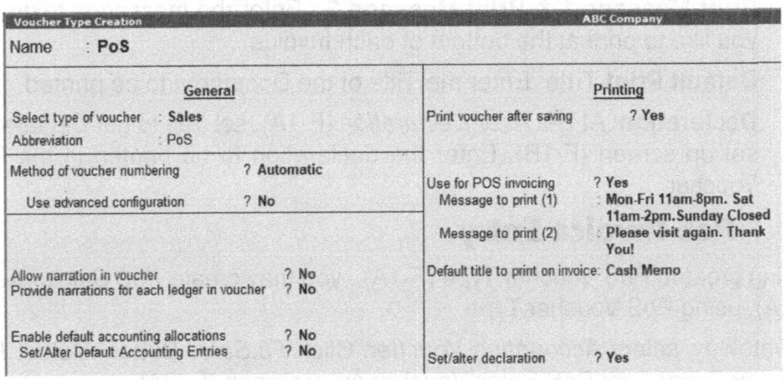

F- 1A : PoS Voucher Type Creation

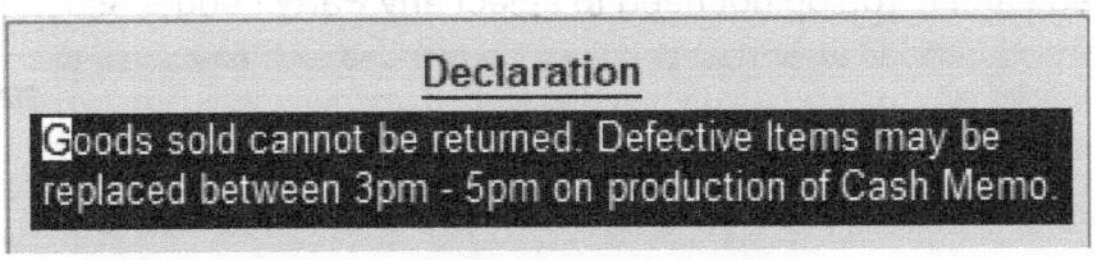

F-1B: Declartion set up

At the *Left Part*, set the options as follows (F- 1A) :

- **Voucher Type Name** : At *Name*, enter the Voucher Type Name.
- **Voucher Type** : At *Type of Voucher*, select *Sales* as PoS is a type of Sales Voucher.

- **Abbreviation** *:* At *Abbr*, enter short name (Abbreviation) of the Voucher Type. This is printed in all Books of Accounts, for the Voucher Type.
- **Method of Numbering :** At *Method of Numbering* field, select *Automatic.* The voucher numbers will be automatically posted serially as per Date.
- **Mode :** At *Use Advance Configuration,* set *No.*
- **Common Narration :** At *Use Common Narration,* set *No* (In PoS, normally no Narration is entered for faster entry).
- **Ledger Narration :** At the field *Narration for each entry,* set *No* (In PoS, normally no Ledger is entered for faster entry).

Printing Options set up : Under the *Printing* section at the *Right Part,* set the Printing options as follows:

- **On-line Printing** : At *Print after Saving,* set *Yes* so that you may directly print the PoS Invoice immediately on entry.
- **Use for PoS Invoicing** : Set *Yes* to define it as PoS Type Voucher, to inherit special characteristics of PoS voucher
- **Print Message 1 & Print Message 2** *:* Enter the messages texts that you like to print at the bottom of each Invoice.
- **Default Print Title**: Enter the Title of the Document to be printed.
- **Declaration**: At *Set Alter Declaration* (F-1A), set Yes to get Declaration set up screen (F-1B). Enter the declaration to be printed in the PoS Voucher

03 PoS Invoice Entry

Having created PoS Voucher Type (F-1A) , you may create *PoS Sales Invoice* (F-2A), using PoS Voucher Type.

At Gateway, select *Accounting Voucher.* Click *F8:Sales* Button. Select *PoS Voucher Type* to get PoS Sales Voucher entry screen (F- 2A).

Now enter the PoS Voucher (F-2A) in same way as Sales Invoice Entry described earlier. You do not need to select any Party Ledger Account.

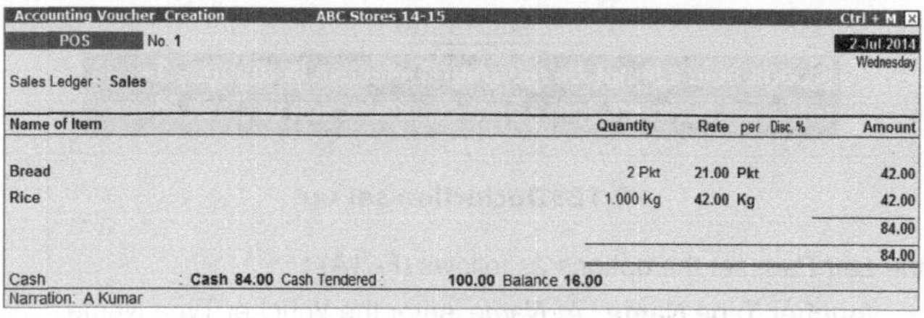

F-2A: PoS Voucher entry

Payment Details : After entry of Item details, enter the Payment details as follows :

- **Cash Ledger Account :** At *Cash*, select the Cash Ledger Account from list.
- **Tendered Amount**: At *Cash Tendered*, enter the amount Tendered by the customer in payment of the Invoice (which must not be less than the amount of the Bill)
- **Balance Amount** : At *Balance*, the excess amount received & refundable to the customer (Cash Tendered – Cash Account), if any, would be shown, to make refund quickly without mistake

PoS Entry Configuration

At *PoS Entry screen* (F-2A), click *F12:Configure* to get *PoS Entry Configuration* screen (F-3A), to set PoS entry configuration

POS Invoice Configuration	
Enable supplementary details *(Address details, despatch details, etc.)*	? No
Print default name and address of party	? No
Display Quantity Godown-wise	? No
Provide additional descriptions for stock item name	? No
Skip quantity during POS invoicing for faster entry	? Yes
Allow modification of rate field during POS invoicing	? No
Skip Discount field during POS invoicing for faster entry	? Yes
Enable entry of party details in POS invoice	? Yes
Other Options	
Allow modification of all fields during entry	? No
Calculate tax on current sub-total *(else calculations are on inventory total only)*	? No

F-3A: PoS Entry Configuration

04 PoS Invoice Printing

Normally PoS invoice are printed on line during entry. After the PoS voucher entry is over, you get PoS Voucher printing screen (if you have set *Yes* at *Print after saving voucher* at the respective voucher Type creation screen)

At *PoS Invoice Printing* screen, set *Yes* at *Print Yes / No* to print the PoS Invoice as per current printing configuration set.

PoS Invoice Printing Configuration

At PoS Invoice printing screen ,click *F12:Configure* to get PoS Printing Configuration screen (F-4A) to set the printing configuration.

POS Invoice Printing Configuration

Title of Document	: Cash Memo
Format to use for stock item	? Name Only
Print Item Name in one line	? Yes
Print serial number	? Yes
Print part number	? No
Print Quantity Units	? Yes
Print rate column	? Yes
Print rate units	? No
Print Discount as a column	? Yes
Print Additional Description(s) for Item Name	? No
Print Card / Cheque No.	? Yes
Print whole Card Number	? No
Print narration	? No
Print base currency symbol for total	? No
Print Time in Invoice	? n

F-4A: PoS Printing Configuration

Having set the PoS Printing Configuration (F-4A), at PoS Invoice printing screen, type Y to print the PoS Invoice (F-5A).

ABC Stores

Cash Memo

Bill No. : 1 Time : 06:36 hrs
Date : 2-7-2014

Sl	Description	Qty	Rate	Amount
1	Bread	2	21.00	42.00
2	Rice	1.000	42.00	42.00
	Total			₹ 84.00

Cash	:	84.00
Cash Tendered	:	*100.00*
Balance	:	*16.00*

Goods sold cannot be retruned. Defetive Items may be replaced between 3pm-5pm on production of Cash Memo

Mon-Fri (11am-8pm). Sat(11am-2pm)

Please visit again. Thank You !

F-5A: PoS Invoice in print

05 PoS Register

Having entered the PoS Invoice, you may print the PoS Register listing the PoS Invoices.

POS Register Ctrl + M

List of All POS Vouchers 1-Apr-2014 to 31-Aug-2014

Date	Vch Type	Vch No.			Gift Vouchers	Credit/Debit Card Pymt	Cheque	Cash	Total
2-7-2014	POS	1						84.00	84.00
	Sales			84.00					
	Bread		2 Pkt	42.00					
	Rice		1.000 Kg	42.00					
	Total:							84.00	84.00

F-6A: PoS Register (with Inventory Details)

At Accounts Books Menu (*GoT>Display> Account Books)*, select *PoS Register* to get *PoS Register* (F-6A).

Summary

- **PoS Voucher Type set Up** : Create PoS Voucher Type
- **PoS Voucher Entry :** Enter PoS Voucher using PoS Voucher Type
- **PoS Voucher Printing :** On entry of PoS Voucher, print the voucher instantly from Voucher entry screen, setting the PoS Invoice printing configuration.
- **PoS Register Printing** : Print PoS register for specified period, showing the details of each PoS invoice, setting the PoS Register printing configuration.

Orders **02-07**

01 Orders

Orders are Trade Contracts for transactions between the Seller & Buyer. Ordering System helps better inventory control & impart better planning and control for Sales & Purchase Activities,

Ordering System Activation

To activate Order System, Click *F11:Feature>Inventory Feature* set the options as follows :

- Set Yes at *Enable Purchase Order processing* to activate Purchase Orders. Consequently, *F4: Purchase Order* button would also appear at Inventory Voucher Entry screen to enter Purchase Orders
- Set Yes at *Enable Sales Order processing* to activate Sales Orders. Consequently, *F5: Sales Order* button would also appear at Voucher Entry screen to enter Sales Orders

02 Orders Entry

The process of Sales Order Entry & Purchase Order Entry is similar. At Main Menu (GoT), Select *Order Vouchers*:

- **Purchase Order** : Click *F4: Purc. Order* button to get Purchase Order entry screen (F-5A), quite similar to Purchase Invoice Entry screen
- **Sales Order :** Click *F5: Sale Order* button to get Purchase Order entry screen, quite similar to Sales Invoice Entry screen

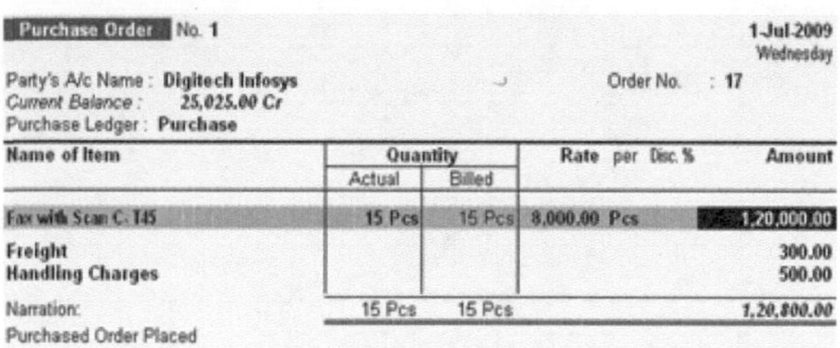

Purchase Order No. 1 — 1-Jul-2009 Wednesday

Party's A/c Name : **Digitech Infosys** — Order No. : 17
Current Balance : 25,025.00 Cr
Purchase Ledger : **Purchase**

Name of Item	Quantity Actual	Quantity Billed	Rate	per	Disc. %	Amount
Fax with Scan C-T45	15 Pcs	15 Pcs	8,000.00	Pcs		1,20,000.00
Freight						300.00
Handling Charges						500.00
	15 Pcs	15 Pcs				*1,20,800.00*

Narration:
Purchased Order Placed

F-1A:Purchase Order entry

Now enter the respective details at various components of Order Entry screen

a. **Header Part :** In Header Part (F-1A), enter the details common to the entire Order, as follows :

- **Party's A/c** : At *Party's A/c Name*, select the Party Name (Supplier / Customer) from the list of Party Ledger Accounts
- **Order Ref** : At *Order No.* enter your Order Reference (or Party's Reference) as Order Reference (the Order Voucher Number is carried as default, which you may change).

b. **Item Details :** After entry of Header details, the following Item Details are entered. On entry of Item Name, a pop up window appears (F-1B) to enter the Item details as follows :

- **Delivery Due Date** : At *Due on* field, enter the Delivery Due Date of the Item. In case of staggering delivery plan (Item to be delivered in parcel on different dates), you have to enter the Item details separately for each Delivery Date.
- **Quantity** : Enter the Order Quantity for the Item.
- **Rate** : The Standard Rate (or the price list Rate) is carried, which you may change in the Order
- **Discount** : Enter the Discount Rate (in %), if Discount option is activated.
- **Amount** : The computed amount as per Quantity & Rate (& Discount) is displayed, which may be changed (in case of lump sum value, the Amount may be entered without entering the Rate)

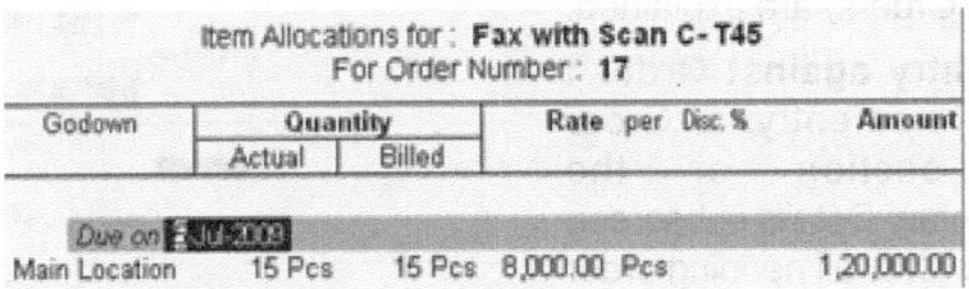

F-1B: Item Allocation in Order Entry

This way, enter the details of each Item in the Order.

c. **Other Ledger Details** : After completing the entry of all Item details, at Voucher Entry screen (F-1A), enter the details for other ledger accounts (like Freight, Tax etc, if any). The process is similar to Invoice Entry

- **Ledger Account** : Select the Ledger Account
- **Rate** : Enter the Rate in % (or may leave zero and fill up amount figure directly)
- **Amount** : The computed amount as per Rate specified (according to rule specified in the Ledger Account), is displayed which you may change.

This way, enter the details of each ledger account.

d. **Voucher Narration:** If you set *Yes* at *Use Common Narration* at the Order Voucher type, then you may also enter Narration for the voucher, giving more details. The Narration entered may be optionally printed in Order / Day Book.

Order Configuration

At order entry screen, click *F12:Configure* to get Order Configuration screen. The options are almost similar to invoice entry Configuration.

Order Printing

Having entered Order, you may print the Order (currently being entered) on-line immediately after entry (while saving). The process of Order Printing is similar to Invoice Printing explained earlier.

03 Order Processing

Order Processing means transaction of goods as per Order (Order Fufilment). The vendor supplies the goods against their Sales Order and the buyer receives the goods against their Purchase Orders.

- **Sales Order Processing:** Creation of Sales Invoice against Sales Order
- **Purchase Order Processing :** Creation of Purchase Voucher against Purchase Order

The entry process of Sales / Purchase Invoice have been explained above. Now the additional part of Execution of Order (Invoice Entry linking the respective Orders) are explained.

Invoice entry against Order : During Invoice entry, at Order Details section of the Supplementary Details subscreen (F-2A), the list of all pending order numbers appear at *Order No(s)* field. Select the Order number against which the Invoice is created, from the list of Pending Order. You may select several Orders one by one in one Invoice.

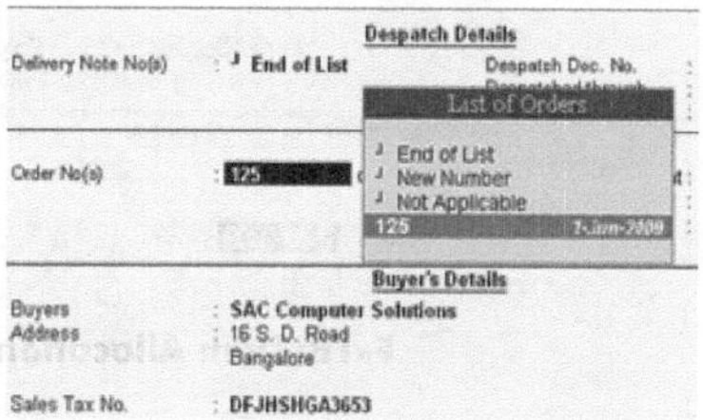

F-2A: Sales Invoice against Sales Order

04 Pre-Closure of Order

In natural course, the contract would be executed in full. However, sometimes, Buyer / Seller may decide that the balance undelivered quantity of an order (full or partial) will not be further delivered by Seller and the Balance Order Quantity be cancelled and the Order is closed (treated like fully executed). Pre Closure of Order may be done at during Voucher Entry or at Order Details screen.

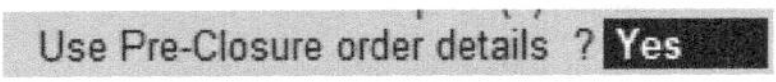

F-3A: Order Pre Closing Configuration option

F-3B : Pre Closure button at Order Entry screen

Pre Closure at Order Alteration : You may pre close order (before Order Completion), in following ways

- **Pre Close the entire Order** : At Order Alteration screen, click *C:Pre Close* (or pres *Ctrl+C*) button (F-3B) to get Pre Closure screen (F-4B).
  - o **Pre Closure Reason** : At Reason, specify the Reason.
  - o **Pre Closure Date** : At *Closed On*, enter the Date of Pre Closure

  The entire Order (in respect of all the Items) is closed.
- **Pre Close Balance of selected Item** : To get Pre Close Order at Item Level, at *Order Configuration* screen (Click *F12:Configure* at Orders Alteration screen), set *Yes* at *Use Pre Closure Order details* (F-3A). Consequently, at *Item Allocation* screen (F-4A), the column *Pre – Close Quantity* appears. Now, enter as follows :

o **Pre Closure Quantity** : At *Pre Close Quantity Column*, enter the Quantity to be reduced from the Balance Order

o **Reason** : At *Reason for Pre Closure*, enter the Reason

The Balance of Order of the Item gets reduced by the specified Pre Closure Quantity.

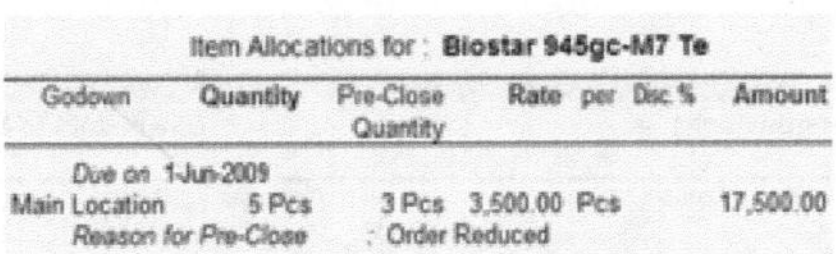

F-4A: Item Level Pre Closing

F-4B : Entire Order Pre Closing from Order

Pre Closure from Voucher Entry : If during Orders Entry, it is decided that Balance Order (full or Partial) will not be fully executed, the Pre Closure Quantity may be entered at respective Voucher Entry screen.

At Voucher Entry (Delivery Note / Receipt Note / Purchase Invoice / Sales Invoice), you may pre –close Order at Item Level. At Voucher Entry Configuration (at current Voucher entry / Alteration screen, click *F12:Configure* to get respective Voucher Entry Configuration screen), set *Yes* at *Use Pre Closure Orders Details* (F-3A).

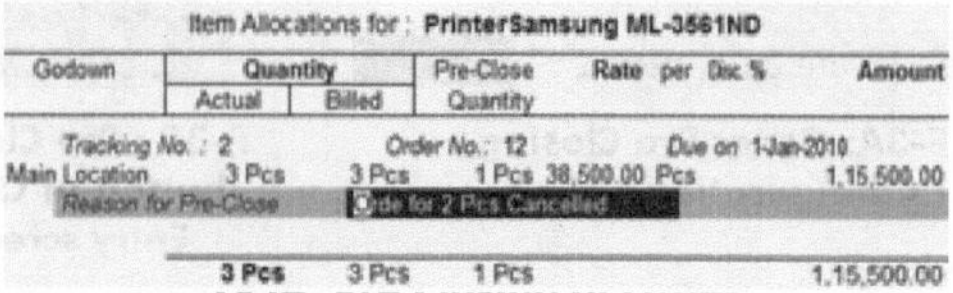

F-5A: Pre Closing of Order

Consequently, at Item Allocation screen, a new Column Pre Close Quantity appears (F-5A). At the Item Allocation screen of the Item for which Order to be cancelled, enter as follows:

- **Pre Closure Quantity** : At *Pre Close Quantity Column*, enter the Quantity to be reduced from the Balance Order.
- **Reason** : At *Reason for Pre Closure*, enter the Reason.

The Balance of Order for the Item gets reduced by the specified Pre Closure Quantity.

05 Orders Outstanding

At *GoT>Display>Statements of Inventory* :

- **Sales Order Outstanding** : Select *Sales Order Outstanding* to get Sales Order Menu. Select *All Orders* to get Due Sales Orders Report (F-6A)
- **Purchase Order Outstanding** : Select *Purchase Order Outstanding* to get Purchase Order Menu. Select *All Orders* to get Due Purchase Orders Report, similar to Due Sales Orders Report.

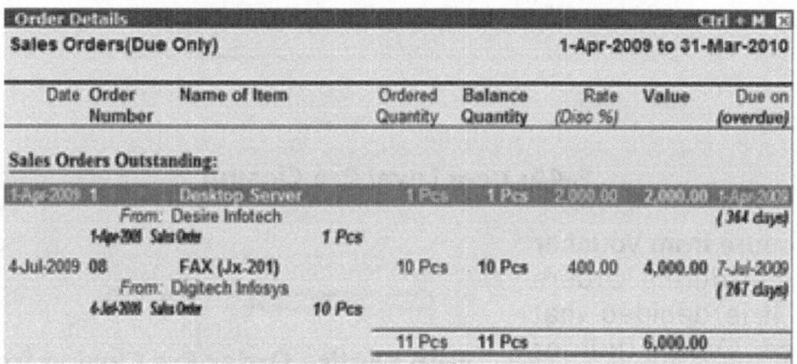

Order Outstanding Analysis

Like Outstanding analysis, by selecting the respective Buttons and setting the Outstanding report Configuration (Click F12:Configure at Order Outstanding Report), you may print Stock Category Sales & Purchase Order Outstanding (Stock Category wise Order Outstanding), Stock Group Sales & Purchase Order Outstanding (Stock Group wise Order Outstanding), Stock Item Sales

& Purchase Order Outstanding (Stock Item wise Order Outstanding). Similarly, you may also print Account Group Outstanding (Sales / Purchase Orders Outstanding for Items transacted for ledgers under selected Account Group) & Account Ledger Outstanding (Sales / Purchase Orders Outstanding for Items transacted for selected Account Ledger)

Summary

- **Activation of Order System** : At *Inventory Features*, activate Ordering System
- **Orders Entry** : Enter Sales / Purchase Orders
- **Invoice Entry** : Enter Invoices selecting the relevant orders against which the Invoice is being created
- **Pre Closure of Order** : If the balance order is not to be executed, through Order Alteration, Pre Close the order, cancelling the balance of the outstanding order
- **Stock Category Order Outstanding** : Display / Print Stock Category wise Sales & Purchase Order Outstanding
- **Stock Group Order Outstanding** : Display / Print Stock Group wise Sales & Purchase Order Outstanding
- **Stock Item Order Outstanding** : Display / Print Stock Item wise Sales & Purchase Order Outstanding .
- **Account Group Outstanding** : Display / Print Sales / Purchase Orders Outstanding for Items transacted for ledgers under selected Account Group)
- **Account Ledger Outstanding** : Display / Print Sales / Purchase Orders Outstanding for Items transacted for selected Account Ledger)

Assignments : Invoicing & Inventory 02

02-01 Inventory Masters

- **Activate Inventory** : Click *F11:Features>Accounting Features.* Set *No* at Maintain Accounts only to maintain Accounts with Inventory.
- **Create Company with Inventory System**

  Select *GoT>F3:Cmp Info >Create Company* to get Company Creation screen. Press Shift+Tab (at name field) to go to *Directory* field and change the Directory Name to d:/T/data. At *Name*, enter your Roll Number, Name – Inv (like 014 A K Sinha-Inv). At *Mailing Name*, remove the Roll Number but keep the Name (e.g AK Sinha - Inv). At *Maintain*, select *Accounts with Inventory.* At *Financial Year From*, enter 01-4-2016. Press Ctrl+A to save the Company.
- **Create Stock Item UoM**

  Select GoT>Inventory Info>Unit of Measure > Create. At *Symbol* select *Kg.* At *Formal Name*, Enter *Kilogram.* At *Number of Decimal Places*, enter 3.
- **Create Stock Item Group**

  Select *GoT>Inventory Info > Stock Group > Create.* At *Name*, enter *Food Grains.* At *Under*, select *Primary.* At *Can Quantities of Items be Added*, set *Yes*
- **Create Stock Item**
  - o Select *GoT> Inventory Info > Stock Item > Create.* At *Name* , enter Wheat. At *Under*, select *Food Grains.* At *Units* , select *Kg.*
  - o At *Opening Balance*, at *Quantity*, enter 100.000. At *Rate*, enter 16.00. At *Value*, the Computed Amount 1600 is displayed. Press *Ctrl+A* to save.
- **Print Chart of Stock Items**

  Select *GoT>Display> List of Accounts.* Click *I:Stock Item* to get list of Groups / Stock Item in hierarchical order. Click *P:Print* and type Y to print on printer.
- **Print Opening Stock Statement Check List**

  Select *GoT>Display> Stock Summary.* Click *F1:Detailed* button. Click *P:Print* to get *Stock Summary Printing* screen. Set *Yes* at *Show*

Quantities, Show Rates, Show Values. Show Opening Balance. Set *No* at all other options. Set *Yes* at *Expand all Levels in Detailed Format* to get Opening Stock Statement showing hierarchal structure of Stock Group/ Stock Items as entered in Stock Item Master. This is useful to print check list of data entered at Stock Item Masters.

02-02 Inventory Voucher

- **On 2-4-2016, Purchased 50 kg of Wheat @ 18.00 / kg by Cash by Cash Memo Number 35 dt 2.4.2016**
    - o Select *GoT> Accounts Voucher.* Click *F9:Purchase.* Click *V:As Voucher* button (at Button Bar) to get Purchase Voucher entry screen (in Voucher Mode). Enter 2-4-2016 at Voucher *Date.* At *Supplier Invoice Number*, enter *35.* At *Date* enter 1.4.2016. Click F12:Configure to get Purchase voucher Configuration screen. Set *No* at *Accept Supplier details* to suppress Supplementary Details screen.
    - o At *Particulars*, select *Cash* ledger account. At *Amount* enter 900 at Credit column, to get *Item Allocation* screen.
    - o At *Nature of Item* column, select Wheat, At *Quantity*, enter 50.000, At *Rate*, enter 18.00. At *Amount*, the computed value (i.e 900.00) is shown. Press <enter> to get back the Purchase Voucher main screen
    - o Enter Voucher Narration (purchased in Cash from Sundar Singh). Press Crl+A to save the Voucher.
- **On 1-5-2016, 10 Kg of Wheat was spoiled as the Wheat Bag was torn.**

  Select *GoT>Inventory Voucher* get Stock Journal entry screen (Click *F7:Stk Jrnl* button). At *Source (Consumption)* at left part, at *Name of Item* column, select *Wheat.* At *Quantity*, enter 10.000, At *Rate* enter zero. and at Value, leave zero (loss). Press *Ctrl+A* to save he voucher

02-03 Invoicing

- **Set Up Invoicing Feature for Sales, Credit & Debit Note**

  Select *F11:Fetaures>Accounting Features* and set *Yes* at *Allow Invoicing, Use Invoice Mode for Debit Note and Use Invoice Mode for Credit Note.*
- **On 2-4-2016, sold 40 kg of Wheat @ 20.00 / kg to A K Mondal, in Cash**
    - o Select *GoT> Accounting Voucher.* Click *F8:Sales.* Click *V:As Invoice* button and click I:Item Invoice (at Button Bar) to get Sales Invoice entry screen . Enter 2-4-2016 at Voucher *Date.* Click *F12:Configure* to get *Sales Invoice Configuration* screen. Set *No* at *Accept Supplementary details.*

o At Party's A/c Name, select *Cash*, At *Particulars*, select *Wheat*, At *Quantity*, enter 20.000. The UoM *Kg* is displayed. Enter 20.00 at Rate. At Amount column, the value Rs 400.00 is displayed. Press <enter> at next line at *Particulars* column to terminate Items entry. Enter 'Sold to A K Mondal' at *Narration*. Press *Ctrl+A* to save the Invoice.

02-04 Invoice Printing

- **Set Instant printing option of Sales Invoice after entry**

  Select *GoT>Accounts Info>Voucher Type>Alter*. Select *Sales* from the list of Voucher Types to get *Sales Voucher Type Alteration* screen. Set *Yes* at *Print After Saving Voucher*, to instantly print *Sales Invoice* immediately on Entry / Alteration.

- **Print Sales Invoice # 4 dt 2.4.2016**

  Select *GoT>Display>Day Book*. Click *F2:Date* and enter the Date 2.4.2106 get the list of Vouchers for the specified Date. Select the Sales Invoice (#4) and press <Enter> to get the Invoice # 4 in Alteration mode. Click *P:Print* Button to get Invoice Printing screen. Type *Y* to print the Invoice.

- **Print All Sales Invoices of a Date (or period) in one shot**

  Select *GoT>Multi Account Printing>Multi Voucher Printing* to get *Multi Voucher Printing* screen. At *Name of Voucher Type*, select *Sales*. At *Select Vouchers to print*, select *Regular*. At *From* and *To*, enter the Dates (e.g 2-4-2016) to print all Sales Invoices of the specified Date in one shot.

02-05 Inventory Reports

- **Print Customer Ledger with Inventory Details**

  Select *GoT>Display>Account Books>Ledger* and select the Customer Ledger (i.e A K Traders) . Click *P:Print* Button. Set Yes at *Show Inventory Details* also, to print Inventory details of the respective vouchers (like Sales, Purchase, Debit Note, Credit Note etc).

- **Print Sales Register for a specified period**

  It is recommended to print Sales Register using Multi Accounts Printing, though you can as well print from Display option also.

  o **Printing from Display :** Select *GoT>Display>Account Books>Sales Register*. Drill down through any month. Click *F2:Period* and enter the *From* & *To* dates for the Period. Click *F1:Detailed* and click *P:Print* Button to get Sales Register Printing screen. Set *Yes* at Show *Inventory Details* also (and other options as required). Type *Y* to Print the Sales Register.

  o **Multi Account Printing :** Select *GoT>Multi Account*

Printing>Account Books>Sales Register. Enter the *From* & *To* dates for the Period. At *Format*, select *Detailed.* Set *Yes* at *Show Inventory Details* also (and other options as required). Type *Y* to Print the Sales Register.

- **Print Stock Summary**
  - o You may print Stock Summary from Display (which is simpler) or from Multi Accounts Printing (which provides some additional advanced options).
- **Printing from Display :** Select *GoT>Stock Summary.* Click *F2:Period* and enter the *From* & *To* Dates for the Period. Click *F1:Detailed* and click *P:Print* Button to get Stock Summary Printing screen.
- **Multi Account Printing :** Select *GoT>Multi Account Printing>Inventory Books>Stock Item.* Select All Items / One Item / Group of Items (and select the Item/ Group of Items (and select the Stock Group) to get Sock Summary Printing screen. Enter the *From* & *To* dates for the Period. At *Format*, select *Detailed.*
  - o Set *Yes* at relevant options (like *Expand All levels in Detailed Format, Show Quantities, Show Opening balance, Show Goods Inwards, Show Goods Outwards, Show Closing balance*) which you like to print in the Report and set other options, as required. Type *Y* to print

02-06 Point of Sales

- **Create Point of Sales Voucher Type CsV**
  - o Select *GoT>Accounts Info>Voucher Types>Create* to get *Voucher Type* creation screen. At *Name*, enter CntSales. At *Type of Voucher*, select *Sales.* At *Abbr*, enter CsV. At *Method of Numbering* field, select *Automatic.* At *Use Advance Configuration,* set *No.* At *Use Common Narration*, set *No.* At *Narration for each entry*, set *No.*
  - o At *Print after Saving*, set *Yes.* At *Use for PoS Invoicing*, *Yes* . At *Print Message 1 & Print Message 2,* enter the messages texts to be printed at the bottom of Invoice. At *Default Print Title*, enter 'Cash Memo'. At *Declaration*, enter the text that would be printed at the end of the Invoice. Press Ctrl+A to save the PoS Voucher Type
- **On 1-5-2016, 5 kg of wheat sold @ 19 /kg.**
  - o Select *GoT>Accounting Voucher.* Click *F8:Sales* and then select *CsV* from list of Voucher Types. Enter 1-5-2016 at Voucher Date. Click *F12:Configure* to get *PoS Configuration* screen. Set *Yes* at *Allow Modification of Rate* during Entry. At Party A/c Ledger, select *Not Applicable.* At *Sales Ledger*, select *Sales.*

- o At *Name of Item*, select *Wheat*, At *Quantity*, enter 5 (press Backspace if Quantity field is skipped). The UoM Kg is displayed. At *Rate*, enter 19. At Amount, 95 is displayed. At next line, at *Name of Item*, press <enter> to terminate Sock Item entry. At *Cash*, select Cash Account. At *Amount Tendered*, enter 100. At *Balance*, 5 is displayed. Type *Y* to Save and print the PoS Invoice.

- **Print PoS Register**

  Select *GoT>Display> Account Books>PoS Register* to get *PoS Register* printing screen. Click *P:Print* button. At *Format*, select *Detailed*. At *Show Inventory Details*, set *Yes*. Type *Y* to print *PoS Register*

02-07 Orders

- **Activate Ordering System**

  Click *F11:Feature>Inventory Feature* and set Yes at *Allow Purchase Order processing* and set Yes at *Allow Sales Order processing*

- **On 1-6-2106, Sales Order No 1 for Sale of 100 kg of Wheat @20 to A K Traders, is created**
  - o Select *GoT>Order Voucher*. Click *F5:Sales Order* to get *Sales Orders* Entry screen. The Sales Order number 1 is displayed. At *Party's A/c Name*, select A K Traders. At *Order No.* enter 34 (Party's Order Reference Number)
  - o At *Item Name*, select *Wheat* to get Order details screen. At *Due on*, enter 1-7-2016. At *Quantity*, enter 100.000. The UoM Kg Is displayed. At *Rate*, enter 20.00. The value 2000 is displayed at Amount column. At next line, at *Name of Item*, press <enter> . Press *Ctl+A* to save the Voucher.

- **On 1-7-2016, 60 kg of Wheat @ 20 was sold to A K Traders against Sales Order #1**
  - o Select *GoT>Accounting Voucher*. Click *F5:Sales* to get *Sales Invoice* Entry screen. At Party Name, select A K Traders to get Supplementary details screen. At Order Number, select the Pending Order from list (i.e.Sales Order # 1). At *Party's A/c Name*, select A K Traders. At *Order No.* enter 34
  - o At *Item Name*, select *Wheat*, At *Quantity*, select 60.000. At *Rate*, enter 20.00. The value 1200.00 is displayed at *Amount* column. At next line, at Name of Item column, press <enter>
  - o Press Ctrl+A to save the Sales Invoice.

- **Display Sales Order Outstanding Report**

  Select *GoT>Display>Statement of Inventory>Sales Order Outstanding>All Orders*. Click *F1:Detailed*

PART 3

Tax Accounting

Almost all organisations are to comply with statutory requirements to Deduct Tax / Charge Tax in Invoices, deposit such Tax with Government under Tax Challans and submit Tax Returns. This module covers the aspects of Tax Accounting, describing the steps of Company & Masters Set Up, Invoicing, Tax Deposit, Tax Challans and Tax Reports printing.

Goods & Services Tax (GST) describes General Rules and Compliance, Company Set Up, Rates Set, Tax Ledger, Party Ledger, Invoicing, Input Tax adjustment, Tax payment, Challans, Reports printing: Reports and Data Upload in GST Portal.

Tax Deducted at Source (TDS) describes Company Set Up, creation & set up for Ledger Accounts related with TDS transactions, Vouchers with TDS transactions, Tax realisation from Payee, Tax Deposit with Government, Tax Challan & TDS Reports

Tax Collected at Source (TCS) describes Company Set Up, creation & set up for Ledger Accounts related with TCS transactions, Invoicing, Tax Payable Computation, Tax Deposit with Government, Tax Challan, TCS Certificate Printing & Statutory Reports.

Introduction 03-1-01

01 GST

GST is a destination based tax on consumption of goods and services. It is proposed to be levied at all stages right from manufacture up to final consumption with credit of taxes paid at previous stages available as setoff. Only value addition will be taxed and burden of tax is to be borne by the final consumer.

GST eliminates the present following taxes and introduces news Tax of CGST, IGST and SGST:

- Service Tax
- Central Excise Tax
- Additional Excise Duties
- CVD (Countervailing Duty), SAD (Special Additional Duty of Customs)
- The Excise Duty levied under the Medicinal and Toiletries Preparation Act
- Surcharges, and Cesses
- VAT / Sales tax
- Luxury tax
- Taxes on lottery, betting and gambling.
- Entertainment tax (unless it is levied by the local bodies).
- State Cesses and Surcharges relating to supply of goods and services.
- Entry tax not in lieu of Octroi.

Customs is outside GST and hence would continue on imports. GST is not charged on exported goods and services

02 Benefits of GST

- **For Business and Industry**
    - o **Easy compliance**: Through a robust and comprehensive IT system, all services like registrations, returns, payments, etc. would be available online, enabling easy and transparent compliance.
    - o **Uniformity of tax rates and structures**: GST will ensure that indirect tax rates and structures are common across the country, business in the country tax neutral of business place.

  - o **Elimination of Tax cascading**: A system of seamless tax-credits throughout the value-chain, and across boundaries of States, would eliminate cascading of taxes.
  - o **Improved competitiveness:** Reduction in transaction costs of doing business would eventually lead to an improved competitiveness for the trade and industry.
  - o **Gain to manufacturers and exporters**: The subsuming of major Central and State taxes in GST, complete and comprehensive set-off of input goods and services and phasing out of Central Sales Tax (CST) would reduce the cost of locally manufactured goods and services. This will increase the competitiveness of Indian goods and services in the international market and give boost to Indian exports. The uniformity in tax rates and procedures across the country will also go a long way in reducing the compliance cost.
- **For Central and State Governments**
  - o Easier Administration: Replacement of Multiple indirect taxes at the Central and State levels by GST, backed with a robust end-to-end IT system, would ease the government administration.
  - o **Better controls on leakage**: GST will result in better tax compliance due to highly controlled input tax credit from one stage to another in the entire chain of value addition, for better tax compliance and tracking evaders.
  - o **Higher revenue efficiency:** GST is expected to decrease the cost of collection of tax revenues of the Government, leading to higher revenue efficiency.
- **For the Consumer**
  - o **Single transparent tax:** GST will be only one tax, from the manufacturer to the consumer.
  - o **Relief in overall tax burden:** Due to efficiency gains and prevention of leakages, the overall tax burden on most commodities will come down, which will benefit consumers.

03 Essential Features of GST

- **Input Tax Credit**: Credits of input taxes paid at each stage of production or service delivery can be availed in the succeeding stages of value addition. This means that the end consumer will thus only bear the GST charged by the last point in supply chain, with set-off benefits at all the earlier stages.
- **GST Rates**: GST rates on goods and services have been classified into broadly four tax rates: 5 per cent, 12 per cent, 18 per cent and 28 per cent. Some goods and services have been exempted. Precious metals like gold will attract a separate tax rate of 3 per cent. A cess will be levied over the peak rate of 28 per cent on specified luxury and sin goods.

- **Components of GST** : For transactions within the State, tax revenue collected under SGST is meant for State Government. Similarly, Union Territories will get the tax collected under UTGST.

  Integrated GST (IGST) would be levied on inter-state movement of goods or services, collected by the Centre. Import of goods would be treated as inter-state supplies and would be subject to IGST in addition to the applicable customs duties. Exports will be treated as zero-rated supplies which means no tax will be payable on exports of goods or services. However, exporters can claim input tax credit.
- **Person Liable** : Businesses with an annual turnover of Rs. 20 lakh (Rs.10 lakh for special category states) would be exempt from GST. A composition scheme (to pay tax at a flat rate without input credits) is available to some businesses having an annual turnover of up to Rs. 75 lakh. The composition scheme is optional.
- **Stocks in transition**: On stocks unsold before GST rollout, input tax credit would be allowed to be carried forward for 90 days. On such goods, they can claim 60 per cent of the input tax credit on stocks lying unsold up to June 30.
- **Anti-profiteering mechanism**: To ensure that manufacturers and service providers pass on the benefit to the final customer, the government has included an anti-profiteering clause in GST. Under this, it becomes mandatory to pass on the benefit of tax reduction due to input tax credit to the final customer.
- **Decision mechanism**: GST Council, constituted by representative of Tax & Finance department of Centre and States, will make recommendations on matters related to GST including laws, rules and rates etc.

  Union Finance Minister heads the panel while ministers of finance or taxation of each state are its members. Decisions in the Council are taken by a 75 per cent majority. Centre and a minimum of 20 states are required for majority. Centre would have one-third weightage of the total votes cast and all the States taken together would have two-thirds of weightage.
- **Products not part of GST**: Petroleum products such as petrol, diesel and aviation turbine fuel have been kept out of GST as of now. Alcohol has also been kept out of GST.
- **Administrative control**: To ensure single interface, all administrative control of 90 per cent of taxpayers having turnover below Rs. 1.5 crore would vest with state tax administration, while 10 per cent will vest with the central tax administration. All administrative control over taxpayers having turnover above Rs. 1.5 crore will be divided equally between central and state tax administrations. States will be compensated for any revenue loss from GST implementation for five years.

GST Registration Rules 03-1-02

01 Registration

Any person having aggregate pan-india turnover of threshold limit (currently reported as Rs 20 Lakhs / 10 lakhs in North East), across all locations in India will need to obtain registration in the States from where they make a supply.

The following persons would be required to obtain GST registration irrespective of turnover: • person making inter-state supply • casual taxable persons and non-resident taxable persons • person required to pay tax under reverse charge • agents supplying on behalf of other registered taxable persons • input service distributors • all e-commerce operators • Person supplying online information and database access or retrieval services from outside India to an unregistered person in India • Persons responsible to deduct TDS

One registration for each State is required, unless the taxpayer chooses to obtain separate registrations for its different business verticals in the State.

Small dealers with turnover below Rs 50 Lakh have the option of adopting the Composition scheme and pay at flat rate on turnover.

02 Existing registered dealers – Registration under GST

All existing dealers registered with central or state tax authorities and having a valid PAN will be auto-migrated and allotted with a provisional certificate of registration in Form GST REG-21. Within 6 months, dealers are required to submit Form GST REG-20 in the GST Portal along with information and documents as prescribed. If the information provided is complete and satisfactory, final registration certificate will be issued in Form GST REG-06.

If the details submitted are not satisfactory, a show cause notice will be issued in Form GST REG-23, and there will be a hearing before cancelling the provisional registration. If the show cause hearing is not successful, or if the details are not provided within the stipulated period, the provisional registration allotted in Form GST REG-21 will be cancelled by issuing an order in Form GST REG-22.

During transition, if a taxable person is not required to register under GST, but was previously registered (Central and State law), he has an option to cancel the provisional registration issued by submitting the **Form GST REG-24.**

03 New Registration under GST

- Fill Form GST REG-01 (Part-A). Provide your PAN, mobile number, and E-mail ID, and submit the form. The PAN is verified on the GST Portal. Mobile number, and E-mail ID are verified with a one-time password (OTP). You will receive an application reference number on your mobile and via E-mail.
- Fill GST REG-01 (Part- B) and specify the application reference number you received. Attach other required documents and submit the form.
- Documents to be uploaded :
  - o **Photographs** : Photographs of proprietor, partners, managing trustee, committee etc. and authorized signatory
  - o **Constitution of taxpayer** : Partnership deed, registration certificate or other proof of constitution
  - o **Proof of principal / additional place of business :**
    - ▪ **For own premises** – Any document in support of the ownership of the premises like latest property tax receipt or Municipal *Khata* copy or copy of electricity bill.
    - ▪ **For rented or leased premises** – copy of rent / lease agreement along with owner's (landlord) documents like latest property tax receipt or Municipal *Khata* copy or copy of electricity bill.
  - o **Bank account related proof** : Scanned copy of the first page of bank pass book or bank statement
  - o **Authorization forms** : For each authorized signatory, upload authorization copy or a copy of resolution of managing committee or board of directors in the prescribed format.

If additional information is required, Form GST REG-03 will be issued to you. You need to respond in Form GST REG-04 with required information within 7 working days from the date of receipt of Form GST REG-03. If all required information are provided via Form GST REG-01 or Form GST REG-04, a certificate of registration in Form GST REG-06 will be issued within 3 days from date of receipt of Form GST REG-01 or Form GST REG-04. If the details submitted are not satisfactory, the registration application is rejected using Form GST REG-05.

04 Existing Composition Dealer registering under GST

All registered taxable persons under the existing indirect tax regime will be automatically transitioned to GST.

Under GST, a registered taxable person whose aggregate turnover does not excess Rupees 50 lakhs during the financial year can opt for composition levy, subject to certain conditions.

On transition to GST, a Composition Dealer may switch over as a Regular Dealer, in following situations :

- Voluntarily opts to become a regular dealer
- The aggregate turnover exceeds the prescribed threshold limit (Rs.50 Lakhs)
- On switching from being a Composition Dealer to a Regular Dealer under GST, the dealer must adhere to compliance requirements of a Regular Dealer, will avail input tax credit and charge GST on outward supplies.
- Composition Dealer becoming a regular dealer under GST, can avail Tax paid on closing stock, on fulfilling following conditions :
    - o The closing stock held either in the form of raw materials, semi-finished goods or finished goods, to be used or intended to be used for taxable supplies.
    - o The VAT paid on inputs held in the closing stock should be allowed as credit under the earlier law. This is applicable only for claiming credit of VAT.
    - o You have invoices or any other prescribed duty/tax paying documents in respect of the closing stock of inputs (including semi-finished goods and finished goods).
    - o The date of invoices or any other prescribed duty/tax paying documents is within 12 months from the date of transitioning to GST.

GST – Registration Process

03-1-03

01 Submission of Application

Registration of GST is mostly digital process and normally can be finished in 5 working days, provided the concerned officer find the application or documentation in order.

- **GST REG -01 (Part A) :** Submit the following particulars
  - o Legal Name of the Business (As mentioned in PAN)
  - o PAN (PAN of business or PAN of Individual for Proprietorship business)
  - o E-mail address
  - o Mobile Number

  On successful verification of e-mail / mobile number on OTP, the application reference number would be generated and communicated to the applicant.
- **GST REG -01 (Part B) :** Using the Application Reference number as received, submit the desired particulars, along with documents as specified in the Form, at the common portal directly or through a facilitation centre. On receipt of the Application, an acknowledgement shall be issued to the applicant in Form GST REG -02

Applicants for Casual Registration shall be given a temporary identification number by the common portal for making advance deposit of tax.

The following persons shall submit the application in other forms (in lieu of GST-REG-01).

- Non Resident Taxable person - GST-REG-09,
- Person required to deduct TDS u/s 51 or u/s 52- GST-REG-07,
- A person supplying online information and data base access or retrieval services from outside India to a non-taxable on line recipient - GST-REG-09A

02 Documents to be submitted alongwith Form GST REG -01

- **Photograph of key persons as applicable :** (a) Proprietary Concern – Proprietor (b) Partnership Firm / LLP – Managing/Authorized/ Designated Partners (personal details of all partners is to be submitted but photos of only ten partners including that of Managing Partner is to be submitted) (c) HUF – Karta (d) Company – Managing Director or the Authorised Person (e) Trust – Managing Trustee (f) Association of Person or Body of Individual –Members of Managing Committee (personal details of all members is to be submitted but photos of only ten members including that of Chairman is to be submitted) (g) Local Authority – CEO or his equivalent (h) Statutory Body – CEO or his equivalent (i) Others – Person in Charge

- **Constitution of Taxpayer** : Partnership Deed in case of Partnership Firm, Registration Certificate/Proof of Constitution in case of Society, Trust, Club, Government Department, Association of Person or Body of Individual, Local Authority, Statutory Body and Others etc.
- **Proof of Principal/Additional Place of Business** :
  - o **For Own premises :** Any document in support of the ownership of the premises like Latest Property Tax Receipt or Municipal Khata copy or copy of Electricity Bill.
  - o **For Rented or Leased premises :** A copy of the valid Rent / Lease Agreement with any document in support of the ownership of the premises of the Lessor like Latest Property Tax Receipt or Municipal Khata copy or copy of Electricity Bill.
  - o **Other premises not covered as above :** A copy of the Consent Letter with any document in support of the ownership of the premises of the Consenter like Municipal Khata copy or Electricity Bill copy. For shared properties also, the same documents may be uploaded.
- **Bank Account Related Proof** : Scanned copy of the first page of Bank passbook / one page of Bank Statement Opening page of the Bank Passbook held in the name of the Proprietor / Business Concern – containing the Account No., Name of the Account Holder, MICR and IFSC and Branch details.
- **Authorization Form** :- For each Authorised Signatory mentioned in the application form, Authorization or copy of Resolution of the Managing Committee or Board of Directors to be filed.

03 Issue of Certificate

- **Approval of Application** : On receipt of Application, if the particulars and attached documents are found in order, the concerned officer would approve the Application with 3 working days. If deficiencies found, the officer will intimate the applicant in Form GST-REG-03, within 3 days. The Applicant would respond to the deficiencies, electronically in Form GST-04, within 7 working days.
- **Deemed Approval** : If the officer fails to take any action (a) Within three working days from the date of submission of application, or (b)

Within seven working days from the date of receipt of clarification, information or documents furnished by the applicant, the application for grant of registration shall be deemed to have been approved.

- **Issue of Certificate** : On approval of the application, the officer would issue certificate of registration in Form REG-GST-06.
- **Rejection of Application** : If not satisfied with the response received from applicant in Form GST-REG-04, the officer would reject the application in Form GST-REG -05 within 7 working days.

04 Separate Registration for multiple business verticals

Any person having multiple business verticals within a State, requiring a separate registration for any of its business verticals shall be granted separate registration in respect of each of the verticals. However, none of the vertical verticals of the same person would be registered under composition scheme, if any of them is registered under regular scheme.

05 Other important provisions

- **Format of Registration Number :** The registration number will be of 15 characters, comprising of – 2 character State Code, 10 characters for PAN / TAN, 2 characters for entry code and the last character for checksum character.
- **Signatory of the Application Form** : The application form shall be signed by – **1. Individual** : By himself or by other person authorized by him. **2. HUF :** Karta or by adult member of family duly authorized by Karta **3. Company :** CEO or authorized signatory thereof 4. **Government, Government Agency, Local authority** - Officer authorized in this behalf. **5. Partnership firm :** Any Partner (not being minor) or Authorized signatory**. 6. Trust :** Any Trustee (not being minor) or Authorized signatory. 7. Any other person : By a person competent to act on his behalf, or by a person authorised as per provisions of s.48
- **Physical verification of business premises in certain cases :** Where the proper officer considers that the physical verification of the place of business of a registered person is required after grant of registration, he may get such verification done and the verification report along with other documents, including photographs, shall be uploaded in FORM GST REG-29 on the Common Portal within fifteen working day***s*** following the date of such verification.
- **Amendment to Registration :** Where there is any change in any of the particulars furnished in the application for registration, either at the time of obtaining registration or as amended from time to time, the registered taxable person shall, within fifteen days of such change, submit an application electronically, duly signed, in FORM GST REG-

11 electronically, along with documents relating to such change at the Common Portal either directly or through a Facilitation Centre, notified by the Board or Commissioner.

- o **Change in key info** : In case of change relates to: **1.** Name of business, **2.** Principal Place of Business, **3.** Details of Partners or directors, Karta, Managing Committee, Board of Trustee, CEO, or person responsible for day to day affairs of business, The officer after proper verification, issue order in Form GST REG- 12 electronically.
- o **Change in other particulars :** Where the change relates to any particulars other than key info, the certificate of registration shall stand amended upon submission of the application in FORM GST REG-11 on the Common Portal.
- o **Change in constitution of firm or PAN** : Where a change in the constitution of any business results in change of PAN, a fresh application for registration in to be submitted in FORM GST REG-01.

- **Suo Moto Registration :** Where, during the course of any survey, inspection, search, enquiry or any other proceeding under the Act, the proper officer finds that a person liable to registration under the Act has failed to apply for such registration, such officer may register the said person on a temporary basis and issue an order in FORM GST REG 13.
- **Cancellation of Registration :** A registered taxable person seeking cancellation of his registration shall electronically submit an application in FORM GST REG-14 including the details of closing stock and liability thereon and may furnish, along with the application, relevant documents in support thereof at the Common Portal either directly or through a Facilitation Centre, notified by the Board or Commissioner.

  Cancellation of registration cannot be considered for the person who has taken voluntary registration.

  Every taxable person, other than a person paying tax under Lump sum Scheme, seeking cancellation of registration under sub-rule (1) shall furnish a final return under GST REG-19.
- **Display of registration certificate and GSTIN :** Every registered taxable person shall display his certificate of registration in a prominent location at his principal place of business and at every additional place or places of business.

  Every registered taxable person shall display his GSTIN in the name board exhibited at the entry of his principal place of business and at every additional place or places of business.

Types of GST

03-1-04

01 Levying of GST

India is a federal country where both the Centre and the States have been assigned the powers to levy and collect taxes. The Centre and States will be simultaneously levying GST, in keeping with the Constitutional requirement of fiscal federalism.

- **SGST (State Goods & Service Tax) :** Different indirect taxes like State Sales Tax, VAT, Luxury Tax, Entertainment tax (unless it is levied by the local bodies), Taxes on lottery, betting and gambling, Entry tax not in lieu of Octroi, State Cess and Surcharge related to in supply of goods and services, are subsumed with SGST.

  The tax revenue collected under SGST is meant for State Government. For Union Territories, **UTGST (Union Territory Goods and Service Tax) is applicable (in place of SGST).**

- **CGST (Central Goods and Service Tax) :** Central taxes of Central Excise Duty, Central Sales Tax CST, Service Tax, Additional excise duties, excise duty levied under the medical and toiletries preparation Act, CVD (Additional Customs duty – Countervailing Duty), SAD (Special Additional Duty of customs) surcharges and cesses are subsumed.

  CGST is charged on the movement of goods and services of standard commodities and services. The revenue collected under CGST is for Centre.

- **IGST (Integrated Goods and Service Tax) :** IGST is charged when movement of goods and services from one state to another (irrespective of sale or stock transfer). For example, if goods are moved from Tamil Nadu to Kerala, IGST is levied on such goods. The revenue out of IGST is shared by state government and central government.

  For inter state transaction (between 2 states) and imports, IGST will be applicable. For intrastate transaction (within the state), CGST and SGST will be applicable.

  Stock transfer (materials belonging to same assesse) will also be subject to GST.

- **Union Territory GST (UTGST) :** A union territory is directly under the governance of the Central Government. This differentiates them from the states, which have their own elected governments. Currently, there are

7 union territories in India, viz : Chandigarh, Lakshadweep, Daman and Diu, Dadra and Nagar Haveli, Andaman and Nicobar Islands, Delhi, Puducherry

Among these, Delhi and Puducherry have their own legislature, with elected members and a Chief Minister, functioning as semi-states.

Under GST, the SGST Act applies to all the states in India. The definition of 'States' in the Indian Constitution includes union territories with their own legislature. Hence, the SGST Act also applies to the union territories of Delhi and Puducherry. So, on supplies within the union territories of Delhi and Puducherry, the taxes levied will be CGST + SGST, and on supplies from Delhi/Puducherry to another state/union territory, IGST would be levied.

As the SGST Act cannot be applied on a union territory without its own legislature, the GST Council has introduced the UTGST Act, to levy a tax, called UTGST, in the union territories of Chandigarh, Lakshadweep, Daman and Diu, Dadra and Nagar Haveli and Andaman and Nicobar Islands. UTGST will be levied in place of SGST in these union territories.

02 GST Rates

Quick glance at Rate structure

- **No tax (0%)**
  - o ***Goods*** : No tax will be imposed on items like Jute, fresh meat, fish chicken, eggs, milk, butter milk, curd, natural honey, fresh fruits and vegetables, flour, besan, bread, prasad, salt, bindi. Sindoor, stamps, judicial papers, printed books, newspapers, bangles, handloom, Bones and horn cores, bone grist, bone meal, etc.; hoof meal, horn meal, Cereal grains hulled, Palmyra jaggery, Salt - all types, Kajal, Children's' picture, drawing or colouring books, Human hair
  - o ***Services*** : Hotels and lodges with tariff below Rs 1,000, Grandfathering service has been exempted under GST. Rough precious and semi-precious stones will attract GST rate of 0.25 per cent
- **5%**
  - o ***Goods*** : Items such as fish fillet, Apparel below Rs 1000, packaged food items, footwear below Rs 500, cream, skimmed milk powder, branded paneer, frozen vegetables, coffee, tea, spices, pizza bread, rusk, sabudana, kerosene, coal, medicines, stent, lifeboats, Cashew nut, Cashew nut in shell, Raisin, Ice and snow, Bio gas, Insulin, Agarbatti, Kites, Postage or revenue stamps, stamp-post marks, first-day covers
  - o ***Services*** : Transport services (Railways, air transport), small

restraurants will be under the 5% category because their main input is petroleum, which is outside GST ambit.

- **12%**
  - *Goods* : Apparel above Rs 1000, frozen meat products, butter, cheese, ghee, dry fruits in packaged form, animal fat, sausage, fruit juices, Bhutia, namkeen, Ayurvedic medicines, tooth powder, agarbatti, colouring books, picture books, umbrella, sewing machine, cellphones, Ketchup & Sauces, All diagnostic kits and reagents, Exercise books and note books, Spoons, forks, ladles, skimmers, cake servers, fish knives, tongs, Spectacles. corrective, Playing cards, chess board, carom board and other board games, like ludo,
  - ***Services*** : State-run lotteries, Non-AC hotels, business class air ticket, fertilisers, Work Contracts
- **18%**
  - ***Goods*** *:* Footwear costing more than Rs 500, Trademarks, goodwill, software, Bidi Patta, Biscuits (All catogories), flavoured refined sugar, pasta, cornflakes, pastries and cakes, preserved vegetables, jams, sauces, soups, ice cream, instant food mixes, mineral water, tissues, envelopes, tampons, note books, steel products, printed circuits, camera, speakers and monitors, Kajal pencil sticks, Headgear and parts thereof, Aluminium foil, Weighing Machinery [other than electric or electronic weighing machinery], Printers [other than multifunction printers], Electrical Transformer, CCTV, Optical Fiber, Bamboo furniture, Swimming pools and padding pools, Curry paste; mayonnaise and salad dressings; mixed condiments and mixed seasonings
  - ***Services*** *:* AC hotels that serve liquor, telecom services, IT services, branded garments and financial services, Room tariffs between Rs 2,500 and Rs 7,500, Restaurants inside five-star hotels.
- **28%**
  - ***Goods*** *:* Bidis, chewing gum, molasses, chocolate not containing cocoa, waffles and wafers coated with choclate, pan masala, aerated water, paint, deodorants, shaving creams, after shave, hair shampoo, dye, sunscreen, wallpaper, ceramic tiles, water heater, dishwasher, weighing machine, washing machine, ATM, vending machines, vacuum cleaner, shavers, hair clippers, automobiles, motorcycles, aircraft for personal use.
  - ***Services*** *:* Private-run lotteries authorised by the states, hotels with room tariffs above Rs 7,500, 5-star hotels, race club betting, cinema.

Supply of Goods & Services

03-1-05

01 Supply

The taxable event under GST is supply of goods and services. The term 'supply' includes all forms of supply, such as sale, transfer, barter, exchange, license, rental, lease or disposal made in the course of business, and importation of service.

- Transactions between principal and agents are deemed to be supplies.
- 'Supply' also includes specified transactions such as permanent transfer of business assets, temporary application of business assets to a non-business use, services put to non-business use, assets retained after deregistration, and supply by a taxable person to another taxable or non-taxable person in the course of business.
- Sale of under construction properties, temporary transfer of intellectual property rights, works contracts (including transfer of property in goods involved in execution of works contracts), transfer of right to use any goods and development, upgradation, customisation etc., of software would be supply of service.

However, supply of goods to a job worker would not be treated as supply.

Illustrations

Type of Transaction	Nature of Supply
Any transfer of the title in goods (e.g Sale of Refrigerator)	Supply of Goods
Any transfer of goods without transfer of title (Renting of Refrigerator)	Supply of Services
Any transfer of title of goods where property in goods is pass at a future date upon payment of full consideration as agreed (Hire Purchase)	Supply of Goods
Any lease, easement, tenancy, and licence to occupy land	Supply of Services
Any lease or letting out of the building including a commercial, industrial or residential complex for business or commerce, wholly or partly	Supply of Services

Job work – Any treatment or process which is being applied to another person's goods	Supply of Services
Permanent transfer or disposal of business assets transferred with or without consideration	Supply of Goods
Business assets put to private use or non- business use whether or not for a consideration	Supply of Services
Renting of immovable property	Supply of Services
Development, design, programming, customisation, adaptation, up-gradation, enhancement, implementation of information technology software	Supply of Services
Works contract, including transfer of property in goods (whether as goods or in some other form) involved in the execution of a works contract of immovable property	Supply of Services

02 Place of Supply

The place of supply of goods is the place where the goods are delivered, except in few cases. The place of supply of services to a registered person, is the location of such registered person. For services provided to an unregistered person, it is the address of recipient, and if it is not available, the location of the supplier of services.

- ABC Caterers of Mumbai, Maharashtra, gives catering service to PQR of Ahmedabad. In this case, the place of supply is Ahmedabad, Gujrat. So, it is considered an Inter State supply (IGST applicable).
- ABC Event Management of Mumbai, Maharashtra, organises the Annual Event of PQR Limited of Bangalore, Karnataka, at Jaipur, Rajasthan. The place of supply is Jaipur, Rajasthan. So, it is considered an Inter State supply (IGST applicable).
- ABC Event Management of Mumbai, Maharashtra, organises the Annual Event of PQR Limited of Bangalore, Karnataka, at Pune, Maharashtra. The place of supply is Pune, Maharashtra . So, it is considered an Intra State supply (CGST+SGST applicable).
- ABC Event Management of Mumbai, Maharashtra, organises the Annual Event of PQR Limited of Pune, Maharashtra, at Port Blair, Andaman & Nicobar Islands. The place of supply is Port Blair, Andaman & Nicobar Islands. So, it is considered Inter Union Territory supply (CGST+UTGST applicable).

03 Time of supply

- **Time of supply of goods :** It is the earliest of: (i) date of removal/ making available goods by the supplier; (ii) date of issue of invoice; (iii) date of receipt of payment by the supplier; or (iv) date on which the recipient shows the receipt of goods in his books of accounts.

- **Time of supply of services :** It is the earliest of: (i) date of issue of invoice or date of receipt of payment, if invoice is issued within prescribed period, (ii) date of completion of service or date of receipt of payment, if invoice not issued within the prescribed period, (iii) date on which recipient shows the receipt of services in his books of accounts, where (i) or (ii) above does not apply.
- **Time of supply under reverse charge :** It is the earliest of: (i) date of receipt of supply; (ii) date of payment; (iii) date of receipt of invoice; or (iv) date of debit in the books of accounts.

04 Value of Supply

Transaction Value is the basis to compute the value of supply of goods/ services for levy of GST.

- To determine transaction value, specific additions are prescribed to be made to the price charged, like, value of goods/ services supplied free/ at concessional rates by the recipient to the supplier, subsidies linked to the supply, reimbursable expenditure, etc. In addition, royalties or license fees related to the supply of goods and/ or services are to be added to the value of taxable supplies.
- The discounts, including the post-sale discounts known at the time of supply (and linked to specific invoices), are allowed as deduction from transaction value.

Computation of Taxable value

- **Sale Value** : GST is charged on sale value, irrespective of MRP value.

  X supplies Y some genuine Maruti auto parts @ Rs 2000, whose MRP value is Rs 2800. X would charge GST on Rs 2000 at the prevailing rate.
- **Incidental charges** : Incidental charges like delivery, packing charges etc, included in the bill would be chargeable to GST.

  X supplies some glassware costing Rs 12,000, and charges Rs 1000 for wooden packing boxes and Rs 500 for delivery charges. X would charge GST on 12000+1000+500=13500, at prevailing GST rate on glassware.
- **Discount** : Discount allowed in the bill, or known at the time of sale / purchase would be allowed. But discount allowed later conditionally, not known at the time of trade, would not be allowed.

  X sold goods to Y for Rs. 10000, and allowed trade discount @ 1% in the bill. X also agreed to allow another 1% cash discount on the due amount if the payment is made through net banking within 7 days. In this case, X would charge GST on 10000 -100 (1% on 10000) = on 9900. Though the cash was committed and made known at the time of deal,

X would not give any GST benefit on additional cash discount, as it was conditional on timely payment through net banking.

- **Exchange of Goods** : In case of transaction, involving exchange of goods (or service), in part, or in whole, GST would be charged on the value of goods (or services) exchanged also.

  X supplied an Air Conditioner to Y, at Rs. 20,000 after taking back his old AC. Now GST would be charged on Rs. 20000 + value of old AC taken back (as old AC taken is also a part of price taken for supply of new AC).

  The value of old AC be computed on following rules:

  - o Open Market Value of such supply.
  - o If the open market value is not available, the sum total of consideration in money and the monetary value of consideration not in money, if such monetary value is known at the time of supply.
  - o If the value cannot be determined by applying above rules, the value of supply of goods or/and services of like kind and quality will be considered.

  In this case, GST would be valued on the normal sale value of similar AC, where no old AC is taken back, or if the value of old returned AC can be determined fairly (e.g. Rs 2000), then its value would be added to the met cash price received (i.e on 20000+2000=22000).

- **Unpriced goods** : XYZ offered a new model of phone 'Alisa' before pre launch (price not yet fixed) to its first customer of its VEEVA model of Phone costing Rs 29000, on the launch day. As price of Alisa was not known (as its price was not fixed yet), the price of a phone similar in feature of Alisa (e.g 4000) would be added to the price of VEEVA. GST would be charged on Rs.29000+4000=Rs.33000 at the prevailing GST rate.

Types of Invoices

- **Tax invoice** : Tax invoice is to be issued by a registered taxable person for the supply of taxable goods or services.
- **Bill of Supply** : Bill of Supply is to be issued by a Registered Taxable Person for the supply of exempted goods or services, and for supplies by a Composition Tax Payer.

05 Advance Payments Received

- **Buyer Paying Advance** : If anyone paid advance before the supply of goods or services will have to pay GST on it.

  Ex:. Buyer gives order for buying goods amounting to Rs. 5 Lakhs and gave advance of Rs. 1 Lakhs, then he have to pay GST on that advance of 1 Lakh.

- **Supplier Receiving Advance** :
  - o **Receipt Voucher** : At the time of receiving advance, supplier will issue a Receipt voucher. The receipt voucher should contain Name of supplier, address, GST number, unique alphanumeric receipt voucher number of less than 16 characters, date of issue, name of the person who gave advance, his address, GST number, description of goods or services, amount of advance, rate of GST, amount of GST, and signature of supplier.
  - o **Tax Invoice** : Supplier will prepare a tax invoice after supplying of goods or services and deduct the amount of advance received from it and will charge GST on remaining amount.

    Ex. If a supplier supplied stationery of Rs. 10 Lakhs and he already received an advance of Rs. 5 Lakhs before 3 months then he have to charge GST on remaining amount of Rs. 5 Lakhs in the tax invoice. He should mention the information about Advance already received in tax invoice.
  - o **GST Return** : At the time of filing of GST return the details of such receipts are to be mentioned in the return also.
- **Input Credit** : After giving the advances to the supplier, the buyer will get the Input credit, only after supplier supplies goods or services and gives the tax invoice to the receiver.

  Ex. "A" gives Rs. 10 Lakhs as advance on 5th July to "B" for buying machinery of Rs. 15 Lakhs He is to pay Rs. 1 Lakh on it as GST @10%. Later on, "B" supplies the Machinery and issues Tax invoice for goods value Rs. 15 Lakhs, charging GST 50,000 (@10% on balance of Rs 5,00,000). "A" will get input credit of Rs. 1.5 Lakh on receipt of Tax Invoice.
- **GST rate not determinable** : At the time of taking advances,
  - o If the rate can not be ascertained at the time of taking advances, then GST should be charged @ 18% Ex. If the person gave orders and advances to make a thing. But if the GST rate is not fixed on that, then 18% GST will have to be paid on those advances.
  - o If the type of supply cannot be ascertained while taking advance, consider this supply as interstate supply. E.g. The place of manufacturing in two different states but if the state is not confirm from where supply will be made at the time of taking advance, then it should considered as inter-state supply.
- **Impact of Advance payment**
  - o **Buyer** : Before buying goods or services, the buyer will have to pay GST on the advance amount and he will receive the credit at the time of supply of goods or services. The money will be blocked for this until the supply is completed.

- o **Supplier** : The supplier will have to charge GST on the remaining amount by deducting advance from the total amount.

Every business (big or small) will have to keep special track for the accounting in place of even for small amount to comply with the law.

06 Transportation of goods without issue of invoice

In following cases, goods may be transported without issue of an invoice:

- Supply of liquid gas, where the quantity at the time of removal from the place of business of the supplier is not known.
- Transportation of goods for job work.
- Transportation of goods for reasons other than supply.
- Any other notified supplies.

In these cases, the consigner should issue a *Delivery challan* in place of an invoice at the time of removal of goods for transportation.

The Delivery Challan should contain the details of Goods supplied. It should also contain the details of Tax in case of Supplies. If the exact quantity is not available, the delivery challan should show estimated quantity.

When a delivery challan is issued in place of Tax Invoice, the reference should be made in e-way bill. In case of supply, the corresponding tax invoice should be issued later on.

Delivery Challan / Invoices are printed in 3 copies. Original for Consignee / Buyer, Duplicate for Carrier, Triplicate for Seller / Consignor.

e-Commerce 03-1-06

01 E-Commerce Operator

An *e-commerce operator* is a person who owns, operates or manages digital or electronic facility or platform for electronic commerce.

- **Mandatory registration :** All e-commerce operators are mandatorily required to register under GST, irrespective of their turnover.
- **Tax to be paid by e-commerce operator on notified services :** Certain service categories may be notified, on supply of which, tax shall be paid by the e-commerce operator, and not the supplier. If the e-commerce operator does not have an establishment in a state, any person representing the e-commerce operator for any purpose in the state will be liable to pay the tax (if it does not have a representative in the state, a person must be appointed in the state for the purpose of paying tax, who shall be liable to pay the tax.
- **E-commerce operator has to collect tax at source :** Every e-commerce operator should collect tax @ 2% on the net value of taxable supplies made through their platform, where the consideration, with respect to such supplies, has to be collected by the operator.

  Net value of taxable supplies = Value of taxable supplies made by all registered taxable persons through the operator, other than notified supplies on which tax is paid by the operator (-) Value of taxable supplies returned to the suppliers
- **Returns and tax payment process :** An e-commerce operator has to furnish Form GSTR-8 containing details of *outward supplies* made through the platform in the previous month, including supplies returned by 10th of the month,. Form GSTR-8 should contain invoice-wise details of supplies to registered taxable persons and aggregate value of supplies to unregistered persons. The e-commerce operator also has to pay the tax collected from suppliers.

Any discrepancy between supplies reported by the e-commerce operator and suppliers on the platform must be submitted in **Form GST ITC-1 by 21st of the month**. The discrepancy must be rectified in the return for the month in which it is communicated

02 Suppliers on e-commerce platforms

Suppliers on e-commerce platforms are persons who supply goods or services on an e-commerce platform, irrespective of their turnover.

- **Mandatory registration :** All suppliers on e- commerce platforms are mandatorily required to register under GST, Hence, even e-commerce suppliers whose aggregate turnover does not exceed the threshold limit for registration will have to compulsorily register.
- **Non-eligibility for Composition Scheme :** A person who supplies goods or services through an e-commerce operator will not be eligible for registration under composition Scheme. Hence, even if the person's aggregate turnover does not cross the threshold limit (of Rs. 50 Lakhs), such person does not have the option to become a composition tax payer
- **Returns process :** A supplier on an e-commerce platform, must follow. In addition, following are the details to be provided with respect to supplies through e-commerce platforms :
  - **Form GSTR-1** containing details of *outward supplies* made through e-commerce platforms, by **10th of the month**, containing invoice-wise details of supplies to registered taxable persons and aggregate value of supplies to unregistered persons made through the e-commerce platform, during the previous month.
  - **Form GSTR-2A** showing the figures of aggregate amount of tax collected by e-commerce operators in the previous month will be auto populated, based on Form GSTR-8 filed by the e-commerce operators, by 11th of the month.
  - The supplier has to furnish Form GSTR-2, by 15th of a month, in which the details of tax collected by the e-commerce operator can be accepted or modified. The tax collected will be credited to the supplier's electronic cash ledger on provisional basis, which can be set-off against the tax liability.

Form GST ITC-1 is made available to a supplier by 21st of a month. Any discrepancy in supplies furnished with supplies reported by the e-commerce operator will be shown. The discrepancy must be rectified in the return for the month in which it is communicated. If not rectified and the value of supplies furnished by the operator is more than the value furnished by the supplier, the differential amount along with interest will be added to the tax liability of the supplier for the succeeding month.

Input Tax Credit 03-1-07

01 Input Tax Credit Claim

The GST law provides for credit of GST paid on all the inputs, barring some exceptions, like services received and used by employees and also vehicles (except when they are used for specified purposes), supplies received for execution of works contract for construction of immovable property. Supplies used for personal consumption are ineligible for credit.

The following procedural conditions also need to be fulfilled for claiming credit:

- Possession of tax invoice;
- Receipt of the underlying supply of goods/ service;
- Payment of tax charged in invoice by supplier;
- Filing of GST return

The credits claimed need to be matched with the tax liability of the supplier. In case of any discrepancies, the amount of excess credit claimed will be added in the tax liability of the recipient. The time limit for claim of credit is one year from the date of the invoice.

02 Input Tax credit on stock held

Dealers can avail Input Tax credit held in your closing stock if : the closing stock is held either in the form of raw materials, semi-finished goods, or finished goods, and must be used or intended to be used for taxable supplies, the date of invoices or any other prescribed duty / tax paying documents is within 12 months from the date of transitioning, and the supplier of services is not eligible for any abatement under the act, the benefit of such credit must be passed on, by way of reduced prices, to the recipient.

03 Reverse charge

Reverse charge means the liability to pay tax is by the recipient of goods/ services instead of the supplier. Reverse charge may be applicable on specified categories of Goods & Services as notified by government.

04 Set off of Credits

- CGST to be set-off against CGST and IGST,
- SGST against SGST and IGST
- IGST against IGST, CGST and SGST (in that order)

However, CGST credit will not be allowed to be set-off against SGST and vice versa.

05 Receipt of Advance Payments for Supply

Liability for payment of GST would arise at the *Time of Supply* of goods and service. As per definition of the term supply, Receipt of *Advance Payments for Supply* of goods and/or services would be considered as 'time of supply' and tax liability would arise on such advance receipt. Even through GST would be paid on advance payments, credit for the same would be available only on receipt of goods and services.

Payment of Tax 03-1-08

01 GST Payment Liability

Every registered regular tax payer must furnish GST returns on monthly basis and pay the tax due by the 20th of the month. Delay Interest on the tax due will be applicable for delayed payment of Tax, from the day on which the tax was due to be paid.

Any monthly return submitted by dealer, without paying tax due, will be considered Invalid. Monthly Return cannot be submitted before submitting the previous month's return & Tax payment. So, tax liabilities under GST must cleared to avoid the penalties of non-payment of tax.

02 GST Portal Tax Accounts

Every registered dealer will have following ledgers in GST portal:

- **Electronic tax liability register :** All liabilities of a person towards tax, interest, penalty, late fee or any other amount will be debited here.
- **Electronic cash ledger :** Every deposit made by a person towards tax, interest, penalty, late fee or any other amount will be credited here.
- **Electronic credit ledger :** Input tax credit, as self-assessed and claimed in Form GSTR-2 by a person, will be credited here. This can only be used by a person for paying tax, but not for other amounts such as interest, late fee, and so on.

To pay the liabilities shown in the Electronic tax liability register, a person can use the balance in the Electronic cash ledger and Electronic credit ledger.

Accounting entries in GST portal Tax Accounts

The Electronic credit ledger will be debited by credit used for making the payment. the Electronic cash ledger will be debited by the amount deposited, and the Electronic tax liability register will be credited by the corresponding amount.

Example : the tax liability was Rs 1,00,000 in Electronic tax liability register, Input Tax credit balance was Rs 20,000 in Electronic credit ledger. Rs 80,000 is deposited in Electronic cash ledger. On deposit of Rs 80,000, the amount would be adjusted against liability of Rs 1,00,000 in Electronic tax liability register, and the balance of Rs 20,000 input Tax credit would be adjusted in Electronic credit ledger. Now all the 3 accounts would be adjusted showing NIL balance.

Set off of Tax Liability : However, set off of Input Tax credit can be made as per set off rules for each component of GST (IGST, CGST & SGST / UTGST) as explained under set off of Tax Liability.

03 GST Payment Modes

Dealers may pay tax in 3 modes of payment: a) Payment by taxpayers through Internet Banking (Retail Internet Banking and Corporate internet Banking) through authorized banks. b) Payment by taxpayers through credit card/debit card; c) Over the Counter payment (OTC) through authorized banks; (for payments up to Rs. 10,000/- per challan only.) d) Payment through NEFT/ RTGS .

Through debit in the credit ledger, only Tax can be paid by (Interest, Penalty and Fees cannot be paid)

04 Tax Payment Process

- **Generate Tax Challans** : Challan for the payment can be generated from the GST portal using Form GST PMT-06, entering respective details of tax, interest, penalty, fees & other amount, if any. The challan generated will be valid for 15 days.
- **Payment Modes** : Having generated the Challan, the payment with reference to the challan can be made through various payment modes, through authorised Bank:
  - o Internet Banking through the customer's Net banking facility
  - o Bank Debit / Credit Cards
  - o NEFT or ITGS (by generating a mandate, valid for 15 days)
  - o OTC (over the Counter) of the authorised Bank (for payment upto Rs 10000 per challan), by Cash, Cheque, DD etc
  - o CIN / Credit in Electronic Cash Register : Upon credit of the Tax deposited in bank, to the Government account by the Bank, a CIN (Challan Identification Number) would be generated, posted in GST portal, and credited to Electronic cash ledger account of tax payer.

Generation of CPIN

- The challan so generated will have a 14-digit (yymm followed by 10-digit) Unique Common Portal Identification Number (CPIN), assigned only when the challan is finally generated. After the challan is generated, it will be frozen and will not be allowed to be modified.
- The CPIN/challan so generated would be valid for a period of seven days. In case of payment through NEFT/RTGS, CPINs would remain live with RBI for a period of 30 days. GSTN would purge all unused CPINs on the day immediately after the date on which the validity period is over (i.e. 7 days if CC/DC and OTC payment is selected and 30 days if NEFT/ RTGS is selected for payment)

- After the successful completion of a transaction, the concerned bank will create a 17-digit CPIN generated by GSTN for the challan (14-digit number & and 3-digit Bank code)

05 Forms related to GST Payment

The GST forma related to Payment have prefix GST-PMT and numbered from 01 to 07, as below:

- **GST-PMT-01 :** Electronic Tax liability
- **GST-PMT-02 :** Electronic credit ledger
- **GST-PMT-03 :** Rejection of claim for refund in Electronic credit / Electronic cash ledger,
- **GST-PMT-04 :** Discrepancy in Electronic credit ledger
- **GST-PMT-05 :** Electronic Cash Ledger
- **GST-PMT-06 :** Payment Challan
- **GST-PMT-07 :** CIN not generated / not posted in GST Portal

Data Upload & Returns 03-1-09

01 Transaction Data Upload

Under GST, every assessee would have to upload invoice level outward supply details for B2B transactions (between registered assesses under GST). Details of inward supplies and tax credit would be auto-populated based on sales details uploaded by the vendor.

02 Filing of Returns

A person who has not opted for composition, is required to file returns, separately for outward supplies made, inward supplies received. In addition to these returns, separate returns are required to be filed by input service distributors and by a person deducting tax at source. An annual return is also required to be filed.

03 Audit of Accounts

The taxpayers having turnover exceeding the prescribed limit will also be required to get their accounts audited by a Chartered / Cost Accountant

- **Submission of Audited Annual Accounts** : They should submit a copy of the audited annual accounts with the annual return
- **Reconciliation Statement** : They would submit a reconciliation statement, reconciling the value of supplies declared in the return furnished for the year with the audited annual financial statement, and any other documents as may be prescribed.

04 Due Dates of Filing of Returns

Return Form	Description	Due Date
GSTR1	Outward supplies made by taxpayer (other than compounding taxpayer and ISD)	10th of next month
GSTR2	Inward supplies received by a taxpayer (other than a compounding taxpayer and ISD)	15th of next month
GSTR3	Monthly return (other than compounding taxpayer and ISD)	20th of next month
GSTR4	Quarterly return for compounding Taxpayer	18th of next month

GSTR5	Periodic return by Non-Resident Foreign Taxpayer	Lat day of Registration
GSTR6	Return for Input Service Distributor (ISD)	13th of next month
GSTR7	Return for Tax Deducted at Source	10th of next month
GSTR8	Annual Return	31st December of next financial year

Most of the returns are auto generated by the GSTN system and the dealer is expected to validate the data (and fill missing data, if any).

If a taxpayer submits a Return without paying the tax liability is paid in full, the return is considered invalid. A taxable person who has not furnished a valid return shall not be allowed to utilize such credit till he discharges his tax liability.

Assessment

03-1-10

01 Modes of Assessment

GST rules provides for various modes of Assessment. It is important for a taxable person to be aware of the different types of assessment under GST and adhere to the compliance requirements. In a case where an assessment is initiated by the tax authorities, a dealer must ensure to furnish the information asked for by the time given. Businesses must make use of the facilities of compliance and technology to remain compliant under GST.

02 Self Assessment

Every registered taxable person must assess the tax payable by himself/herself and furnish the relevant return for each tax period. Self-assessment is most important for every registered person. It is important to furnish accurate information and pay tax due on a timely basis, as per the due dates laid down. Self-assessment done appropriately ensures that assessment is not initiated by the tax authorities

03 Assessment by the Tax Authorities

In following cases, assessment may be initiated by the tax authorities :

- **Provisional Assessment :** If a taxable person is unable to determine the value of goods and/or services or determine the rate of tax applicable, the person can request an officer to allow payment of the tax on a provisional basis (submitting a Bond to pay the difference in tax, if any). The officer will pass an order allowing the person to pay the tax on a provisional basis. Within **6 months** from the date of the provisional assessment order, the officer must pass the final assessment order.
- **Scrutiny Assessment :** Under scrutiny assessment, an officer can examine the return and other information furnished by a person, to verify the correctness of the return. If any discrepancy is noticed, the officer will inform the person and seek his explanation. If the explanation is satisfactory, no further action will be taken. In case no satisfactory explanation is given within **30 days** of being informed or if the person does not make corrections in the return after accepting the discrepancies, the officer will initiate appropriate action.
- **Best Judgement Assessment :** In following circumstances, an officer may assess the tax liability of a person to the best of his/her judgement.
    - o **Assessment of non-filers of returns**– If a person fails to furnish a return, even after a notice is served to the person, an officer will

assess the tax liability of the person to the best of his judgement, on the basis of all relevant material available to him.

- o **Assessment of unregistered persons**– If a taxable person fails to obtain registration even though he/she is liable to do so, an officer will assess the tax liability of the person to the best of his judgement for the relevant tax periods, and issue an assessment order

- **Summary Assessment :** In certain special cases, an officer may, on finding any evidence showing tax liability of a person, with the permission of the Additional/Joint Commissioner, assess the tax liability of the person to protect the interest of revenue, and issue an assessment order

Export / Import 03-1-11

01 Treatment of Export / Import in GST

Under GST, importer of goods has to pay customs duty and IGST. IGST will be levied at the rate applicable to the imported goods in India. Importer can claim full tax credit of IGST paid on imports. However, no tax credit will be given on customs duty paid and it remains a cost for the importer under GST.

- **Import of Services :** Under GST, a supply will be considered as an import of service by a service recipient located in India, for service received at India, from a supplier of service located outside India.
- **Export of Goods :** Under GST, exports will be zero rated. An exporter can also claim refund of the tax paid on inputs used to manufacture/ purchase/provide the exported goods or services.
- **Export of Services :** For Services delivered from a supplier located in India, to a service receiver located outside India, for services received outside India, for which Payment is received in convertible foreign exchange, the GST rate is zero, provided the supplier & receiver of service are not related to same entity.

02 Refund of Input Tax Credit in Case of Export of Goods

In case of zero rated exports (including Deemed Exports), made without payment of tax, refund of input tax credit will be available subject to fulfilment of certain conditions :

- No refund of unitized input tax credit shall be allowed in cases other than exports including zero rated supplies or in cases where the credit has accumulated on account of rate tax on inputs being higher than the rate of tax on output supplies, other than nil rated or fully exempt supplies.
- No refund of unutilized input tax credit shall be allowed in cases where the goods exported out of India are subjected to export duty.
- No refund of input tax credit shall be allowed if the supplier of goods or services avails duty drawback of CGST / SGST / UTGST or claims refund of IGST paid on such supplies.

03 Instances of Supplies Outside India Not Constituting Export

- Supply of service to a person located outside India where place of supply of service is in India. For example, a property rented out in Mumbai to a person residing in Dubai; agent located in India providing service to a New York based exporter for selling goods to China.

- Supply of services where consideration is received in Indian currency or a currency other than convertible currency. For example supply of consultancy service by an Indian consulting firm to an overseas entity, payment for which is made in Indian rupees by Indian branch of overseas entity.
- Services provided to overseas branch would not be eligible as export of services.

Input Service Distributors 03-1-12

01 Centralised Billing

Many large companies have centralized Business Head Office (HO) & Branches (BO) spread over many places (in same or in different States). Such organisation may have centralized billing at HO, for procurement, for better control. So, the input credits are accumulated at central place, utilized by Branches.

02 Distribution of Input Credit

Under GST Rules, Input Service Distributor is an Office of supplier of goods / services, which has received *inputs (goods / services) under the cover of tax invoice, and is allowed to distribute the said tax credit to the supplier of goods and/or services registered under the same PAN'.*

03 Input Service Distributors

As per GST, ISD is an office (like head office, administrative office, corporate office, regional office, depot) belonging to registered taxable person who intends to distribute the credit.

- It receives tax towards the receipt of inward supply of services
- It distributes the tax credit paid of inward supplies of services to the branch units which have consumed the services, and issues invoices for the distribution of credit

04 Registration of ISD under GST

An ISD is must obtain a separate registration, irrespective of turnover. Businesses who are already registered as an ISD under the existing regime (i.e. under Service Tax), will be required obtain a new ISD registration under GST (as existing ISD registration will not be migrated to the GST regime).

05 Mode of Distribution

In intrastate transaction, CGST and SGST will be applicable. In transaction within a union territory, CGST and UTGST will be applicable. In interstate transactions and imports, IGST will be applicable.

The unit to which the input tax credit is distributed is referred to as the 'recipient of credit'.

- **ISD and recipient of credit are located in the same state**

  When the ISD and recipient of credit are located in the same state/ union territory, the input tax credit of IGST, CGST, SGST, and UTGST should be distributed to the recipient in same category. This means that IGST with ISD would be distributed to IGST of Recipient, CGST with ISD would be distributed to CGST of Recipient, SGST with ISD would be distributed to SGST of Recipient, UTGST with ISD would be distributed to UTGST of Recipient.

- **ISD and recipient of credit are located in different state**

  When the ISD and recipient of credit are located in different state/union territory, the input tax credit of IGST, CGST, SGST, and UTGST should be distributed to the IGST of recipient. This means that IGST, CGST, SGST & UTGST with ISD would be distributed to only IGST of Recipient

06 Return Forms for ISD

- **Form GSTR-6A** : This monthly return showing the Details of inward supplies made available to the ISD recipient, on the basis of FORM GSTR-1 furnished by the supplier, should be submitted by 11th of the next month.
- **Form GSTR-6 :** Monthly Return showing the details of Input Credit distributed should be submitted by 13th of the next month

07 Conditions for distribution of input tax credit by an ISD

- An ISD invoice is issued only for distribution of input tax credit, by the distributor to the unit to which the input tax credit is distributed (referred as the 'Recipient of credit'), contain following details;
  - o Name, address, and GSTIN of the Input Service Distributor
  - o A consecutive unique serial number (only alphabets and/or numerals), for a financial year
  - o Date of its issue
  - o Name, address, and GSTIN of the supplier of services for which credit being distributed, serial number and date of invoice issued by such supplier.
  - o Name, address, and GSTIN of the recipient to whom the credit is being distributed
  - o The amount of credit distributed
  - o Signature or digital signature of the supplier or his authorized representative
- The amount of credit distributed shall not exceed the amount of credit available for distribution.
- The input tax credit available for distribution in a month shall be distributed in the same month, and the details of the same shall be furnished in Form GSTR -6.

08 Addition / Reduction in Input Credit

- **Supplementary Input Credit** : Any additional amount of input tax credit on account of issuance of a 'debit note' by a supplier to the ISD shall be apportioned to each recipient in the same ratio in which the input tax credit contained in the original invoice was distributed.
- **Reduction in Input Credit** In case the input tax credit already distributed gets reduced for any reason, an ISD credit note should be issued for the reduction of credit. The following details have to be captured in the ISD credit note :
  - o Name, address, and GSTIN of the ISD
  - o A consecutive SL.No containing alphabets or numerals or special characters such as hyphen or dash or slash, symbolized as, "-" "/" respectively, and any combination thereof, unique for a financial year
  - o Date of its issue
  - o Name, address, and GSTIN of the recipient to whom the credit is distributed
  - o The amount of credit distributed, and
  - o The signature or digital signature of the ISD or his authorized representative

  Apportionment of reduction amount :
  - o Reduced from the amount to be distributed in the month in which the credit note is included in the return in FORM GSTR – 6 and
  - o Added to the output tax liability of the recipient, in case the amount so apportioned is negative.

09 Method of input tax distribution

- **Distribution to Single Receiver** : The input tax credit should be distributed only to that branch which has consumed the input services.

  Example : ABC Ltd, located in Bangalore, Karnataka, have branches in Mysore (Karnataka), Chennai (Tamil Nadu), and Mumbai (Maharashtra). The unit in Bangalore is the Head office and they procure common services in bulk which are used by the other branches too.

  ABC Ltd receives an input invoice of Rs.1,00,000 + GST of Rs.18,000 towards services provided exclusively to the Mysore branch. The total credit of Rs. 18,000 will be distributed only to the Mysore branch.
- **Distribution to Multiple Receiver** The credit of tax paid on input services, availed by more than one recipient of credit or all, should be distributed only amongst such recipients or all recipients.

The distribution shall be on pro rata basis based on the turnover for the previous year of such recipients. In the absence of turnover in previous financial year, the turnover of the last quarter of the month in which ITC is distributed, will be considered

Example :

- Amount of credit to be distributed : Rs.90,000
- Aggregate turnover of Mysore unit in previous financial year (PY) : Rs.60 Lakhs
- Aggregate turnover of Chennai unit in previous financial year (PY) : Rs.90 Lakhs
- Aggregate turnover of all recipients of credit : Rs.150 Lakhs

The credit of Rs.90,000 will be distributed in the following manner :

- Mysore : (60,00,000 / 1,50,00,000) x 90,000 =36,000
- Chennai : (90,00,000 / 1,50,00,000) x 90,000 = 54,000

Electronic Way Bill

03-1-13

01 e-Way bill

e-Way bill (Electronic Way Bill). is a unique bill number generated for the specific consignment for movement of goods. Under GST, a registered person who intends to initiate a movement of goods of value exceeding Rs 50,000 should generate an e-Way bill.

When an eway bill is generated, a unique e-way bill number (EBN) is allocated and is available to supplier, recipient, and the transporter.

- **Applicability** : It is applicable for any consignment of value exceeding Rs.50,000 (even in case of inwards bill from unregistered person). Generation of e-way Bill for consignment of lower value is optional.
- **Time of Generation of e-way bill** : The e-way bill is to be generated before the commencement of movement of goods. A unique e-way bill number (EBN) will be allotted for each e-way bill.
- **Forms** : GST INS-01 is used as e-way bill form. Part-A contains details of the goods, and Part-B contains details of transporter.

02 Persons responsible for generation of e-way Bill

- When goods are transported by registered person, either acting as a consignee or consignor in his own (or hired) vehicle, the supplier or recipient of the goods should generate the e-way Bill, by filling Part A of GST-INS-1. If the consignor does not generate the e-way bill, the transporter must generate the e-way bill based on info submitted in the related documents submitted (like Invoice / Delivery Note etc), by filling B of GST-INS-1.
- When the goods are handed over to a transporter, the e-way bill should be generated by the transporter (if the consignor does not generate the e-way Bill, by filling GST-INS-1) In this case, the registered person should declare the details of the goods in a common portal.
- In case of inward supplies from an unregistered person, either the recipient of supply or the transporter should generate the e-way bill.

A registered person may submit a tax invoice in Form GST INV-1 on the common portal. If a registered person has uploaded the invoice, information in Part A of Form GST INS-1 is auto populated from GST INV-1. Information in Part A of Form GST INS-01 is used for preparing GSTR-1.

03 Salient Features of e-way Bill

- **Multiple Consignments** : The transporter should generate a consolidated e-way bill in the Form GST INS 02 and separately indicate the serial number of e-way bills for each of the consignment.
- **Transfer of goods from one vehicle to another** : Before transferring the goods to another vehicle and making any further movement of such goods, a transporter should generate new e-way bill in Form GST INS 01 by specifying the details of the mode of transport.
- **Acceptance of Goods by Recipient** : The recipient of goods (registered person) should communicate acceptance or rejection of the consignment covered by the e-way bill within 72 hours of the details being made available. If the recipient of goods does not communicate acceptance or rejection within 72 hours, it will be deemed as accepted by the recipient.
- **Validity of e-way bill** : The validity of e-way bill would depend on distance covered, upto 100 km, - 1day, 100-300 km – 3 days, 300-500 km – 5 days, 5-1000 km – 10 days & more than 1000 km-15 days. Validity period of specific goods may be extended by Commissioner, by notification.
- **Cancellation of e-way Bill** : If e-way bill is generated but goods are not transported, the e-way bill may be cancelled. An e-way bill cannot be cancelled after being verified by an office during transit.

04 Administration

- The transporter or the person in charge of a conveyance should carry the copy of Invoice / Bill / Delivery Challan, e-way bill (or the e-way bill number).
- At the place of verification, the officer may intercept any vehicle to physically verify the e-way bill / e-way bill number, for all movement of goods (interstate and intrastate).
- To avoid verification of the physical copy of the e-way bill, RFID (Radio Frequency Identification Device) may be fixed to the vehicle, mapping the e-way to the device. At the place of verification, the e-way bill mapped to this device will be verified through RFID readers. For certain class of transporters, fixing of RFID devices to the vehicle and mapping of e-way bill to device are mandated, as notified by commissioner.
- On the ground of suspicion of tax evasion, a physical verification of the vehicle can be carried out by an officer after obtaining necessary approval from the commissioner (or an officer authorized on his behalf). Once a physical verification of vehicle is done at any place (*within the state or in any other state)*, no further physical verification will be carried out again during the transit, unless specific information of tax evasion is reported subsequently.

- After every inspection, the officer needs to record the details of the inspection of goods in Part- A of Form GST INS-03 within 24 hours of inspection and the final report must be recorded in Part B of Form GST INS 03 within 3 days of inspection. If the vehicle is detained for more than 30 minutes, the transporter may complain by uploading the details in Form GST INS 04.
- With GST, e-way bill becomes the ultimate mode of verification and the functions of numerous check post across the country would be done away with, resulting easier movement of goods.

GST Refund 03-1-14

01 Situations for Refund under GST

The assessee may claim refunds of excess payment / excess credit, in following cases:

- Excess payment of tax due to mistake or inadvertence.
- Export (including deemed export) of goods / services under claim of rebate or Refund of accumulated input credit of duty / tax when goods / services are exported.
- Finalization of provisional assessment.
- Refund of Pre – deposit for filing appeal including refund arising in pursuance of an appellate authority's order (when the appeal is decided in favor of the appellant).
- Payment of duty / tax during investigation but no/ less liability arises at the time of finalization of investigation / adjudication.
- Refund of tax payment on purchases made by Embassies or UN bodies.
- Credit accumulation due to output tax being exempt or nil-rated.
- Credit accumulation due to inverted duty structure i.e. due to tax rate differential between output and inputs.
- Year-end or volume based incentives provided by the supplier through credit notes.
- Tax Refund for International Tourists.

02 Refund Process under GST

Procedures for claiming / processing of refund claimed :

- Application form for claiming refund can be filed through the GSTN portal.
- An acknowledgement number would be shared with applicant via sms or email, once the application is filed electronically.
- Adjustment would be made to return and cash ledger and reduce the "carry-forward input tax credit" automatically.
- Refund application and documents submitted shall be scrutinized within a period of 30 days of filing the refund application.
- Concept of "unjust enrichment" would be examined for reach refund application. If it does not qualify, then the refund would be transferred to CWF(consumer welfare fund).

- If refund claimed exceeds the predetermined amount of refund then it will go through pre-audit process for sanctioning the refund.
- Refund will be credited electronically to the account of applicant via ECS, RTGS or NEFT.
- Application for refund can be made at end of each quarter.
- No refund shall be provided for an amount of less than Rs 1000.

03 Delay in Refund and Interest

As per recommendation of the committee, Refund application must be processed within a period of 90 days, otherwise, interest @6% is recommended.

GST Activation & Set Up 03-2-01

01 GST Set Up

In previous sections we have described the salient aspects of GST rules & compliance.

So far we have explained the operational details of Accounting with Tally, for organizations to which GST is not applicable. Now, we discuss about the exclusive additional points regrading activation, set up, Accounts & Inventory masters, Transaction entries & reports relating to maintenance of GST.

In this part, matters exclusive to GST are explained, without repeating the common points which have already been discussed in earlier chapters.

02 GST Activation for the Company

First, activate GST for each company, to which GST is applicable (i.e organisations registered under GST) rules.

Company Features set up

At gateway, Press *F11:Features* to get Company Features Menu (F-1A). Select *Statutory & Taxation* (or GoT>F11>F3) to get *Statutory & Taxation* screen (F-2A).

Statutory & Taxation Features set up for Company

At *Statutory & Taxation screen* (F-2A), set as follows:

- **GST Activation** : Set Yes at *Enable Goods & Services Tax (GST)* to activate GST
- **GST details entry** : At Set / Alter GST details, set *Yes* to get GST Details entry screen (F-3A)

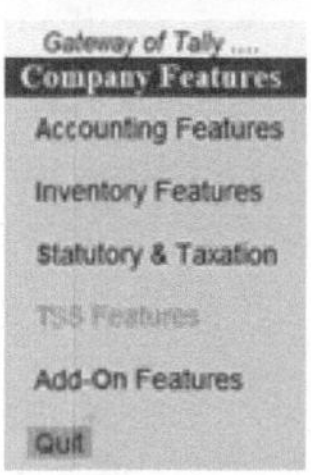

F-1A: Company Features Menu

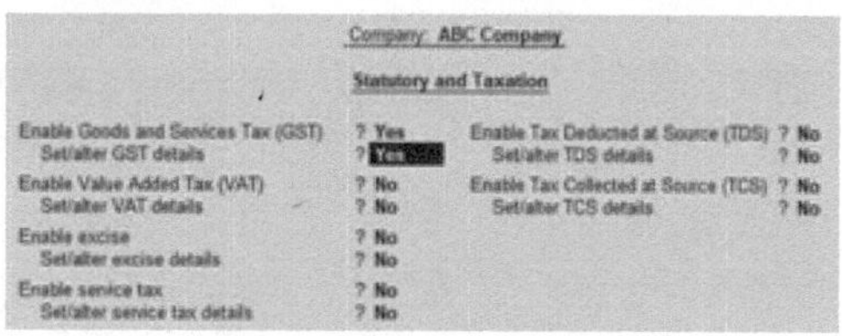

F-2A: GST activation at Statutory & Taxation set up

GST Details entry screen

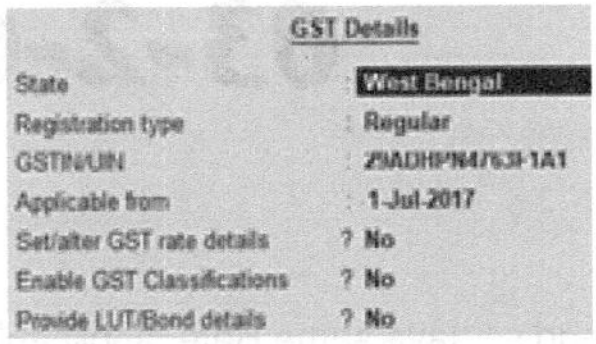

F-3A: GST details entry

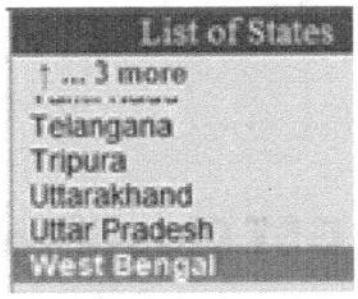

F-3B: List of States

At *GST Details* entry screen (F-3A), enter as follows:

- **State** : The State as selected at Company creation screen appears as default, otherwise select the State / UT, from the *List of States* (F-3B), in which the company is registered with GST (from the list of States and Union Territories).
- **Registration Type** : *Regular* appears by default. You cannot change it.
- **GSTIN/UIN** : Correctly enter the complete 15 digit State /UT GSTIN allotted.
- **Applicable From** : Enter the date of applicability (e.g 1 July 2017).
- **Activate GST rate Details** : At *Set / Alter GST rate Details* set Yes,

  You should set Yes at Activate GST rate details, if only one tax rate is applicable for all the items dealt with by the company. In that case, you may next set the Tax Rate at Company level, which would be applicable for all Items.

  If multiple GST Rates are applicable, then set *No* at this option. You may later on enter the Tax Rates at Stock Item Group or Stock Item. Even if you have single applicable rate, you may set *No* at this option and set the Tax Rate at Item level. That is more flexible.
- **Activate GST Classification** : At *Enable GST Classification* set Yes.

  You may set Yes to create Classification, set GST details at Classification and link Stock Items with Classification, else set No
- **LUT/ Bond details** : At *Provide LUT/ Bond details,* set No. This option is applicable for Importer / Exporter only

Summary

GST Activation : GST Activation for Company.

Company Features set Up : Set up of Statutory info related to GST for Company.

GST Masters 03-2-02

01 GST Classification

Many Items may be of similar nature and so have same Rate applicable (e.g various models and brands of TV. The Stock Items would be different but classification & GST rate would be same. Instead of setting rates and related info for each Item, you may create Item Classification Master and then link the Item with related Classification. The Rates and related details would be carried from the linked Classification, and you need not enter these details at Stock Item.

However, you may enter these details at Stock Item level also. So, create Classification Master if you have large number of Items under various classification, else enter the classification details at Stock Item Master creation.

At gateway of Tally, select Accounts Info>Statutory Info>GST Classification>Create to create GST Classifications (F-1A & F-1B). Now enter as follows:

- **Classification Name** : At *Name*, enter Classification Name. As you have to link specific tax rate for each Classification, create a classification for each applicable rate.
- **Transaction Nature** : At *Nature of Transaction*, select the applicable nature from the list (F-1D)
- **Taxability** : Select the *Taxability* from the list (F-1C). Select Taxable or Nil Rates, as the case may be.
- **GST Rate** : At Integrated Tax, enter the GST rate. Enter zero for Nil Rated classification.

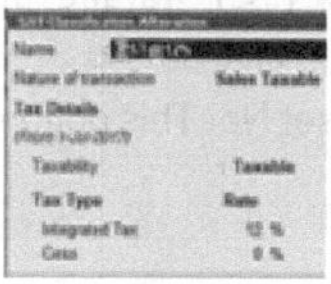

F-1A: GST Classification

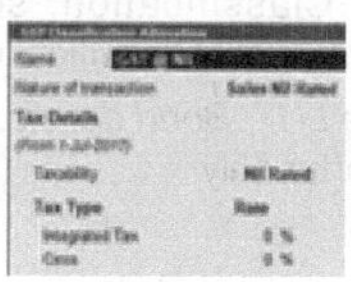

F-1B: GST Classification

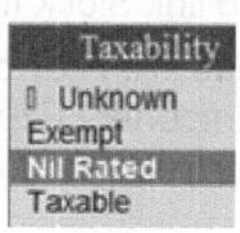

F-1C: Taxability list

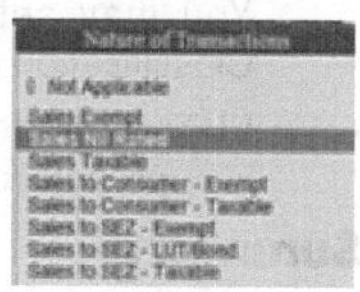

F-1D: Trasnsaction Nature

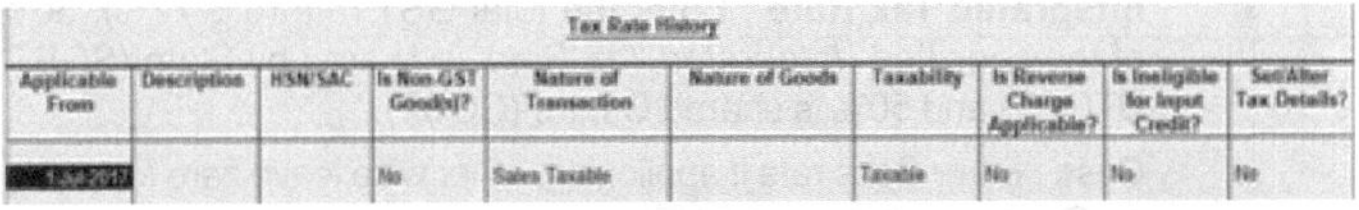

F-2A: Tax Rate History

To view GST Rate History (F-2A), press At+L. click *F12:Configure* to get Configuration screen (F-3A) to set up set up GST Configuration.

At Configuration (F-3A), set Yes at Allow HSN/ SAC details to enter HSN details of the Item

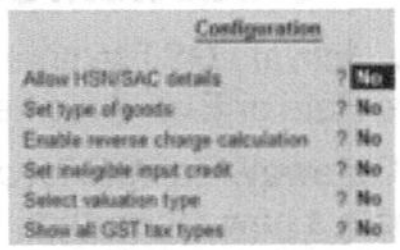

F-3A: GST Configuration

02 Stock Group Set up

If you have grouped your Stock Items as per GST classification (Items of same GST Rates placed under same Stock Group), then you may specify GST Rates at Stock Group, for convenience. The GST Rate would be carried when you create Stock Item under the Stock Group. Otherwise, specify GST Rate for each Stock Item, described next (do not enter GST rates for Stock Group).

To set up GST rates for Stock Groups, at Gateway, select *Accounts Info>Stock Group* and then select *Create* (to create a new Sock Group) or *Alter* (to enter GST Rate details for the Stock Group) to get Stock Group Entry / Alteration screen (F-4A).

F-4A: Stock Group Entry / Alteration

At Group entry / alteration screen (F-4A), at *Set / Alter GST Details*, set Yes to get *GST Details* entry screen, to enter GST Rates for the Stock Group (F-5A).

The Rates entered at Stock Group would be applicable for all Stock Items placed under the Stock Group. So, set Yes at this option if all Stock Items under the Stock Group bear same GST Rate. Otherwise set No.

Stock Group GST Rate entry

At GST Details entry screen (F-5A), enter GST rate for the related Stock Group, as follows:

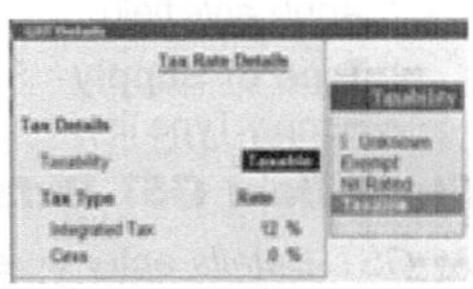

F-5A: Stock Group GST rate Entry

- **Taxability** : Select the GST Taxability as applicable for the Stock Group from the drop down list. Select *Taxable* for Taxable Items (Tax not zero), *Exempt* for Exempted Items, and *Nil Rated* for Zero rated items (Exempt and Zero Rated are different, though no Tax is chargeable for both of them. Be careful!).
- **Tax Rate** : Enter the Tax Rate for Taxable Stock Groups (these fields do not appear for *Nil Rated* and *Exempted* Stock Groups):

- o **Integrated Tax Rate** : Enter the total GST rate (e.g 12%). 50% of the specified *Integrated Tax Rate* is shared by State (SGST/ UTGST) and 50% is shared Centre (CGST).
- o **Cess** : Enter Cess rate if applicable, other wise leave zero (currently no Cess is charged on GST).

03 Stock Item Set Up

Now Activate GST features and enter GS details for each Stock Item (even for Zero Rate or Exempted Items).

At Gateway, select *Accounts Info>Stock Item* and then select *Create* (to Create a new Stock Item) or *Alter* (to enter GST Rate details for existing Stock Item) to get Stock Item Creation / Alteration screen (F-6A).

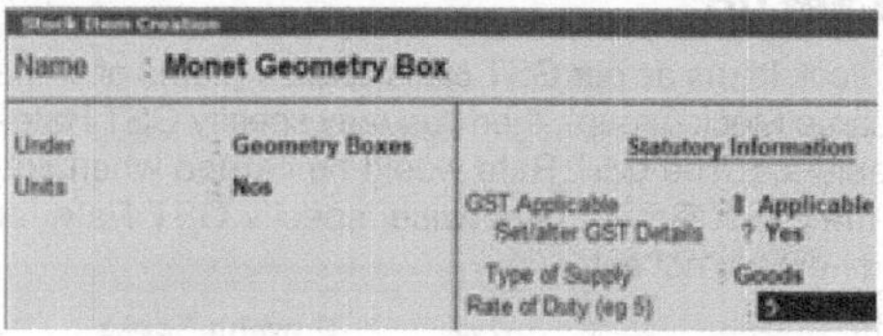

F-6A: Stock Item creation / alteration screen

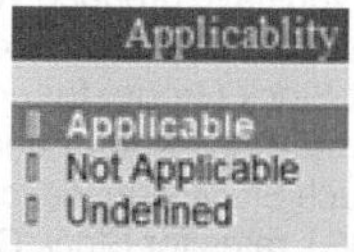

F-6B: GST Applicability List

At *Stock Item Creation / Alteration* screen (F-6A), under *Statutory Information* section, set as follows:

- **GST Applicable** : Select the *Applicability* from the list. Select *Applicable* for Items to which GST is applicable, *Not Applicable* for Non Taxable Items (F-6B).

F-6C: Supply Type List

- **GST Rate Details** : At *Set / Alter GST* details, set *Yes* to get GST Details screen to set up *GST Details* screen to enter GST rate details for the Stock Item (For Items for which you have set *Applicable* at *GST Applicable* field).
- **Type of Supply** : Select Goods / Service (F-6C) as applicable from Supply Type list.

Stock Item GST Rate entry

At *GST Details* entry screen (F-7A), enter the Stock Item GST Rate, as follows:

- **Calculation type :** At Calculation type, select the applicable Type from the list. Normally, GST is applicable on sale value (select *On value*) of the Item
- **Taxability:** Select *Taxability* from the list (F-7B)

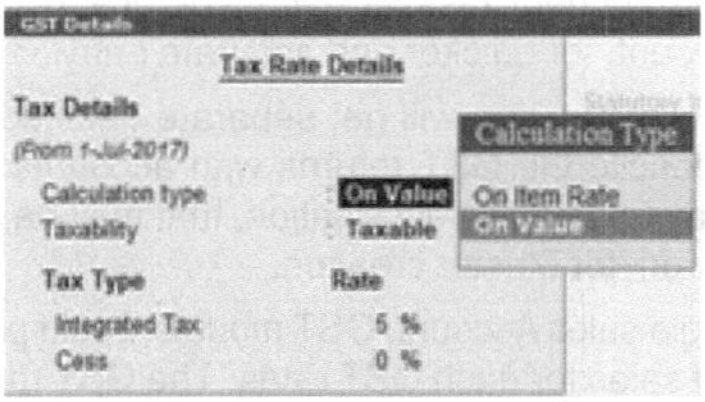

F-7A: Stock Item GST rate details entry

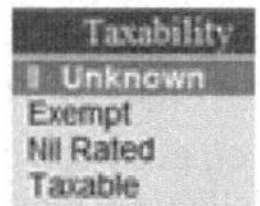

F-7B: Taxability Type List

- **Tax Rate** : As explained for Stock Group, for Taxable Stock Items, enter the Tax Rate for the Stock Item as follows (these fields do not appear for *Nil Rated* and *Exempted* Stock Groups):
    - o **Integrated Tax Rate** : Enter the total GST Rate (e.g 12%). 50% (i.e 6%) is shared by State (SGST/UTGST) and 50% (i.e 6%) is shared by Centre (CGST).
    - o **Cess** : Enter Cess rate if applicable, otherwise leave zero (currently no Cess is charged on GST).

Enter the details of Opening Stock for the Stock Item, as usual.

Other details : At GST details entry screen (F-6A),

- **GST History** : Press *Alt+L* to view History of past changed Tax Rate (F-8A), if any.
- **GST Configuration** : Press *F12:Configure* to set up Configuration details of GST (F-8B)

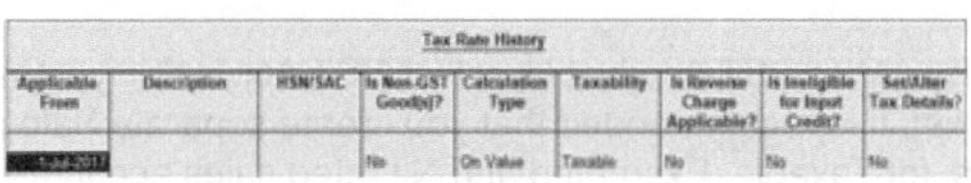

F-8A: GST Rate History List

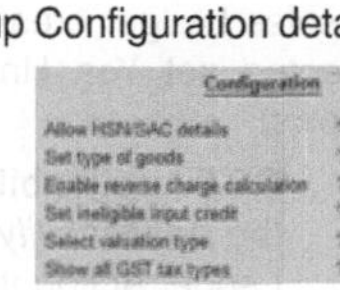

F-8B: GST Configuration

04 GST activation for Sales Ledger Account

Now set up GST details in Sales Ledger, to charge GST in sales Invoice and account for the GST. At Gateway, select Accounts Info > Ledgers. Now select *Create* to get sales Ledger creation screen (F-9A), or select *Alter* and select the Sales ledger to get Sales Ledger Alteration screen (F-9A) .

If multiple GST rates are applicate for various types of goods, it is upto you to create a single sales account, for all the Items, or create separate sales account for each type sales (like Local, Inter State) etc, and also separate Sales Account for each Tax rate for each sales type.

In that case, you should create Voucher Class for each type of sales to pre-set the Sales & Tax Ledger Account, for quicker and accurate entry.

If you create separate sales accounts, you will get separate detailed break up which may be useful to reconcile the GST returns with accounts. If you have large volume with many tax rates and classification, that may be useful, though it requires a little more work for Master creation.

However, even you create a single sales Account, GST module would properly compile figures for each type of sales for each GST rates. The GST rates are entered in Stock Item and States are entered at Party Master (Buyer & Seller) ledger accounts. Combing these two info together, Tally would properly compile the break up figures in various statutory returns.

So, decide accordingly, whether you would create a single Sales Account and enter the Sales & Tax Accounts at Invoice level.

We have explained the various info that you need to enter at various fields in sales ledger account master creation in respect of GST.

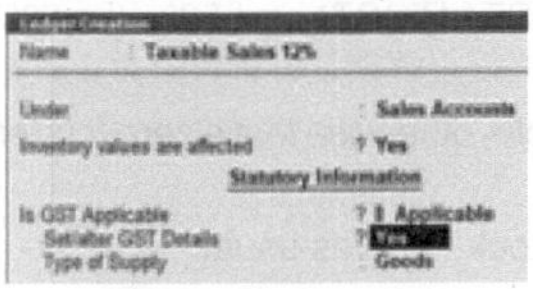

F-9A: sales Ledger Activation

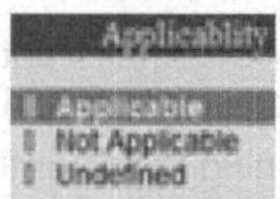

F-9B: Applicability List

F-9C: Supply Type List

At sales Ledger creation / alteration screen (F-9A), at *Inventory values are affected*, set *Yes*. Under *Statutory Information* section, set GST details as follows:

- **GST Applicability** : At *Is GST Applicable*, select GST Applicability from the *Applicability* list. It is recommended that you create separate Sales Ledger Accounts, for Taxable, Exempted and Nil rated sales accounts, and select the respective option from the applicability list.
- **GST Rate Activation** : At *Set / Alter GST details*, set Yes to get *GST Details* screen (F-10A) to enter GST rates

  If you create a common sales account for Items with different GST Rates, then set No at this field, as GST rates are entered in Stock Item Master as explained.

  Set Yes at Set/ Alter GST details, if you have a single GST rate for the sales account (when same rate is applicable for all Items, or you create separate Sales Ledger for each GST Rate).
- **Type of Supply** : Select Goods as explained for Stock Item (F-9C)

GST Details entry

Having set Yes at Set / Alter GST rates at Sales Ledger Account entry (F-9A), At *GST Details* entry screen (F-10A), enter as follows:

- **Transaction Nature**: Select the transaction nature from the list (F-10B). Since, you can select only one transaction nature for a Sales Ledger Account, create separate Sales Ledger Account for each type of sales Transaction and select the respective Transaction nature from the list.
- **Tax Details** : Set the Tax details, as explained for Stock Item.

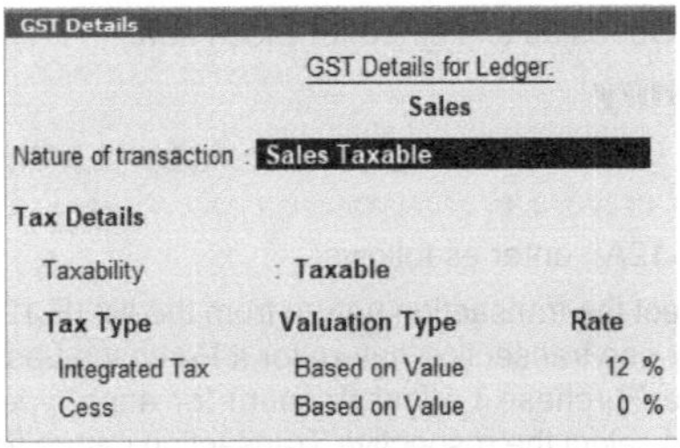

F-10A: Sales GST rate set up

F-10B: Transaction Nature list

Similar to Stock Item, you may view GST Rate History (press At+L) and set up GST Configuration (press F12:Configure).

05 Purchase Ledger Account Set Up

As explained for Sales, you may create one Purchase Account or separate Purchase Accounts as per nature of purchase (local, Interstate etc) and for each Tax Rate. Now set up GST details in Purchase Ledger, to charge GST in Purchase Invoice and account for the GST. At Gateway, select Accounts Info > Ledgers. Now select *Create* to get Purchase Ledger creation screen (F-11A), or select *Alter* and select the Purchase ledger to get Purchase Ledger Alteration screen

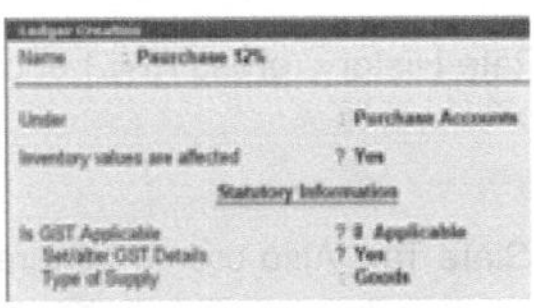

F-11A: Purchase Ledger Activation

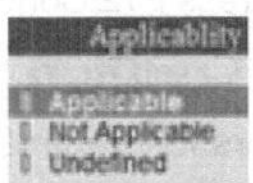

F-11B: Applicability List

F-11C: Supply Type List

At Purchase Ledger creation / alteration screen (F-11A), at *Inventory values are affected*, set *Yes.* Under *Statutory Information* section, set GST details as follows:

- **GST Applicability** : At *Is GST Applicable*, select GST Applicability from the Applicability list (as explained for Sales Ledger). It is recommended that you create separate Purchase Ledger Accounts, for Taxable, Exempted and Nil rated sales accounts, and select the respective option from the applicability list (F-11B).
- **GST Rate Activation** : At *Set / Alter GST details*, set *Yes* to get GST Details screen (F-12A) to enter GST rates on Purchase.

  Set No for common Purchase Account for Items having different GST rates, as GST rates are specified in Stock Item, as explained.
- **Type of Supply** : Select Goods as explained for Stock Item

Purchase GST details entry

Having set Yes at Set / Alter GST details, at Purchase Account entry at F-11A

At *GST Details* entry screen (F-12A), enter as follows:

- **Transaction Nature**: Select the transaction nature from the list (F-12B). Since, you can select only one transaction nature for a Purchase Ledger Account, create separate Purchase Ledger Account for each type of Purchase Transaction and select the respective Transaction nature from the list.
- **Tax Details** : Set the Tax details, as explained for Stock Item.

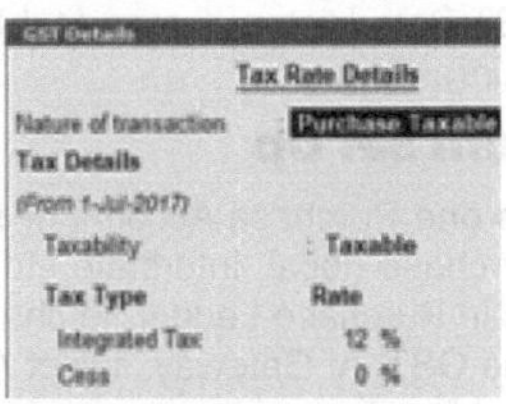

F-12A: Purchase GST rate set up

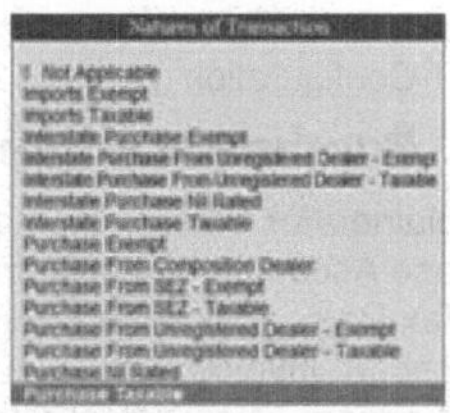

F-12B: Transaction Nature list

Similar to Stock Item, you may view GST Rate History (press At+L) and set up GST Configuration (press F12:Configure).

06 Tax Ledger Creation

Now create GST Ledgers for Central Tax, State Tax. Also create Integrated Tax for Inter State transactions.

At Gateway, select *Accounts Info>Ledger* and create the Tax Ledger Accounts as follows (F-13A to F-13C)

Tax Ledger Account Name : At *Name*, enter the Tax Ledger name

- **Parent Group** : At *Under*, select Duties & Taxes at Parent Group

- **Type of Tax / Duty** : At *Type of Tax / Duty*, select GST
- **Tax Type** : At Tax Type, select the Tax type applicable from the list, for the Tax Ledger

This way, create a Tax Ledger for each Tax component of GST.

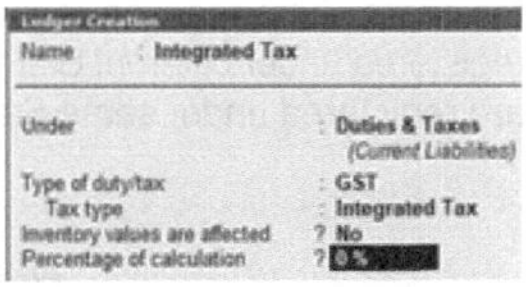

F-13A: Tax Ledger Account

You may create separate Tax Accounts for Input and Output, like Input CGST, Input SGST, Input IGST (applicable for Purchases) and Output CGST, Output SGST and Output IGST (applicable for Sales).

You may even create separate Tax accounts for each rate, etc, in respect of each these accounts. This may involve some more work for Tax Accounts creation, but reconciliation and identification of discrepancy would be easier if the volume of transaction is quite high (use Voucher Classes with pre- defined accounts when such multiple accounts are used).

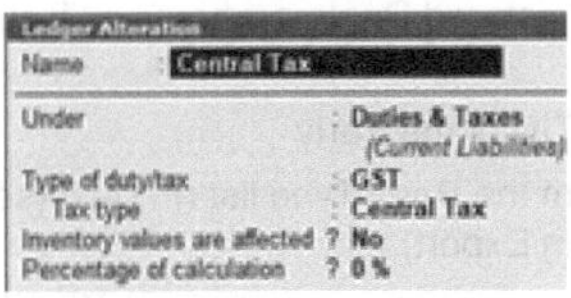

F-13B: Tax Ledger Account

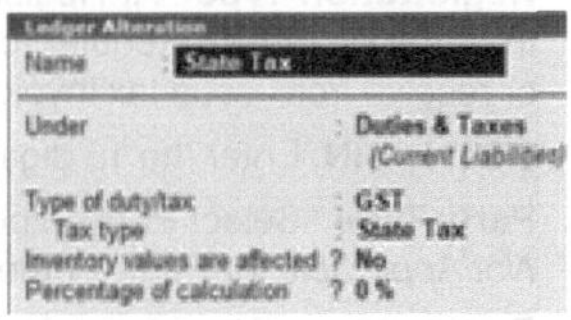

F-13C: Tax Ledger Account

07 GST activation for Party Ledger

Set up GST details of Customer & Suppliers registered under GST. You may enter the details individually in each Ledger Account (useful for new edger creation) or enter for Multiple Ledger Accounts under a Group (convenient for quick entry of GST details, for already created Ledger Account Masters).

GST Details entry in individual Ledger Account : At Gateway, select *Accounts Info > Ledgers*. Now select Create to get Ledger creation screen, or select *Alter* and select the Party ledger to get Ledger Alteration screen (F-14A)

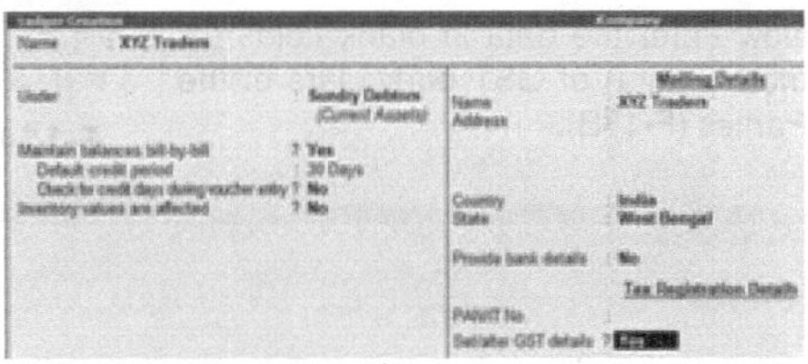

F-14A: GST Activation for Party Ledger Accounts

At Country, normally India is carried as default. At State, select the State with which the party is registered with GST. The first 2 digits of GSTIN indicates the State. A transaction is treated Inter-State, when the seller and buyer is registered under different State) and Intra-State sales (when the both the parties are registered under same State).

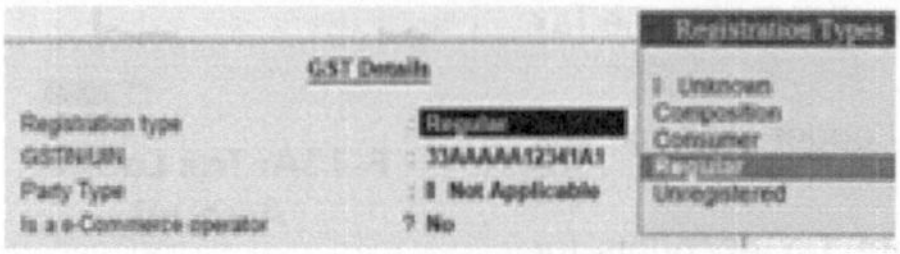

F-14B: Party Ledger Account GST details entry

F-14C: Party Type List

At *Set/ Alter GST details* (F-14A), set Yes to get GST Details screen to enter GST details of the Part Ledger Account (F-14B)

GST Details entry for Party Ledger : At *GST details* screen of the Party Ledger Account, enter as follows (F-14B):

- **Registration Type** : At *Registration Type*, select the appropriate type from the list (select Regular for Registered Dealers whom you issue to or receive from issue tax invoice).
- **GSTN / UIN**: Enter the 15 digit GSTIN of the Party
- **Party Type** : Select Party Type form the Party Type list (F-14C) (select *Not Applicable* for Parties other than Export)
- **E-commerce Operator** : At *Is e-commerce operator*, set Yes if the Party is e-commerce operator, otherwise set No.

Multiple Party GST Details updation

For Parties Ledger Accounts already created, to quickly enter the GST details for multiple parties in a list, at Gateway, select *Display>Statutory Reports>GST>Update Party GSTIN*, select the desired Ledger Group / Ledger to to get Update Party GSTIN screen. Showing the Ledger Accounts of selected Account Group.

Now enter the data in blank fields (or modify data) of GST particulars of the Parties (F-15B).

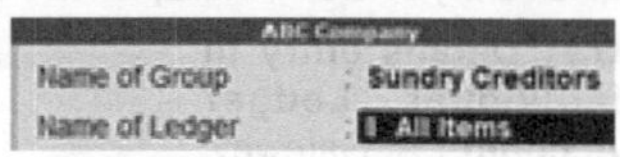

F-15A: Multiple Party GSTN

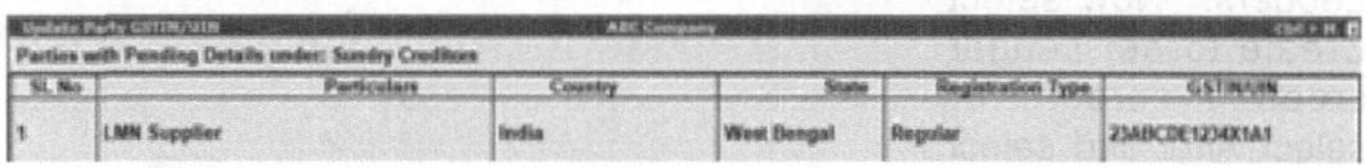

F-15B: Multi party GSTN / UIN updation screen

List of GST State / UT Code

The first 2 letters of GSTIN represent State / UT code, as per list below:

01: Jammu & Kashmir, 02 : Himachal Pradesh, 03 : Punjab, 04* : Chandigarh, 05:Uttaranchal, 06 : Haryana, 07* : Delhi, 08 : Rajasthan, 09 : Uttar Pradesh, 10 : Bihar, 11: Sikkim, 12 : Arunachal Pradesh, 13 : Nagaland, 14 : Manipur, 15 :Mizoram, 16 : Tripura, 17 : Meghalaya, 18 : Assam, 19 : West Bengal, 20 : Jharkhand, 21: Odisha, 22 : Chhattisgarh, 23 : Madhya Pradesh, 24 : Gujarat, 25* : Daman & Diu, 26* : Dadra & Nagar Haveli, 27 : Maharashtra, 28 : Andhra Pradesh, 29 : Karnataka, 30 :Goa, 31* : Lakshadweep, 32 : Kerala, 33 : Tamil Nadu, 34*: Pondicherry, 35* : Andaman & Nicobar Islands, 36 : Telangana

Union Territories (UT) Codes are marked with *

Summary

GST Classification : Classification of Items dealt with by the Company for proper organisation as per HSN and GST Rate

Stock Group Set Up : GST set up for Stock Group

Stock Item Set Up : GST set up for Stock Item

Sales Ledger Account Set Up : GST set up for Sales Account Master

Purchase Ledger Account Set Up : GST set up for Purchase Account Master

Sales Ledger Account Set Up : GST set up for sales Account Master

Tax Ledger Account Set Up : GST set up for each GST Account Master

Party Ledger Account Set Up : GST set up for Party Account Master

GST Transactions 03-2-03

01 Sales Invoice Entry

Having activated GST features and having set required GST related info in all the Masters, you now enter details of sales & purchase transactions. We describe details exclusively related to GST.

Having entered the Party and Item details (item name, Quantity, Rate, Value etc) of all the items in the Invoice, select Accounting Invoice, Click *F8:Sales* and then enter the details of Item sold (Item Name, Quantity, Rate, value), as usual (F-1A).

Local Sales Invoice Entry

In Local Sales Invoice (F-1A), select *State Tax* and *Central Tax*. The amount is equally divided into both the Tax Accounts.

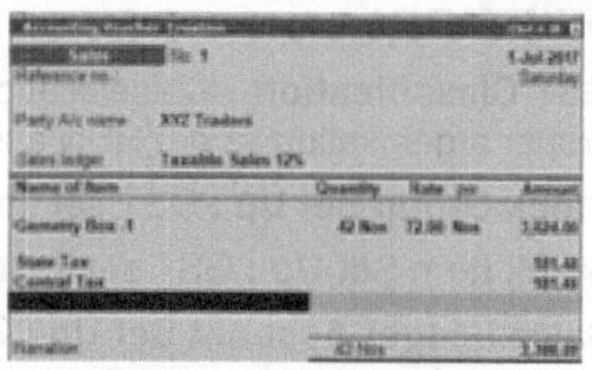

F-1A: Local sales Invoice

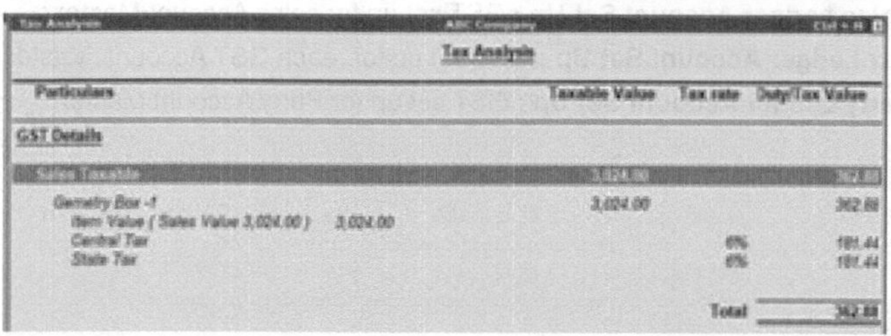

F-1B: Tax Analysis of Local sales Invoice

Interstate Sales Invoice Entry

In Interstate Sales (F-2A), select *Integrated Tax* (instead of Local and Central Tax).

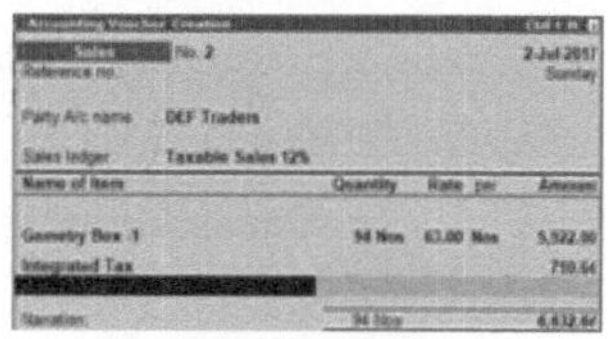

F-2A: Inter State sales Invoice

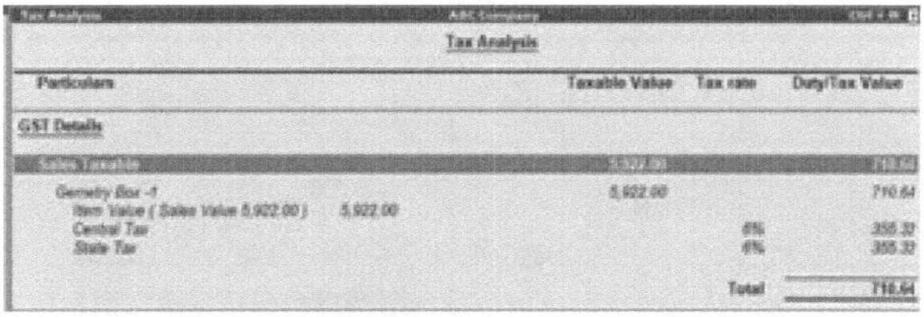

F-2B: Tax Analysis of Local sales Invoice

To view Tax Details, at Invoice entry (F-1A & F-2A), click *A:Tax Analysis* button to get Tax Analysis screen (F-1B & F-2B). Click *F1:Detailed* to get details

02 Invoice Printing

To instantly print the invoice after entry, at Invoice entry screen, Click *P:Print* button and then type *Yes* to print Invoice (F-3A), as per current configuration set. To set configuration, click *F12:Configure* to get Invoice Printing Configuration options (F-3B). At Invoice Printing Configuration screen (F-3B), you may further click *F12:Configure* to get Advanced Invoice Printing Configuration screen (F-3C). Set the configuration options as desired.

F-3A : Sales Invoice in print

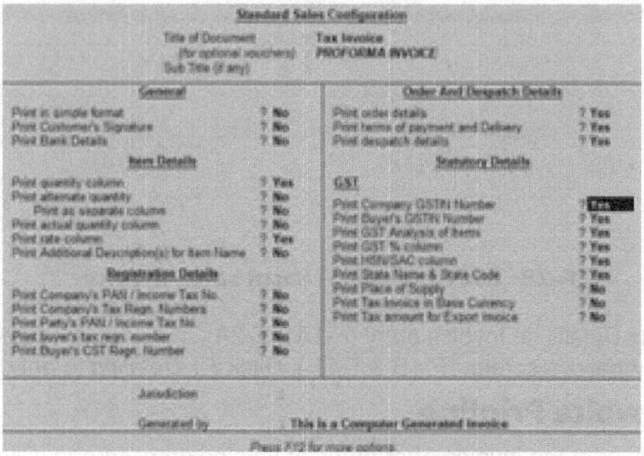

F-3B: Invoice printing Configuration options

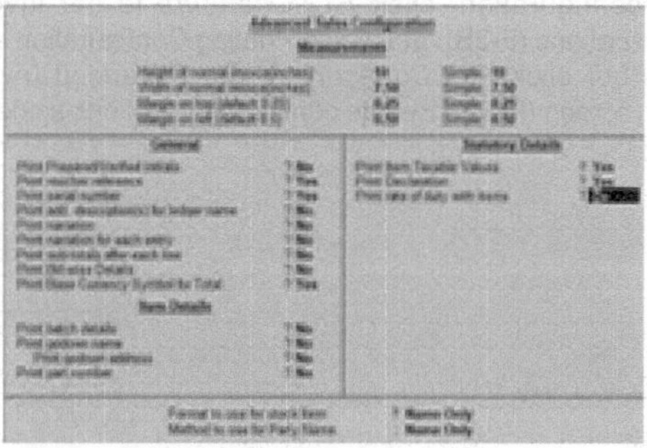

F-3C:Invoice printing Advanced Configuration options

03 Purchase Invoice Entry

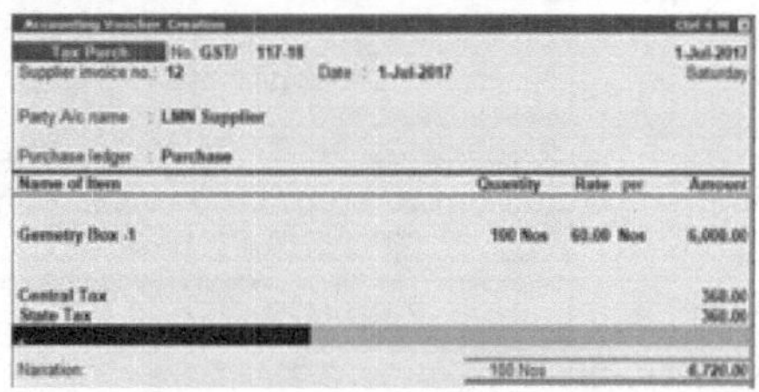

F-4A: Taxable Local Purchase entry

Having entered the Party and Item details (item name, Quantity, Rate, Value etc) of all the items in the Invoice, select Accounting Invoice, Click F9:Purchase (select the underlying Purchase voucher type) and then enter the details of Item purchased (Item Name, Quantity, Rate, value), as usual.

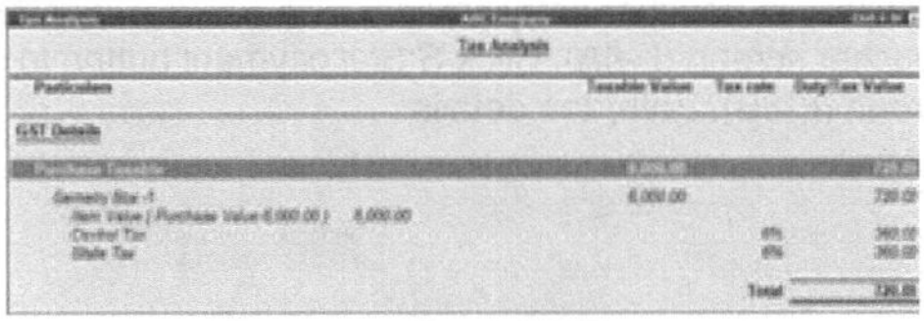

F-4B: Purchase Invoice Tax Details view

In Local Purchase Invoice (F-4A), select *State Tax* and *Central Tax*. The amount is equally divided into both the Tax Accounts.

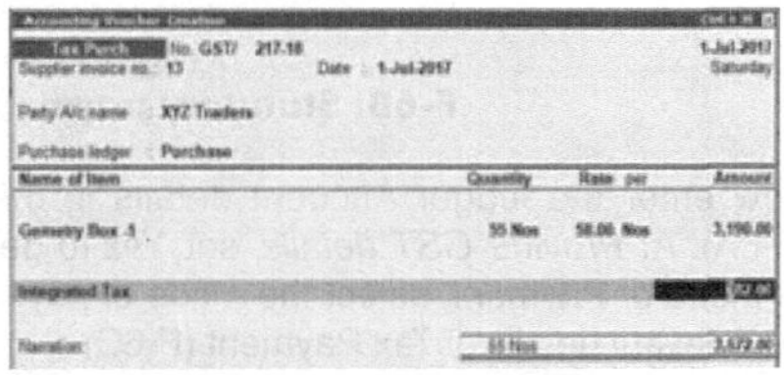

F-5A: Taxable Interstate Purchase entry

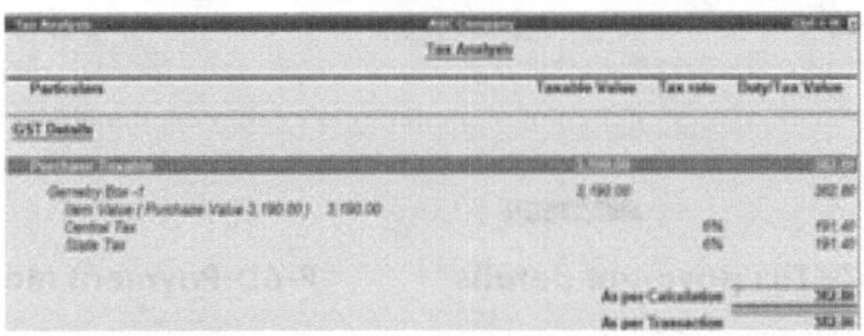

F-5B: Purchase Invoice Tax Details view

In Interstate Sales, select Integrated Tax (instead of Local and Central Tax).

To view Tax Details, click *A:Tax Analysis* button to get Tax Analysis screen (F-5A & F-5B). Click F1:Detailed to get details.

04 Tax Payment

At the end of the month, you have to deposit the Tax payable after adjustment of input Tax from the output Tax.

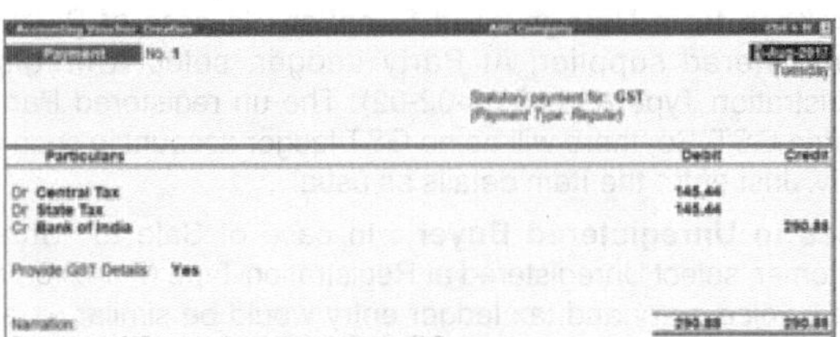

F-6A: Tax payment Voucher

For deposit of Tax, at Voucher entry screen, click *F5:Payment* Voucher to get Payment Voucher screen (F-6A). Click *S:Stat* payment button to get Statutory payment screen (F-6B). Enter the details.

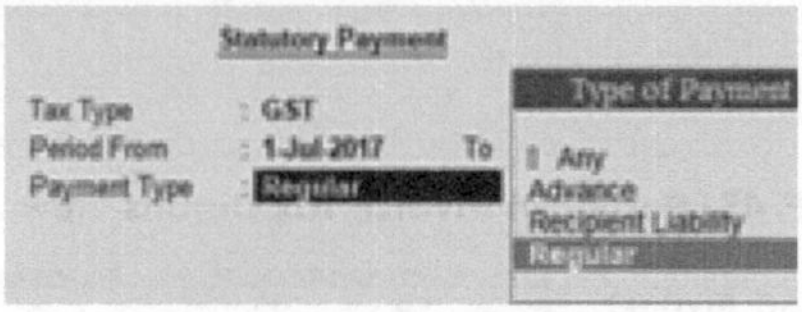

F-6B: Statutory payment details

Now enter the ledger Account details in the main voucher entry screen (F-6A). At *Provide GST details*, set *Yes* to get Bank Details screen (F-6C). At *Mode of Payment*, select the mode of payment from the list (F-6D). Enter the relevant details of Tax Payment (F-6C).

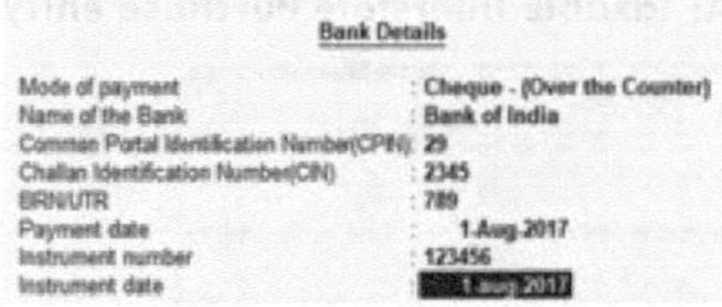

F-6C: Tax payment details

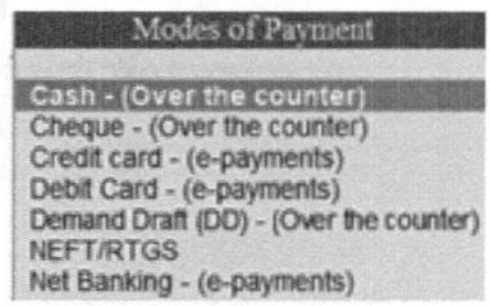

F-6D:Payment Modes list

Save the Payment Voucher.

05 Other types of Domestic Sales / Purchase

We have explained B2B (Business to Business) sales and purchase between two registered dealers. You should keep in mind in case other types of sales / purchase.

Trade with Unregistered Parties : For sale / purchase for resale of goods to / from unregistered parties, the sale / purchase voucher entry should be dome **as** follows:

- **Purchase from Unregistered Supplier** : In case of Purchase from Unregistered supplier, At Party Ledger, select Unregistered at Registration Type (F-14B/03-02-02). The un registered Party will not charge GST. So, there will be no GST ledger account in such purchase entry. Just entre the Item details as usual
- **Sales to Unregistered Buyer** : In case of Sale to Unregistered customer, select Unregistered at Registration Type (F-14B/03-02-02) at. The invoice entry and tax ledger entry would be similar as explained. Select CGST / SGST / UTGST for Intra State / Union territory sales, or

IGST in case of Inter State, as explained, for sale to unregistered Party also.

Cash Sale / Purchase : For Cash sale / purchase to / from Unregistered dealer, for consumption, the sale / purchase voucher entry should be dome **as** follows:

- **Cash Sale** : Cash Sale means sale to consumer, who will not use the Tax charged as Input credit. At any ledger Account, you should select Cash Account (or Bank account when paid by cheque). If you want to record details of Cash Party (like Name, Address etc), click F12:Configure to get Configuration screen, Set Yes at *Supplementary Details.* and enter the Party details, at Supplementary Details screen, select *Consumer* at *Registration Type.* Even if a registered B2B dealer buys your products in Cash for resale, you should create a regular Sale Invoice selecting the Party at Buyer, as usual (not Cash Account), and enter the money received against the sale bill, through receipt Voucher. Don't create such sales Invoice as Cash Sale Invoice.
- **Cash Purchase** ; Cash Purchase (from Unregistered Parties) should be entered like Purchase from Unregistered supplier. Cash Purchase from registered dealer, for which GST charged would be taken as input credit, should be treated as Regular Purchase and enter the payment made through payment Voucher, in usual way. You may record Party details in Supplementary details screen, as explained.

06 Invoice entry using Voucher Class

You can do error free faster entry using Voucher class as explained. You may create several voucher class, as follows, for example :

Transaction Type	Voucher Type Sale	Voucher Class	Pre selected Ledger Accounts in Voucher Class	
			Sales / Purchase	Tax Accounts
Local Party Registered Sale	Sale	RgLSI	Sale	O_SGST / O_UTGST O_CGST
Inter State Party Registered Sale	Sale	RgCSI	Sale	O_IGST
Local Party Registered Purchase	Purchase	RgLPu	Purchase	I_SGST / I_UTGST I_CGST
Inter State Party Registered Purchase	Purchase	RgCPu	Purchase	I_IGST

We have assumed that separate GST Accounts are created for Input Tax (prefixed by I_) for Purchase, and Output Tax (prefixed by O_).

Having created the Voucher Classes, select the Voucher Class (after selecting the Voucher Type button) from the class list to get the Voucher entry screen, with ledger accounts pre-selected. Just select Party Ledger, enter Item details. The Tax amount would be auto computed and allocated to the respective Account. The entry would be very fast, Tax account auto selected. For fast Invoice entry in busy counter, it is recommended that Voucher class should be created and entry be made through Voucher class (particularly sales Voucher which should be made very fast, accurately).

07 Sales Invoice with Inclusive Price

Often retailers would charge the price inclusive of Tax (for sale to consumer). In that case, Voucher Class would be useful. Split the 100% sales / purchase value to Sales Tax Accounts. The sale value and tax values would be automatically allocated to the respective ledger accounts.

The following table shows the computed % allocation for respective Ledger Accounts

Tax %	Sale A/c %	SGST %	CGST %
5%	95.24 [(100/105) x 100%]	2.38 [(2.5/105) x 100%]	2.38 [(2.5/105) x 100%]
12%	89.28 [(100/112) x 100%]	5.36 [(6/112) x 100%]	5.36 [(6/112) x 100%]
18%	84.74 [(100/118) x 100%]	7.63 [(9/118) x 100%]	7.63 [(9/118) x 100%]
28%	78.12 [(100/128) x 100%]	10.94 [(14/128) x 100%]	10.94 [(14/128) x 100%]

For high value transactions, set the % rate in 4 places of decimal (instead of 2 digits as shown above) for more accurate computation.

08 Advance from customers

Under GST, advance received against supply of Taxable Goods or Services are taxable and the receiver must pay tax, like a sales transaction. Sometimes, the customer may cancel the order. In that case, the advance is to be refunded to the customer and necessary adjustment entries be made.

- **Receipt Voucher creation** : On receipt of advance from customer, the supplier should first create a Receipt Voucher. In Receipt Voucher, click *V:Advance Receipt* button, select the Party from which advance received to get *Advance Receipt Details* screen. Select the Stock Item (for which advance received), amount of advance received. The Tax on advance received is auto computed as per Tax Rates applicable for the Item.
- **Sales Voucher creation** : On supply of goods or services, the supplier would create the Sales Voucher, adjusting the advance received, in Bill Ref adjustment section, as usual (to square up the Advance).

  When Sale Bill is created in the same month in which advance is received, then the entire series of transactions (receipt of advance & issue of sale invoice) is properly captured in the GST Statutory Reports.
- **Journal Voucher creation**: If the Sales Bill is not created in the same month in which advance is received, to properly account for the liability of GST on advance received and to carry the unadjusted amount in the next month, for adjustment against subsequent sales bills, create a journal entry at the end of month, to regularize everything properly in the monthly statutory reports for that month.
  - o **Journal Voucher** : Create a Journal Voucher (normally at the end of month), click *J:Stat Adjustment* to get *Stat Adjustment* screen. At Type of Duty, select GST. At Nature of Tax Liability, select Increase of Tax Liability from the List (as you want to create Tax

Liability in respect of GST to be paid on Advance Received, for the current month itself (though supply not made). At *Additional Details*, select On *Account of Advance Received* from the list. These selections are reflected at the header of the Voucher.

Now enter the ledger accounts to be adjusted in the Journal Voucher. At Debit, select *Tax on Advance* ledger (under Group Current Asset) and enter the total GST applicable on the advance received, for which supply invoices are yet to be created. At credit, select the GST Accounts (SGST / CGST / IGST) as applicable and the amount in respect of each GST Tax ledger.

The Tax liability would be included in the Tax Liability report for the month. To deposit the Tax on Advance during that month, create a Payment Voucher. At Statutory payment screen (after you click *S:Stat Payment* at Payment Voucher screen), at *Payment Type*, select *Advance.* At ledger Account details, select the Tax Ledger Accounts (CGST / SGST / IGST) and enter the amount of Tax payable on unadjusted Advance portion, to deposit the Tax on Advance.

- o **Sales Bill** : In subsequent period, at the time of supply, create the sales bill, in which tax on total Sale Value would be charged as usual. At *Bill Ref* section, adjust the advance received (balance bill amount after adjustment of advance is placed under New Ref). The tax on advance adjusted is captured under *Set off of Tax paid on Advances* in the GSTR return, and the liability is reduced by the tax amount on advance already paid and adjusted in earlier month.
- o **Journal Reverse entry** : To properly adjust the balance of the ledger account *Tax on Advance* (as entered at the time of receipt of advance), create a Journal Entry to reverse the tax amount. So, debit the Tax on Advance amount (by the amount of total GST applicable on the Advance, as entered in the Advance Receipt Voucher), and credit the Tax Ledger Accounts (CGST / SGST / IGST) by the respective Tax Amount. The ledger accounts (Tax on Advance and the GST tax accounts like CGST, SGST, IGST) are properly adjusted.

- **Cancellation of Advance** : Sometimes, the customer may cancel the order, and the advance may be returned to the customer.

If the advance is to be returned after creating the Journal entry for increase in Tax Liability on receipt of advance, as explained, create another Journal voucher reversing the entries for refund of Advance. At Journal Voucher entry, at *Stat Adjustment* screen, at *Nature of Adjustment*, select *Decrease of Tax Liability* from the list, and at *Additional Details*, select *Cancellation of Advance Receipt*, from the list. Now create a payment for refund of Advance to the Party.

09 Reverse Charge on Purchase from Unregistered Dealer

Reverse charge means buyer liable to pay tax to government. When a registered dealer buys goods from unregistered seller (hence without paying GST), the registered buyer would pay the GST.

- **Supplier Set Up** : At Supplier master, at State, select the State of the supplier. At GST details section of the Party, at Registration Type, select Unregistered. Depending on the State of the supplier, CGST / SGST (if within state) or IGST (if from other State), would be applicable. As the Party is unregistered, there is no GSTIN applicable for the Party.
- **Purchase Account** : Create separate Purchase Account for *Local Purchase from URD* & *Inter State Purchase from URD* (under Purchase Group), as usual. At *Tax Rate details* screen, at *Nature of Transaction*, for Party within the same State, select *Purchase from Registered Dealer - Taxable*, from the list, while in case of Party outside the State, select *Inter State Purchase from Registered Dealer - Taxable*, from the list. Further, at *Is Reverse Charge Applicable*, set *Yes* (if the option does not appear, click F12:Cinfigure and then set Yes at Enable Reverse Charge Calculation) to get the option. Such separate ledgers would help you better reporting and tax reconciliation.
- **Purchase Voucher** : The process of Purchas entry in usual way, as explained. If you created separate Purchase Accounts, as recommended above, select the appropriate Purchase Account in respective case. Select the Item and enter the Item details, as usual. As it is purchase from Unregistered Party (who does not charge GST), there is no entry for GST Accounts. However, the GST Tax liability for Reverse Charge is auto created, which is reflected in GST Statutory Reports through Tax Analysis report (like usual Invoice with Tax charged), as explained earlier. The Tax liability is also reflected in GST Return.
- **Journal Voucher :** To account for the liability in Accounts, create a Journal Voucher, for increase in Tax Liability for Reverse Charge (You may also do this by drilling down through the tax Liability entry in GSTR Return, after the Purchase Voucher entry). At *Stat Adjustment* screen, at Nature of Adjustment, select *Increase in Tax Liability* from the list, and at Additional Details, select *Purchase under Reverse Charge*, from the list.

10 Voucher Numbering for GST Invoices

As Tally renumbers the Vouchers on deletion. Do not delete any voucher. All subsequent voucher would be renumbered. The Sale / Purchase Bills are uploaded in GST portal. All Bills are subsequently matched in GST portal. So, it will create huge problems (and even legal problem), if the Bill Numbers are disturbed subsequently.

Here we discuss about how to plan for sale / purchase Bill Numbering for GST Invoices, for smooth implementation & avoid change in Voucher Numbers

- **Voucher Cancellation :** Do not delete any Invoice. If you have created any Invoice which you need to delete, instead of deletion, cancel the voucher. At Voucher Alteration mode, press Alt+X to cancel a voucher. The voucher, with voucher number remain listed (to indicate that the voucher was cancelled), but all details are removed, (as if the voucher was not entered). The Voucher Numbers of subsequent vouchers would remain intact, and would not be changed. Even you can create a new Bill against a cancelled Bill.
- **Separate Bill Series with Prefix / Suffix**: To reduce the problems of insertion / deletion of voucher, at Voucher Type, in advanced mode, create separate series of vouchers, with different prefix & suffix, re-start numbering each month, with starting number 1. Consequently, deletion / insertion (due to some mistake), would have minimal problems affect numbers of subsequent months vouchers. In suffix, you may allot different identification for Local & Inter State, Registered & Unregistered etc.
- Such numbering scheme would help you smooth uploading and working, as you have to upload the GST Invoices in the portal, for each calendar month.

11 Input Tax Credit on Closing Stock

Dealers registered under Excise and VAT, may avail credit of CENVAT & VAT paid on closing stock lying on 30th June 17, as per return filed under respective rules, if Input Tax credit is also available on the Item, under GST rule. They have to provide the original bills of purchase (in proof of VAT / Excise having paid) in respect of the closing stock. The input tax credit would also be available on semi finished or finished goods (which he has not purchased but produced) also, provided he can submit evidence of VAT / Excise Duty having paid on materials consumed for such Finished / Semi Finished Goods. These bills must have not been earlier than 1.7.16 (i.e, 12 months before introduction of GST).

Tax paid (Excise Duty, Service Tax, VAT and local Taxes), for which input credit is not availed and is included in the closing stock, would be carried forwards in GST regime for Input Credit. To carry forward unavailed Input Tax credit from the previous Tax regime to current GST system and to avail Input Tax credit on element of Tax paid in Stock held as on 30th June 2017, the registered person has to submit Tran-1 and Tran-2 Form.

Full Tax credit would be available if Excise documents are available, otherwise, a part of Tax paid would be available for credit as follows:

- 60% towards CGST / SGST or 30% towards IGST if the Item is chargeable at GST rate 18% or higher
- 40% towards CGST / SGST or 20% towards IGST if the Item is chargeable at GST rate below 18%

12 Capital Goods Purchase & Input Tax Credit thereon

Credit of Input Tax on Capital Goods purchased will be available where Capital Goods is used in business for effecting taxable supplies. The input tax credit would be spread over useful life of the asset (5 years).

- **Stock Item** : For Capital Goods stock Item creation, set *No* at *Inventory values are affected,* at *Nature of Goods*, select *Capital Goods.* Enter other details and Tax Rate as usual.
- **Fixed Asset Account** : Create the Fixed Asset Ledger Account (like Machinery), under *Fixed Asset.* Ser yes at *Set / Alter GST*. At *Tax Rate Details* screen, at *Nature of Goods*, select *Capital Goods.* Enter GST Rates
- **Purchase Voucher** : Create a Purchase Voucher. Click V:As Voucher to get the purchase voucher entry in Voucher Mode. Click F12:Configure and set Yes at Allow Expenses / Fixed Assets in Purchase Voucher, to enable entry of Ledger Accounts under Fixed Assets.

  Now select Supplier Ledger Account and enter the total Bill Amount (which is to be credited to the Party Account) in credit column. Next select the Machinery Ledger Account and enter the value of machinery in Debit Column. Next select the Tax Account (CGST & SGST or IGST). The Tax amount would be auto computed as per Tax rate specified in Assets Ledger Account.

  Advance GST Ledger Account : Since the whole GST Amount would not be available for Input credit, create a ledger Account under Current Asset to set aside the total Input Tax available and take out the apportioned amount of Input Tax periodically. Create a Ledger Account (like Advance GST), under *Current Asset.*
- **Journal Voucher** : Only 1/5th of the Input Tax would be available for Input Credit during the year. The balance 4/5th would be carried forward to subsequent years.

  For such adjustment, create a Journal Voucher. Click *J:Stat Adjustment* button to get Stat Adjustment entry screen. At *Type of Duty / Tax*, select *GST*. At *Nature of Adjustment*, select *Reversal of Tax Credit.*
- Select Advance GST Account and enter the amount of the rest of the amount (4/5th) to be carried in next year (1/5th for current year, 4/5th to be carried forward) in debit side.
- In credit side, select CGST and SGST (in case of purchase of Machinery within the Sate) and enter the 50% amount (50% of the 4/5th amount debited to Advance GST Account) for each Ledger Account, or select IGST and enter the entire amount to IGST Account, in credit column (in case of purchase of Machinery from outside the Sate).

13 Zero Rated Purchase Invoice

There are instances where supplier has not charged any GST in their Invoice. So, you do not enter any GST in Purchase Invoice.

- **Stock Item :** In *Stock Item* creation screen (Click F12:Configure and set Yes at Set Type of goods to get option for all types of Goods), at *Tax Rate details* screen:
  - o At *Taxability*, select *Exempt* for Exempted Item on which GST is not chargeable (like Books), select *Nil Rated* for goods on which Tax is zero (Exempted and Nil rated are different concept though No Tax is chargeable on both of them).
  - o At *Is Non GST Goods,* set Yes for Non GST Items.
- **Supplier Ledger** : In case of Composition Dealer, at GST details screen, at *Registration Type*, select *Composition.*
- **Purchase Voucher** : Now create the Voucher as usual.
- **Purchase of Exempt, Nil Rated or Non GST Items** : Select the Item (Nil Rated, Exempted, Non GST). On selecting the Tax ledgers (CGST/ SGST) or IGST, the Tax amount would be zero for purchase of Nil rate or Exempted Items (irrespective of Type of Dealer : Registered, Unregistered, Exempted or Composition).

In GSTR, the entries would be shown with respective break up, under Nil Rated Invoices (drill down and get break up).

14 GST on Additional Charges in Invoice

When Additional Charges are added (like Packing Charges, Freight, Cartage, Delivery Charges etc), GST would be added in the same way like principal goods or services sold. The amount for additional charges may be computed as On value of the goods, on Quantity of the Goods (be careful, the UoM of all the Items should be same, otherwise there would be computation mistake when computed on Quantity), or user defined value. If the Invoice contains multiple tax rates, the GST on additional charges would be computed as per individua amount, at rate applicable for each Item.

- **Additional Charges Ledger Account** : Create Leger Account for such additional charges. Such additional charges ledger, should be placed under *Indirect Income* group (do not place under Indirect Expenses).

  At *Inventory Values are affected,* set *No.* At *Method of Appropriation in Purchase Invoice*, set *No* (you are entering Sales Invoice, not Purchase Invoice).

  At *GST Applicable*, set *No.* At *Include in Assessable Value Calculation for*, select GST from the list. At *Apportion to*, select *Goods* (when such charge is added in Sale of Goods). At *Method of Calculation*, select the appropriate method from the list (like Based on value).

- **Sales Invoice** : Select the Additional Charges first, get the amount computed and then select The Tax Accounts (CGST/ SGST / IGST), as Tax would be computed inclusive of expenses.
- **Tax Computation** : Press F12:Configure at Voucher Entry screen, at *At Calculate Tax on current Subtotal* set *No*, to compute Tax on Additional Charges on sale Value only, else set *No*, to compute Tax on Amount including successive additional charges also.

  The Tax is computed on Sales Value and also on additional charges as per method selected, and shown together against respective Tax Accounts (CGST/ SGST / IGST).

  In case of multiple tax rate invoice (for example in invoice with 12% & 18% tax rate Items), the common expenses charged at the end, in respect of entire amount, would be computed proportionately and then added together for all the Items.

GST Reports

03-2-04

01 Data Validation

After all transaction data entry, Sales, Purchase, Payments etc, you may print the GST Statutory Reports for filing with the authorities within specified period.

At the time of printing of Statutory Reports, Tally.ERP 9 first validates the GST data for data consistency. In Statutory reports, data anomalies, if any, are first shown in the Report (F-1A to F-1C).

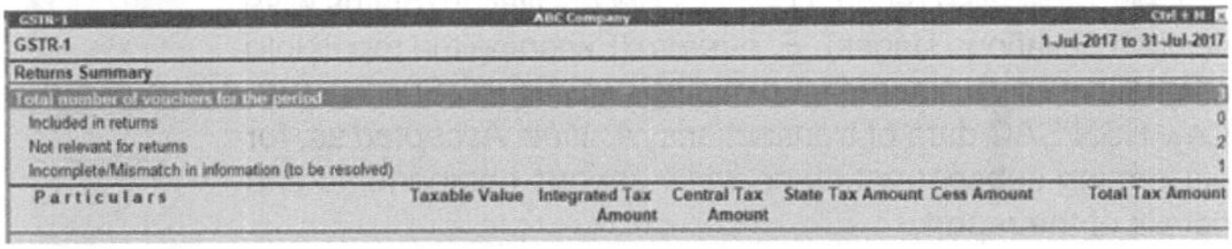

F-1A: GSTR-1 – Monthly report

Mismatch & Exception Resolution

Details of data anomalies, as indicated in the reports (F-1B & F-1C), if any, must be rectified first. The subsequent reports are produced only when the inconsistencies are resolved.

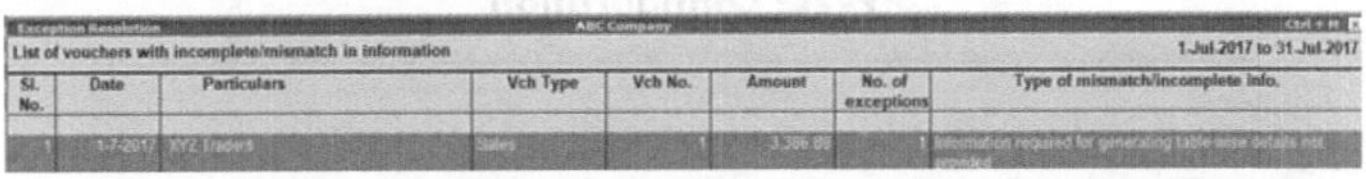

F-1B: GSTR-1 – Mismatch details – Voucher list for Exception resolution

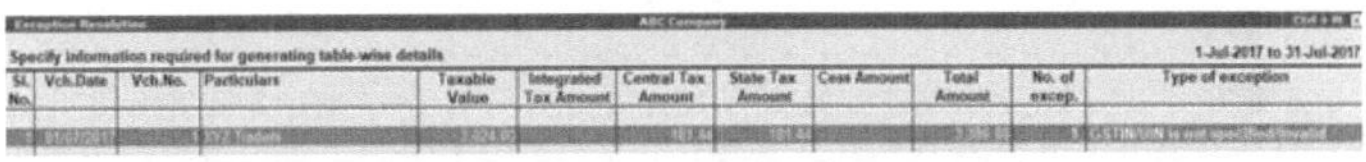

F-1C: GSTR-1 – Mismatch details for Exception resolution

02 GSTR-1

GSTR-1 is monthly report of Outward supplies made by taxpayer (other than compounding taxpayer and ISD). This is to be filed by 10th of the following month.

At Gateway, select Display>Statutory Reports>GST>GSTR-1 to get GSTR-1 report (F-2A).

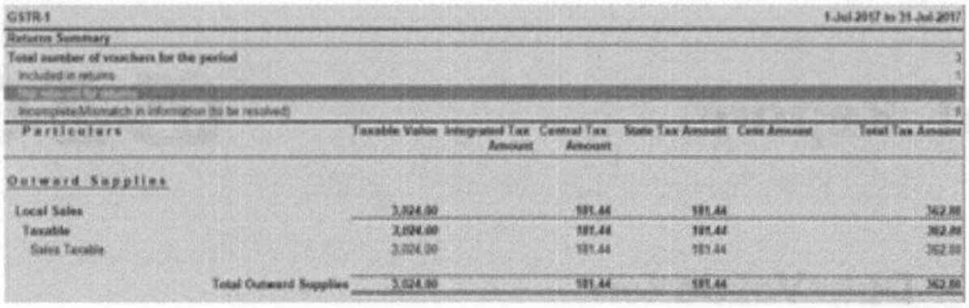

F-2A: GSTR-1 Report of outward supplies

Buttons

F-2B: Buttons

The report provides buttons (F-2B) for various task like *J:Stat Adjustment* (for accounting adjustments of credit / reversals), *V: View Table wise report*, *U: Status Reconciliation* (Status wise position of various stages), *E: e-return* (Exporting the report into compatible Excel Sheet for uploading), *HSN/SAC Summary* (to view HSN/SAC data of transactions, *A: View Accepted* as, for performing subsequent steps, view various components and details of the report.

Click *F12:Configure* to get Configuration screen (F-2C).

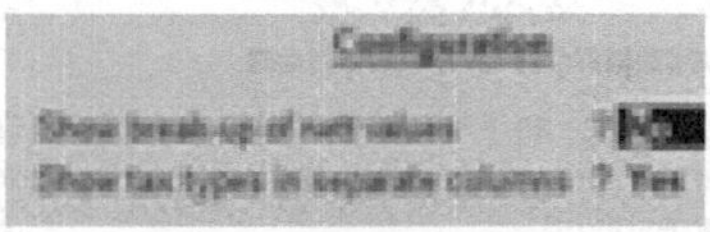

F-2C: Configuration

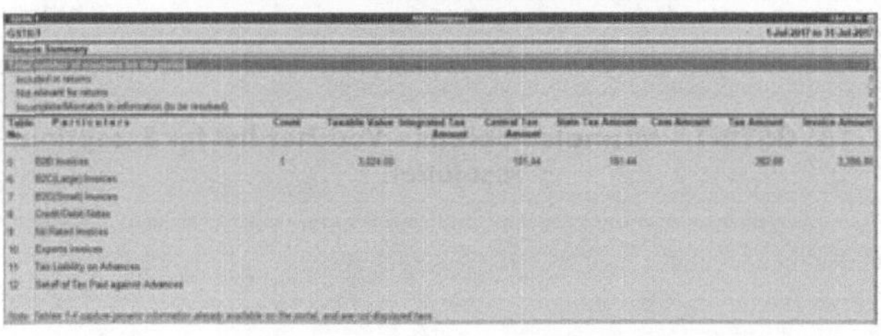

F-3A: GSTR-1 Report : Table View

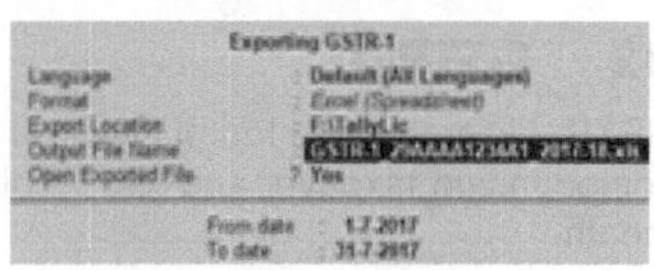

F-4A: Exporting GSTR-1 into Excel Sheet for uploading

Exporting Report in Excel Sheet for uploading : To create the compatible Excel Sheet for uploading of Report to the GST site, at *GSTR-1* report, click *E: e-return* button, to get Exporting GSTR-1 screen (F-4A). Now set the values as required, to store the Excel Sheet, at the desired folder.

Accounting Adjustment of Liabilities & Credits : To make adjustment of various liabilities & credits, At *GSTR-1* report, click *J:Stat Adjustment* button (F-2B), to get *Stat Adjustment* screen (F-5A). Select the desired option from the respective list (F-5A & F-5B).

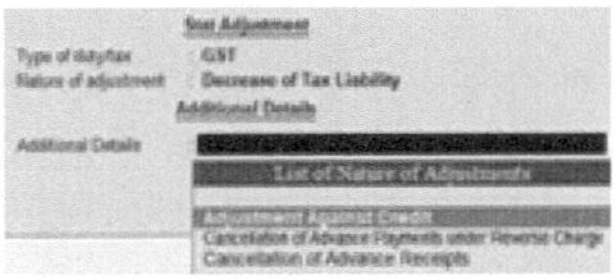

F-5A: Stat Adjustment screen

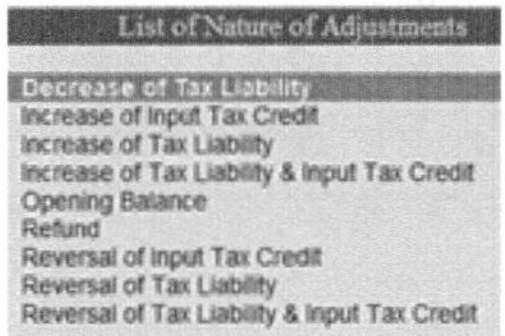

F-5B: Adjustment Nature list

On selecting the options, you get a Journal Voucher screen to make necessary accounting adjustments.

Status set up : At GST Status reconciliation report (Click *U:Status Reconciliation* button at GSTR-1 report), drill down to get Voucher Register (F-6A). At Voucher Register, click S:Staus button to get Status Set up screen (F-6B). Set the status for the vouchers.

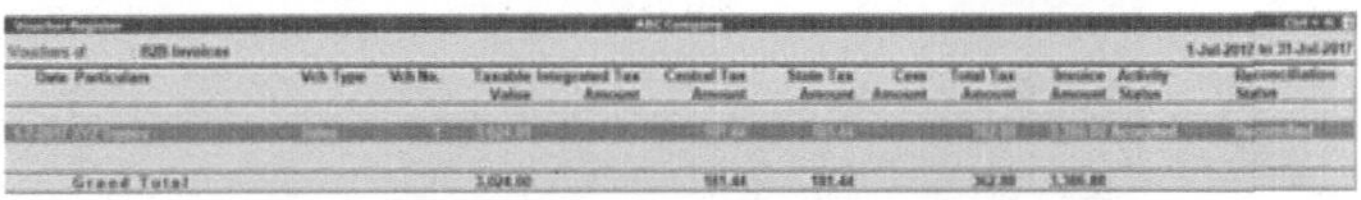

F-6A: Voucher Register

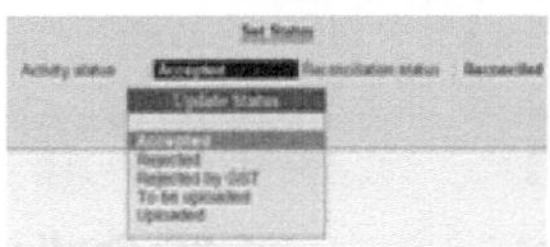

F-6B: Status set up

HSN / SAC Summary : At GSTR-1 report, click N:HSN/SAC summary button to get HSN/SAC summary report (F-7A).

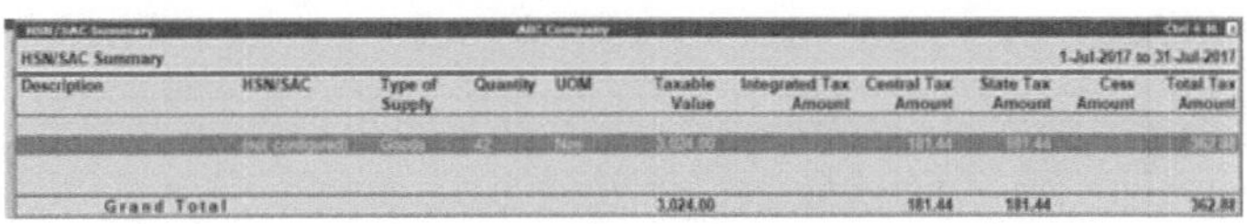

F-7A: HSN/SAC summary

03 GSTR-2

GSTR-2 is monthly report of Inward supplies received by a taxpayer (other than a compounding taxpayer and ISD). It is to be filed by 15th of the following month.

At Gateway, select *Display>Statutory Reports>GST>GSTR-2* to get GSTR-2 report (F-8A).

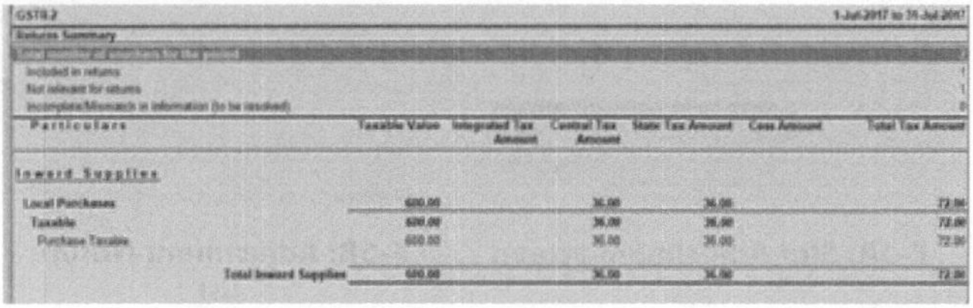

F-8A: GSTR-2 Report

The buttons (F-8B) and configuration (F-8C) options of GSTR-2 are similar to GSTR-1

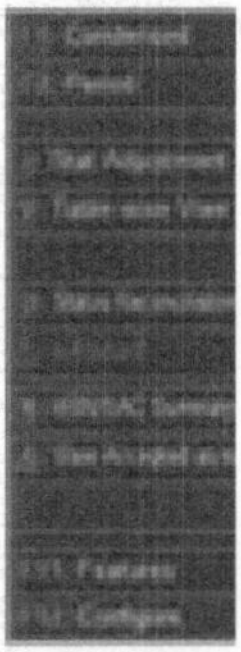

F-8B: Buttons

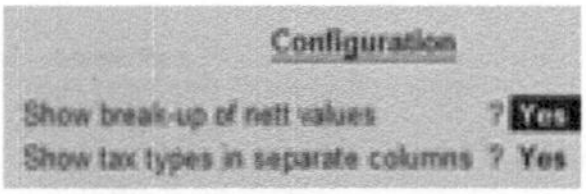

F-8C: Configuration

Uploading of Data to GST Portal

03-2-05

Classification of Transaction as per GSTR-1

Open the site www.gst.gov.in in your browser (F-1A). Click on *Download* tab.

Select *Returns Offline Tools* from the list (F-1A), to get Returns Offline Tools screen (F-2A).

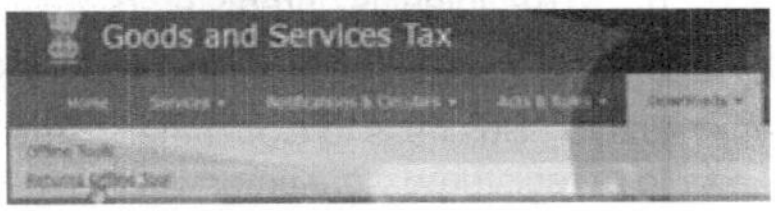

F-1A : GST portal

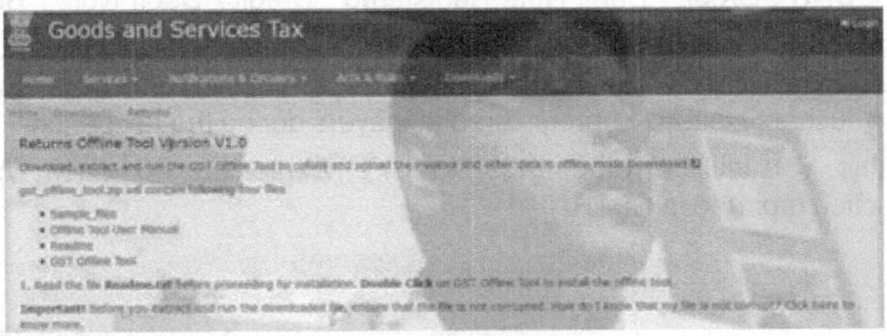

F- 2A: GST Portal

Click on Download link, Click Proceed (and then save) to get a zip folder gst_offline_tool downloaded in your Computer in the specified folder (F-3A).

You will get a folder named gst_offline_tool. Extract files of the folder to get the files (including an excel file like GSTR1_Excel_Workbook_template-v.1). Open the Excel file. It contains tabs for data for B2B, B2CL, B2CS, CDNR etc.

Direct data entry in GST portal : Those who have not entered GST Sales data in Tally, instead of working with Excel template, you may install the gst_offline_tool (it is an application) and enter data directly at the GST portal).

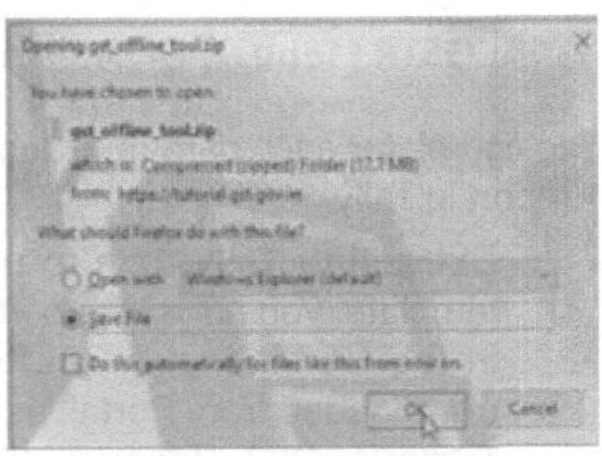

F- 3A : GST Portal

GST Data Classification

This excel template file is portal created file in its own format (not Tally created Excel Format), with Tabs for transaction types as follows:

- **B2B** : Taxable Supplies to other registered Suppliers
- **B2CL**: Business to Consumer Large (CL) – Taxable outward supplies where:
  - o Place of Supply is outside the State where the supplier is registered
  - o Recipient is unregistered.
  - o Invoice value more than 2,50,000
- **B2CS** : Business to Consumers Small (CS) – Taxable outward supplies to unregistered Consumer where :
  - o Place of supply is same State (any value)
  - o Outside State Rs 2,50,000 or less
- **CDNR** : Credit / Debit Note Registered ; Credit / Debit Note / Refund vouchers issued to registered taxpayers during the tax period.
- **CDNUR** : Credit / Debit Note Un Registered ; Credit / Debit Note / Refund vouchers issued to unregistered taxpayers during the tax period.

Like this, you will get other tabs like *Exp, Exmpt* etc. for each type of transaction reported in GSTR-1

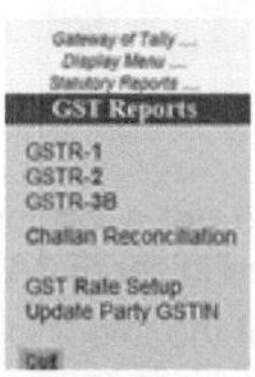

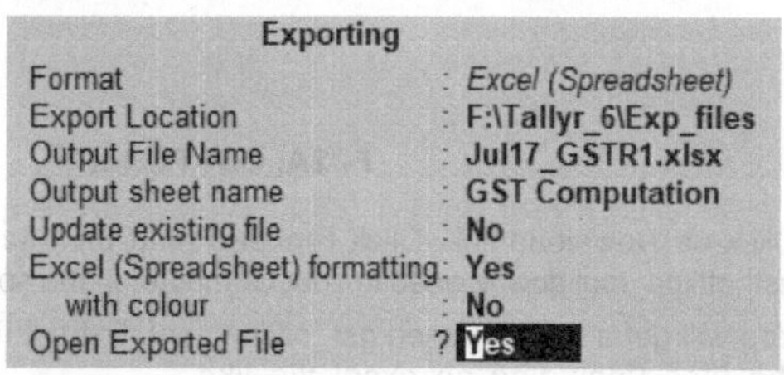

F-4A: GSTR Menu **F-5A: Exporting GSTR-1 Report to Excel format**

The figures for each para (and sub para) of GSTR-1 will be reflected in GSTR-1 report in Tally.

- **Extracting Tally data to upload in portal** : Having saved the Excel template, you have to export data from GSTR report in Tally, and upload in the GST portal (place the data into the Excel Template of GST downloaded from Portal, as explained). Select *GoT>Display>Statutory Reports>GST Reports> GSTR-1* (F-4A) to get GSTR-1 Report, as explained earlier.
- **Data creation for Upload**: At GSTR-1 report, click e:e-Return or Click

E:Export button (or press Ctrl+E) to get Exporting GSTR-1 screen (F-5A). At Format, select *Excel*. At *Export Location*, select the folder (the default export data folder as set would appear). The default export filename appears, which you may change (you may specify filename as per your choice). The data would be exported in the specified Excel File at specified folder. You may open the Excel Sheet (F-6A), view and quickly check if the things are alright.

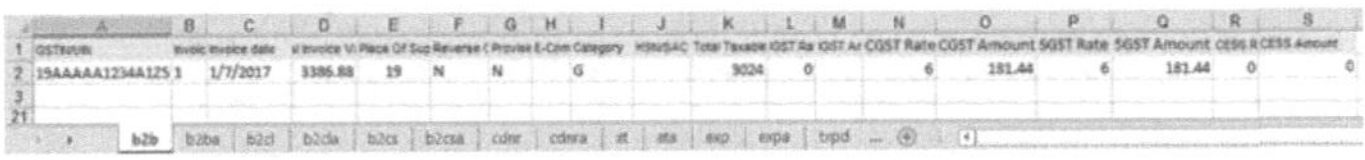

F-6A: Exported GSTR-1 data in Excel Sheet Format

Having checked all data, at Summary section, click on the Generate File button. Click save specifying a filename as per your choice, at designated folder.

Uploading Data on Portal

The exported Excel Sheet data (F-6A) are in Tally's own format, containing all columns that are necessary to be uploaded in GST portal. Copy the data from Excel File generated from Tally (F-6A) and paste in the Portal Excel sheet at *Copy & Paste* section, to upload data for Generation of Return (you may get error message like Data invalid if there is any inconsistency in the Excel data, which you have to resolve first). If data is correct, you will get message "Return Details added successfully". You may now check summary to ensure that the data is uploaded correctly. If any inconsistency is found, check the data and make corrections.

Uploading Return : Now at GST portal (gst.gov.in), login entering your Username & Password (F-7A) and then upload the file following the instructions.

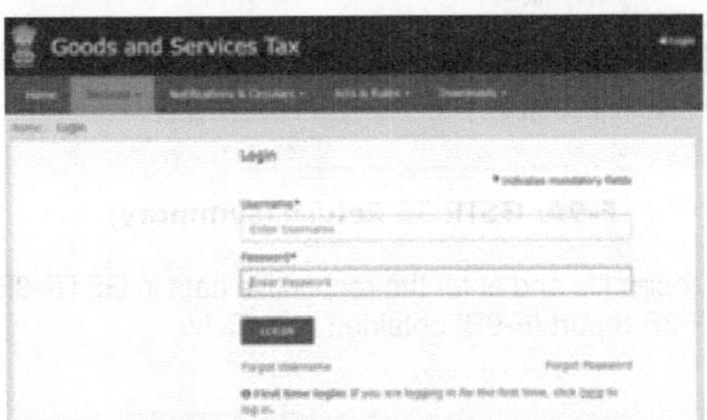

F-7A: GST user login screen

GSTR-2 : GSTR-2 contains data of Inward transactions. Extract data of GSTR-2 and upload the data in same manner, as explained for GSTR-1.

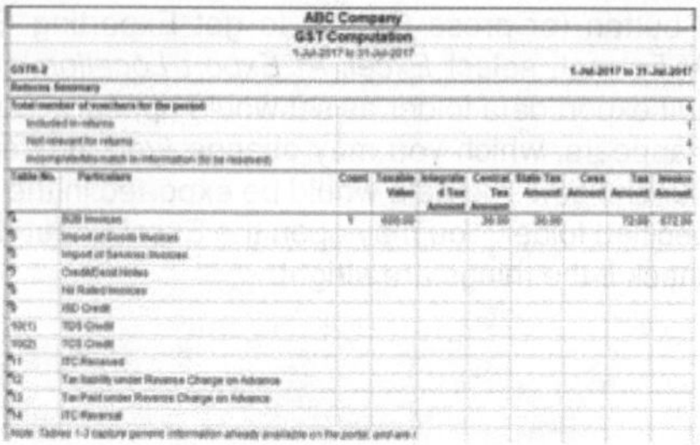

F-8A: GSTR-2 Summary

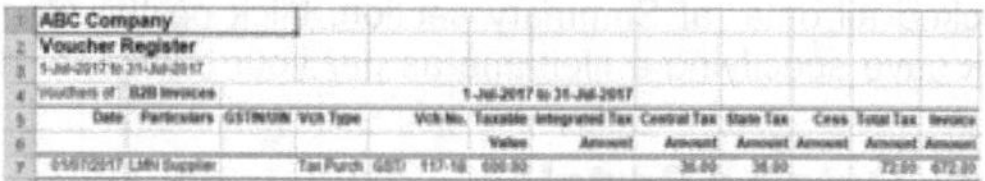

F-8B: GSTR-2 : Tally Exported Data

GSTR-3B : Government have issued format of GSTR-3B (for July & Aug 17). You have to input data in GSTR-3 in portal in the prescribed format, from the GRST-3B report.

Select *GoT>Display>Statutory Reports>GST Reports> GSTR-3B* to get the GSTR Report printing screen. Click *E:Export* and save the report in desired format (PDF / Excel).

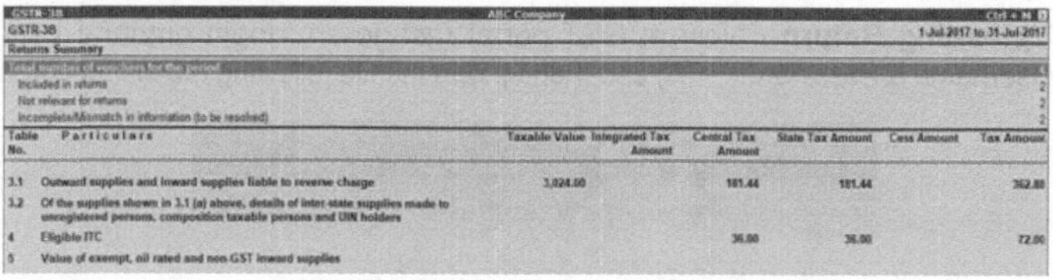

F-9A: GSTR 3B Return (summary)

Now open the report file and enter the respective data in GSTR-3B in the portal from the GSTR-3B report (F-9B) obtained from Tally.

Table No.	Particulars	Taxable Value	Integrated Tax Amount	Central Tax Amount	State Tax Amount	Cess Amount	Tax Amount	
3.1	**Outward supplies and inward supplies liable to reverse**	3024.00		181.44	181.44		362.88	
a	Outward taxable supplies (other than zero rated, nil rated		3024.00		181.44	181.44		362.88
b	Outward taxable supplies (zero rated)							
c	Other than Outward supplies (Nil rated, exempted)							
d	Inward supplies (liable to reverse charge)							
e	Non-GST outward supplies							
3.2	**Of the supplies shown in 3.1 (a) above, details of inter-**							
	Supplies made to Unregistered Persons							
	Supplies made to Composition Taxable Persons							
	Supplies made to UIN holders							
4	**Eligible ITC**			36.00	36.00		72.00	
A	ITC Available (whether in full or part)							
	(1) Import of goods							
	(2) Import of services							
	(3) Inward supplies liable to reverse charge (other than 1							
	(4) Inward supplies from ISD							
	(5) All other ITC				36.00	36.00		72.00
B	ITC Reversed							
	(1) As per rules 42 & 43 of CGST Rules							
	(2) Others							
C	Net ITC Available (A) - (B)				36.00	36.00		72.00
D	Ineligible ITC							
	(1) As per section 17(5)							
	(2) Others							
5	**Value of exempt, nil rated and non-GST inward supplies**							

F-9B: GSTR 3B Return (Detail)

TDS 03-02

01 TDS Set up for the Company

Certain payments are subjected to tax deduction at source. Such Tax (TDS or Tax Deducted at Source) will be deducted at time of payment or credit, whichever is earlier. Here we describe maintenance of TDS (Tax Deducted at Source) deducted and deposited to Government, for such specified payments made (other than Salary).

Click *F11:Features* button, select *Statutory & Taxation* to get *Statutory & Taxation* screen

- **TDS Activation** : At *Enable Tax Deducted at Source*, set *Yes* to Activate TDS Features for the Company
- **TDS Details** : At *Set / Alter TDS Details*, set *Yes*, to get *Company TDS Deductor Details* screen (F-1A), to enter the Company TDS Details'
- **PAN / CIN** : At *PAN / Income Tax Number*, enter the Company PAN & Company Identification (CIN), where applicable.

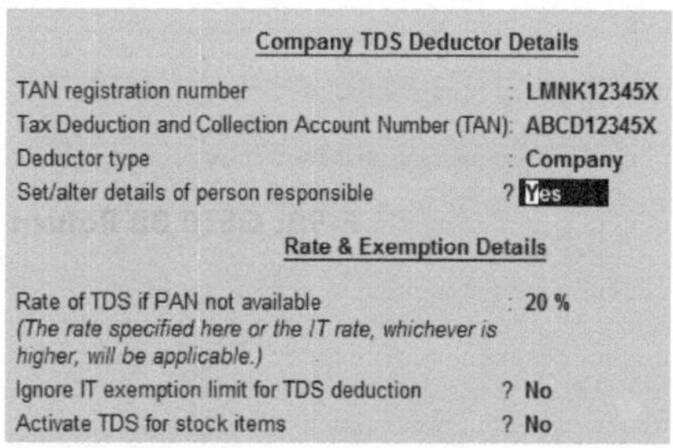

F-1A: TDS Deductor Details entry

At *Company TDS Deductor Details* screen (F-1A), at *Set / Alter details of persons responsible*, type *Yes* to enter details of the person responsible to deduct TDS on behalf of the Company (F-1B). Entr other details in the *Company TDS Deductor Details* screen (F-1A),

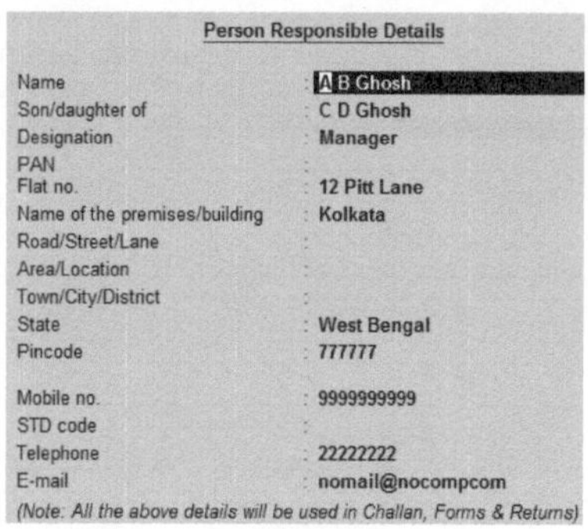

F-1B: Responsible persons details entry

02 TDS nature of Payment

First create all the relevant Nature of Payments (press Ctl+C at name to select the TDS name form the list) under various sections of I Tax, that would be applicable in your case for deduction of TDS (F-2A). Enter the details and the threshold limit and date of applicability

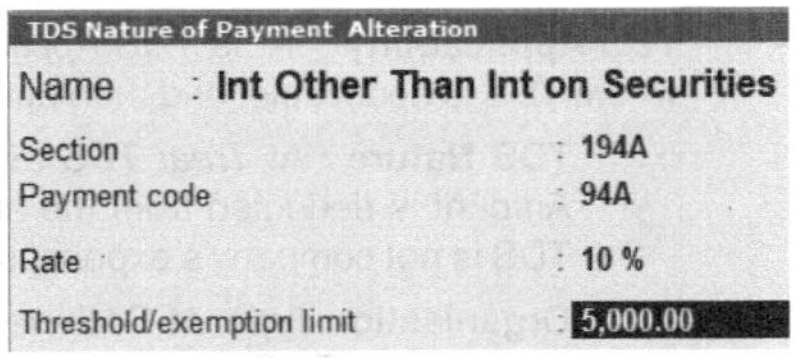

F-2A: TDS nature of Payment

Click F12:Configure to set up additional options, if required.

03 TDS Ledger Account

Create separate TDS Ledger Account for each TDS nature (F-3A). At TDS Ledger Account creation / alteration screen (F-2A), enter the following details:

- **Parent Group** : At *Under*, select Duties & Taxes (or a Group created under Duties & Taxes)
- **TDS Type**: Select from the list
- **Nature of Payment**: At *Nature of Payment*, select from the list of TDS Nature of Payment, applicable for the respective TDS Account.

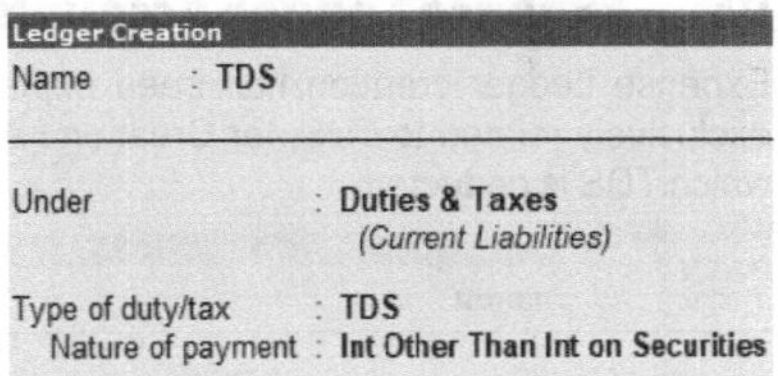

F-3A: TDS Ledger Account creation

04 Party Ledger Account

Party Ledger creation has been explained earlier. We describe points exclusively related to

Ledger Creation / Alteration of the Party from whom TDS is deducted (F-4A).

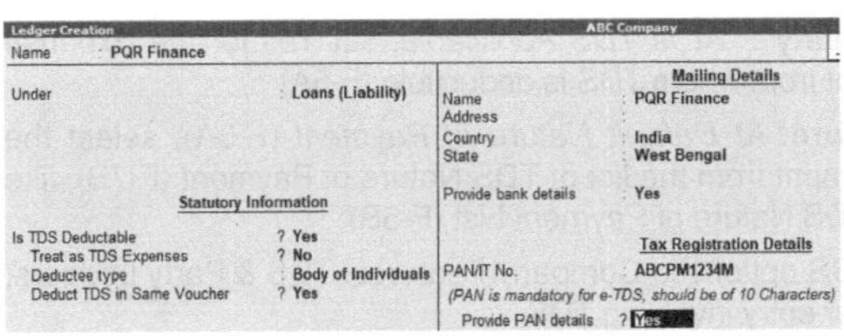

F-4A: Party Ledger Entry

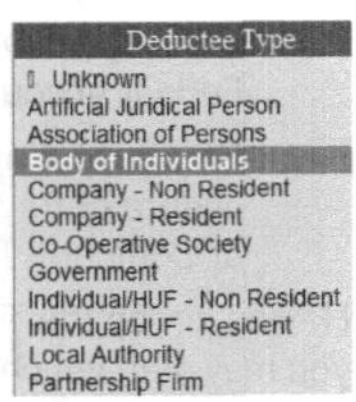

F-4B: Deductee Type List

At *Statutory Information* section of the Party Ledger creation screen (F-4A), enter as follows:

- **TDS Applicability** : At *Is TDS Applicable*, set *Yes* for the Party from whom TDS is deductible, and then enter as follows:
  - o **TDS Nature** : At *Treat TDS as Expenses* set *No* (where TDS Amount is deducted from the amount Payable to the Party. So, TDS is not company's expenses)
  - o **Organisation Type**: At *Deductee Type,* select the *Deductee Type* from the list (F-4B), according to the nature of constitution of the Party.
  - o **TDS Voucher** : At Deduct TDS in same Voucher, set Yes if TDS is deducted in same Voucher

At right part, enter Address & PAN Details (PAN is mandatory). Set *Yes* at *Provide PAN details* and Enter *Effective Date* and *Name of Deductee* as per I Tax records.

05 Expense Ledger Accounts set up

Expense Ledger creation has been explained earlier. We describe points exclusively related to TDS, for Creation / Alteration of Expense Ledger from which TDS is deducted.

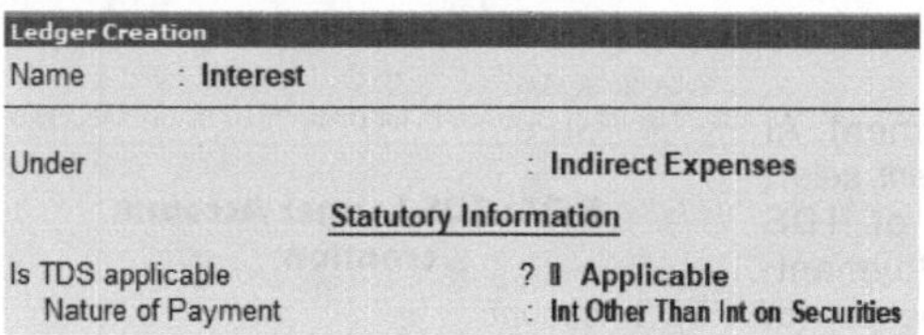

F-5A: TDS Ledger creation

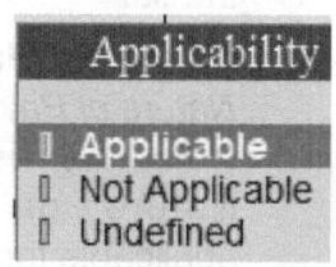

F-5B: Applicability List

At *Statutory Information* section of the Expense Ledger Account creation / alteration screen (F-5A), enter as follows :

- **TDS Applicability** : At *Is TDS Applicable*, set *Yes* for the Expense Ledger Account from whom TDS is deductible (F-5A)
- **Payment Nature**: At *Default Nature of Payment* (F-5A), select the Nature of Payment from the list of TDS Nature of Payment (F-7B), like at Company TDS Nature of Payment List (F-5B)

Having set up the TDS options in Company Features, TDS & Party Ledgers, you may start voucher entry involving TDS.

06 TDS Adjustment Journal Voucher

Create a Journal Voucher (F-6A) to book the expense and adjust the TDS.

At Main voucher screen (F-6A), enter Other Ledger Accounts (if any). Save the Voucher.

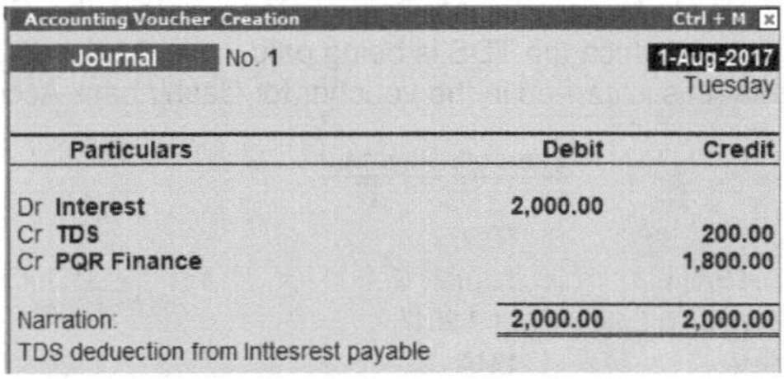

F-6A: Journal Voucher for Expense

07 TDS Deposit Payment Voucher

Create a Payment Voucher for Deposit of TDS to Government (F-7A). At *Payment Voucher* entry screen (F-7A), Click *S:Stat* Payment button to get Statutory Payment screen (F-7B). Fill up the details. At main voucher screen (F-7A), enter the ledger account details as usual

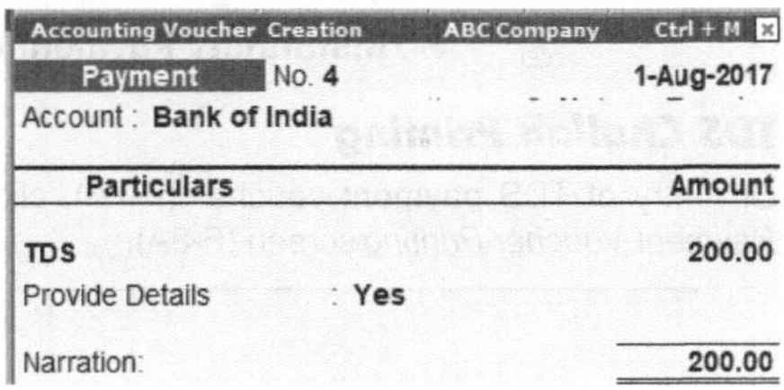

F-7A: TDS Payment Voucher

At *Statutory Payment* Screen (F-7B), enter as follows :

Duty / TaxType : At *Type of Duty/Tax*, select TDS from the list of Duty / Tax Type

Mode of Entry : At *Auto Fill Statutory Payment*, select *Yes* to get the fields to fill up the Payment details as below:

- **Period** : Enter the period for which TDS is being deposited
- **Period End** : At *Deducted Till Date*, enter he Date upto which the TDS deducted is being deposited through the current voucher. Accordingly the amount of TDS deducted would be carried in the voucher, for TDS Deposit.
- **I Tax Section** : At *Section*, select the I Tax section under which the TDS is being deposited from the list
- **Payment Nature** : At *Nature of Payment*, select the Nature of Payment from the list, for which TDS is being deposited.

- **Company Type** : At *Deductee Status*, select the Status (Company / Non Company) from the list, as per constitution of the Company)
- **Cash / Bank Account** : At *Cash / Bank*, select the Cash / Bank Account from which the TDS is being paid, from the list of Cash / Bank Accounts (this is carried in the voucher for Cash / bank Account)

Statutory Payment

Tax Type	: TDS		
Period From	: 1-Jul-2017	To	31-Jul-2017
Deducted Till Date	: 31-7-2017		
Section	: 194A		
Nature of Payment	: Int Other Than Int on Securites		
Deductee Status	: Non Company		
Residential Status	: Resident		
Cash/Bank	:		

F-7B:Statutory Payment details

TDS Challan Printing

On entry of TDS payment voucher (F-7A), click *P:Print* button to get the *Payment Voucher Printing* screen (F-8A).

Report Titles

Payment Voucher

Print as TDS Challan	? Yes
TDS/TCS Regular Assessment (Raised by I.T. Dept.)	? No
Filing Date	: 1-Aug-2017
Print Payment Advice	? No
Payment Advice Date	: 4-Jul-2017
Start fresh page for each bank allocation	? No
Include Bill Details	? No
Print Party's Contact Details	? No
Show Transferred to	? Yes
Print Instrument Date	? Yes
Print Due Date	? No
Print Company's PAN/IT Number	? No

F-8A: Challan Printing screen

At *Payment Voucher printing* screen (F-8A), set the relevant details. Type Y to print challan (F-9A).

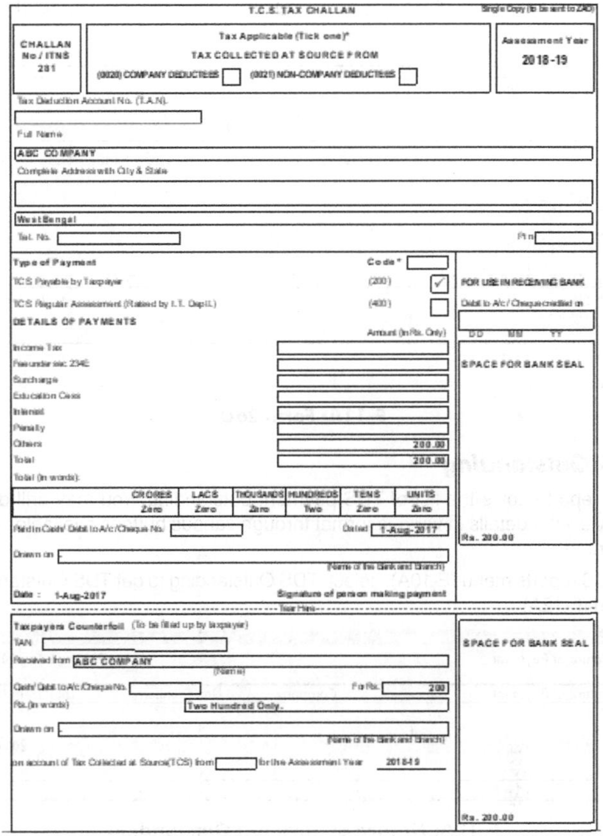
T.C.S. TAX CHALLAN

Single Copy (to be sent to ZAO)

CHALLAN No./ ITNS 281

Tax Applicable (Tick one)*

TAX COLLECTED AT SOURCE FROM

(0020) COMPANY DEDUCTEES (0021) NON-COMPANY DEDUCTEES

Assessment Year 2018-19

Tax Deduction Account No. (T.A.N.)

Full Name

ABC COMPANY

Complete Address with City & State

West Bengal

Tel. No. Pin

Type of Payment Code*

TCS Payable by Taxpayer (200) ✓

TCS Regular Assessment (Raised by I.T. Deptt.) (400)

FOR USE IN RECEIVING BANK

Debit to A/c / Cheque credited on

DD MM YY

DETAILS OF PAYMENTS

Amount (in Rs. Only)

Income Tax	
Fee under sec 234E	
Surcharge	
Education Cess	
Interest	
Penalty	
Others	200.00
Total	200.00

Total (in words):

CRORES	LACS	THOUSANDS	HUNDREDS	TENS	UNITS
Zero	Zero	Zero	Two	Zero	Zero

SPACE FOR BANK SEAL

Paid in Cash/ Debit to A/c /Cheque No. Dated 1-Aug-2017

Rs. 200.00

Drawn on

(Name of the Bank and Branch)

Date : 1-Aug-2017 Signature of person making payment

Tear Here

Taxpayers Counterfoil (To be filled up by taxpayer)

TAN

Received from ABC COMPANY

(Name)

Cash/ Debit to A/c /Cheque No. For Rs. 200

Rs. (in words) Two Hundred Only.

Drawn on

(Name of the Bank and Branch)

on account of Tax Collected at Source(TCS) from for the Assessment Year 2018-19

SPACE FOR BANK SEAL

Rs. 200.00

F-9A: TDS Challan

06 TDS Reports

Select *Display>Statutory Reports>TDS* Reports to get TDS Reports Menu (F-10A).

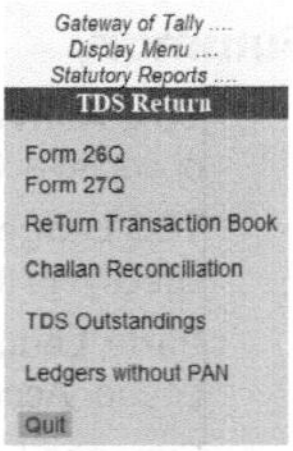

F-10A: TDS Reports Menu

Form 26Q

Form 26Q is Quarterly return of TDS in respect of all payments other than salaries. The top portion shows the statistics of vouchers from where you may drill down to view the related voucher list.

At TDS reports menu (F-10A), select 26Q to get the Form 26Q report (F-11A)

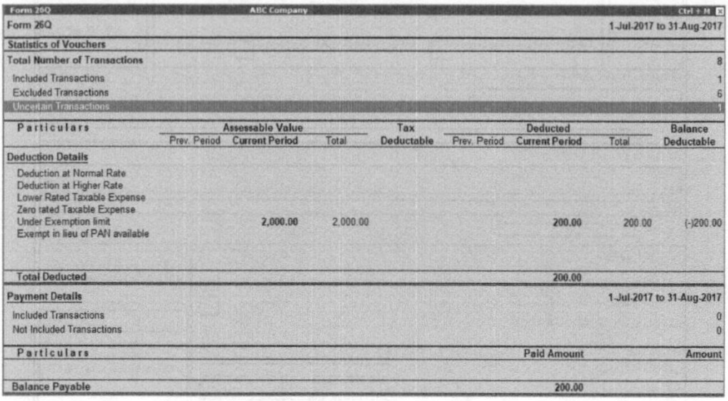

F-11A: Form 26Q

TDS Outstanding

This report shows the list of TDS payment outstanding. You may drill down and view the details in various format through various buttons available in the report.

At TDS reports menu (F-10A), select TDS Outstanding to get TDS Outstanding report (F-12A)

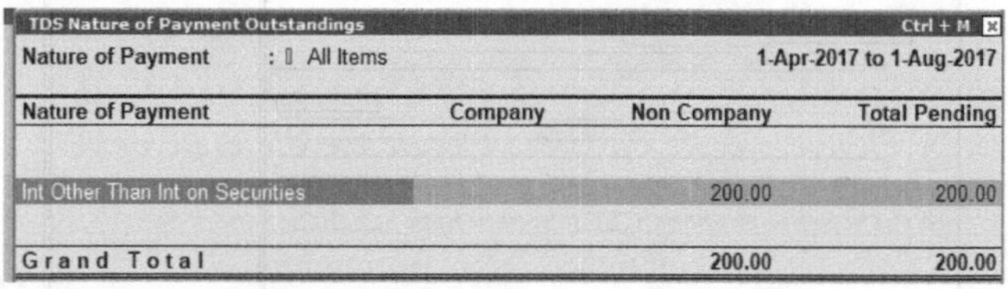

F-12A: Nature of Payment Outstanding

Summary

- **TDS Activation** : At *F11:Fetaures>Statutory Features*, set up TDS option to activate TDS Features, enter the related details of the Company
- **TDS Ledger Account Masters** : Create TDS Ledger Account masters, specifying the TDS Payment Types for the TDS Ledger Account
- **Party Ledger Account Masters** : Create TDS deductible Party TDS Ledger Account masters, setting the TDS related options
- **Expense Ledger Account Masters** : Create TDS deductible Expense Ledger Account masters, setting the TDS related options.

- **Expenses Voucher** : Create Journal Voucher for Expenses, deducting TDS in the Voucher. Set up various TDS details in the Voucher.
- TDS Adjustment Voucher : Create Journal Voucher for TDS Dedcution.
- **Party Payment Voucher after TDS Deduction** : Crate Payment voucher for the amount payable to the Party after TDS Deduction, like usual Payment Voucher. You may also print the Payment Advice.
- **TDS Deposit** : Create Payment Voucher for TDS deposit with Government.
- **TDS Challan Printing** : Having created the payment Voucher for TDS deposit, print the TDS Challan which is to be used to deposit the TDS with the Government.
- **TDS Report** : You may print various TDS Reports under TDS Reports menu (Display>Statutory Reports> TDS Reports).

TCS 03-03

01 TCS Activation

TCS means *Tax Collected at Source* by the seller (or lessor, licensor – commonly referred as *Collector*) from the buyer/ lessee (collectee/ payee), on sale of specified goods (defined u/s 206C of the Income Tax Act,1961).

Create a Company (Accounts with Inventory). Click *F11: Features> Statutory and Taxation* to get *Statutory & Taxation* screen.

At *Statutory & Taxation screen*, set :

- **Activate TCS** : At *Enable Tax Collect at source*, set Yes
- **TCS Details** : Having set *Yes* at *Enable Tax Collect at source, at* set *Yes* at *set/Alter TCS Details*, to get *Company Deductor/ Collector Details* (F-1A).

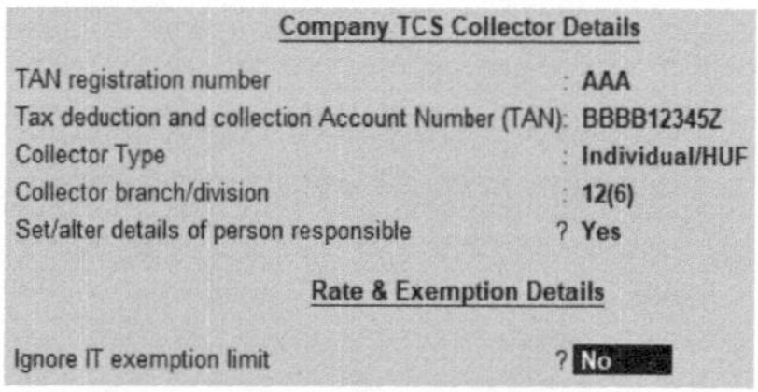

F-1A: TCS Details entry

02 Collectee Ledger Creation

Create Customer Ledger from whom TCS is collected (through Sales/ Service Bill). At Party Ledger entry screen, at *Is TCS applicable*, set *Yes* for the Customer Accounts from whom TCS is to be collected (F-2A) and enter the TCS details for the Party (F-2B).

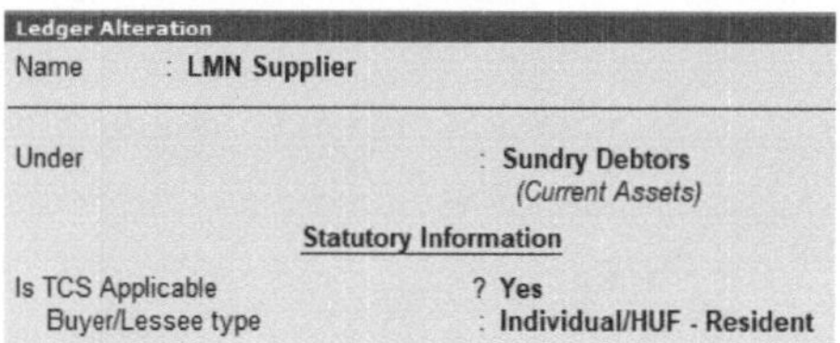

F-2A: Collectee Ledger Creation

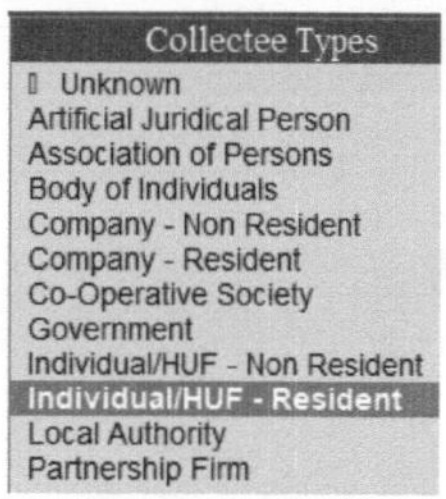

F-2B: Collectee Type List

03 TCS Ledger creation

Create TCS Ledger (F-3A). At *Nature of Goods/ Contact/ License/ Lease*, select the respective Item from list (you should create separate TCS Ledger Accounts for each type of Goods)

Create Sales & Purchase Ledger as usual

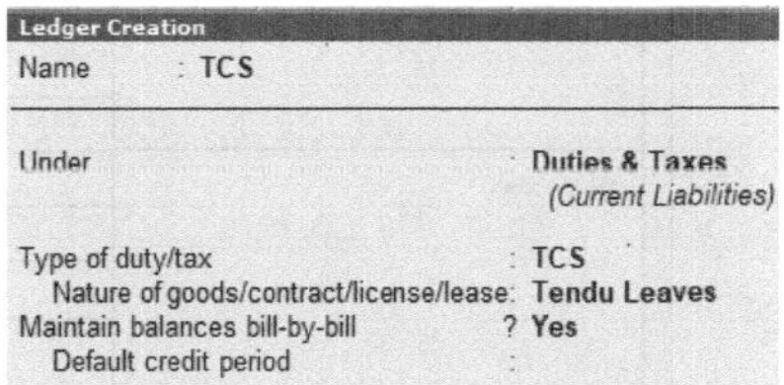

F-3A : TCS Ledger Creation

04 TCS Applicable Stock Item

Create Stock Item for TCS Chargeable Goods. At *Stock Item Creation* screen (F-4A), at Tax *Information* section, at *TCS Nature of Goods*, select the Goods Type from the *TCS Goods Type* list.

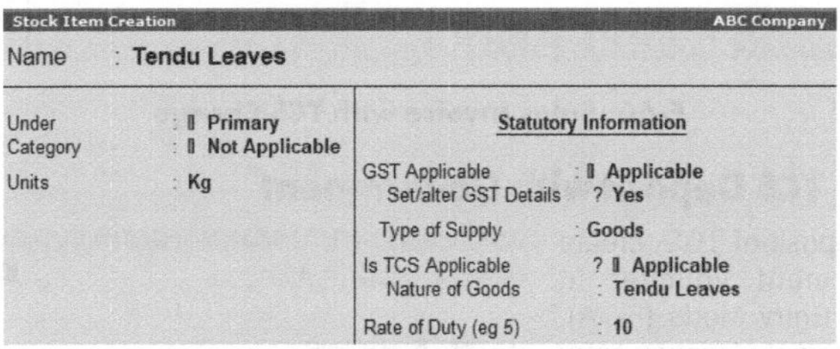

F-4A: TCS Stock Item creation

05 Sales Invoice Entry

Create Sales Invoice collecting TCS (F-5A).

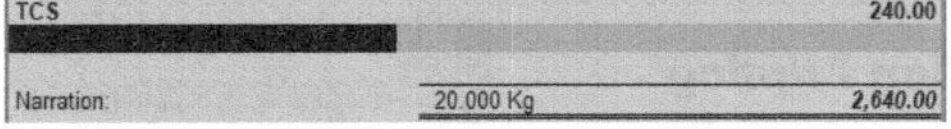

F-5A: Sales Voucher entry

Sales Invoice Printing

On entry of Sales Invoice, click *P:Print* to print the Sales Invoice (F-6A)

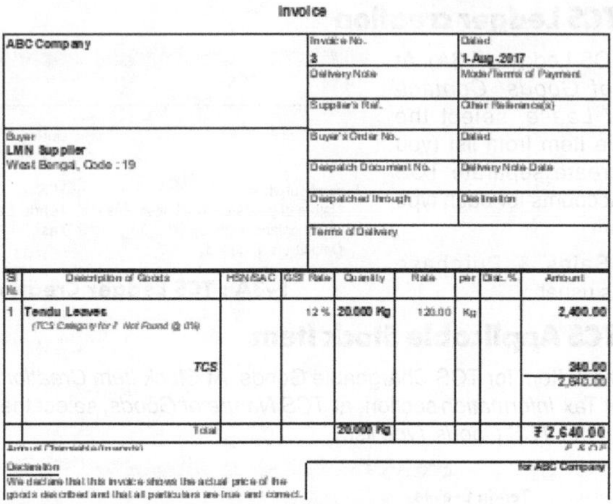

Invoice

ABC Company

Invoice No. 3 | Dated 1-Aug-2017
Delivery Note | Mode/Terms of Payment
Supplier's Ref. | Other Reference(s)

Buyer
LMN Supplier
West Bengal, Code : 19

Buyer's Order No. | Dated
Despatch Document No. | Delivery Note Date
Despatched through | Destination
Terms of Delivery

Sl No.	Description of Goods	HSN/SAC	GST Rate	Quantity	Rate	per	Disc. %	Amount
1	Tendu Leaves (TCS Category for 1 Not Found @ 0%)		12 %	20.000 Kg	120.00	Kg		2,400.00
	TCS							240.00
								2,640.00
	Total			20.000 Kg				₹ 2,640.00

Amount Chargeable (in words) E. & O.E

Declaration
We declare that this invoice shows the actual price of the goods described and that all particulars are true and correct.

for ABC Company

F-6A: Sales Invoice with TCS Charge

06 TCS Deposit with Government

For Deposit of TCS, create a Payment Voucher in Single Entry Mode (F-7A). At Payment Voucher entry screen, click *<u>S</u>:Stat Payment* button to get *Statutory Payment Screen* (F-7B).

At Statutory Payment screen (F-7B), enter the details to get TCS payment Voucher entry screen (F-7A).

At TCS payment Voucher entry screen (F-7A), set *Yes* at provide details and enter the cheque details

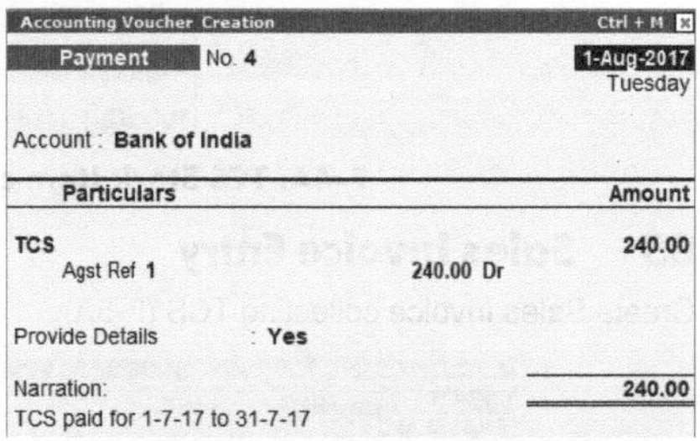

Accounting Voucher Creation Ctrl + M

Payment No. 4 1-Aug-2017 Tuesday

Account : **Bank of India**

Particulars		Amount
TCS		**240.00**
Agst Ref **1**	240.00 Dr	

Provide Details : **Yes**

Narration: **240.00**
TCS paid for 1-7-17 to 31-7-17

F-7A : TCS Payment Voucher Entry

Statutory Payment

Tax Type	: TCS	
Period From	: 1-Jul-2017	To 31-Jul-2017
Collected Till Date	: 31-7-2017	
Section	: 206	
Nature of Good(s)	: Tendu Leaves	
Collectee Status	: Non Company	
Residential Status	: Resident	
Cash/Bank	:	

F-7B: TCS Payment Details

TCS Challan Printing

At TCS Payment Voucher entry screen (F-7A), click *P:Print* and enter the details to print the TCS Challan (F-8A)

T.C.S. TAX CHALLAN Single Copy (to be sent to ZAO)

CHALLAN No./ITNS 281	Tax Applicable (Tick one)* TAX COLLECTED AT SOURCE FROM (0020) COMPANY DEDUCTEES ☐ (0021) NON-COMPANY DEDUCTEES ☐	Assessment Year 2018-19

Tax Deduction Account No. (T.A.N).
BBBB12345Z

Full Name
ABC COMPANY

Complete Address with City & State

West Bengal

Tel. No. Pin

Type of Payment Code*

TCS Payable by Taxpayer (200) ✓

TCS Regular Assessment (Raised by I.T. Deptt.) (400) ☐

FOR USE IN RECEIVING BANK

Debit to A/c / Cheque credited on

DD MM YY

DETAILS OF PAYMENTS

	Amount (in Rs. Only)
Income Tax	
Fee under sec 234E	
Surcharge	
Education Cess	
Interest	
Penalty	
Others	240.00
Total	240.00

Total (in words):

CRORES	LACS	THOUSANDS	HUNDREDS	TENS	UNITS
Zero	Zero	Zero	Two	Four	Zero

Paid in Cash/ Debit to A/c /Cheque No. Dated 1-Aug-2017

Drawn on

(Name of the Bank and Branch)

Date : 1-Aug-2017 Signature of person making payment

SPACE FOR BANK SEAL

Rs. 240.00

---Tear Here---

Taxpayers Counterfoil (To be filled up by taxpayer)

TAN BBBB12345Z

Received from ABC COMPANY (Name)

Cash/ Debit to A/c /Cheque No. For Rs. 240

Rs. (in words) Two Hundred Forty Only.

Drawn on

(Name of the Bank and Branch)

on account of Tax Collected at Source(TCS) from for the Assessment Year 2018-19

SPACE FOR BANK SEAL

Rs. 240.00

F-8A: TCS Deposit Challan

07 TCS Reports

Having created the Vouchers for TCS Sales & Tax Deposit, you may print various periodical Reports & Returns of TCS.

At Gateway, select *Display> Statutory Reports>TCS Reports* to get TCS reports menu (F-9A). Select the desired menu item to display /the report.

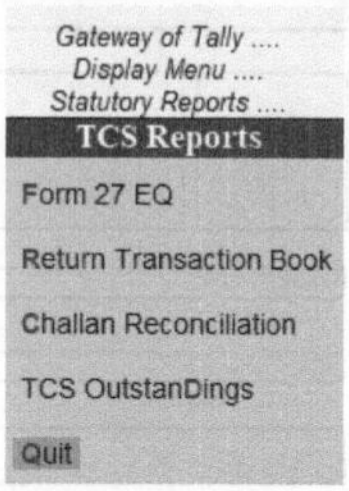

F-9A :TCS Payable Reports Menu

Summary

- **TCS Activation** : At *F11:Features>Statutory Features>TCS* activate TCS option
- **Company Details of TCS**: Having activated TCS for the Company, set the Company (Collector) Details for TCS
- **Party Ledger** : Set up TCS features at Party Ledger from whom TCS is collected
- **TCS Ledger** : Create TCS Ledger Account, setting up TCS features. You should create separate Ledger for each type of Goods, Lease, License, etc.
- **Stock Item** : Create Stock Item Master, setting up TCS features in the Stock Item in which TCS is applicable.
- **Income Ledger** : Like Stock Item, you have to create TCS Ledger Account for granting Lease / License etc, on which TCS is chargeable.
- **Sales Invoice** : Create Sales Invoice charging TCS, print the Invoice. In the same way, you may Sales Voucher for Lease / License, charging TCS.
- **TCS Deposit** : Create Payment Voucher for TCS Deposit, entering details of the Bills for which TCS is being paid. Print TCS Tax Challan to Deposit TCS to government.
- **TCS Reports** : Print TCS Reports

Assignments : Tax Accounting 03

03-01 GST

- **Set GST Features and Company Details**

  Click *F11:Features* button, select *Statutory & Taxation* to get *Statutory & Taxation* screen. At *Enable Goods & Services Tax (GST)*, set *Yes.* At *Set / Alter GST*

  Details, set *Yes*, to get *Company GST Details* screen. Enter the Company GSTDetails as per your own records.

- **Create GST Ledger Account :** Select *GoT>Account Info>Ledger> Create* to get Ledger Account creation screen.
  - o Create the 3 GST Ledger Accounts (State, Central & Integrated).
  - o Set GST Features for Sales & Purchase Accounts.
  - o Set GST Features for Party Ledger Accounts
- Create Stock Item and set the GST info in the Stock Items, GST rates
- Create Intra state Sales Voucher charging SGST and CGST
- Create Intra state Purchase Voucher with SGST and CGST
- Make adjustment voucher for Input credit of Purchase against liability of saes
- Create Payment Voucher for net payment of GST
- Upload data of Sales Purchase
- Print GST Reports

03-02 TDS

- **Set TDS Features and Company Details**

  Click *F11:Features* button, select *Statutory & Taxation* to get *Statutory & Taxation* screen. At *Enable Tax Deducted at Source*, set *Yes.* At *Set / Alter TDS Details*, set *Yes*, to get *Company TDS Deductor Details* screen. Enter the Company TDS Details as per your own records.

- **Create TDS Ledger Account**

  Select *GoT>Account Info>Ledger>Create* to get Ledger Account creation screen. At *Name*, enter *TDS on Interest.* At *Under*, select *Duties & Taxes.* At *Type of Duty /Tax*, select *TDS* from the list. At *Nature of Payment*, select *Interest other than Interest on Securities*

- **Set TDS related info at Deductee Ledger Account**

- o Select *GoT>Account Info>Ledger>Alter* and then select the Party Ledger (A K Traders) from whom TDS is to be Deducted to get Ledger Account Alteration screen.
- o At *Statutory Information* section, at *Is TDS Applicable*, set *Yes.* At *Treat TDS as Expenses* , set *No.* At *Deductee Type,* select *Individual / HUF - Resident.* At *Deduct TDS in same Voucher*, set Yes. At right part, enter Address & PAN Details as per records.

- **Set TDS related info at TDS Deductible Expenses Ledger**

Select *GoT>Account Info>Ledger>Alter* and select the *Interest* Account for which TDS is to be deducted from specified Payees to get Ledger Account Alteration screen. At *Statutory Information* section, At *Is TDS Applicable*, set *Yes.* At *Default Nature of Payment* (F-7A), select *Interest other than Interest on Securities* from the list of TDS Nature of Payment.

- **On 1-1-2017, Interest of Rs 5000 to be paid to A K Traders on 1,00,000 @ 10% for July 16 to Dec 16**

- o Select *GoT>Accounting Voucher.* Click *F7:Journal* button to get Journal Voucher creation screen. At Date enter 1-1-2017. Voucher No 1 is displayed. At *Particulars*, select *Interest* Ledger Account. Enter 5000 at Debit column., to get TDS Nature of Payment Details screen. Select *Interest other than Interest on Securities* from the list of TDS Nature of Payment . At Assessable Value, 5000 is carried. Press <enter>.
- o At 2nd entry, select A K Traders Ledger Account to get the *TDS Details* screen. At *Type of Ref* column, select *New Ref.* At *Name* column, the Voucher Ref #1 is shown. At *Nature of Payment*, *Interest other than Interest on Securities* is shown. At *Assessable Amount*, 5000 is shown. At *Deduct Now*, set *Yes.* At *TDS Amount*, 500 (showing TDS / Surcharge / Cess / SE Cess breakup) is shown. At *Payable Amount*, 4500 (5000-500=4500) is shown.
- o You get Bill Details screen, as usual. At Type of Ref, the Journal Ref is carried. At Amount 5000 is carried with Cr sign. Press <enter> to accept. At Next line, at *Type of Ref*, the Journal Ref is carried. At Amount 500 is carried with Dr sign. Press <enter> to accept.
- o You get back to the main Voucher screen. At Main voucher screen, select TDS Ledger Account and enter 500 at Credit column. At *Narration*, enter voucher Narration (Interest payable to A K Traders on 1,00,000 @ 10% for July 16 to Dec 16). Press *Ctrl+A* to save the Voucher
- o At *TDS Ledger*, select *TDS on Interest Ledger Account.*

- **On 2-1-2017, the amount of TDS (500) is deposited with Government by Ch# 123456 on HDFC bank and the Challan is printed.**

- o Select *GoT>Accounting Voucher*. Click *F5:Payment* button. Click *F12:Configure* and set *Yes* at *Use Single Entry Mode for Pymt/ Rcpt/Contra*). Click *S:Stat Payment* button to get *Statutory Payment* Screen
- o At *Type of Duty/Tax*, select TDS from the list of Duty / Tax Type. At *Auto Fill Statutory Payment*, select *Yes* to fill up the Payment details. At *Deducted Till Date*, enter 31-12-2016. At *Section*, select 194A. At *Nature of Payment*, select *Interest other than Interest on Securities*. At *Deductee Status*, select *Non Company*. At *Cash / Bank*, select HDFC Bank Account.
- o You get back to the main voucher screen showing the amount of TDS deposit with details of each related reference. Set *Yes* at *Provide Details* to get Payment Details screen. Enter the relevant details. You get back to main voucher entry screen.
- o Click *P:Print* button to get Voucher / Challan Printing screen. At *Print as TDS Challan*, set *Yes* to print Challan. At *TDS / TCS Regular Assessment (raised by IT Deptt)* : Set *Yes.*

- **Display TDS Computation Report**
  - o Select *GoT>Display>Statutory Reports>TDS Reports> Computation* to get *TDS Computation* showing the details of TDS Deducted, Paid, Payable etc,
  - o Drill down from *Expenses & Advances* head to get Partywise Statement of TDS, from *Paid* head to get TDS Payment details, from *Balance Payable* head to get Balance Payable details

03-03 TCS

- **Activate TCS and set Company TCS Details**

  Select *F11: Features> Statutory and Taxation* to get *Statutory & Taxation* screen. At *Enable Tax Collect at source*, set *Yes* and at *set/Alter TCS Details*, set *Yes* to get *Company Deductor/ Collector Details* to enter the relevant TCS details of the Company.

- **Create Customer Ledger**

  Select *GoT>Account Info>Ledger> Alter* and then select the Customer (Deductee) Ledger (i.e *A K Traders*), from whom TCS is collected to get Ledger Alteration screen. At *Is TCS applicable*, set *Yes* to get TCS details screen. At *Buyer / Lessee*, select *Individual / HUF- Resident.* At *Is Lower / No Tax Rate applicable* set *No.* At *Ignore Surcharge Limit,* set *No.*

- **Create TCS Ledger**

  Select *GoT>Account Info>Ledger> Create.* At Name, enter TCS. At Under, select *Duties & Taxes.* At *Type of Duty Tax,* select *TCS.* At *Nature of Goods/ Contact/ License/ Lease*, select *Tendu Leaves*

- **Set Up Stock Item for TCS**

  Select GoT>Inventory Info>*Stock Item> Create* to get Stock Item creation screen. At Tax *Information* section, at *TCS Nature of Goods*, select *Tendu Leaves*

- **On 1-12-2016, 100 kg of Tendu Leaves were sold to A K Traders @ 120 / kg, charging TCS @ 5%. Enter & print the Sales Invoice**

  o Select *GoT>Accounting Voucher* and click *F5:Sales*. Click V:As Invoice to get Sales Invoice entry screen. Enter Voucher Date. Invoice No. 1 is shown

  o At *Party Ledger*, select A K Traders. At *Sales Ledger*, select Sales.

  o At *Name of Item* column, select *Tendu Leaves*, at *Quantity* enter 100, at *Rate*, enter 120.00. The computed value 12000.00 is shown in *Amount* column. In the next line, at *Name of Item* column, press <enter> to terminate Stock Item entry

  o Select the TCS ledger to get the TCS details sub screen, showing Rs 12000 at Gross Amount. At next line, against Income Tax, 1200 is shown. At the bottom part, at *Type of Ref*, the Invoice Number is shown. The amount 1200 is carried against TDS Ledger account in the main voucher screen.

  o Click *P:Print* to get Invoice printing screen. Click *F12:Configure* to get *Invoice Printing Configuration* screen. Set *Yes* at *Print TCS Details*, *Print TCS Analysis of Items*, *Print Party PAN / Income Tax Number* etc., to print the TCS related details in the Invoice. Set other options as required.

PART 4

Payroll

Payroll Masters explains Activation & Set Up of Payroll Features for the Company, Pay Heads creation, Employee Masters and Employee Pay Structure set up

Payroll Vouchers explains Pay Voucher Entry and auto computation of Pay from the Employee Pay structure

Pay Reports explains preparation of Pay Slip, Pay Sheet and other Pay Reports

Payroll Masters

04-01

01 Pafmyroll Activation

Company Features set up : You may maintain Payroll for any type of Company (*Accounts Only Company*, or *Accounts with Inventory*).

At *Gateway of Tally,* Click *F11: Features >Accounting Features* to get Accounting Features screen. Under the Cost / Profit Centres Management section (F-1A), set *Yes* at *Maintain Payroll features* (F-1A)

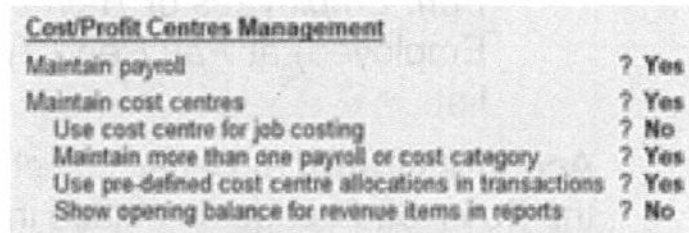

F-1A: Accounting Features Set Up

You may further set Yes at *Maintain more than one payroll or cost category*, for parallel allocation of employee cost/cost centre, if required

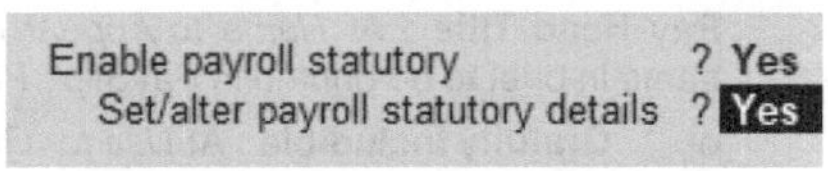

F-1B:Statutory & Taxation Features Set Up

Statutory Features set up : At *Gateway of Tally,* Click *F11: Features >Statutory & Taxation* to get *Statutory & Taxation* screen (F-1B).

If any Statutory provision for Payroll like PF, ESI, Pension, I Tax is applicable in your company, you may set Yes at the options *Enable Payroll Statutory* and then set *Yes* at *Set Alter Payroll details* to get Payroll Statutory Details of the Company (F-1C).

At *Payroll Statutory Details* screen (F-1C), enter the relevant details of the Company

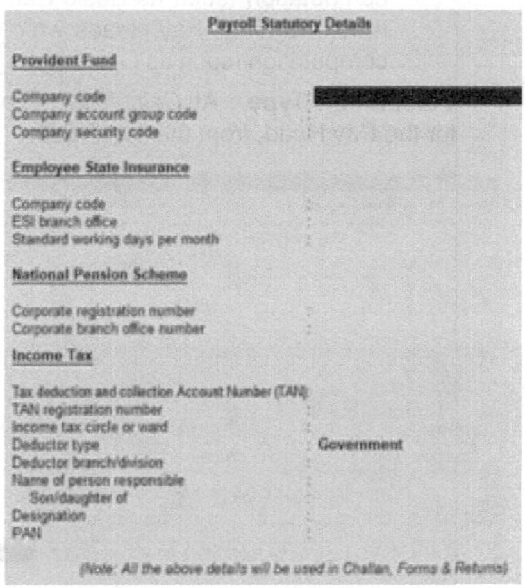

F-1C: Payroll Statutory Details

02 Pay Head Creation

At *Gateway of Tally,* Select *Payroll Info > Pay Heads> Create* to create a Pay Head (F-2A) :

- **Pay Head Name :** At *Name*, enter the Name of Pay Head. A Ledger Account of this Name would be automatically created on saving the Pay Head.
- **Pay Head Type** : At *Pay Head Type*, select the Pay Head Type from the list.
    - o **Income Type** *:* This field appears only when you select *Earnings from Employees* or *Reimbursement to Employees* (*Incomes* for Employee) at *Pay Head Type*. Select the *Income Type* from the list.
- **Account Group:** At *Under*, select the parent Account Group under which the Pay Head Ledger is placed in Chart of Accounts.
    - o **Pay Head Nature :** At *Affect Net Salary*, set *Yes* for Cash Heads which affect Net Pay in Pay Slip (like Basic, DA, I Tax, P tax, P F Deduction, ESI Deduction etc)
- **Pay Head Title :** At *Name to Appear in Payslip*, write the Payhead name in brief to be printed in PaySlip / Pay Register
    - o **Gratuity Includible :** At *Use for Gratuity* (this appears only when you select Earnings for Employees at Pay Head Type (F-1B), set *Yes* for those Earnings Pay Heads which are included in Gratuity computation (such as Basic Salary, HRA, etc.), else set *No* for those Earnings Pay Heads which are NOT included in Gratuity computation (such as Overtime).
- **Calculation Type :** At *Calculation Type*, select the Calculation Type for the Pay Head, from the list (F-2B).

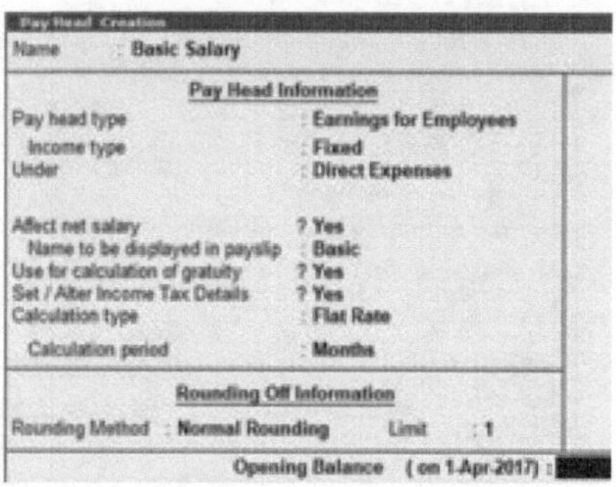

F-2A: Pay Ledger Creation

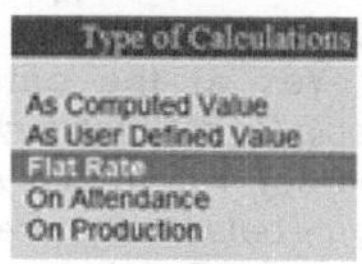

F-2B: Calculation Type

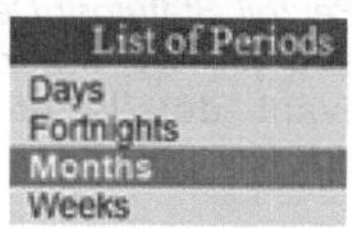

F-2D: Periods Type

- **Periods :** This option appears for Calculation Type *Flat Rate* or *Computed Value* (depending on selection of Calculation type, the next options vary)
- **Income Tax details :** At set / alter Income Tax details set Yes (if Income Tax is to be computed), to get the Income Tax Details screen (F-2E)
- **Rounding Info :** At *Rounding Method*, select the *Rounding Method* and then select the Rounding Limit

Income Tax Details

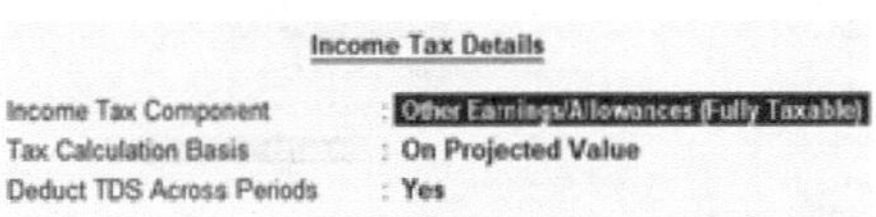

F-2E: Income details

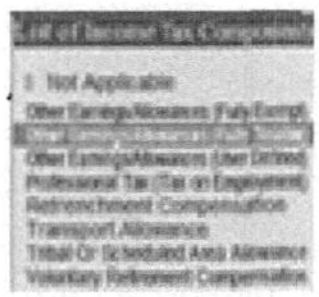

F-2F: Income Tax components

03 Employee Group

Employee Group refers to a Class of Employees having quite similar Pay Structure.

At Gateway, select *Payroll Info>Employee Group* to get *Employee Group Menu.* At *Employee Group Menu,* select *Create* to get *Employee Group Creation* screen. At *Employee Group Pay Structure* screen, to enter the Employee Group Pay Structure

04 Employee Category

Employee Category is a parallel classification of employees independent of Employee Group. To enable creation of Employee Categories, at Gateway, click *F11:Features > Accounting Features.* At *Accounting Features* screen, Under *Cost / Profit Centres Management*, set *Yes* at *More than ONE Payroll / Cost Category.*

To create a new Employee Category, at *Gateway,* select *Payroll Info>Employee Category* to get Employee Category creation Menu. At Employee Category Menu, select *Create* to get Employee Category creation screen. Employee Category Creation is very similar to Cost Category creation.

05 Employee Master

At *Gateway of Tally,* Select *Payroll Info>Employees>Create,* to get Employee Master screen (F-3A) to enter Employee Master Data.

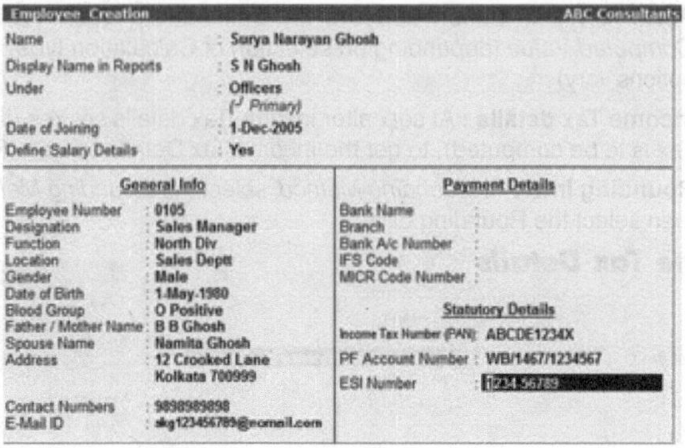

F-3A: Employee Master creation screen

- **Employee Full Name**: At *Name*, enter the complete Name of the Employee. Employee Name must be unique. If two names are similar, you must distinguish them by some distinctive letters.
- **Employee Short Name**: At *Display Name in Reports*, enter the short Name of the Employee, for unique identification, which is printed in all Payroll Reports
- **Under** : Select the parent Employee Group(not account group) of the Employee (or select *Primary*)
- **Date of Joining** : Enter the Date of Joining in dd-mm-yyyy format (like 1-4-1976). This is an important field used for first payslip computation and for computation of length of service for the purpose of Gratuity.
- **Pay Structure** : At *Define Salary Details*, set *Yes* to get the Pay Structure screen (F-3B), to enter Pay Structure Data

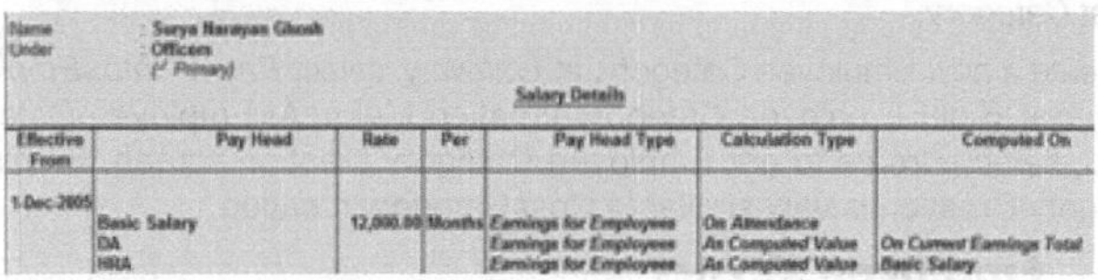

F-3B : Employee Master Pay Structure screen

06 Attendance Head

At *Payroll Info* Menu, select *Attendance / Production Types* to get *Attendance Master* Menu. At *Attendance / Production Types* Menu. Select *Create* to get *Attendance / Production* Head creation screen to create Attendance / Production Heads (F-4A)

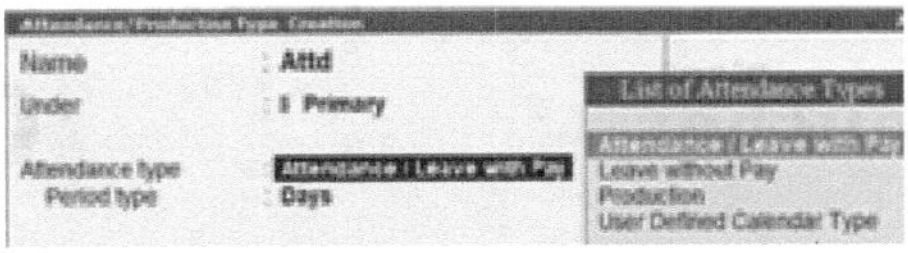

F-4A: Attendance / Production Head Entry

Summary

- **Payroll Activation** : At *F11:Fetaures > Accounting Features*, activate Payroll Features for the Company
- **Pay Heads** : Create Pay Heads for Earnings & Deductions, specifying the Pay Head types, Pay Head Nature, Calculation Type, Computation Rules, Computation Basis, etc. You may also create Pay Heads , and for Expenses Reimbursements. and User Defined Pay head to be specified in Pay Voucher only.
- **Employee Group** : You may create Employee Group, specifying Employee Group Pay Structure. You may copy Employee Group Pay Structure to another Employee Group Structure, avoiding repeated entry for each Employee Group
- **Employee Category** : You may also activate Employee Category Features and create *Employee Category* Masters (parallel classification of employees independent of Employee Group).
- **Employee** : Create Employee Master, specifying Employee Pay Structure, specifying Employee Particulars, Pay Structure, Bank Details, Statutory details, You may copy Employee Pay Structure to another Employee Structure, avoiding repeated entry for each Employee Master. Print Employee Profile.
- **Attendance / Production Heads** : Create Attendance / Production Heads

Pay Voucher

04-02

01 Attendance Voucher Entry

At Gateway, select *Payroll Voucher* to get Payroll Voucher Entry screen. At Payroll Voucher Entry screen, click *F5:Attendance* to get *Attendance Entry* screen. Enter the Attendance for the Employee in respect of each Attendance / Production Head (F-1A).

During Attendance Entry, you may also enter the period specific Earnings / Deduction amount.

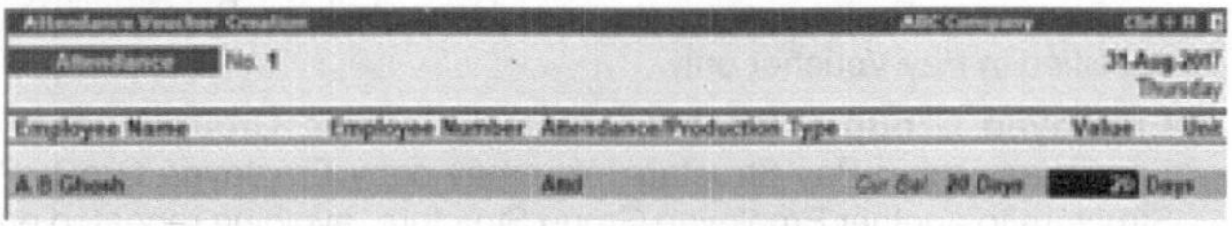

F-1A : Attendance Entry

02 Payroll Voucher Manual Entry

At Gateway, select *Payroll Vouchers* to get Payroll Voucher Entry screen (F-2A):

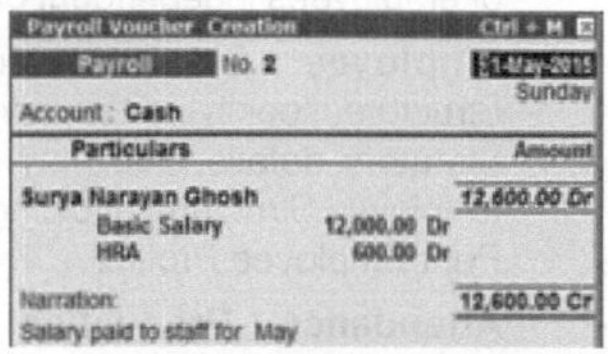

F-2A: Payroll Voucher Manual Entry

- **Header Account**: At the Header, select the Account (Cash / Bank or Salary Payable) from the list of Ledger Accounts.
- **Employee Account** : At *Particulars* column, select the Employee from list of Employees, in the same way as Attendance Entry.
  - o **Pay Head Details** : Now enter the Pay Head details of the employee, as follows:
    - ▪ **Pay Head** : Having selected the Employee, at Particulars column, select a Pay Head for which you like to enter the amount for the Employee
    - ▪ **Amount** : Now enter the Amount for the Account Head. The Dr / Cr will be auto set according to the Type (Earnings / Deductions) as defined in the Pay Head Master.

This way, select the Heads one by one, for which amount is to be entered in respect of the employee. Finally select *End of List* from the list of Pay Heads to terminate he Pay Head entry

This way, select the Employees one by one, and enter the respective Pay Head details as explained above. Finally select *End of List* from the list of Employees to terminate the Employee selection.

- **Voucher Narration** : Enter *Voucher Narration* and save the Voucher.

03 Payroll Voucher Auto Fill

Instead of manually entering Amount for each Employee, you may get the Voucher Auto computed from the Pay Heads and Rates specified in Employee Pay Structure in Employee Master, and the Attendance Production data.

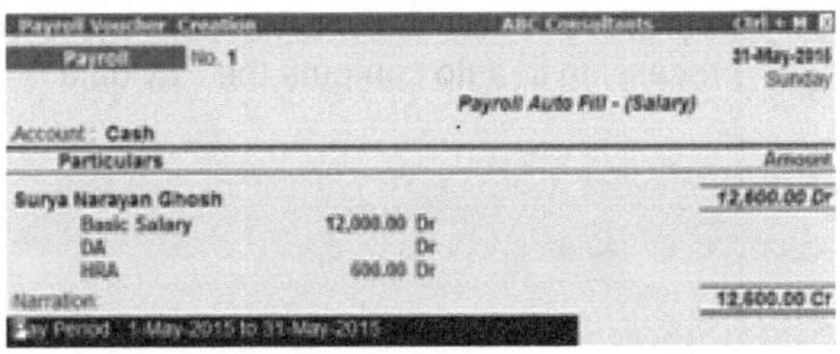

F-3A: Payroll Voucher (Auto Fill)

At Payroll Voucher Entry screen (F-3A), click *A:Auto Fill* button to get *Payroll Auto fill* Screen (F-4A) to enter as follows :

- **Salary Process** : At *Process For*, select *Salary* from the Process List to Process Salary
- **Pay Period** : At *From* & *To*, enter the Start & End Date of Pay Period, as follows:
  - o **Period Start Date** : At *From*, enter the Start Date of Pay Period
  - o **Period End Date**: At *To*, enter the End Date of Pay Period
- **Employee Range**: At *Employee Group*, Select Employee / Employee Group from the List
  - o **Employee Group** : Select the Employee Group. The Payroll will be processed for all Employees of the selected Employee Group.
  - o **One Employee**: Select an Employee. The Payroll will be processed for the selected Employee
  - o **All Employees** : Select *All Items* to process the Payroll for All Employees
- **Account Ledger** : At *Payroll Ledger*, select Cash / Bank or Salary Payable Ledger from the list of Ledgers
- **Payment Mode**: At *Use Mode of payment / Transaction Type*, set *Yes* to select the Mode of Payment Type
- **Payment / Transaction Type** : Having set Yes at *Use Mode of payment / Transaction Type*, select the Transaction Type from list (F-4B)

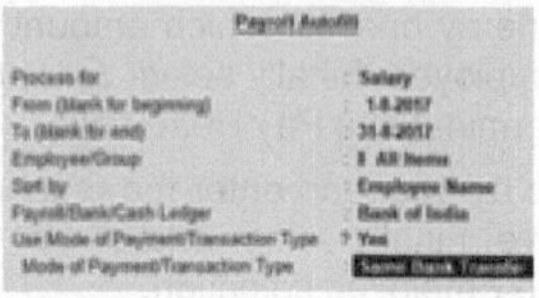

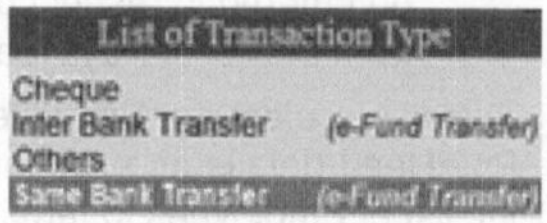

F-4A : Payroll Auto Fill **F-4B: Transaction Type**

Summary

- **Attendance** : Enter Attendance & period specific Earnings / Deduction data for each Employee
- **Payroll Voucher** : Create Manual Payroll Voucher or Perform Payroll processing to auto compute the Pay data.

Pay Reports

04-03

01 Payroll Reports Menu

Select GoT>Display > Payrll Reports to get Payroll Reports Menu

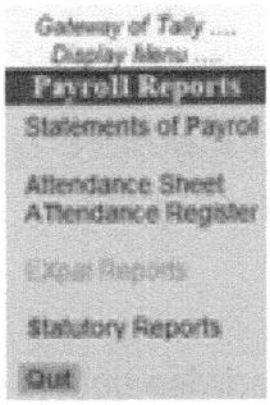

F-1A: Payroll Reports Menu

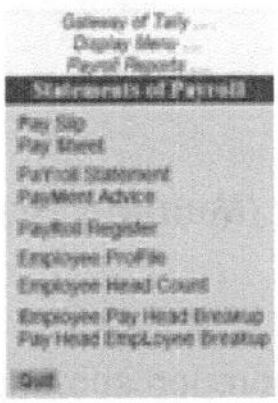

F-2A: Statement of Payroll Menu

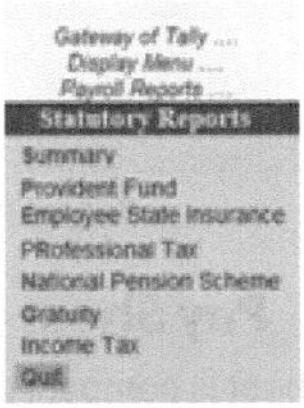

F-3A: Payroll Statutory Report

At Payroll Repots menu (F-1A):

- Select *Statement of Payroll* to get Statement of Payroll Menu (F-2A).
- Select Statutory Reports to get Statutory Reports menu (F-3A)

02 Pay Slip

Pay Slip (F-4A) contains the details of Pay & Deduction for the Employee for the Pay Period.

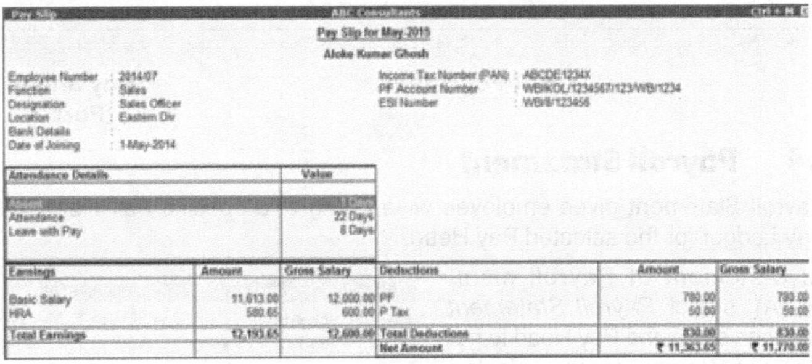

Pay Slip — ABC Consultants

Pay Slip for May 2015

Aloke Kumar Ghosh

Employee Number : 2014/07
Function : Sales
Designation : Sales Officer
Location : Eastern Div
Bank Details :
Date of Joining : 1-May-2014

Income Tax Number (PAN) : ABCDE1234X
PF Account Number : WB/KOL/1234567/123/WB/1234
ESI Number : WB/8/123456

Attendance Details	Value
Attendance	22 Days
Leave with Pay	8 Days

Earnings	Amount	Gross Salary	Deductions	Amount	Gross Salary
Basic Salary	11,613.00	12,000.00	PF	780.00	780.00
HRA	580.65	600.00	P Tax	50.00	50.00
Total Earnings	12,193.65	12,600.00	Total Deductions	830.00	830.00
			Net Amount	₹ 11,363.65	₹ 11,770.00

F-4A : Employee Pay Slip Display

Single Payslip : At Statement of Payroll menu (F-2A), select *Payslip > Single Payslip* and then select the Employee to get the Payslip for the selected

Employee (F-4A). Payslip is normally delivered to the concerned employee at each Pay Period, showing complete details of each of Pay Head & Net Pay, for the Employee.

Multiple Payslip: At Statement of Payroll menu (F-2A), select *Payslip > Multi Payslip* then select the Employee / Employee Group to get the *Pay List* (Multi Payslip) for the selected Employee Group (F-5A). *Pay List* (Multi Payslip) shows the details of Bank Account Details and Net Pay.

Multi Pay Slip — ABC Consultants — Ctrl + M

For All Employees — 1-Apr-2015 to 31-Mar-2016

Particulars	Employee Number	Account No.	Bank Name	Branch	Amount	E-Mail ID
Primary Cost Category					30,103.65	
Officers					24,943.65	
Aloke Kumar Ghosh	2014/07	1234567890	HDFC Bank	Kalighat	24,943.65	bechu@nomail.com
Workers					5,160.00	
Ram Prasad	W013	234567812	HDFC Bank	Kalighat	5,160.00	bbb@abcco.com
Grand Total					30,103.65	

F-5A: Pay List (Multiple Pay Slip) Display

03 Pay Sheet

Pay Sheet is compact columnar report showing Pay headwise details of each employee.

At *Statement of Payroll* menu (F-2A), select *Paysheet* and then select the Employee Filter to get Pay Sheet for the selected Employee / Group of Employees (F-6A)

Pay Sheet shows the complete details of each element of Pay Head and Net Pay amount, as they appear in Pay Slip.

PaySheet — ABC Consultants — Ctrl + M

For All Employees — 1-Apr-2015 to 31-Mar-2016

Employee Name	Basic Salary	HRA	Canteen	PF	VPF 4%
Aloke Kumar Ghosh	11,613.00	580.65		780.00	
Grand Total	11,613.00	580.65		780.00	

P Tax	Net Amount
50.00	11,363.65
50.00	11,363.65

F-6A: Pay Sheet **Pay Sheet (Part 2)**

04 Payroll Statement

Payroll Statement gives employee wise listing of a specific Pay Head, like Pay Ledger for the selected Pay Head.

At Statement of Payroll menu (F-2A), select *Payroll Statement* and then select the Pay Head to get Payroll Statement for the selected Pay Head(F-7A). The total amount for the Pay Head in respect of each Employee is shown under the column of selected Pay Head

Payroll Statement — Ctrl + M

For All Employees — 1-Apr-2015 to 31-Mar-2016

Particulars	Basic Salary
Primary Cost Category	23,613.00
Officers	23,613.00
Aloke Kumar Ghosh	23,613.00

F-7A: Payroll Statement

05 Payroll Voucher Register

At *Statement of Payroll menu* (F-2A), select *Payroll Register* to get Payroll Register (F-8A). Initially the Payroll Register shows the number of Payroll Vouchers for each Month. Select any Month to get Voucher Register showing the list of Payroll Vouchers for the selected month.

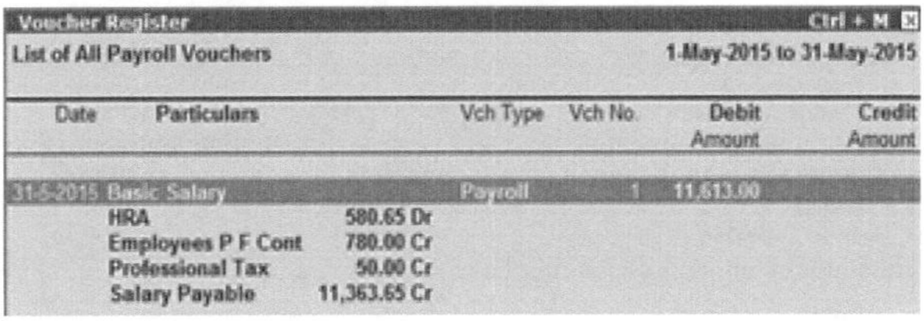

Voucher Register — Ctrl + M

List of All Payroll Vouchers — 1-May-2015 to 31-May-2015

Date	Particulars		Vch Type	Vch No.	Debit Amount	Credit Amount
31-5-2015	Basic Salary		Payroll	1	11,613.00	
	HRA	580.65 Dr				
	Employees P F Cont	780.00 Cr				
	Professional Tax	50.00 Cr				
	Salary Payable	11,363.65 Cr				

F-8A: Payroll Voucher Register

06 Employee Pay Head Breakup

At *Statement of Payroll* menu (F-2A), select *Employee Pay Head Break Up* and then select a Pay Head to get *Employee Pay Head Break Up* Report for selected Pay Head (F-7A). This report shows the details of employee wise Account Ledger figures for the selected Pay Head.

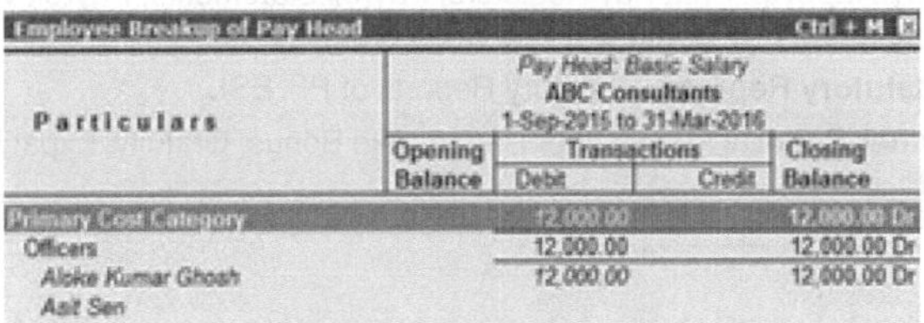

Employee Breakup of Pay Head — Ctrl + M

Pay Head: Basic Salary — ABC Consultants — 1-Sep-2015 to 31-Mar-2016

Particulars	Opening Balance	Transactions Debit	Transactions Credit	Closing Balance
Primary Cost Category		12,000.00		12,000.00 Dr
Officers		12,000.00		12,000.00 Dr
Aloke Kumar Ghosh		12,000.00		12,000.00 Dr
Asit Sen				

F-7A: Employee Pay Head Break Up

07 Pay Head Employee Breakup

At *Statement of Payroll* menu (F-2A), select *Pay Head Employee Break Up* and then select *Pay Head Employee Break Up* Report for selected Employee (F-8A). This report shows the Account Group/ Ledger Account Summary (like Extract), in respect of Pay Roll Vouchers.

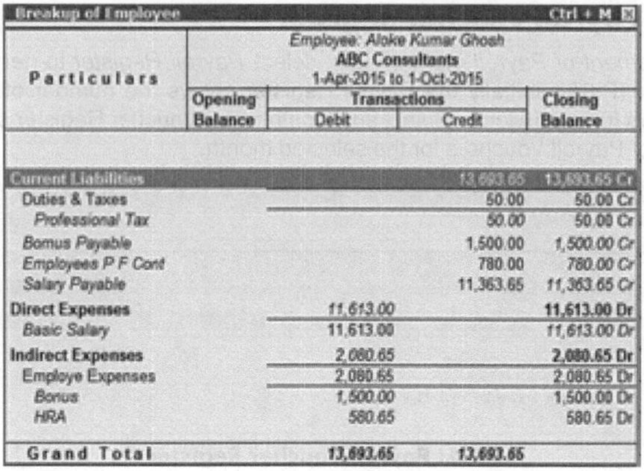

Breakup of Employee — Ctrl + M

Employee: Aloke Kumar Ghosh
ABC Consultants
1-Apr-2015 to 1-Oct-2015

Particulars	Opening Balance	Transactions Debit	Transactions Credit	Closing Balance
Current Liabilities			13,693.65	13,693.65 Cr
Duties & Taxes			50.00	50.00 Cr
Professional Tax			50.00	50.00 Cr
Bomus Payable			1,500.00	1,500.00 Cr
Employees P F Cont			780.00	780.00 Cr
Salary Payable			11,363.65	11,363.65 Cr
Direct Expenses		11,613.00		11,613.00 Dr
Basic Salary		11,613.00		11,613.00 Dr
Indirect Expenses		2,080.65		2,080.65 Dr
Employe Expenses		2,080.65		2,080.65 Dr
Bonus		1,500.00		1,500.00 Dr
HRA		580.65		580.65 Dr
Grand Total		13,693.65	13,693.65	

F-8A: Pay Head Employee Break Up

Summary

- **Pay Disbursement** : Print Pay Slip, Pay List, Bank Advice in respect of Payment to Employees
- **Pay Reports**: Print Pay Registers, Payroll Statements, Payroll Voucher Registers, Pay Summary, Pay Head break up etc.
- **Statutory Reports** : Statutory Reports of PF, ESI.
- **Other Reports** : Print Other Reports like Bonus, Gratuity, Expat Repots etc.

Assignments - Payroll 04

04-01 Payroll Masters

- **Activate Payroll Features for the Company**

  Select *F11: Features >Accounting Features.* Under the Cost / Profit Centres Management section, set *Yes* at *Maintain Payroll*

- **Create Basic Salary Pay Head**

  Select *GoT>Payroll Info > Pay Heads> Create* to get Pay Head creation screen. At *Name*, enter *Basic Pay.* At *Pay Head Type*, select *Earnings for Employees.* At *Income Type*, select *Fixed.* At *Under*, select *Indirect Expenses.* At *Affect Net Salary*, set *Yes.* At *Name to Appear in Payslip*, enter *Basic.* At *Use for Gratuity* set *Yes.* At *Calculation Type*, select *On Attendance.* At *Rounding Method*, select the *Rounding Method* and then select the Rounding Limit.

- **Create Employee Master**

  o Select *GoT>Payroll Info>Employees>Create,* to get Employee Master creation screen. At *Name*, enter *Asok Kumar Das.* At *Display Name in Reports*, enter *A K Das.* At *Under*, select *Primary.* At *Date of Joining*, enter 1-1-1990. Enter other details of the Employee as per record. At *Define Salary Details*, set *Yes* to get the Pay Structure screen

  o At *Effective From* column, enter 1-1-1990. At *Pay Head* column, select *Basic Pay.* At *Rate* column, enter 12000. Other info are carried from the Pay Head master

- **Create Attendance Master**

  Select *GoT>Payroll Info> Attendance / Production Types>Create* to get *Attendance* Head entry screen. At *Name*, enter *Paid Days.* At *Under*, select *Primary.* At *Attendance Type*, select *Attendance / Leave with Pay.* At *Period*, select *Days.*

04-02 Pay Voucher

- **Enter Attendance Voucher**

  o Select *GoT>Payroll Voucher* . Click *F5:Attendance* to get *Attendance Entry* screen. Enter 31-12-2106 at Voucher Date.

  o At *Employee Name*, select *Asok Kumar Das.* At *Attendance / Production Head Type* column, select *Paid Days.* At *Value* column, enter 28

- **Create Payroll Voucher**

  Select *GoT>Payroll Vouchers*. Enter 31-12-2016 at Voucher Date. At Account, select *Cash*. Click *A:Auto Fill* button to get *Payroll Auto fill* Screen. At *Process For*, select *Salary*. At *From* & *To*, enter 1-12-2016 to 31-12-2016. At *Employee Group*, select *All Items*. The computed Pay, Basic Salary Rs 10838.78 [(12000/31)x28] is shown.

04-03 Payroll Reports

- **Print Payslip**

  Select *GoT>Display > Payroll Reports> Statement of Payroll> Payslip>Single Payslip*. Click *F2:Date* and select the Pay Period. Select *A K Das* to get Payslip. Click *P:Print* to get Payslip printing screen. Set the printing options and type Y to print the Payslip.

- **Print Pay Sheet**

  Select *GoT>Display > Payroll Reports> Statement of Payroll> Paysheet* and then select *All Item* to get Pay Sheet for All Employees. Click *P:Print* to get Paysheet printing screen. Type *Y* to print the Paysheet

Appendix A : Shortcut Keys

(**Keyboard Convention** : F_n (with no underline) means press the Function Key button (e.g F12 :Configure), $\underline{F_n}$ (with single underline) means press the Alt key+Function Key button together (e.g H:Help), $\underline{\underline{F_n}}$ (with double underline) means press the Ctrl key+Function Key button together (e.g H:Support Centre),

01 Function Keys

F1 : To select a company (At all masters menu screen), To select the Accounts Button (At the Accounting Voucher creation / Alteration screen)

F1 (ALT+F1) : To select the Inventory (At the Inventory/Payroll Voucher creation / alteration), To toggle detailed / condensed report (At Inventory/Payroll Voucher creation alteration).

F1 (CTRL + F1) : To open Payroll Vouchers screen (At the Accounting/Inventory voucher creation /alteration)

F2 : To change the current date (at almost all screens), To select company inventory features (At F11: Features screen)

F3 : To select the company (At almost all screens), To select Company Statutory & Taxation features (At F11: Features screen)

F4 : To open Contra voucher (At Accounting / Inventory Voucher creation / alteration screen)

F5 : To open Payment voucher (At Accounting / Inventory Voucher creation / alteration screen)

F6 : To open Receipt voucher (At Accounting / Inventory Voucher creation / alteration screen)

F7 : To open Journal voucher (At Accounting / Inventory Voucher creation / alteration screen)

F8 : To open Sales voucher (At Accounting / Inventory Voucher creation / alteration screen)

F8 (CTRL+F8) : To open Credit Note voucher (At Accounting / Inventory Voucher creation / alteration screen)

F9 : To open Purchase voucher (At Accounting / Inventory Voucher creation alteration screen)

F9 (CTRL+F9) : To open Debit Note voucher (At Accounting / Inventory Voucher creation / alteration screen)

F10 : To open Reversing Journal voucher (At Accounting / Inventory Voucher creation / alteration screen)

F10 (Ctrl + F10): To open Memorandum voucher (At Accounting / Inventory / Payroll Voucher creation alteration screen)

F11 : To select the Functions and Features screen (At almost all screens)

F12 : To open Configure screen (At almost all screens)

02 Special Keys

ALT + 2 : To Duplicate the selected voucher (At List of Vouchers)

ALT + A : To Add a voucher (At List of Vouchers), To Alter the column (At columnar report)

ALT + C : To create a master at a voucher screen (at Master selection field). To invoke Calculator and paste computed value (at numeric input field)

ALT + D : To delete a voucher (at Voucher alteration screen), To delete a master (at Master alteration screen), To delete a column (at Columnar Report)

ALT + E : To export the report (At all reports screens)

ALT + I : To insert a voucher (At List of Vouchers), To toggle between Item and Accounting invoice (at sales and purchase invoice screen)

ALT + G : To set Language Configuration (At almost all screens)

ALT + K : To select Keyboard Configuration (At almost all screens)

ALT + M : To Email the report (At all reports screens)

ALT + N : To view the report in automatic columns (At columnar reports)

ALT + O : To upload the report at website (At all reports screens)

ALT + P : To print the report (At all reports screens)

ALT + R : To repeat the narration in different voucher type (At all Vouchers)

ALT + S : To restore removed line (At all reports screens)

ALT + U : To retrieve last deleted line (At all reports screens)

ALT+ V : To select VAT Payment Voucher (At Payment Voucher screen). From Invoice screen to bring Stock Journal screen

ALT + X : To cancel a voucher (in Day Book/List of Vouchers)

ALT + R : To repeat the narration in similar voucher

CTRL + A : To instantly save and exit (At almost all screens)

CTRL + B : To select Budget (At Accounts Groups/Ledgers/Cost Centres/ Budgets/Scenarios/Voucher Types/ Currencies creation / alteration screen)

CTRL + ALT + B : To display Tally info (Build, release, stat version) at Message / Calculator section (at all Menus)

CTRL + C : To select the Cost Centre (At Groups/Ledgers/Cost Centres/ Budgets/Scenarios/Voucher Types/ Currencies creation / alteration screen, To select the Cost Category (At Stock Groups/ Stock Categories/ Stock Items/ Reorder Levels/ Godowns/ Voucher Types / UoM creation /alteration)

CTRL+ E : To select the Currencies (At Groups/Ledgers/Cost Centres/ Budgets/Scenarios/Voucher Types/ Currencies creation / alteration)

CTRL + G : To select the Group (At Groups/Ledgers/Cost Centres/ Budgets/ Scenarios/Voucher Types/ Currencies creation / alteration)

CTRL + H: To invoke Help (At Almost all screens)

CTRL + I : To select the Stock Items : At Stock Group/ Stock Categories/ Stock Items/ Reorder Levels/ Godowns/ Voucher Types / UoM creation/ alteration)

Ctrl + Alt + I : To import statutory masters (At all menu screens)

CTRL + K : To Login as Remote Tally.NET User (At Almost all screens)

CTRL + L : To mark a Voucher as Optional (At the creation and alteration of Vouchers), To select the Ledger (At Groups/Ledgers/Cost Centres/ Budgets/ Scenarios/Voucher Types/ Currencies creation / alteration)

CTRL + O : To select the Godowns (At Stock Group/ Stock Categories/ Stock Items/ Reorder Levels/ Godowns/ Voucher Types / UoM creation /alteration

CTRL + Q : To abandon the screen without making any changes (At almost all screens)

CTRL + R : To repeat narration of similar voucher (At creation/alteration of voucher)

CTRL + Alt + R : To Rewrite data for a Company (At GoT)

CTRL + S : To alter Stock Item master (At Stock Voucher Report / Godown Voucher Report)

CTRL + U : To select the Units (At Stock Groups/ Stock Categories/ Stock Items/ Reorder Levels/ Godowns/ Voucher Types / UoM) creation/alteration screen

CTRL + V : To select the Voucher Types (At Groups/Ledgers/Cost Centres/ Budgets/Scenarios/Voucher Types/ Currencies (Accounts Info) creation and alteration screen). To toggle between Invoice and Voucher (At creation of Sales/ Purchase Voucher)

CTRL + K : To login to Control Centre (At almost all screens)

CTRL + H : To invoke Help (At almost all screen)

Alt + Enter : To view Voucher display (At Day Book, other Voucher Reports)

Alt + S : To view Stock Query report (At all Voucher Creation and Alteration screens (with Inventory details)

Alt + Z : To zoom in print preview to 100% (At all print preview screens that appear on pressing Alt+P with the option I: With Preview enabled. To zoom in to the print preview (At all print preview screens that appear after pressing Alt+Z). To zoom out of the print preview (At all print preview screens that appear after pressing Alt+Z)

CTRL + Scroll wheel (Mouse Wheel) : To zoom in to the print preview (At all print preview screens that appear after pressing Alt+Z)

SHIFT + Scroll wheel (Mouse Wheel), SHIFT + Right or Left arrow : To scroll horizontally - left to right or right to left (At all print preview screens that appear after pressing Alt+Z)

+ : To zoom in at Print Preview ((At all print preview screens that appear after pressing Alt+Z)

- : To zoom out at Print Preview ((At all print preview screens that appear after pressing Alt+Z)

03 Special Function Keys

ALT + F1 : To Shut a company (At all menu screens), To view detailed report (At almost all report screens) , To explode a line into its details (At almost all screens), To open Inventory vouchers to alter (At the Inventory/ Payroll voucher creation or alteration screen).

ALT + F2 : To change the period (At almost all screens)

ALT + F3 : To select the company info menu (At Gateway of Tally screen)

ALT + F4 : To open the Purchase Order Voucher Type (At Accounting / Inventory Voucher creation and alteration)

ALT + F5 : To open the Sales Order Voucher Type (At Accounting / Inventory Voucher creation and alteration screens. To view monthly / quarterly report (At almost all reports)

ALT + F6 : To open the Rejection Out Voucher Type, To open the Sales Order Voucher Type (At Accounting / Inventory Voucher creation and alteration)

ALT + F7 : To open the Stock Journal Voucher Type (Inventory Voucher creation / alteration). To accept all the Audit lists (At Tally Audit Listing screen)

ALT + F8 : To open the Delivery Note Voucher Type (At Inventory Voucher creation / alteration screens), To view the Columnar report (At Ledger Voucher screen)

ALT + F9 : To open the Receipt Note Voucher Type (At Inventory Voucher creation and alteration)

ALT + F10 : To open the Physical Stock Voucher Type (At Inventory Voucher creation / alteration)

ALT + F12 : To invoke Range Button (At almost all reports)

CTRL + F1 : To open payroll vouchers for alteration (At the Accounting/Inventory Voucher creation or alteration)

SPACE : To select the line (At almost all reports)

CTRL + SPACE : To select multiple lines at a time (At almost all reports)

CTRL + ALT+ A : To select all the line at a time (At almost all report screens)

04 Navigation Keys

PgUp : Display previous voucher during voucher entry/alter (At voucher entry / alteration)

PgDn : Display next voucher during voucher entry/alter (At voucher entry and alteration)

ESC : To remove what you typed into a field, To come out of a screen (At almost all screens)

SHIFT + ENTER : Collapse next level details (At Voucher Register, Trial Balance report), To explode a line into its details (In almost all Reports).

CTRL + ENTER : To alter a master while making an entry or viewing a report (At voucher entry / alteration)

Appendix B: Tally Software Download and Installation

01 Tally ERP 9 Rel 6 Download

Login to Tallysolution.com. Select Downloads Tab. Click Install now (F-1A)

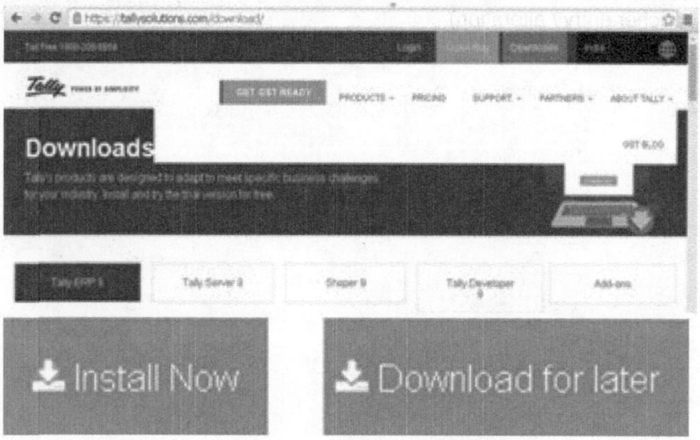

F-1A: Tally.Erp9 rel 6.x download

Download process starts. You see the progress bar of download process (F-2A).

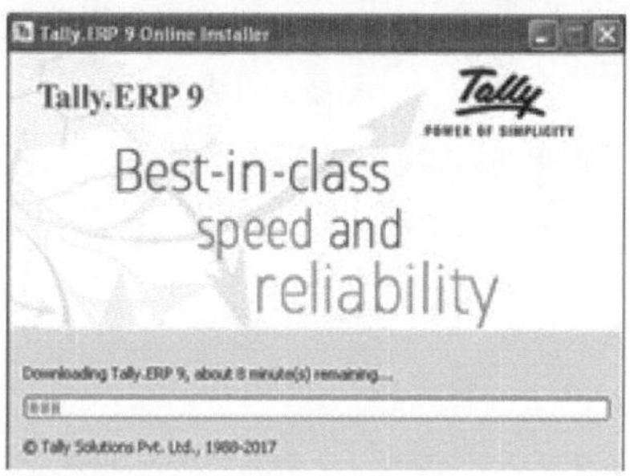

F-2A: Tally.Erp9 rel 6.x download process

02 Tally.ERP 9 Installation

On download, you get Setup.exe placed at the specified folder. Now click *Setup.exe* to get the SetUp installation screen (F-3A) to specify the folder where Tally.exe is to be placed. Enter the folder path (you may select using folder selection wizard).

The folder where Tally.exe is to be installed (F-3A) should be different from where the Set Up file is installed, (except in case of upgradation). Click *Install* to run the SetUp execution application.

You get Installation progress screen. You will get a number of files (including tally.exe) in the folder.

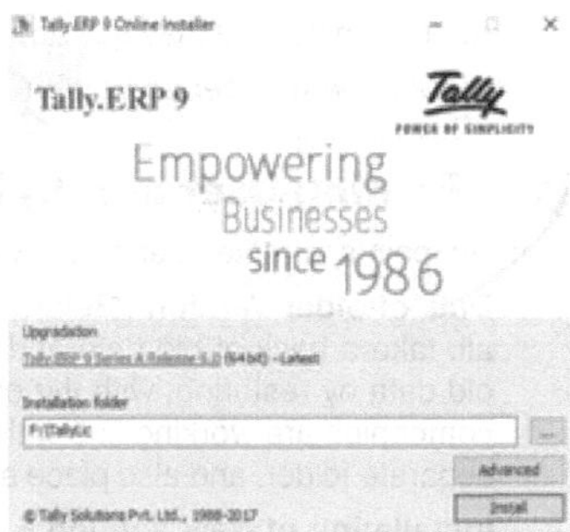

F-3A: Tally software location set up

To quickly load Tally from Desktop, Create a shortcut of tally.exe at the desktop.

Click *Tally.exe* icon (shortcut) at Desktop to get Tally.ERP 9 Start Up screen (F-4A).

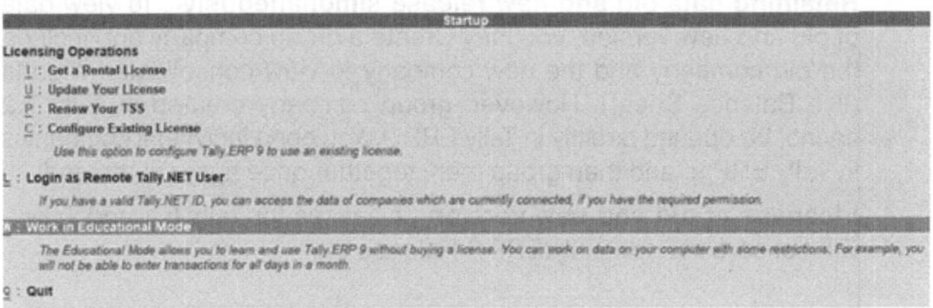

F-4A: Tally Start up screen

03 Working in Educational Mode

At Tally.ERP 9 Start Up screen (F-4A), select as follows:

- **Working with Educational Mode** : Select W:Work in educational modeand then select *I: Silver Edition Mode (Single user)*

  You may work in Educational Mode to learn all the aspects and features of Tally. ERP9. Though the Educational version has some operational restrictions, you may enter data and perform almost all operations in Educational Version to enter data, run the processes and display reports. In educational version you cannot enter any date other than 1,2, or 31.

It does not provide multi account reports printing (but you can view and print all reports from Display option available in Educational Version).

After learning, you may buy and activate license.

- **Working with License version** : Select other options to activate/ install / Buy license

04 Existing User of Tally.ERP 9 rel 5.x

Important points to remember before you install new release 6

- **Data of older Version** : Before you install the new release 6.0, first of all, take a back of old data and place in a separate folder. Check the old data by restoring, with the older release and check that the all the companies are working fine with restored data. Keep the back up in a separate folder, and also place a copy in some safe place.
- **Installation of New Version 6.0** : If you are using any old release of Tally ERP 9 (like Tally ERP 9 rel 4.91), just renew your subscription to get the upgraded license version. If you are using old version (Tally 9, not ERP 9), then buy an upgrade version. If you are first time Tally User, download and install Tally ERP 9 release 6.
- **Opening of old data in new release 6.0:** To open the old data, open the Tally company with new release 6. The data would be upgraded to release 6. Once upgraded, you will not be able to open thee data with your old tally version
- **Retaining data old and new release simultaneously** : To view data of old and new version, you may Create a group company and include the old company and the new company to view consolidated reports (like Balance Sheet). However, group company created in Tally 7.2 cannot be opened directly in Tally.ERP 9. You open individual companies in Tally.ERP 9, and then group them together once again at the end.
- **Licenses of old and new version** : Licenses for Tally 8.1 and Tally 9 will not co-exist with Tally.ERP 9 Release 6.